Acclaim for the Authors

"A book of this nature helps balance our Wheel, with honor, respect and gratitude as guides, not to mention a heaping dose of fun and fulfilling activities."
—**Patricia Telesco**
Author: *Charmed Life*

"I have known Oberon Zell-Ravenheart for over 35 years. He is one of the pioneers of Paganism in the United States. With his many decades of experience he, more than anyone, is uniquely qualified to write this book, having been teaching for the majority of his life. His name is greatly respected in all of the varying fields of Paganism and Witchcraft. He is truly an Elder…of Paganism, Witchcraft, and Magick." —**Raymond Buckland**
Author: *Buckland's Complete Book of Witchcraft*

"Morning Glory's introduction to the magickal ways of the Goddess, manifest in our time, has enlarged my understanding of Pagan ways, enriching my spirit and imagination." —**Elinor Gadon**
Author: *The Once and future Goddess*

"I couldn't imagine someone more appropriate to write this book than Oberon Zell Ravenheart. I have worked with him personally for over 30 years, and have found him to be an excellent teacher, craftsman, artist, scholar, and general creative genius. His ability to organize information into nifty charts and easy-to-access language remains unequaled in the magickal community."
—**Anodea Judith**
Author: *Waking the Global Heart*

"Oberon Zell-Ravenheart is not only one of the founders of contemporary Neo-Paganism but remains one of its most respected spokesmen. The Goddess herself shines through Morning Glory as she shares the joy and passion of her scholarship and worship. There is no more enthusiastic and delightful interpreter of the Goddess."
—**Patricia Monaghan**
Author: *The Book of Goddesses and Heroines*

"Morning Glory Zell knows more about Goddesses than almost anyone I've ever encountered!"
—**Margot Adler**
Author: *Drawing Down the Moon*

"To those who study the occult, the name of Oberon Zell-Ravenheart is internationally known and respected. He is a genuine Wizard. One of the pioneers of Paganism in the United States, he shares his lifetime of learning and information with readers from all walks of life." —**Lee Prosser**
Fate Magazine

"Morning Glory Zell is one of the most knowledgeable people I know on Goddess cultures of the world." —**Joan Marler**
Editor: *From the Realm of the Ancestors: An Anthology in Honor of Marija Gimbutas*

"There is no more important task than the awakening of wonder, magick, and love for the inspirited Earth in the greater culture. And no one more ideal to pull it off than Oberon. Oberon has the talents as well as experience to make it happen, the way he brought together a church, a movement...and our Grey Council. He awakens a fire in everyone he comes into contact with, having long lived the life of a Wizard not only in image but in service. His enchanting art, writings, and talks are themselves a magical manifestation, and his influence on our community is legendary."
—**Jesse Wolf Hardin**
Author: *Gaia Eros*

"Morning Glory is a charismatic ritual priestess with a great sense of humor." —**Z Budapest**
Author: *Grandmother of Time*

"Oberon Zell-Ravenheart has been personally involved with many important historic events in the creation of the Earth-based spirituality that is important to so many people today. Oberon has the unique distinction of being probably the most influential male in the Goddess movement! He is a gifted storyteller, a powerful magician, and is young at heart. I have known Oberon, or known of him, since 1969, and I am eagerly looking forward to this book and to what I can learn from it! Viva Oberon!" —**John Sulak**
Co-Author: *Modern Pagans*

"Morning Glory displays a generosity of spirit that has always welcomed newcomers into the magic of the Great Goddess and empowered them to explore the feminine divine within themselves and in the universe. Her Goddess sculptures are among the finest in the world and incorporate her deep understanding of sacred ritual and her wisdom of an experienced high priestess." —**Abby Willowroot**
Goddess 2000 Project

"Oberon and Morning Glory recreated living unicorns, traveled to the remote South Seas in search of genuine mermaids, and created the Church of All Worlds. If there is anyone who can bring magick to life for a million aspiring Wizards, it is Oberon and Morning Glory." —**Amber K**
Author: *True Magick: A Beginner's Guide*

CREATING CIRCLES & CEREMONIES
EDITED BY KIRSTEN DALLEY AND ARTEMISIA
TYPESET AND FORMATTED BY OBERON ZELL-RAVENHEART
COVER ILLUSTRATION AND DESIGN: SCOTT FRAY
PRINTED IN THE U.S.A. BY BOOK-MART PRESS

To order this title, please call toll-free 1-800-CAREER-1 (NJ and Canada: 201-848-0310) to order using VISA or MasterCard, or for further information on books from Career Press.

The Career Press, Inc., 3 Tice Road, PO Box 687,
Franklin Lakes, NJ 07417
www.careerpress.com
www.newpagebooks.com

Library of Congress Cataloging-in-Publication Data

Zell-Ravenheart, Oberon, 1942-
    Creating circles & ceremonies : rituals for all seasons and reasons / by Oberon Zell-Ravenheart and Morning Glory Zell-Ravenheart.
        p. cm.
    ISBN-13: 978-1-56414-864-3
    ISBN-10: 1-56414-864-5
    1. Magic. 2. Ritual. I. Zell-Ravenheart, Morning Glory. II. Title: Creating circles and ceremonies. III. Title.

BF1623.R6Z45 2006
299'94—dc22

                                                                    2006014337

Creating Circles & Ceremonies
Rituals for All Seasons & Reasons

Oberon Zell-Ravenheart &
Morning Glory Zell-Ravenheart

NEW PAGE BOOKS
A division of The Career Press, Inc.
Franklin Lakes, NJ

Foreword: Always Coming Home

By LaSara WakeRobin Firefox

In the early days of my existence, the land, the seasons, and my family's ties with them held sway. We lived, as Oberon writes in his preface, "the semi-mythical lives of our ancient Pagan tribal forebears." Not all of it was easy, not all of it was idyllic. There is little romance to the Earth sometimes, and days of back-breaking work just to get food on the table and nights of not enough dry firewood have their cost.

The warmly-lighted moments that find purchase in the folds of memory are evenings telling "The Stories" by candle and kerosene lamp. The first solid memory I have of Oberon was from such an evening.

In those days, in the life that had been chosen by my parents, and by Oberon and Morning Glory, Anodea Judith, and many other latter-day "pioneers," a visit to another's home meant a two-hour hike and often a two-day stayover. Roads were not roads; they were logging tracks that were impassable for sometimes months at a time. Many of us had cars that were not always working, and even the best of what any of us could afford was not built for the terrain.

My family had the distinction of being at the end of one such not-a-road, with a waterway that was somewhere between creek and river. When it was in its river phase, we were land-locked. The only way in or out was overland hiking to the one bridge that crossed the river.

On one such pilgrimage that Oberon and Morning Glory made to our home, I recall all of us—Morning Glory, Oberon, my parents, three siblings, and myself—sitting very cozily in the Cook House, the central element of our homestead, around the beautiful, antique round table that served as our dinning set. Though I was only four or five at the time, I still remember the fire burning warmly in the cooking stove and the soft quality of the natural candle and kerosene light. I remember the stories and songs, and Oberon washing the dishes after the large and hearty supper my family had prepared for our visitors.

Visitors were a rare treat, and these visitors were a god/dess-send after weeks of isolation.

That was three decades ago. Through the years roads were improved, bridges installed, dynasties rose and fell. Many of the people who had chosen this rustic life grew tired of it, went back to work for "The Man," put their kids in private or public schools, and moved back toward the middle ground, the middle class, the middle road.

A few people held onto their dreams, even through all the transformations—the births and deaths, the love affairs and heartbreaks, the break-ups and breakdowns.

As I grow older I recognize more and more that the path of the visionary is not a path that is easy. Walking a path outside the circumscribed, circumspect "way things are" is not something that is often greeted with fame and fortune, as much as we might want to look for examples of the rare occasions where it is. There are a few strong souls who feel the call of the wild, the call of the heart, the call of the Goddess, the call of God. There are even fewer willing ones who hear the call and are willing to answer.

My forebears were not some mythical Pagan tribe; they were an actual tribe of spirit and soul who made magick with the bare land, made dreams real, made vision an integrated part of our cultural definition.

I am a product of tribe, of community. I was born to the land, fostered by forest spirits, faeries, and phantoms. I was let to run free in the wild lands of my youth, where we were in relationship with each element of it. My forebears eschewed the notion of domination, and found new frameworks upon which to build a co-creative relationship with the land, with entities beyond the physical, and in ideal moments of communion, with one another. Out on the edges of the domina-tor culture, we were building a new way of being *with* the Earth.

Ritual helped us to create and honor these bonds. Learning to listen to the land, the plants, each other, and with our hearts was what I was raised believing to be the natural way of things. My memories are laced through with nights spent around the balefire under the moon and stars, images of the Maypole, ribbons flying and dancers laughing as we wound the ribbons joyously around the pole, tying our new May King to it. I reigned as Queen of the May twice, the first time at 19, the second at 25. As a community, we mourned the cyclical loss of the Year King at Samhain, wept with the Queen, said our goodbyes, and went into the world of Spirit. We ate silently and fed the spirits who gathered as the veils grew thin.

First my younger brother, and later my firstborn, served as the Robin, the new year's Child King, atop the Yule log. (Yeah, my child is a girl. We're flexible!) We sang and told stories, exchanged gifts, then wandered in the snowy fields to call in the shifting season. We greeted the dawn after the darkest of nights, making sure the sun still rose.

I served twice as Persephone's vessel (with my third and final round approaching—a girl must have her limits!), and sat on Her throne in the dark and drear underworld of Erebos, and watched the myths unfold as we participated in the regeneration of deities more ancient than written history. I grew chthonic, found my roots, and stood with Her in me to find the stars again.

We held and beheld the Mysteries, and tied ourselves securely to the Earth with them. Ritual offered a space for recognition of the sanctified ground upon which we built our dreams of new worlds, new words, a new age, a new Aeon.

I grew up finding rhythms in the natural order of things: birth, life, and death all had their time and place. We grew a garden, helped our animals birth new broods every springtime, and buried our dead in the soil. Of course, by our dead I don't mean human relations, but our animal counterparts. My pony died one spring and became fertilizer for the raspberry patch. The remains of animals we took for food were honored with a resting place deep in the soil that would offer up next year's harvest.

There was no mediation between our lives and the seasons, and the lives of the lands and creatures we cohabitated with were part of the whole. This inherent witnessing of cycles was a pattern that we brought into the creation of our ritual cycles and myths.

My mother practiced a wide array of indigenous practices, and we honored the teachings of all paths. We celebrated Ostara and Easter, Yule, Christmas, and Chanukah. We prayed to the rocks and trees, and to the gods and goddesses for wisdom and assistance.

My parents encouraged faith and belief. I was told we were descended from the Pixies. I later figured out that the Picts may have been the origin of the mythical Pixies, and if that is so, what I believed was the truth. In magick there are many truths.

The ritual structures we founded were organic, just as the land and the seasons are organic. Just as human relationships and the process of aging and growth, births, rites of passage and deaths are organic.

We studied the Ancient Stories, created and recreated rituals that taught the Old Teachings. We pulled together paths and followed them all at once. We initiated Mysteries and learned from them as we taught; experienced the Mysteries as we performed them.

The loose-knit traditions of the Church of All Worlds offered space for intuitive ceremony, and encouraged the eclectic recombination of structure and experience, form and limitless expansion. In learning the basic elements of ritual structure, I became adept at creating and adapting ritual formats to make room for as many points of reception as possible. Using the Celtic-Hellenic hybrid that formed the basis of the CAW cosmology, and the ease of integration of the "Wing-It Tradition," I was given the tools to adapt, amalgamate, update, and re-vision mythical structures and ritual formats.

On numerous occasions I have pulled together a ritual at a moment's notice. I take the elements desired, the deities to be honored, and the purpose of the Rite, place it in the cauldron of mind and spirit, and pull out a fully-formed ritual outline in minutes. Once we have the desired end-point in mind, the rest is dressing. But that dressing works best when it is flexible and strong, inclusive and focused.

I sought ordination in the Church of All Worlds after years of training, and my path to that ordination was ten years long from start to finish. I was the first, and as far as I am aware, the only second-generation CAW member to be ordained.

It wasn't easy, but it was mostly good. My stepping up, stepping into a position of adulthood made the elders nervous perhaps, or at least led them to recognize the movement of time. I was 29 when I was finally ordained. I was older than Oberon was when he started CAW. But I grew up into an existing structure, and we are all products of our environment.

At some point we grew into a multi-generational sense of tribe. Somewhere along the way the wisdom of age and the wisdom of youth made peace, and we all learned how to learn from one another. We all claimed our positions as visionaries, dreaming a new age into being.

The people you will read writings from in these pages were, and are, those visionaries: outlaws, renegades, anarchists, hippies, teachers, dreamers. They are ones who heard the call of the Divine, and answered that call. Hearts open, eyes wide and wild, and minds churning, these pioneers took to the path of Spirit, and emerged as both gods and seekers.

I'm the result of a social experiment. I am one piece of proof that this experiment worked. The revolution of the heart lives on in the lives we build, the rituals we create, the dreams we live, and the communities we invest in. Generation to generation the vision takes deeper purchase in the soil. It gestates, seeds, and grows.

And we grow continually closer to the Earth, closer to the gods, closer to living with our hearts. We are always coming home.

—LaSara WakeRobin Firefox, Beltaine, 2006

Acknowledgements

First off, we'd like to thank everyone who contributed chants, invocations, workings, and rituals to the original loose-leaf compilation of *HOME Cooking* (1997) as well as to the present work. There are too many to list here individually, but each piece is credited.

And thanks also to Meliny Hansen and Wynter Rose, who each spent volunteer days at the *Green Egg* office collating the *HOME Cooking* books.

But most importantly, the genesis of this book, as with its predecessor, emerged organically out of decades of rituals developed and performed in the context of the Church of All Worlds, and its subsidiary, the Holy Order of Mother Earth (HOME). These rites especially blossomed into full manifestation when a number of us came to live and work magick together on the sacred lands of Coeden Brith, Annwfn, and the encompassing Greenfield Ranch in the Misty Mountains of Mendocino County, NorCalifia, from the mid-1970s to the present day.

Significant contributors to the evolving HOME liturgy during that formative period include Gwydion Pendderwen, Anna Korn, Anodea Judith, Eldri Littlewolf, Tom Williams, Avilynn Pwyll, Marylyn Motherbear, LaSara Firefox, Diane Darling, Sequoia Greenfield, Ayisha Homolka, Aeona Silversong, Orion Stormcrow, Maerian Morris, Starwhite, Night An'Fey, Wendy Hunter-Roberts, Buffalo Brownson, and D.J. and Rick Hamouris. All of these are deeply appreciated, and you will find some of their inspired work within these pages.

We would also like to acknowledge and thank other authors, teachers, mentors, and creative ritualists whose works have inspired and informed our own. These include Aleister Crowley, Gerald Gardner, Doreen Valiente, Robert A. Heinlein, Robert H. Rimmer, Frederick MacLauren Adams, Webster Kitchell, Robert Graves, Deborah Bourbon, Paul Huson, Ed Fitch, Carolyn Clark, Gavin and Yvonne Frost, Isaac Bonewits, Marion Zimmer Bradley, Bran & Moria Starbuck, Victor Anderson, Z Budapest, Kenny and Tzipora Klein, Aidan Kelly, Diana Paxson, and Starhawk.

And finally, special extraordinary thanks go to Jack Crispin Cain and Tamar Kaye, who have devoted over a decade of their lives to being caretakers on Annwfn. Without their dedication to ensuring the maintenance and survival of Gwydion's 55-acre legacy, we'd have had no place to hold many of these rituals, and they might never have come to be.

May you all Never Thirst!

Oberon Zell-Ravenheart   5/1/2006
Morning Glory Zell-Ravenheart   www.CAW.org

Table of Contents

Preface: A Brief Personal History of HOME
By Oberon Zell-Ravenheart

HOMEward Bound

Morning Glory and I have been creating and participating in ceremonies for most of our lives. We were both very active in our respective families' churches when we were children, as we were fascinated by the mystique and magick of the rituals. We enjoyed all the seasonal holiday celebrations (especially Hallowe'en!), birthdays, church retreats, and other annual events. As teenagers, we created our own little rituals for many occasions: funerals for pets, initiations, taking new names, full moons. I joined the Boy Scouts, and attended summer camps where I was introduced to Native American-inspired campfire circles and other "tribal" rituals—which I loved!

Approaching adulthood, we each discovered Paganism and Witchcraft, which led us into creating group rituals for others. In 1962, I co-founded a Pagan Church—the Church of All Worlds (CAW)—which necessitated developing an entire liturgy for our weekly services. In the earliest phases of this process, my ritual constructs were largely derived from my childhood experiences in church and Scouting, combined with ideas from the fantasy, science fiction, and mythology I was reading at the time. Robert Heinlein's *Stranger in a Strange Land* (1961) and Robert Rimmer's *The Rebellion of Yale Marrat* (1964) were particularly influential.

In the late 60s, living in St. Louis, Missouri, I became involved for a few years with the local Unitarian Church, whose pastor, Webster Kitchell, became a close friend. Unitarian liturgical structure and music—especially the hymnal, *Songs for the Celebration of Life*— became another source of inspiration. I also came upon the brilliant work of Feraferia founder Frederick Adams, and incorporated much of his ritual concepts and artwork into the ceremonies I was creating. All of this experience came in very handy when, as a Pagan Priest, I started being asked to perform public wedding ceremonies in those halcyon days of Hippiedom!

In 1970, I was introduced to modern Wicca and Ceremonial Magick, with all of its formal and complex ritual structures. I took classes in these traditions from Deborah Letter at her St. Louis occult store, The Cauldron, and received initiation in April of 1971. CAW's new High Priestess, Carolyn Clark, had been trained in Ozark "Druidic" Witchcraft, and I studied with her as well.

During this period, my publication of *Green Egg* magazine and my articles on "TheaGenesis" (the earliest published writings on what later became known as "The Gaia Thesis") brought me to wider attention, and I started getting invitations to travel and lecture. Thus it came to be that while I was presenting a series of such talks at Llewellyn's 3rd Gnostic Aquarian Festival in Minneapolis, Minnesota, over Autumn Equinox, 1973, I met my lifemate, Morning Glory. The saga of our romance is mythic, but I will not recount it here.

Our wedding at Llewellyn's Spring Witchmoot the following Easter Sunday was an enormous event—attended by hundreds of magickal people and Pagan luminaries. CAW High Priestess Carolyn Clark and Arch Druid Isaac Bonewits officiated, with Margot Adler singing songs by Gwydion Pendderwen. It was covered by local news media and Japanese television, and appeared on the front page of the *Minneapolis Star Tribune,* upstaging the Pope! Morning Glory and I had created the ceremony, and we subsequently printed it in the pages of *Green Egg*. Evidently, this was one of the first Pagan "handfasting" rituals to be published, and it became widely adopted as a model throughout the Pagan community.

After a few years together in St. Louis, Morning Glory and I bought and fixed up a 1958 Chevy school bus ("The Scarlet Succubus"), sold our house, and hit the road for the West Coast. In the Fall of 1976 we arrived in Eugene, Oregon, where we met Anna Korn. She had been trained in Texas in a pre-Z Budapest British Tradition of Dianic Witchcraft by Mark Roberts and Morgan McFarland. I had been trained in an Italian Strega-Qabalistic tradition by Deborah Letter, while MG had pieced together her own "Shamanic Wicca" path out of personal experiences and published materials. The three of us organized all our respective training into a coherent amalgam, and formed the Coven of Ithil Duath to practice it. That Winter and the following Spring, Morning Glory and I developed and refined these materials and practices into an organized study course, which we taught at Lane Community College under the title of "Witchcraft, Shamanism, and Pagan Religions."

HOME Coming

In 1977, Morning Glory and I moved to *Coeden Brith,* a 220-acre parcel owned by Alison Harlow on the 5,600-acre home-steading community called Greenfield Ranch, near Ukiah, Northern California. *Coeden Brith* ("speckled forest" in Welsh) was adjacent to the 55-acre parcel recently acquired by legendary Pagan Bard Gwydion Pendderwen, which he called *Annwfn* (the Welsh Underworld). The Holy Order of Mother Earth was conceived there as a magickal monastic order of stewardship and ritual. HOME was officially chartered "as a subsidiary organization" of the Church of All Worlds on September 21, 1978, "for the purpose of establishing and maintaining a wilderness sanctuary and religious retreat/training center." The first appointed Directors were Alison, Morning Glory, and me.

When Morning Glory and I moved to Greenfield Ranch, other Pagan residents included Bran and Moria Starbuck, Anodea Judith, Sequoia, and Molly. Shortly thereafter, Eldri Littlewolf brought her green step-van (and several fruit trees) up to Coeden Brith from Berkeley. Mari Shuisky rode her bicycle all the way up from San Francisco with her parrot, Rima, on her shoulder. When my old friend Orion decided to leave St. Louis and join us, and Anna Korn moved in with Gwydion, we had a foundation for a solid working magickal group—but one composed of people from several distinctly different Traditions!

Gwydion, Eldri, and Alison were all Faerie Tradition—trained by Victor Anderson. Sequoia was Feminist Dianic—trained by Z Budapest. Anna was also Dianic, but from a British Tradition that included men, formed in Dallas, Texas, in the late 60s by Morgan McFarland and Mark Roberts. Molly came out of Aiden Kelley's New Reformed Orthodox Order of the Golden Dawn (NROOGD). Bran and Moria embraced Mohsian Tradition, Morning Glory practiced an eclectic Celtic/Shamanic brand of Wicca, Orion was pure Church of All Worlds, and I was trained in Ceremonial Magick, Strega, and CAW—with a bit of Ozark "Druidic" Witchcraft, Feraferia, and Egyptian (Church of the Eternal Source) thrown in for good measure.

With all these Pagans in the neighborhood trained in magick and ritual, we weren't about to miss out on Sabbats and Esbats just because we came from different magickal backgrounds! We just began meeting and celebrating together, and during the eight years that many of us lived communally in the Misty Mountains—through full Moons, rites of passage, seasonal celebrations, and daily practice—we wove all these disparate strands together into a unique practice that was rooted in our own daily and seasonal lives in the Magick Land. This gave rise to a new magickal working tradition and shamanic path: the "HOME Tradition." The written course materials that M.G. and I had developed for our classes in Eugene—particularly the "Tables of Correspondence"—provided the foundation for our first personal *Book of Lights and Shadows,* which Morning Glory assembled.

A very important aspect of our evolving Tradition developed in the form of poetry, songs, and chants—many composed by Gwydion, our first Bard (and the first Bard in the Pagan community to record albums of his original performances). So we became a "Bardic Tradition" in which entire rituals would be sung, chanted, or recited as poetry.

In time, other members of the Greenfield Ranch community came to join our HOME Circles, such as Marylyn Motherbear and her wonderful family (which included LaSara FireFox, an eventual two-time May Queen). We planted trees and gardens, raised unicorns and deer, sang our songs and told our stories around the campfire. Babies were born on the land, blessed in ritual, and raised up in Circle, assimilating our customs and traditions into a new generation. In our growing magickal community we actually lived the semi-mythical lives of our ancient Pagan tribal forebears. Several *"Letters from HOME"* were published over the next few years, mainly dealing with the cycles of seasons, plants, animals and arboriculture of Coeden Brith.

The HOME Tradition

HOME continued the tradition, already established by Alison and Gwydion, of hosting a large Summer Solstice festival on the land. At one such, we had over 200 attendees! Alison and Gwydion had also been holding a "Grape Harvest Festival" each Autumn Equinox, which we continued and expanded into Mabon. We also began holding Beltane (Mayday) celebrations at Coeden Brith, which eventually became our main annual event.

Greenfield Ranch held a number of major parties throughout the year, and Summer Solstice and Halloween were the biggest of these. Morning Glory and I developed an elaborate "Underworld Journey" Samhain Mystery Play for Halloween and a great "Bubble of Protection" ritual for Midsummer. Yule became a moving all-night vigil of sharing songs and stories around the enormous Ranch House fireplace.

The biggest event in which we participated during that period was the total eclipse of the sun on February 26, 1979. The location was a full-scale replica of a restored Stonehenge, erected by railroad tycoon Sam Hill (1857-1931) on a bluff overlooking the Columbia River Gorge ("The Dalles"), about 100 miles East of Portland, Oregon. The site had been selected as the only place in North America where two total eclipse paths would cross—one in 1918 and the other in 1979. The altar stone had been laid and the site dedicated for the first of these eclipses, but the construction of the entire monument wasn't completed until 1930. And all those years it had stood there awaiting the second eclipse.

On the morning of the eclipse, nearly 4,000 people were in attendance! Morning Glory and I had previously designed the core ritual, and along with Isaac Bonewits, we served as

High Priestess and High Priests at the "Stone Table." But dozens of other Priests, Priestesses, and Elders of various Traditions contributed to the liturgy and wove the magick. A photo of us appeared on the cover of the first edition of Margot Adler's book, *Drawing Down the Moon* (1979). (right)

HOME joined the Covenant of the Goddess as a charter member in 1979, and participated actively in organizational meetings from Los Angeles to Seattle, as well as the local NorCal CoG Council.

In June of 1981, Gwydion organized a great public Pagan Litha Festival in Berkeley, which was sponsored by CAW, HOME, and Nemeton. It included his "Faery Shaman" ritual, and was quite successful. The following year, Gwydion released his second album, "The Faerie Shaman," containing many wonderful and moving songs of our lives together on the land. When he was killed in a car wreck at Samhain of 1982, our community was plunged into deep grief as for the first time we dealt with Death in our own family. Our rituals developed a darker aspect as we created funerary rites and wakes, exploring the Underworld through the mythic Mysteries of Samhain, Walpurgisnacht, and the Eleusinia.

In 1983, Anodea Judith founded Lifeways, creating a course program ("Magic 101") based on the rituals, traditions, and materials we had all developed under the auspices of

HOME. Many people in the San Francisco Bay Area took these classes and were trained in the HOME liturgy. As they became more proficient, many composed and added their own contributions to this growing body of materials. Anodea herself blossomed as a Bard during this period, composing and performing many hauntingly evocative poems, songs, and rituals that enriched our liturgy and our ceremonies. She became High Priestess of the Church of All Worlds, as well as President of the Board, and served in those roles for many years

Perhaps the most remarkable factor of the HOME Tradition was that we never created a "Common Book of Shadows," which would provide a compendium of set rituals to be used for every purpose. Indeed, each ritual we conducted over these past three decades was a unique creation, never performed before, and likely never to be performed again.

When Morning Glory and I moved from Coeden Brith in 1985, the original envisioned purpose of HOME—that of "establishing and maintaining a wilderness sanctuary and religious retreat/training center"—was transferred to Annwfn, which Gwydion had bequeathed to the Church of All Worlds. Our unique HOME Tradition continued to be the unifying designation for the rites and rituals we had developed during those years on the land, and which we have continued to practice, refine, and expand upon to the present day.

A "Branch Description" of HOME dated March 28, 1992, listed HOME's purpose as "being responsible for making the CAW vision real through well-conducted and appropriate rituals and festivals." The responsibilities of HOME were listed as: "ensures that each Sabbat, festival or other ritual occasion is properly scheduled, staged, promoted and staffed," and "keeps a library of ritual scripts, Books of Shadows, props and other pertinent information." "Functions" were listed as: "creates, reviews, stages public festivals and rituals; assembles guidelines for rituals; engages in outreach to other Pagan and religious groups; provides coordination for Clergy."

Over the years, people inspired and trained in the HOME Tradition have continued to "create and conduct the CAW's rituals and ceremonies." These have included not only our own Wheel of the Year cycle of Sabbats—especially Beltane, Litha, Samhain, and Yule—but also special events, ceremonies, initiations, handfastings, and rites of passage. Lifeways continued to conduct classes and disseminate rituals using the materials developed as the HOME Tradition.

HOME Cooking

In the Spring 1993 issue of CAW's membership newsletter, *Scarlet Flame*, there appeared the first solicitation for a "CAW Book of Shadows," asking CAW members ("Waterkin") to submit their contributions to Aeona Silversong. As materials came in, Aeona organized them into basic categories, from which emerged a provisional Table of Contents. Morning Glory went through our personal collection of HOME ritual materials as well as Books of Shadows from the various Traditions we had studied and worked with, selecting appropriate additions and conceptualizing the organizational structure and presentation. Meanwhile we continued to solicit, collect, organize, and create new materials. When Liza Gabriel joined our family in the mid-90s, she began working with Morning Glory to sort and categorize the growing collection, scanning many pages of typed materials onto disk so they could be used, and spending many hours correcting the errors of such scans.

By Autumn of 1996, we had enough materials to determine that *HOME Cooking* would comprise a three-volume set, to be published in loose-leaf format. At the Highlands of Tennessee Samhain Gathering that year, we arranged with Nybor for cover art. Anodea contributed many of her lessons from "Magick 101," and wrote up introductions to various sections, while I drew a bunch of illustrations. In December, as soon as we got an office and computer set up at our new home on the V-M Ranch, I began compiling and formatting the book, finally presenting the first draft of *Book One: The Magick Circle,* to Brigit , our patron goddess, at Oimelc of 1997. It contained 66 pages in a hard loose-leaf binder with cover art by Nybor. Each copy had to be hand-copied, punched, collated, and bound—by me and a few dedicated volunteers.

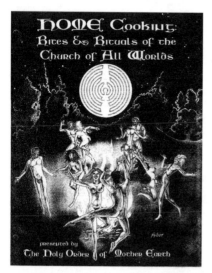

HOME Cooking:
Rites & Rituals of the
Church of All Worlds

presented by
The Holy Order of Mother Earth

But this material was so important, and the contributions so wonderful, that I felt it worthwhile to go to this much trouble just to make it available. Unfortunately, as we found ourselves having to move several times, the effort of copying and binding each edition soon became too overwhelming to keep up, and I had to let it lapse after running off maybe a couple hundred copies. Regardless, materials were collected for two more volumes. Book II was to comprise a collection of actual rituals for Esbats, Rites of Passage, Nest meetings, magickal workings, blessings, etc., and Book III was to cover the Wheel of the Year. However, conflicts within the Church at that time precluded further publication, and the entire project was shelved.

But each copy of *HOME Cooking* has been a treasure to those who managed to get them, and I still get requests from those who haven't. So at the International New Age Trade Show (INATS) in June of 2005, I showed my dog-eared copy of *HOME Cooking Book I* to my Publishers at New Page Books. With the phenomenal success of my first book, *Grimoire for the Apprentice Wizard* (2004), and a second *Companion* volume on the way, they immediately snapped up the proposal for publishing the entire three-volume set of *HOME Cooking* materials as a single book, to be re-titled: *Creating Circles & Ceremonies: Rituals for All Seasons & Reasons.*

So as soon as *Companion for the Apprentice Wizard* was off to the printer, I fired off an e-mail to all the folks who had contributed to the original *HOME Cooking*, explaining the new project, and asking their permission to include their materials. That was about 100 people. However, some of those who received my post thought it would be helpful to forward it on to various lists of Pagan writers, and soon we were deluged with wonderful submissions from some of the most creative minds of the magickal community! All of us felt honored to have some our own inspired poetry, spells, invocations, chants, workings, and rituals, etc., become a permanent part of the liturgy of the fastest-growing religious movement in the English-speaking world. This is like getting your songs into the hymnal of your church! And after all, that's why we create such works in the first place...so that others will use them to enhance our collective magick in healing and awakening Gaia.

Hence this present compilation, while including most of the original *HOME Cooking* materials, has expanded to include significant contributions from throughout the worldwide Neo-Pagan community—and beyond, as you will find here ritual resources from other ceremonial traditions as well. Some of these pieces entered our rituals and collections anonymously; we decided to include some that have been important parts of our liturgy, even if we couldn't determine where they came from. Every effort has been made to locate and contact authors and copyright holders, but for any omissions that can be properly attributed, we would appreciate being informed for corrections and credits in future printings.

In this new manifestation, we go beyond the original premise of focusing just on decades of accumulated rituals developed in the Church of All Worlds, to produce a general "kit" with mix-'n'-match components for creating rituals and ceremonies for every conceivable purpose. We intend this book to be both a tribute to our amazing magickal community, and a quintessential resource for any ritualist, of any magickal Tradition or Path, be they Pagans, New Agers, Unitarians, Solitaries, Wiccans, Gaians, and other spiritual folk.

We hope you will find it a treasure trove to enrich your ceremonies, and your life!

And if you want to learn more about CAW and Annwfn, go to: *www.CAW.org.*

Book I: The Magick Circle

Table of Contents

1. Welcome to the Circle of Magick!

Introduction to Magick & Ritual
By Anodea Judith

Welcome to the realm of magick and ritual! Here in these pages you are invited to enter into an enchanting convergence with the raw forces of Life, exquisitely combining your Will and Intention for the sake of achieving transformation and balance. This is no small task, and as such it requires the application of both science and art. These three books in one volume are designed to aid you in this process—a set of tried and true recipes, if you will—that can be used according to your own taste and practice. Pick and choose, sample and muse your way through these offerings—offerings to the temple of the sacred circle, the field in which magick occurs. Use what you will, add to it, change it, enhance it, or discard it. But do enjoy the process, for the elements of magick are the spiritual language of the Gods, and the building blocks of the world we create.

Why Study Magick?
By Sheila Attig

The path of the Western Mysteries is not for everybody. It requires extraordinary honesty, dedication, persistence, and a deep commitment to change. Real magick requires a fundamentally balanced personality willing to take on the challenges of accelerated growth. The decision to embark on the magickal path should never be taken lightly—once begun, there is no turning back. It is a decision to trust one's individual experience, and to take responsibility in all areas of one's life.

From the beginning, the student will perceive that the lessons he/she most needs to learn are delivered with astonishing clarity. Along the way, the student will be presented with many tests and difficulties unique to the Magickal path. The ability to learn from these experiences and thrive is the true measure of Initiation.

Unlike most forms of religion, Magick has no central written codex of laws, and offers no easy answers. The laws under which it operates are uniform, but are discovered only through direct experience. To truly begin the path, then, is to commit oneself to a lifetime of discovery and sacrifice offered without reservation. For those few with the honesty and courage to choose this path there is no turning back. One can cease to practice, but the lessons will still be delivered on schedule in the life of the person who turns away.

Opening oneself to the Innerworld opens the way to change at the deepest inner levels. Without the courage to confront and change all the aspects of your own Innerworld that will be presented, the risk of confusion and self-deception is great. Undertaking such study without the foundation of a balanced personality, and without clear knowledge of the best and worst aspects of one's self, could be gambling with your sanity. Until you know firmly who you are, why take such a risk? Magick has a way of calling in old business that must be cleared before serious work can begin, and many who approach it decide to stop when they first experience encounter such obligations. Not everyone will find that dire consequences immediately ensue when they choose the Magickal Path. For those who choose it rightly, the speed at which things clear in their lives will be experienced with a distinct sense of relief.

Magick is powerful, but it is foolish to undertake it as a quest for increased personal power. If you desire to be a master, rather than a servant, Magick is not for you. Before beginning, ask yourself, "What do I intend to do with my Magick?" Make no mistake, the only true answer for real magicians is "I desire to serve Spirit and humankind, and I am willing to take the risks to complete that service."

Creating Rituals
by Hallie Iglehart

Ritual is a metaphor for all of conscious living. It is a way to focus and acknowledge energy and awareness. We all perform rituals throughout the day—some more conscious than others—that influence and support our attitudes and behavior. We get dressed in the morning, we celebrate our birthdays, we meet with others, and we mark major events in our lives. The quality that makes "ordinary" life a ritual is very subtle. Lighting a candle and burning incense does not by itself make a ritual, but the state of mind and awareness accompanying or resulting from the action does.

Our Ritual Heritage

Mythology, archeology, linguistics, art, and history tell us of the rituals that our foremothers performed. Paleolithic caves, as metaphorical "wombs" of the Earth Mother, were natural sites for birth and rebirth rituals, and the carved and painted breasts and vulvas, paintings of animals and plants, and markings of the cycles of the moon and seasons still preserved in some of these caves are vivid reminders of these ancient rituals.

Right up until the classical period, arguably the most powerful and important religious experience in ancient Greek culture was the Eleusinian Mysteries, traditionally founded by the Earth Goddess Demeter to celebrate Her reunion with Her daughter Persephoné/Koré. The Mysteries were brilliantly designed to facilitate a psychic rebirth in the participant, corresponding to Koré's return from the Underworld and the re-emergence of Spring.

Since the beginnings of time, ritual has been a comprehensive, holistic expression and celebration of human creativity and cyclic regeneration. Many of our arts—theater, poetry, and song—originally evolved as parts of one unified ritual-making process. As people became more alienated from nature and their inner selves, the arts became isolated from each other and fragmented from their original unifying spiritual source, much as one primal female spiritual energy became, over time, fragmented into many goddesses. However, we can still feel the spiritual power of ritual in the best of art. The energy of performance art in particular is very similar to that of ritual: witness the intense focus, the channeling of energy, and the exchange of energy between performers and audience.

HOME Cooking: The Magick Circle
By Anodea Judith

The first and most basic element of conducting formal magickal ritual is the creation of Sacred Space. Formal ritual is something made special, set apart from everyday, requiring a focused attention. The setting up of sacred space marks this time as different from that time, these words as more significant than mere idle chit-chat, these movements as having deeper meaning. It allows us to alter our consciousness, to redirect our attention.

The Circle is the sacred center in which most formal rituals take place. Like a cauldron in which we mix and stir our magick elixir, the Circle forms the psychic boundaries that keep unwanted energy out, while allowing the magickal energy within to be contained until transformation is complete. As such the Circle is seen as a "place between the worlds"—a place outside the ordinary stream of time and space, yet a place that inevitably influences this stream. Thus we say, *The Circle closes between the worlds, to mark this sacred space, where we come face to face."* (Rick Hamouris, "We Are a Circle")

As the essential foundation of all ritual, the Magick Circle is extremely important. This means that the space in which the Circle is held is purified and consecrated for the rite in question, that care is taken to be as conscious as possible of all words and actions within the Circle, and that there are certain codes of behavior for protecting the sanctity of the Circle.

One of these codes is the law of Perfect Love and Perfect Trust. This means that we only enter into a Circle with the feeling and intention that we can behave toward all members and toward the rite in general with this attitude. It means we agree to open our hearts and minds to each person in an aura of trust, and to not betray the trust of anyone in the Circle. If we cannot enter a Circle in this manner—for instance, if we have a major quarrel with someone in the Circle, or if we are simply in an ornery mood that we can't shake—then we should not enter the Circle at all. In accordance with the Three-Fold Law, our behavior, feelings, or mood may increase exponentially, and possibly contaminate the magick that is trying to happen.

What does this mean when we do not know all of the participants in a large ritual? How can we be in "perfect love" with strangers? My interpretation is that we agree to *behave* as if we had this perfect love and trust. Much as we practice the " suspension of disbelief" in some magickal workings, we practice an assumption of belief about the mutual trustworthiness of the partici-pants with whom we share our Circle. If everyone abides by this law, this should not be a problem, and will eventually create the feeling of total love and trust. In smaller Circles, of course, the level of intimacy and trust is deepened, and consequently the intensity of the magick is also increased.

In my Tradition, the Holy Order of Mother Earth, we often refer to our magickal prac-tices as "HOME Cooking." Therefore I like to use the analogy of baking a cake to represent the various aspects of creating a magickal Circle:

Before baking the cake, it is necessary to clean off the counter. We do not want to prepare food on a counter cluttered with yesterday's dirty dishes or piles of unsorted papers. Similarly, we purify the space we are going to use in our ritual. This may involve magickally banishing unwanted energies, or it may simply entail sweeping the floor and unplugging the phone. Purification may also include ritual baths for the participants, smudging the room or the people who enter, or sprinkling the area with salt water. These acts clear the field in which we wish to work and makes the work proceed more smoothly.

Next we bring out a large bowl in which we are going to mix the ingredients for the cake. The bowl is a container that holds the ingredients so they will mix together. If we simply threw them on the counter, we could not mix them. In this way, the Circle becomes a cauldron that hermetically seals the energies we invoke until they can adequately transform.

This cauldron or bowl is formed by "casting the Circle." This marks the physical area that is now clearly defined as sacred space. It may be marked on the ground or floor by drawing with chalk or cornmeal, or even by a scattering of flowers. Often it is drawn sym-bolically in the air by a Priestess or Priest with some sort of magickal tool, such as a sword, knife *(athamé),* wand, or crystal. Or, it may be delineated simply by the walls of the temple or room. Finally, if need be, it can also be created in the realm of your imagination, without any outward movement or markings at all. Samples of Circle Castings will be given in Chapter 3.

Once we have an adequate bowl and a clean space in which to work, we bring in our ingredients according to the recipe chosen. For a cake, it's eggs, flour, milk, and sugar. For a Circle, this includes the Elements and Directions, the Deities and Spirits chosen for the rite, ancestors, faeries, animal spirits, and whatever else is appropriate for the purpose of the ritual. These ingredients are invoked into the Circle and "stirred" together by the Priestess and/or Priest and the participants.

It is not enough to merely follow a cookbook of ingredients; a talented baker adds that extra special something that makes the recipe unique. The Deities that are called into the Circle are the special magick that makes for a good "cake." The Deities are the archetypal principles that we wish to connect with in ourselves and remember as influences in our working. They bring the essence of the Divine—that mysterious element that we cannot control or completely plan for, but that we can invite. This invitation of a Deity or Deities is called *Invocation.*

Then comes the working. This is where we stir the "ingredients" together. Do we beat them like egg whites for meringue, or gently fold them together, as in a marble cake? Do we add surprise ingredients and stir in one direction, or do we mix some ingredients separately before adding? This is the most creative part of a ritual, and it is the real essence of the magick.

After the working we need to raise energy in order to transform the ingredients into something new. In baking a cake, this is the part where we apply heat by placing the mixed ingredients in the oven. In a Circle, raising energy may entail drumming and dancing, chanting, meditating, or focusing energy on symbolic objects or on the Priestess herself. When this energy is applied, as in the case of heat from the oven, a transformation does indeed take place—the cake now holds a new form.

Once this transformation has taken place, a cooling-off period is needed. In the same way that a cake "sets" better if it is allowed to sit for a bit, a Circle often spends this time sharing food, drink, and discussion that allays the previous intensity of raising energy.

Once cooling has taken place, the cake can be taken out of the pan. It will hold its new shape and can be shared outside the kitchen. In the Circle, this means that the magick has taken place in whatever fashion was intended, and the Circle can be removed to allow that magick to pass on to wherever it is intended. The "pans" are cleaned, the "containers" and "ingredients" put away, and the ritual is ended.

Circle Symbolism
By Bran th' Blessed

The four-quartered Circle of Magick is a central element in most Western magickal rituals. It is called "the portal between the worlds," a means of connecting with the Deities, Spirits, and Elemental Powers of a realm beyond the material universe. It is envisioned as a vortex within which we focus our own innate psychic powers, called forth by ritual actions from the subliminal depths of the mind and soul. It is a "sacred space," a sanctuary for communion with the old ones, the deities of our faith.

Many levels of symbolism are intrinsic to the Magick Circle:. Among these metaphors are metaphysical and mystical concepts that describe the greater reality within which our lives are experienced. The four "corners" of the Circle of Magick correspond with the compass directions and their associated Elements (Earth, Air, Fire or Water). A fifth Element, Spirit, is often associated with the center of the Circle or with the Circle as a whole.

Anaximander of Miletus, a Greek philosopher of the sixth century BCE, proposed that reality had its foundation in an all-pervasive, unending substance which he called the *Infinite* or *Boundless*, the Divine Source of all things. The *Boundless* divided itself into two components by spinning about its center. Its hotter and lighter component was flung outward to form the heavens while its colder and heavier component sank toward the center to form the Earth. Later the Earth separated further into the dry land and the wet oceans. Today we find this same explanation for the formation of planets, stars and galaxies whose shapes are sculpted by the interplay of gravity and energy. Anaximander's *Boundless* is the Spirit of the Circle imagery and the source of Heaven (Air) and Earth. Spirit is the very force and fiber of existence; but in spite of its fundamental importance in our being, it is virtually beyond comprehension.

The realm of wind, water, stone, and flesh is manifest Spirit; the realm of Earth, Moon, Sun, and stars is manifest Spirit; time and space, energy and gravity, the realm of imagination, memory, emotion, and desire—all are Spirit manifest in that they can be named and known. Yet the aspect of Spirit that transcends naming and knowledge, incomprehensible in its mystery, is the ultimate Source of all these things.

Many Pagan groups, Wiccan covens, and the HOME Tradition place Air in the East and Fire in the South. Some believe Water should be assigned the direction of the nearest ocean. Earth is generally assigned to the North, and Fire to the South; but in the Southern Hemisphere, Earth may be assigned to the frozen Antarctic South, and Fire to the hot equatorial North. However the details, Circle symbolism speaks to the heart and mind with images that remind us of our bonds to the universe and its awesome wonders.

Magick Circle Mandala

By Oberon

This Mandala diagrams the Magick Circle with the corresponding alignments of the various cycles of the Sacred Year. A ritual area laid out in this design may serve for virtually any form of magickal ceremony. In the Northern Hemisphere, all cycles begin in the North (at the top of the picture) and move *deosil* (clockwise). In the Southern Hemisphere, North and South should be reversed, and the cycles (and movements in the Circle) go *widdershins* (counterclockwise).

The outermost rings mark the **52 weeks** of the year, each of seven days, totaling **364 days,** plus two intercalary days: *Π* (Pi) following the Winter Solstice each year; and *Φ* (Phi) following Summer Solstice every four years.

The next ring inward marks the **13 Lunar/tree/consonant months** of Robert Graves' Celtic Tree calendar: Beth (Birch), Luis (Rowan), Nion (Ash), Vearn/Fearn (Alder), Saille/Ztraif (Willow/Maple), Huath (Thorn), Duir/Fith (Oak), Tinne (Holly), Coll/Quirt (Hazel/Apple), Muin (Vine), Gort (Ivy), Ngetal (Reed), Ruis (Elder), These are illustrated with "axerian" glyphs.

The third ring in links the **eight Sabbats** and the **Elements of the Four Directions**: Yule (North/Earth)—Winter Solstice; Oimelc (Northeast); Ostara (East/Air)—Spring Equinox; Beltaine (Southeast); Litha (South/Fire)—Summer Solstice; Lughnasadh (Southwest); Mabon (West/Water)—Fall Equinox; Samhain (Northwest).

The fourth ring inward marks the **12 astrological signs of the Zodiac,** with their glyphs: Capricorn, Aquarius, Pisces, Aries, Taurus, Gemini, Cancer, Leo, Virgo, Libra, Scorpio, Sagittarius. (If you would like to use this design to make a henge of wood or stone, the small circles on the inner edge of the astrological ring indicate the positions of Summer Solstice sunrise (NE), Winter Solstice sunrise (SE), Winter Solstice sunset (SW), ad Summer Solstice sunset (NW). These must be adjusted for local latitude.)

The next area inside the astrological ring marks the **four Seasons:** Winter, Spring, Summer, and Fall—with their respective glyphs.

The Pentagram—emblem of magick, Witchcraft, and the Pythagorean Mysteries— marks in its points the **five Celtic vowels**: *Idho, Ailm, Onn, Ura,* and *Eadha.* The Pentagram also represents the five magickal Elements: Spirit, Air, Fire, Water, and Earth.

The center circle marks the **Altar,** and its symbol is the universal glyph representing Earth, our Holy Mother and Sacred Home.

Tables of Correspondence provide the symbolic associations that may be made when addressing any of these aspects. In practice, the Correspondences of the Four Directions are almost universally used in Pagan rituals, while few of the others are.

Axerian glyphs for the Celtic consonants and vowels were designed by Fred Adams of Feraferia. They may be constructed as staves or wands for henge and temple work.

This Mandala may be painted on the floor of a temple, printed on an altar cloth, or used as a design for a stone or wood henge.

Ten Questions to Ask in Planning a Ritual
By Anodea Judith

1. **What is the purpose of the ritual?** (Why am I doing this, what do we wish to accomplish, what is the problem we wish to solve, etc.) Answers can be anything from the removal of nuclear weapons to simply having a good time. This dictates the theme.
2. **What time is it?** (What time of year, season, moon cycle, day or night, time in your life, time in a group's life (i.e. initiation, closing, etc.) or what time in a succession of rituals (such as planetary or chakra rituals, which may go in a certain order)?
3. **Who is it for and who will take part?** This encompasses number of people, level of experience, age, physical capabilities, children, all women, all men, mixed, closed intimate circle, large public ritual, or anything in between.
4. **Who do we wish to influence?** This is slightly different from #1, and may also be skipped, as in a purpose of simply having a good time. If our purpose is to remove nuclear weapons, we may wish to influence politicians in Washington, or we may wish to influence families in the neighborhood to inspire them to write letters to congressman. A word of warning must always be added on this one, namely that what you're doing doesn't become manipulation, which is both exhausting and of questionable ethics.
5. **Where will it be held?** Indoors, outdoors, in a home, temple, classroom, etc.
6. **How long should it last?** This relates to #2 and #5, for outdoor, nighttime rituals may need to be shorter than others. It also must take into consideration who will be there—i.e. children cannot sit through long rituals. Subroutines of the ritual should also be planned (i.e. casting the circle: 5 minutes, invocations: 10 minutes, etc.).
7. **What do we have to work with?** If it's outdoors on a full Moon, you have the time and the place to work with, and whatever elements they invoke. A mountaintop gives you one thing, the ocean another. What tools do you have in the way of invocations, skills, people, robes, dances, chants, etc? Sort through what you have from your Book of Shadows (if you have one) and lay out all the things that are appropriate. You may not use them all but you can sort and order them later when the skeleton comes into play.
8. **What will be the main techniques for working?** Meditation, dancing, chanting, healing, drinking, walking, drumming, etc. Which is most appropriate to the purpose and theme?
9. **How do you symbolize, on a microcosmic scale, what you wish to work?** If you wish to cross the abyss, how can you represent that in the ritual? If you wish to open people's hearts, how can that be symbolized in a subliminal way?
10. **What should be on the Altar(s)?** This comes out of the symbolism of #9. If you are working on Air, then you would have feathers and incense. Conversely, if you are working on Earth, you might have crystals or plants.

By this time, if these questions have been asked and answered, a general thread should start to come through. Be creative. Look for narrative threads, and how one part can flow into another naturally and gracefully while feeding the central theme and purpose that was chosen. Once the theme becomes clear and you know what you have to work with, these answers can be fed into the liturgical structure outline to create the actual ceremony. It is far more important, however, that the ritual *work* on a gut level, than actually having every little thing in place. Give yourself full rein for experimentation, and know there is *no* one true right and only way.

Theatrical Considerations
By Oberon

Morning Glory and I were both very involved in theatre throughout high school and college. As a member of the Thespian Society, I immersed myself in everything from set design, costuming, and makeup, to on-stage acting. Morning Glory and I both regularly got leading roles in many of the school plays, and we remember each of them fondly these many years later. We consider our theatrical experience to be perhaps one of our most important trainings for our later vocations as Priest and Priestess—especially for large public rituals. And we highly recommend this training to anyone who is really serious about wanting to create and perform rituals and ceremonies. Nearly every community has a local community theatre where plays are performed several times a year. Look them up, and go try out for a part. Even a walk-on or extra role will teach you valuable lessons – especially in how to project your voice and your energy – that will lend depth and authenticity to your performance and staging of ceremonies.

Ritual and theatre were originally one. They began around the campfires of our most ancient ancestors, from the time we first learned mastery of this most magickal Element. For our very humanity began with the taming of Fire. All our magick—and all our culture—came first from the Fire. Gathered around our blazing hearths, we sang our first songs, made our first music, danced our first dances, told our first stories, and performed our first plays. These performances recounted the experiences of our lives and adventures for the rest of the clan, enacting, in time, the tales of our ancestors, the mighty deeds of our legendary heroes, the myths of our gods, and the Mysteries of Life, Death, and Rebirth. For hundreds of thousands of years we did this, and only in the past 2,500 years did "theatre" begin to be distinguished from "ritual."

> *If theatre is to be defined as involving the art of acting a part on stage, that is the dramatic impersonation of another character than yourself, we begin with Thespis. A figure of whom we know very little, he won the play competition in honor of the Greek god Dionysus, in 534 BCE. While it is uncertain whether Thespis was a playwright, an actor or a priest, it is his name with which the dramatic arts are associated in our word "Thespian."*
> (from "History of Theatre" http://www.tctwebstage.com/ancient.htm)

All Greek drama was dedicated to Dionysos, and performed in the context of sacred rituals in his honor. And for the next 2,000 years after Thespis, the vast majority of Thespian performances continued to enact religious rituals, pageants, and "Mystery Plays." So there is a rich historical lineage and tradition of dramatic ritual, and ritual drama. Good ritual is good theatre.

Read play scripts to learn how to stage and script your rituals dramatically—and how to write them up so they can be easily understood by the performers. Learn how to designate characters, costumes, sets, props, and stage directions. Learn to make ritual implements ("props"): magickal tools, staves, scepters, streamers, etc. Learn to design and create appropriate costumes, such as simple robes and colored tabards for the four directions, as well as masks, wings, tiaras, helms, and headdresses for different spirits and deities. Learn to create dramatic sets, with altars, gateways, henges, ritual fires, tiki torches, and banners. Learn special effects to add a flair of drama, such as powders to make the fire flare up in different colors. And develop a good stage voice to reach to the outermost fringes of the largest Circle.

And most important, *memorize your lines!* Nothing detracts more from the effect of a ritual than the performers carrying around paper scripts, and reading aloud from them! However, for certain formal rituals (such as handfastings, initiations, dedications, rites of passage, etc.), it is not untoward to have your script bound into an impressive-looking binder as a *Grimoire* or "Book of Shadows" which will sit open on the Altar as a prop—perhaps even on a stand. An image of a Pentagram or Magick Circle Mandala on the cover will give it a real mystical aura of credibility. After all, magickal rites are often referred to as "Bell, Book, and Candle."

Ethics of Magic & Ritual
By Anodea Judith

Within the realm of magick, everything is alive and connected to everything else. All elements of life—the trees, the weather, the emotions we feel, the words we speak, the time of day, and the way we move—all are intimately connected, inextricably interwoven within a greater field that surrounds us. What affects one element affects all, as expressed by the Hermetic maxim: *"As above, so below."* Furthermore, what occurs without occurs within, and vice versa. The various realms are but mirrors for each other, and mirrors for our very souls. In this way, magick is but a microcosm of the larger forces—a microcosm small enough to be influenced by us, but one which in turn influences larger forces which might otherwise seem beyond us.

Magick does not manipulate the world as much as it follows the natural lines of force as Life flows into the stream of Time. In this stream, nothing is stationary or stagnant; everything is constantly moving and changing. It is this fluid movement that allows magick to occur, for in the midst of change we can reach in and create new realities as the forces of Life journey from chaos to manifestation.

As everything in the magickal world is interconnected, it makes for an interesting question of ethics. We ourselves are not separate from this world, nor can our actions be separate, nor their results. Thus, magick contains its own sacred immune system. All that we do within the magick realm we do to the field around us, and hence to our very selves. Magick can, in fact, be one of the quickest karmic feedback systems we experience!

This is summed up in the *Wiccan Rede: "An it harm none, do as ye will"* (*an* is archaic Middle English for "if"). This means that the sovereignty of one's personal will is highly respected as long as it does not cause harm or interfere with the rights of another. To do so would be to harm the basic underlying fabric that connects all things, and reflect back negatively upon the practitioner. Yet to act upon one's own will is also to be responsible for it— to follow up on actions, to avoid blaming others, and to live responsibly and consciously.

This may also be expressed in what is called *The Threefold Law,* which states that whatever we generate magickally returns to us threefold—positively or negatively. Ritual within a Magick Circle is basically an amplifier for energy, multiplying the effects of one's actions. Therefore, whatever we initiate magickally expands exponentially, like ripples from a stone cast into a still pond, into the outer world. If our intentions are not clear, if we do not act with respect and affinity for all that may be affected, then the results of these actions, as they run through the connective web of all Life, eventually return to us magnified in threefold measure.

This requires the magical participant to take full responsibility for any actions initiated within the Circle—and indeed, throughout one's life. This even includes unintentional mistakes, which can happen to anyone. We are still required to be fully responsible for those mistakes, and do so always provides valuable lessons in magickal and spiritual growth.

Pagans recognize a responsibility to treat the Earth with respect, to reuse and recycle, to treat each other excellently, to empower their word by speaking truth at all times, and to be conscious of their behavior. In Paganism, there is no concept of a stern "Father in Heaven" to sit in judgment of us, damning us to some eternal hell. There is merely the state of the world we wish to live in, which we can make into a heaven *or* a hell, depending on our own actions.

Pagan ethics, therefore, are based more on cause and effect than an arbitrary sense of right and wrong. They are intrinsically woven, inseparable from all action. Opinions of right and wrong may vary, but results are the definitive experience for each individual practitioner.

Circle Lore & Etiquette
By Eldri Littlewolf & Wendy Hunter

Someday you will very likely want to attend rituals put on by other people and groups. Here is a guideline for how to behave, along with some information to help you feel comfortable.

The Circle is a manifestation of cyclic energy in the form of a vortex. This holy time and sacred space is separate from the world and contiguous with all other Circles. The Circle is an animate universe between the worlds that we empower by our agreement. Therefore:

1. **A ritual is not a spectator sport.** If you don't wish to participate, please stay far enough away that your conversations, etc. won't interfere in the rite.
2. **Leave your mundane self and earthly business outside the Circle,** and enter with your magickal self. Enter the Circle in "Perfect Love and Perfect Trust," having worked through personal difficulties beforehand.
3. **Meet everyone's magickal self in the Circle as if for the first time,** remembering that we have been partners since life began. Treat everybody and everything in the Circle with respect, tact, courtesy, and love.
4. **A ritual is like a religious service,** one in which considerable power may be raised, so please behave reverently and carefully in Circle.
5. **Keep solemn silence** except when Truth wishes to speak through you. Speak only Truth in Circle, and your magickal affirmations will have the force of that Truth.
6. **A ritual need not be solemn,** yet it should be serious in that humor should be used with purpose. Gratuitous remarks can disrupt the circle's energy and focus, so please refrain from making them.
7. **The best rituals are those that seem spontaneous,** yet they've often been planned carefully. So look to those leading the rite for clues on when to join in with chanting, drumming, etc.
8. **When moving about in the Circle, always move in the direction of the Casting** (usually *deosil*/clockwise). Walk around the Circle if necessary, but don't walk across or against the flow.
9. **Ritual objects and tools are invested with power** and should be treated with respect. A person's tools and musical instruments are private and should not be touched without permission—especially anything wrapped, sheathed, or boxed.
10. **Once the Circle is cast, enter or exit only at great need.** If you must enter or exit the Circle, please cut yourself a door or have one of the ritual officers do so.

One of the Priestess' or Priest's jobs may be to channel the Goddess and/or God in the Circle. Help them by:

- Watching them, listening to them, following them.
- Empowering them and the ritual by your participation. Feed your energy and visualizations through them into the Circle.
- Putting objections aside and saving criticism until later. If you cannot go along with something, leave the Circle.

We are all sisters and brothers in the Circle, but we may work in different ways. Be sensitive to different needs and styles before and during a ritual. Respect the differences between all magickal selves and include them, for they are all needed to complete the Circle.

Basic Ritual Structure
By Oberon Zell-Ravenheart

Magick is the art of coincidence control, or, as Anodea Judith says, "probability enhancement." When we practice magick we deliberately shift the patterns of probabilities in our favor, so that the things we want to happen are more likely to come about. That's why many people cite Aleister Crowley's definition of magick as "causing change to occur in conformity with Will." The way we do this is to focus all our energies in the same direction, the way a laser focuses all the light waves in a single coherent direction. By using the appropriate colors, incense, words, meditations, charms, spells, chants, Elements, and planetary powers, we can maximize the influences on our side – sort of like piling rocks on one end of a balance beam until eventually the whole thing tips. If we do this very precisely, we can achieve a perfect equilibrium of factors that will allow the beam to be pivoted around the fulcrum to the way we want it to go.

Natural magick is magick that works with the forces, fields, and energies of Nature. We do this kind of magick best when we merge ourselves into the natural flow and become one with it. The flow of an effective ceremony can be likened to any other sublime activity, such as sex, a gourmet meal, a concert, a story, a movie, etc. The energy is built through organic stages to a climax, and then returns in mirrored increments to the final anticlimactic finish.

In Wicca and many other forms of Pagan magick, especially when working in a group, we do all this within a Magick Circle. Here is a brief outline of a basic generic 13-part ritual structure commonly used in many rites throughout much of the American, European, British, and Australian magickal community. If you learn this form, you will be at home in just about any Circle anywhere, in all of their infinite variations. There are entire books, tapes, and CDs full of variations on this basic form, with countless different chants, invocations, blessings, etc.—many of which are in the forms of songs and poetry. What I offer here are only samples. This 13-part outline may be used as a starting point for creating an infinite variety of more complex forms. One of the best things about magickal rituals is that they offer so much room for creativity!

I. BANISHING/CLEANSING (*optional; not used in all rituals*)
    A. Smudging
    and/or: B. Asperging *(with salt water)*
II. GROUNDING (*optional; not used in all rituals*)
    A. Guided meditation ("Tree of Life")
    or: B. Physical movement
III. CASTING THE CIRCLE (*Deosil*/clockwise for "doing;" *widdershins*/counterclockwise for "undoing." All movements henceforth within the ritual should follow direction of casting.)
    A. Walk circumference with a tool (*blade or wand*)
    or: B. Caster stands in center and rotates with tool
    C. All dance circumference
    D. Chant/sing while holding hands
    E. Visualization/meditation while holding hands
IV. CALLING THE QUARTERS
    A. East (Air)
    B. South (Fire)
    C. West (Water)
    D. North (Earth)
    Optional: E. The Great Above (or Spirit)
    F. The Great Below (or Abyss)
    G. The Center (Spirit or Faerie)
V. INVOKING DEITIES & SPIRITS
    A. The Goddess
    B. The God
    Optional: C. Ancestors
    D. Guardian Spirits or Angels
    E. The Fae

    F. Animal Totems
    G. Higher Self
VI. STATEMENT OF PURPOSE
    Clarifying the intention of the ritual.
VII. WORKING
    Elements of the ritual are symbolized and/or represented. Dynamics between chosen elements are dramatized, healed, transformed, or energized (this is the most creative part).
VIII. POWER RAISING & RELEASING
    A. Chanting and/or Drumming
    B. Dancing
    C. Grounding
IX. COMMUNION
    A. Charging/Blessing and Sharing:
      1. Food (cakes, bread, fruit, etc.)
      2. Drink (water, juice, wine, etc.)
X. HIATUS
    A. Meditation
    or: B. Sharing, discussion, announcements, business
    C. Silence
XI. THANKS & DISMISSAL OF SPIRITS
    A. Deities/Spirits *(in reverse order of invocation)*
XII. THANKS & DISMISSAL OF ELEMENTS
    A. Directions/Elements *(in reverse order of invocation)*
XIII. OPENING THE CIRCLE *(in reverse direction of casting)*
    Usually done in same manner as it was cast, i.e. by song, dance, blade, wand, etc.

NOTE: Maximum participation is desired. Parts are often shared.

There is usually personal ritual preparation before the rite begins. This may include silent meditation, a purifying bath, fasting, dancing, stretching, etc.

Circles are usually cast *deosil,* starting in the East, but at Samhain, Walpurgisnacht, and for Greek rituals, the Circle and Quarters are cast and called *widdershins,* beginning in the West.

In the Southern Hemisphere, the Directions, movements, and seasons are commonly reversed from those here indicated.

A Universal Inter-Faith Ceremony
By Oberon

In 1990, Morning Glory and I were living near the small town of Ukiah in Mendocino County, Northern California. That April was the 20th anniversary of the first Earth Day in 1970, and Rev. John Crapps, the liberal Minister of the local Methodist Church, decided that it would be a fine thing to create a major interfaith ceremony in commemoration. The word went out through the community, and Morning Glory and I found ourselves representing the Pagan Church of All Worlds at the planning meetings—along with other clergy from the various Protestant Christian denominations, the Catholic Church, the Jewish Synagogue, the Chinese "City of 10,000 Buddhas," the Coyote Valley Pomo Indian Reservation, Sufis, Krishna Consciousness folks, and Tibetan Buddhists. Some of the people there were certainly surprised to see others; in fact, the Evangelical and Orthodox Christians simply got up and walked out of the whole thing when we introduced ourselves as Pagans!

Pulling such a diverse collection of faiths together enough to create a single coherent ritual presented a real challenge! After several unsuccessful go-rounds were unable to come to any resolution or even common ground, Morning Glory and I stood up. We said that we had a fair amount of experience in inter-faith work, and we thought we could help facilitate. By this time, everyone was frustrated enough to let us give it a shot.

So we turned to the Sufis: "What is it that you would most like to contribute to this ceremony?"

"Well," they said, "we'd like to dance a 'Dance of Universal Peace' in a circle around the ritual area."

"Fine," we said. "How about we start with that, then?" And everybody thought that would be okay.

Next, we turned to the Pomo elders: "What would you most like to contribute to this ceremony?"

"We would like to pray the Sacred Pipe to the Four Directions," they said.

"Good. Let's have the Pomos pray to the Four Directions next."

And so we went, singling out each faith group to do what they most wanted, and plugging their part into the basic liturgical structure outlined above. After the Four Directions were called, each group did an invocation or prayer to their respective deities. I think no one will ever forget the magnificent Morning Glory, in her diaphanous blue Priestess gown, standing proudly in the center of the Circle intoning Doreen Valiente's "Charge of the Star Goddess" in her stage-trained voice!

The Working was the planting of a Tree for the Future by the Methodist Youth Group, while Tibetan Lamas intoned a trance-inducing "Auoommm…" The Krishnas served *prasadam* (holy food) for Communion; everyone thanked their respective deities, the Pomos concluded their Pipe ceremony, and the Catholic Priest delivered the final Benediction (blessing).

It had started to rain as the tree was being planted (well, naturally!). The next day the front page of the local newspaper featured a large photo of Pagan Priestess Morning Glory sheltering under a big black umbrella being held by the Catholic Priest. All-in-all, a perfect ritual! And from start to finish it followed the universal structure presented in these pages.

(Following is an exquisite portrayal of a basic ritual following the previous outline, all written in traditional sonnet form by long-time Church of All Worlds Priest, Tom Williams. Read this aloud for best effect. Memorize and recite it for a group, following all the actions, and you will have an elegant and powerful ritual!)

L'Adoration de la Terre
a ritual in sonnets
By Tom Williams

It has begun:

I

And are we met in scented wood,
Betwixt the Earth and air,
And have we sworn by sacred blood,
Our breath and life to share?

And have our souls on silver wing
In starry council met?
And did we speak and forge a ring,
Our common fates to set?

And as we met beneath Her gaze,
And as we found a voice for praise,
Did not we swear an oath so fair?
Did not our hearts with passion blaze,

And shall we not our voices raise,
As now Her altar we prepare?

II

Now raise the sword and walk the round,
By cold blue flame this place we claim,
And banish all that is profane,
Within this round is sacred ground.

Now send the swirling clouds on high,
From censer's depth to starry deep,
Send forth on air our bond to keep,
Cold matter to embrace the sky.

From sacred cup a mystic space,
Where we the threads of magick lace,
Let streams of cleansing water pour.
With rune five-pointed guard this place.

Create a haven for Her grace,
A seat for Her whom we adore.

III

From East on mighty wing be sped,
Wild spirits of the air and storm,
From South with flaming aspect dread,
Let fiery guardians take their form.

From Western seas with tossing foam,
Oh watchers issue from the deep,
From Northern glades, from beds of loam,
Let kobolds granite vigil keep.

Oh Elements receive our call,
And Powers gather to our rite,
And build four mighty towers tall,
To ring us from the world this night.

And guard this circle on the hill,
Where we are met to work our Will.

IV

A sprite, you dash through dappled glade,
As flowers revel in your wake,
And in your joy, oh holy Maid,
You laugh the world awake.

Consumed with sweat and labor's tears,
You push and gasp with Mother's sighs,
And squeeze with will to bridge the years,
A fresh-clad spirit from your thighs.

The spindle drops, the thread is spun,
Your eyes glow soft with wisdom deep,
And as the West receives the Sun,
You sing the dying to sleep.

Oh Goddess, Maiden, Mother, Crone,
Transform our hearts into your throne.

V

When light and dark are met as one,
You leap, a flame that will not die,
Your Mother, Koré, Maid become
Beguiles her hornéd lover's eye.

When Sun finds highest glory's plane,
We feast the joining of your hands,
You swell the heavy heads of grain,
And dance your blessing on the lands.

When dark and light again are met,
You lay your bounty at her feet,
And as the Sun's short courses set,
You fall, the cycle to repeat.

Of lover wild of hoof and horn,
You are the seed that is reborn.

VI

Now are the Powers summoned all,
That we our healing work begin,
And join our wills to heed the call,
To work without what is within.

And from a place of perfect love,
In every heart let healing flow,
To join below with that above,
And as above then so below.

To mend that which is torn apart,
With wisdom that will conquer fear,
With balm to soothe the grieving heart,
And brush away a child's tear.

Let purpose now with power unite,
Let magick be abroad this night!

VII

Now draw from air one golden thread,
Entwined with water's azure blue,
And bind them to a loamy bed,
And strike the spark of life anew.

Now weave them in a spiral cord,
And call dead matter forth to live,
To forge and bind by power of word,
A web of life with life to give.

Now from our hearts send love to tie,
With healing grace the woven strands,
Let open now compassion's eye,
Formed by the joining of our hands.

And raise the power to work the spell,
That all be healed, that all be well.

VIII

By sun and rain you bear the seed,
The grain transformed by miller's toil,
And baked to fill your children's need,
We share the blessings of the soil.

Your heartbeat moves the ocean's surge,
Your laughter drives the rain's tattoo,
And joined, we dance your tidal urge,
And drink of water, and of You.

As now we bread and water share ,
And call the power of Earth and Sea,
We bind with force of Fire and Air,
That life may ever, ever be.

But bond through Mother's blood be first,
Thou art Goddess, never thirst.

IX

Our magick work now well be done,
Fulfilled the purpose of our art,
We shall be gone 'ere comes the Sun,
Ye Powers we hail and bid depart.

From North and South we bid you fade,
Oh Guardians who have watched this night,
From South and East pass back to shade,
Ye witnesses of sacred rite.

Now lift the shimmering Circle's veil,
That all who've worked within be well,
Oh ye divine whose names we hail,
We bid you fond and true farewell.

And as to astral realms you go,
With power we seal the spell and so,

Mote it Be.

2. Creating a Sacred Space

The Circle, Our Magick Temple
By Oberon Zell-Ravenheart

Since the beginning of time, Wizards, Witches, magicians, and other magickal folk have used the Circle to define our area of magickal workings. There are many reasons for this: the Circle leads back into itself and is consequently a symbol of unity, the absolute, and perfection. It therefore represents the Heavens in contrast to the Earth, or the spiritual in contrast to the material. There is a close connection between the Circle and the wheel. As an endless line, it symbolizes time and infinity. The Circle may be represented in the form of *Ouroboros*—the cosmic serpent who swallows his own tail, and who symbolizes the great Mysteries of circular time and continuous creation.

When the Circle is inscribed with a magickal implement it forms a protective barrier against external negativities, becoming a lens with which to focus the energy of the individual or group.

The dimensions of the Magick Circle will largely depend upon the number of people who will be using it. For solitary work, a three to five foot circle will do nicely; for small groups, nine to thirteen feet is usually considered adequate. There should be enough room for an Altar in the middle, and for those in attendance to move (and even dance) around it comfortably.

Ritual Spaces
Rituals may be held in many kinds of spaces, some temporary and others permanent. Temporary Circles may be set up in people's homes, or in public spaces, such as parks or rented halls. Depending on circumstances, a ritual area may be set up quite elaborately, with a Gateway, Quarter Altars, statues, banners, Maypole, bonfire, fountains, tiki torches, etc. Or it may consist of no more than clearing a little space in your living room and placing a simple Altar in the middle of it. The HOME Tradition is very flexible, in that function should determine structure. So here are a few notes on designing appropriate ritual areas for your Circle:

Indoor Temples
Any suitable indoor space may be made into a Temple, as long as it has room enough for the people who want to use it to gather together in a Circle.

Your Temple is the space where you will do nearly all of your magickal workings and rituals. If you are working solitary, you won't really need much space, nor does it have to remain set up all the time. Your bedroom will do fine. The only permanent item in your Temple is your Altar. This can be your own special altar to celebrate your life and the magic around you, and you can put on it anything you find particularly magickal.

Your Temple should have indicators of the four *Cardinal Directions*—East, South, West, and North. Determine which walls or corners of your room most nearly align to those directions, and then decorate them accordingly. Some people get very imaginative with this process, even hanging different colored banners of paper or cloth marked with appropriate sigils. Others put up pictures that remind them of each of these Elemental Directions, such as clouds, birds, or a sunrise for East; an erupting volcano, lightning, or the Sun for South; a seascape or underwater scene for West; and mountains, crystals, or a snowy Winter landscape for North. I have even designed a whole set of directional wall plaques which many people use just for this purpose: a Bird Goddess for East, a Sun God for South, a Sea Goddess for West, and a Green Man for North. And I added a plaque of Psyche for Spirit, in the Center.

Your Temple should also have a space where you can lay out a Magick Circle. Traditionally, these are marked on the floor with a piece of chalk, then cleaned up afterwards with a damp cloth or sponge An easy way to measure and draw such a circle is with a cord, such as a *cingulum,* which has knots tied at measured intervals. By anchoring the first knot at the center of the space, and holding the chalk at one of the other knots, you can draw the circle around like a compass. You can also make a big circle of string.

If you expect to be doing rituals with three or more people, however, you will want to create a larger ritual space. Circles should be odd-numbered feet in diameter. The traditional Witches' Circle, for instance, has a diameter of nine feet to provide room for a full coven of 13 Witches. But smaller groups can certainly get by with smaller Circles, such as seven or five feet.

Some people actually paint a ritual Circle on the floor of their Temples, often inscribing a pentagram within it and marking areas and points in different colors. This can be as simple as a plain circle with the four directions indicated, or as elaborate as the Magick Circle Mandala in Chapter 1. Such a painted Circle may be covered with a rug when not in use, or a round rug may serve to mark the Circle.

A way to make a permanent Magick Circle for your Temple without painting on the floor is to use a large piece of cloth (black is recommended, so it will seem as if you are standing in outer space). A top sheet for a California King-size bed should be just about the right size (8-foot square). Find the exact center of the sheet by folding it carefully into quarters diagonally from corner to corner, and iron it. Put a dot of white chalk at the center, and then spread the whole sheet out on a flat wooden deck or floor that it won't matter sticking thumbtacks or nails into (this may be a bit of a quest!).

Tack or tape down the four corners of the sheet with just enough tension to get rid of the wrinkles. Then insert a thin finishing nail through the knot at the end of your Cingulum. Hammer this into the center of the sheet, but not so far that you can't easily pull it out again. Then hold a piece of chalk at the first knot and draw the circle round. This will be 7 feet in diameter. Draw over the chalk lines with a white fabric marker, and where the ironed creases extend beyond the circle to the corners of the sheet, use the marker to draw symbols of the four Directions.

When setting up an indoor ritual area, be sure to check on the alignment of the Cardinal Directions! (For this reason I think every Wizard should consider a Compass to be a basic magickal tool.) Symbols of the Elements should be placed at the four Quarters. These may be as simple as colored jar candles (E=yellow, S=red, W=blue, N=green), or as fancy as full-scale, semi-permanent Quarter Altars. Determine which walls or corners of your Temple most nearly align to those directions, and then decorate them accordingly. Use your imagination.

Outdoor Circles

Nature magick is meant to be performed in the open air, in forests and meadows, under starry skies, and around an open fire. The HOME Tradition evolved out in the country during the eight years when our core people were living together in a homesteading community in the Mendonesian Mountains of NorCalifia. There was a bunch of us, and we didn't have any large indoor space in which to hold rituals—our biggest homes were 20-foot diameter round *yurts.* So we held almost all of our group rituals outdoors, even in the middle of Winter. We started with the primal Circle—just a fire pit, with space to sit around it. This is the original and most ancient form of ritual Circle, and where our ancestors first became human. Gathering around the magick fire, keeping our bodies warm through the cold nights, seeing each other's faces illumined by the dancing flames, telling our stories, singing our songs, beating our drums, dancing our celebrations, enacting our adventures—ritual, drama, music, poetry, myth—all of this evolved from our prehistoric tribal campfires.

Over the years, our simple campfire Circles acquired more accoutrements. At Annwfn, we refined the fire pits with rocks, cleared the grass, leveled the areas, and made benches to sit on. Later we planted flowering hedges around the perimeters, and built stone and wood Altars at the four Quarters. Gates were made at the entrances to the Faerie Circle and the Maypole Circle of branches woven into archways (when in use, these are festooned with ribbons, bells and flowers). At the Western Gate of the Faerie Circle we built a rocking bridge, over which one can cross into the Underworld at Samhain (during the rest of the year, it is kept roped off and covered with a fishing net). While we kept the fire pits at the center of the Moon Circle and the Sun Circle on Pwyll's Meadow, the one in the Faerie Circle was eventually replaced with a great stone Altar. And, of course, the Maypole Circle has the Pole itself as its centerpiece.

When magickal rituals are regularly performed in a wooded place, especially one remote from "civilization," it will come alive in both obvious and subtle ways. Growing things will prosper, and wild animals will find the area pleasing and appear in greater numbers. Those who are psychically sensitive will soon observe that there is a definite *charge* or aura about the place, and often Faeries, Wood-Sprites, and other Nature Spirits will be seen—first at night, and later even by day. This is the type of "Enchanted Wood" mentioned in classic tales, such as *A Midsummer Night's Dream.*

Of course, you can only do these lasting modifications on land you own. But lots of simple things can work in a wooded park area or even in your own back yard, provided you have privacy and are discreet.

Ritual Altars
By Oberon & Morning Glory

Altars are the primary stages for the microcosm of a magickal ritual. An Altar is a miniature symbolic model of the Universe, containing representations of whatever elements are to be addressed. Various magickal traditions have specific customs regarding the placement and decoration of their Altars. For instance, Hindus, Moslems, Jews, and Christians place their Altars in the East, while several traditions of Witchcraft and Ceremonial Magick put Altars in the North. The Faerie Tradition uses the Western gate. I feel that these arrangements can be flexible, depending on the theme, season, and purpose of the ritual itself. Here are some of the Altars we use in our rituals:

Personal Altar
Each member of our Ravenheart Clan has a personal altar. On it, we keep one or more Goddess and/or God statues, our personal athamés, chalices, wands, etc. Candles are a requisite, and the colors will be changed according to the seasons and the nature of the magick we're working at any given time. All our altars contain at least one crystal or crystal ball, and some also contain something for incense. Other items representing the Elements may be included, such as feathers, seashells, fossils, acorns, stones, geodes, etc. Some of us also have a little D&D figurine representing ourselves—one which we have picked out from a gaming store and painted up (and which we will also use when we're gaming). We also tend to include little totemic animal figurines; some of our favorites come in Red Rose Tea boxes! Addionally, items of our personal magickal jewelry will be kept on our altars when we're not wearing them.

My personal altar (Oberon) has a 6-inch flat *Dearinth,* whereupon sits my favorite crystal. My God & Goddess figurines are the *Millennial Gaia, Aphrodite, Kwan Yin,* and the *Green Man* (represented by a little action figure of the "swamp thing"!). I have a few art cards of Wizards, and a little pewter wizard model of myself , made back when I was touring Renaissance Faires with my unicorns. I have several wands, a lovely "Flying Dragon" athame I bought at Starwood festival, a nice chalice, and a couple of tea candles in fancy holders. Finally, there is my most truly magickal object—a *tektite* shaped like a little kayak (a yoni from the stars) which I found on a riverbank in Mississippi over 40 years ago, and which is a remnant of the asteroid that wiped out the dinosaurs 65 million years ago.

Personal altars are as varied and as individual as the people who have them. There is no really "wrong" way to make one. Any flat horizontal surface can be made into an altar. Many magickal folk use a small table (square, round, or rectangular), a bureau, a dresser or cabinet, the top of a TV, or even one shelf of a bookcase (mine is like that—though our large Ravenheart family altar has been on the mantle over our fireplace). If you have very little space, a particularly convenient way to make a personal altar is a triangular shelf attached to the walls in a corner of your room. An altar can be any size you find convenient, but I recommend one at least two feet wide and a foot deep. And you can always cover a table or shelf with a large bolt of fabric for an instant altar.

Once you have a suitable altar space, you will need an altar cloth. A batik-decorated silk scarf or large handkerchief is ideal, but any piece of pretty material you like will do. If you check your local metaphysical store, you will probably find some lovely altar cloths with magickal designs printed on them. If you buy something ready-made, make sure the symbols are ones you can work with. For color-coded magick, you will want to have appropriately-colored altar cloths. Arrange the cloth on the altar, and let the edges hang over.

There are a few things that go on almost every altar. As I indicated earlier, you should have something to represent each of the Elements (Earth, Air, Fire and Water). Earth may be represented by a crystal, a geode, a little cup of salt, a *pentacle,* bread, fruit, or even a small potted plant. Air might be represented by a feather, a *thurible* (incense burner), a bell, a flute, or a dried butterfly. Water is usually contained in a cup or chalice—but a seashell, starfish, or piece of coral also makes a lovely representation of this Element. Water in your chalice should never be allowed to get stale, but should be refreshed regularly—especially before any working. Fire is universally represented by a red votive candle in a red jar, but a piece of red lava, coal, charred wood, or a polished red stone or gem will also serve. Even a little figurine of a red dragon can be used to symbolize Fire.

NOTE: NEVER leave a candle burning on your altar when you are not in the room! I've known of several magickal folks whose homes burned down from untended altar candles! Also make sure that there is nothing above your candle that could possibly catch fire—including another shelf, curtains etc. And make sure your cat or weasel cannot climb the fabric or leap onto the Altar if you leave the room!

Your magickal tools—such as your wand, *athamé* (ritual knife), jewelry, medicine pouches, amulets, talismans, etc. should also be kept on or around your altar. If you have a lot of such stuff, you might want to fasten a branch or deer antler above your Altar from which you can hang things on chains and cords. Make sure you use good size molly bolts on dry walls to hang anything heavy!

Next, your altar should have some representation of Spirit. This may be in the form of a crystal ball, or statues or pictures of gods and goddesses, which you can make yourself or buy at a metaphysical store. Don't try and crowd your altar with such images—one or a matched set of two will do nicely. Another way to represent Spirit is to have a mirror at the back of your altar, which will reflect your own face when you do your workings. After all, the Divine Spirit is always within you! Your Altar is a little home for Spirit/God/Goddess to dwell with you as an honored guest. Treat Them so, and They will honor you in kind. If you wish to establish an Altar to a particular deity, consider this carefully. Take the time to study Them, and learn Their attributes and symbols.

And finally, your personal altar should have representations of yourself and your loved ones. Photos are the most common way to include them, but some folks use little animal figures to represent themselves and family members—especially those who strongly identify with particular *Totem* critters. Such representations are particularly used in working healing magick.

Other decorations may be added as you like. Pretty stones (especially ones with natural holes through them, which, resembling *yonis,* are considered sacred to the Goddess), crystals, fossils, bones, meteorites, shells, acorns etc. that have the kind of energy you want can be arranged decoratively. However, remember that your altar is a sacred space, and never casually put mundane objects (like your hairbrush, a can of soda, or your wallet) on a consecrated Altar! Keep your Altar clean and fresh.

And when you have it all set up, do a little Rite of Consecration. Light the candle and incense (if you are using them), and say:

> *This altar now be sacred space*
> *Of Spirit and of Mystery*
> *May Magick dwell within this place*
> *And all upon it blessed be!*

Household Altars

It's hard to imagine a magickal home without at least one household altar. Around our place, such altars tend to multiply like tribbles, until every horizontal space has been made into an Altar, and every vertical space has been converted into a bookcase! In our house, we have several altars devoted to the various Gods and Goddesses to whom we personally relate, or to particular purposes. We have, for instance, a special healing altar permanently set up, with a statue of *Kwan Yin.* When we're doing healing work for people we care about, we will try and get a photo or some object link for that person, and we burn candles for their healing.

We also have altars to *Aphrodite* and *Eros* in our bedrooms, an altar to *Ganesha* to help us overcome obstacles, an altar to *Lakshmi* for prosperity (where we keep piles of spare change), and a little altar in our business office to *Tin Hau,* Goddess of seafaring commerce and matron Goddess of Hong Kong.

Seasonal altars are set up in our Gardens (vegetable gardens, flower gardens, herb gardens), with images of the Green Man and various seasonal goddesses (such as *Kore/Persephone, Demeter,* and *Hygeia*), some of which we've gotten at garden shops. Our main herb garden is laid out in the form of a Celtic Cross/Medicine Wheel of four parts, and we call it our "Garden of Heart's Desire." This is where we work our magick to bring us all our personal hearts' desires.

And then there is our main family altar, dedicated to *Brigit* as our patron, benefactor, and inspiration—overseeing hearth and home and our sacred creative work. At our previous home, it was on the beautiful Victorian mantle over the fireplace in the center of our house. Over the top hung our handfasting besom, and two life-sized realistic raven images with real feathers. The back was a mirror, and the images and arrangements thereon were changed seasonally. This is where we did our family magick, and various little scrolls with spells, etc. were rolled up and stuffed into a side compartment after they'd been activated. When we had our large parties and gatherings (100+ people), especially at Samhain, Yule, and Oimelc/Imbolg/Brigantia, we'd gather everyone into the living room around the fireplace and present our ritual enactments, hold our bardics, play music, dance, etc.—all before the great altar.

Household altars may be fairly easily incorporated into bookcases, but they may also be established on the tops of bureaus, dressers, or cabinets. An altar can be kept in a small corner of the bedroom, a niche in a sewing room, or a convenient closet. When Morning

Glory and I lived in a school bus (1975-'79), our Altar was a little cabinet with a mirror in the back and a door hinged on the bottom and held horizontal by small chains. It could be folded down for use, and folded up to be put away when we were driving.

Household Altars are not usually the focus of group rituals, but rather of personal and family observances, prayers, and devotions. The most important thing is to keep them clean and fresh—don't let them get covered with dust and cobwebs!

Central Altar

In the HOME Tradition, we almost always have a central Altar, right in the middle of the Circle. Pretty much the only exceptions are when we have a fire or a Maypole there instead. This Altar is the main focus area around which the entire rite re-volves. We prefer it to be round, like the Earth Herself. Around 18" tall and about 2-3' in diameter is a good size. Perfectly fine low, round end tables or coffee tables of ap-propriate dimensions may be found readily at used furni-ture stores. Or make a collapsible Altar by cutting a circle out of plywood and affixing it to a base (see right).

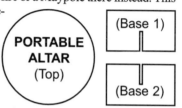

Traditionally, a central Altar is set up to be viewed from the South, just as if it were a map. It should be covered with an Altar Cloth of color and material appropriate to the occasion. Square silk scarves are very popular as Altar Cloths, but other materials may serve as well, as long as they complement the theme of the ritual. Velvets are beautiful, but thick fabric makes it difficult for objects to stand upright. (And we don't recommend paisley prints, checkerboards, or pictures of Mickey Mouse.) Block-printed, tie-dyed, or batik cloths are often available through the magickal marketplace, or you may make your own, painting anything from a simple Pentacle to a full Magick Circle Mandala. You can buy fabric paints at fabric stores or craft shops. As many rituals have seasonal themes, seasonally appropriate colors are always a good idea: red and green for Yule, red for Brigit, gold for Harvest, orange and black for Samhain, and green for almost anything else.

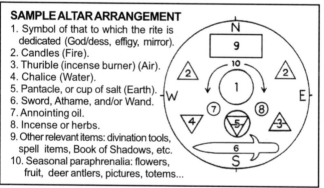

SAMPLE ALTAR ARRANGEMENT
1. Symbol of that to which the rite is dedicated (God/dess, effigy, mirror).
2. Candles (Fire).
3. Thurible (incense burner) (Air).
4. Chalice (Water).
5. Pantacle, or cup of salt (Earth).
6. Sword, Athame, and/or Wand.
7. Annointing oil.
8. Incense or herbs.
9. Other relevant items: divination tools, spell items, Book of Shadows, etc.
10. Seasonal paraphrenalia: flowers, fruit, deer antlers, pictures, totems...

In the middle of our Central Altar we usually place figurines of the God and Goddess we wish to in-vite into the Circle for the ritual (I have created an en-tire line of these over the years; others may be pur-chased at stores, online, or even at flea markets). If we wish to reflect and call forth the Deity within each participant, sometimes we use a mirror instead. We usually place two taper candles to either side of these statues, the colors depending on the season and/or purpose of the rite. In the absence of figures, these candles alone may represent the God and Goddess. In fact, candles in the form of male and female figures are available in most occult shops. Candleholders may be made of metal, glass, or pottery in symbolic shapes. You can get glass candle guards to keep the wax from dripping on your Altar cloths.

Magickal tools or symbols of the four Elements should be placed at the cardinal sides of the Altar. A *Thurible* (incense burner) at the East is very common (be sure to put a layer of sand in your Thurible under the charcoal blocks!), though the magickal tool for Air in the HOME Tradition is a Wand. Or you may have a feather, a burning sage bundle, a bird's wing, a bell—anything to symbolize Air.

In the HOME Tradition, the magickal tool for Fire is the *Athamé* (magickal knife), but I prefer the actual flame of a red candle or a small fire-pot in the South. (A fire-pot may be made by melting all your candle and crayon stubs in an old pot, then pouring the melted wax into a little iron or ceramic cauldron stuffed with torn-up cotton rags, which will act as wicks.) If you use a fire pot, be sure to place it on a fireproof ceramic dish or iron trivet (these are readily available in magickal designs such as pentagrams). And have a lid handy to cover it when you want to put out the flames.

In the West, the traditional symbol for Water is, of course, the Chalice. But a beautiful seashell filled with water may serve as well. And in the North, the traditional symbol for Earth is a *Pantacle* (a disk inscribed with a pentagram). Alternatives might include a bowl of earth or rock salt, a large crystal or geode, a pretty stone, or a potted plant.

Wands or Athamés used for casting the Circle are usually placed across the front of the Altar (in the South) or propped against it (as in the case of a sword, a staff, or a broom used in a Handfasting rite). A plate or bowl of food to be shared in the Communion phase of the ritual, such as bread or fruit, may be kept on the North side of the Altar, or beside it on the ground if there is no room. A bottle and glasses of fruit juice or wine may be kept beside the Altar in the West. Lighter, candles, and charcoal blocks for the incense may be kept under the Altar in the South.

Other items on the Altar would be those to be used in the ritual itself. These might include a bell, anointing oils, smudge sticks and shell or bowl, incense or herbs, a copy of the ritual script (it's particularly cool to do it up as a scroll!), divinatory implements (a Tarot deck, crystal ball, rune stones, black mirror), necessary materials for spell casting, photos of people needing healing (or of the beloved dead in a Samhain rite), totem animal figurines representing people or pets, and many other possibilities too numerous to recount here

We also often weave seasonal paraphernalia among the Altar implements, such as wreaths of holly and ivy at Yule, flowers in Spring, berries and fruit in Summer and Fall, bones at Samhain, etc. Again, use your imagination!

Quarter Altars

Our HOME community is really into Altars, and we have lots of them. For our ritual areas, whether indoors or out, we often have Quarter Altars at the points of the cardinal directions outside the actual Circle. These may range from simple shelves on wall brackets, as in the "Shaggy Mushroom" Temple of Annwfn, to the big stone-and-wood structures at Annwfn's Faerie Moon and Sun Circles. These Altars can be quite imaginative, as their purpose is to honor the Elemental Spirits. An advantage: if you have Quarter Altars outside the Circle, you don't have to have all that Elemental stuff on the Central Altar!

An Eastern Altar may be made of branches festooned with yellow ribbons, bells, feathers, little Faeries, and wind chimes, whereas a Western Altar may be made of driftwood and covered with assorted seashells, with a mermaid sculpture and a large Chalice of water. As the West is the Gateway to the Underworld, we may also have a special Altar to our beloved dead. There we might place a black candle or a skull, as well as photos and other mementos of our discorporate loved ones. A South Altar may be a section of fire-blackened tree with lava stones, red draping, a dragon, and a fire-pot, whereas a Northern Altar is always made of stone—a large, flat stone is ideal. It may be decorated with crystals and potted plants, especially ferns and moss.

For large rituals, especially all-nighters held outdoors, many of our tools are kept on the appropriate Quarter Altars when not in use. All the incense is kept by the Eastern Altar, along with the Temple Sword; spare candles are stashed in the South; extra water, juice, coffee, and other beverages are kept at the West; and the Northern Altar serves as a place to keep the ritual bread, fruit, and other food.

Preparations

By Oberon

It is a good idea in the beginning to mark the Circle with tape or string on the floor, or inscribe it in the dirt with your Wand, Sword, Staff, or Athamé if outdoors. We have even drawn Circles of lime, corn meal, flour, and chalk powder for outdoor rituals in grassy parks. This will serve as a visual aid to focus your attention on the proper boundary line. For small circles, you can mark out a circle using your *Cingulum* (a braided cord worn around the waist, with knots at various lengths) as a compass, with the knots measuring the radius (see above).

A really wonderful way to mark a permanent (and portable!) Circle is to paint it on a piece of canvas, carpet, or other material that can later be folded up and put away when not in use. This is a good idea because the Circle stays the same and will absorb some of the energy created curing the rituals. And you can make a painted design very elaborate, like the one on page 19.

However you decide to mark the Circle, one thing is most important: it must be correctly oriented towards to the Cardinal Directions. Consider a compass an essential working tool of magick, and learn how to use it, including compensating for the difference in degrees between magnetic north and true North (something you will need to look up for your local area). The most ancient and ideal way to orient your Circle is by the stars, with the Northern point of the circle pointing towards the North Star. With the Altar (or a temporary stake) in the center, sight across from the South side to Polaris, the bright star at the end of the handle of the Little Dipper. Then note and mark the points where that line of sight crosses the Circle perimeter, and you have it. For East and West, just mark points halfway between North and South.

In the Southern hemisphere, unfortunately, there is no corresponding South Pole star. The Southern Cross is only an approximation of the general direction, which will vary greatly through the seasons and the hour of the night. So "down under" you will have to rely on your compass.

Purifying the Temple

If the room or area where you will be working is normally used for mundane activities (such as a living room), you may want to cleanse your Temple of any negative thoughts and vibrations before beginning the ritual. Put some water into a small bowl and add a scoop of salt from the blade of your Athamé, stirring it into the water. Use a sprig of herb (rosemary, basil, lilac, or pine) as an *aspergillam* and, beginning in the East, *asperge* (sprinkle) the salt water around the room in a *deosil* (clockwise) direction, saying:

> *Water and Salt, where you are cast,*
> *No spell or adverse purpose last*
> *That is not in accord with me.*
> *As I will, so mote it be!*

Then light a bundle of sage or cedar and, starting in the East, carry it around the room deosil (we hold it in an abalone shell, but a ceramic bowl will do), fanning it into all the corners with a feather fan or bird's wing, while chanting:

> *Fire and Air, this charge I lay:*
> *No phantom in your presence stay*
> *That is not in accord with me.*
> *As I do will, so mote it be!*

As you do this, visualize with your mind's eye all of the negative thoughts and vibrations leaving, with only the pure white light of Spirit remaining to permeate the area. Ring a bell and wait until the vibration fades completely. Your Temple is now ready for whatever ritual or work of magick you wish to perform.

> NOTE: The instructions to conduct these movements *deosil* (clockwise) are appropriate for the Northern Hemisphere. South of the equator, it is considered more appropriate to reverse the direction, and go around the Circle *widdershins* (counter-clockwise). The word *deosil* actually means "sunwise," indicating the direction of the Sun across the sky, from left to right. This is fine if you are standing in the North temperate latitudes, and facing the Southern sky. But if you are below the equator and facing the Sun as it crosses the Northern sky, it appears to move from right to left. So "sunwise" in the Southern Hemisphere *is* actually counter-clockwise! So when you read instructions for the direction of movements in the Magick Circle, please take this into account, and reverse the directions if you are in, say, Australia or South Africa!

Cleansing the Altar
By Crow Dragontree

Take up the wand and level it toward the salt. Begin circling the wand in wide, ever quickening counterclockwise circles while envisioning a bright, white-to-yellow light blasting the impurities from the salt and cleansing it. While this is occurring, say something akin to:
> *Creature of Earth, untainted and pure,*
> *Be fit to dwell within this Circle.*

Once cleansed, reverse the direction of the wand, directing green, earthy energies toward the salt, infusing it with the element of Earth. While doing this, say:
> *Spirit of Earth accept this place,*
> *Dwell within this sacred space.*

Repeat the same thing with the bowl of Water (substituting the appropriate words), then add three pinches of salt to the water.
> *Purity and Purity*
> *Of Earth and of Water, Blessed Be.*

Now turn your attention to the flame of the candle, then the incense. Repeat the same action of purifying and charging, then combining the elements by lighting the incense with the candle flame.

Setting Up and Announcing Intent
Set up your altar, light whatever candles you have for illumination (except for the God and Goddess candles, which will be lit as part of the rite itself). Announce the beginning of the ritual and have everybody ground and center, entering an appropriate state of consciousness with the following regimen or something similar. The announcement may consist of something similar to these words:
> *A Circle of Magick is soon to be cast,*
> *A place of wonder and might,*
> *A place between worlds, the future and past,*
> *Caught between darkness and light.*

The Ritual Bath
By Oberon and Lady Sabrina

For small rituals involving from one to no more than a dozen or so people, it is recommended that everyone take a Ritual Bath before the rite begins in order to cleanse and purify the body, mind, and spirit. This should be a solitary experience. If done in a home, a tub can be prepared that everyone will use in turn, but it is important that all bathers be healthy and carrying no communicable disease!

First, clean your tub thoroughly; then fill it with hot water at a comfortable temperature (101-102°F, or 38°C, is about right). Add ¼ cup of sea salt (or bath salts), saying something like this (you might even write this out in pretty calligraphy on a little laminated card that each bather can see and read aloud as they enter the bath):

> Let salt and water purify
> My body where I resting lie.
> Let all mundane impurities
> Be washed away with gentle ease.
> Let pure creative forces fill
> My soul, my spirit, and my will.
> So mote it be!

A few drops of lavender or rosemary oil may also be added to the water, or (our favorite!) a handful of fresh mint leaves or rose petals from your herb garden. Then turn out all the electric lights, and light a few white candles and some cedar or sandalwood incense. Lower yourself into the water and let the scent and warmth permeate your body. With every breath you take, feel all tension flow out of you and be replaced with a glow of golden light that flows into every extremity and washes away all aches and pains, as well as any negative thoughts and feelings of the day. You might want to put on a nice meditation tape or CD to help you relax, create atmosphere, and get you in the right mood for the ritual. Or you might prefer just the quiet solitude of the bath for meditation and a moment of reflection before you begin the rite.

For group rituals, it will be important to monitor the amount of time allowed for each person in the Ritual Bath, so that everyone gets a turn. Five or ten minutes should be adequate, at which point an attendant should appear with a warm towel to dry the participants when they emerge.

Smudging, Asperging, and Grounding
By Oberon

As people enter the ritual area, or after everyone has assembled into a Circle, we will often have a "Smudging" in which smoking incense (usually sage or cedar) is carried around the Circle in an abalone shell or pottery bowl and fanned over each person with a feather fan or bird's wing. This may be done at the entrance to the Circle, if it is a large event and people are processing in a long line into the ritual area. In such case, it is common to have two people greet each participant as they enter: one with smudging, and the other with *asperging* (sprinkling water from a bowl using an herbal branch). As this is done, the person entering will hold out their arms and turn slowly in a circle, while the smudger will waft the smoke from feet to head. This helps to cleanse our personal auras of any energies we do not want to bring into the Circle.

"Grounding" is done to harmonize the energies of everyone in the Circle and tune us all into the vibrational field of the Earth. In the HOME Tradition, we use a grounding we call "The Tree of Life." We stand in a circle, all holding hands, close our eyes, and visualize that we are trees in the forest. The person who is leading the Grounding will say something like this:

Imagine that you are a tree. Plant your feet firmly on the ground. Now send your roots deep into the Earth. Feel the layers of cold soil and rock beneath your feet. Feel the roots of other plants and trees, as you reach down through the bones of your ancestors, through the pages of the Ages, down, down, to the molten heart of Mother Earth. Now draw that heat up through your roots, up into your trunk. Feel Her life force flow upwards through your body, filling you with Mama's magick. Now stretch your branches up, way up, reaching your leaves towards the Sun, towards a million billion suns, and draw the cosmic radiance from the Universe down into your body, where it meets the hot energy you drew up from the center of the Earth. Feel yourself filled with light and life, with the blended energies of Heaven and Dearth. Take a deep breath, exhale, and be here now!

Everyone opens their eyes, still holding hands, and the Rite proper begins.

Casting the Circle
By Oberon & Crow Dragontree

The Magick Circle defines a space between the mundane and magical worlds. A boundary is created around this space by "casting the Circle." In the Northern hemisphere, this is most commonly done by one person (usually the Priestess) walking *deosil* (clockwise) around the edge of the Circle, usually starting in the East, while chanting a Circle-casting charm (or *rune*). In the Southern Hemisphere, the Circle is usually cast *widdershins* (counter-clockwise), but is still most often started in the East—the realm of new beginnings, birth, and the rising Sun. However, some traditions prefer to start in the North, and others begin in the direction corresponding to the season—especially for Sabbats (the eight solar festivals comprising the Wheel of the Year). Any starting point is okay, as long as everyone understands and accepts the rationale for it.

While everyone else in the Circle takes hands, the person doing the Circle-casting holds a Wand, Staff, *Athamé*, Sword, or Crystal (I will henceforth use "Wand" to refer to any casting tool) and uses it to draw a surrounding ring of astral light, which everyone should visualize together as ultraviolet flames or lightning. This ring will contain the energies raised in the Circle, until it is time for them to be released. When the "Cone of Power" is raised and released in the Working, everyone should visualize the Circle as rising into the form of a clear crystal cone around and over the whole group. Each time we cast the circle anew, our gestures resonate through higher layers of conditioned response, reinforcing a morphic field to awaken the higher self.

To cast a Magick Circle, touch or turn the Wand toward the ground at the starting point, direct a beam of electric blue liquid light from the Wand to the ground, then raise it to shoulder level and point it straight out. Circumscribe a Circle in the air around the celebrants and the ritual area. Raise the wand to where it is pointing above the altar, then circle it toward the ground, drawing a sphere of power with one hemisphere above the ground, and one hemisphere below. When you have come full circle and return to the place you began, once again touch the ground with the tip of the Wand, thus "grounding the Circle."

The Circle itself as cast may be imagined initially as the perimeter of a sphere, but when it is set in motion with the Working, it becomes the base of a double cone—one point reaching up, and the other down.

In a small space, or when for some reason it is impractical to walk around the outside of the Circle, the traditional thing to do is just stand in the center, hold out your Wand, and simply rotate, visualizing the energy flowing from you out through your Wand and shaping itself into a Circle.

While casting the Circle, chant something like this (and see many more elaborate examples on the following pages):

I cast the Circle round and round—
Shadow of Moon upon the ground
I cast the Circle round about—
A world within; a world without!

— Morning Glory

You may also wish to further mark the boundary of the Circle with the Elements, by sprinkling salt and water around the perimeter and carrying the candle and incense around as well.

Motions in the Circle are always conducted *deosil* (sunwise), except during Walpurgisnacht (May Eve), Samhain (Hallowe'en), and Dark Moons (when the gates between the mortal world and the world of faerie stand open). During these times the motions are reverse, or widdershins (contrariwise). In the Northern hemisphere, "sunwise" is from left to right, or clockwise in a circle. But in Australia, South America, and South Africa, as I mentioned earlier, "sunwise" is in the opposite direction from the North, and so all these motions are reversed. Even the seasons are opposite from those in the North, as is the planet's Coriolis Force (Google this...).

Once the Circle is cast, it must not be entered or exited without cutting a Gate. This is done with a Wand, starting at the ground and drawing a line up, over the top, and down the other side to make a "doorway" you can then walk through. Or you may draw a line straight up from the ground to above your head, and just zip it open and step through, like the double sliding doors on the Starship Enterprise. Don't forget to close your door behind you!

Groundings

1. Ground and Center

Let's start by standing up as straight as possible, with your heads tilted slightly back, and taking a few deep breaths—through your nose if you're able—and try to push your belly out as you inhale.

Hold it for a few seconds...

And slowly release...keep your lips only slightly parted as you exhale.

With every exhale, feel yourself sinking deeper and deeper into a deep state of relaxation...

...deeper and deeper into a pleasant state of calm...

Keep breathing in this manner for a few more breaths *(between 2 to 5 breaths, depending on your own comfort level)*...

...and say "ready" when prepared to continue.

(Continue after everyone has said "ready").

"Now, I'd like you to take another deep breath, drawing the deep, strong energy from the Earth up through the sole of your left foot as you inhale...

...through your entire body...

...and down through the sole of your right foot as you exhale...

...leaving you calm, empowered, and ready for magick."

Keep circulating the energy for a few more breaths *(again, between 2 to 5 breaths, depending on your own comfort level)*...

....and say "ready" when prepared to continue.

— Crow Dragontree

2. Tree of Life Grounding

Imagine you are an ancient tree. Feel yourself planted here on this holy ground. Now sink your roots deep into the darkness of the Earth. Feel the layers of cold Earth and rock beneath you as you reach down, down, through the soil, the rocks, past the bones of your ancestors. Reach down through the crust of the Earth, through the fiery mantle, down into the molten core, and the throbbing crystalline iron heart of our Mother. Feel Her heat rising up through your roots. Draw that heat up into you. Feel Her life force flow upwards through your body, filling you with magic. Let it suffuse your body, and warm your heart.

Now stretch your branches up into the sky, way up into the heavens. Reach towards the light of the Sun. Unfurl your leaves to receive the blessings of our Solar Father. Then reach beyond; reach for the stars, and let your consciousness flow out through your infinite twigs to embrace the wonders of the universe, with the different light and blazing energies of a hundred billion suns, nebulae, swirling galaxies, and distant worlds. And now draw all that cosmic radiance back down into your body. Let it infuse every cell. Let it illuminate your mind and flood your heart with light.

And swirl together in your heart the heat of our Mother, the Earth, with the light of our Father, the Sun, and all the vast glory of the infinite cosmos—all the realms of Mother Nature and Father Time. Become filled with light and life, pulsating with the blended energies of Heaven and Earth. Know that you stand right here in the center, halfway between the atoms and the stars. Take a deep breath, exhale, and Be Here Now!

—Oberon, 2001

3. My Roots Go Down

My roots go down,
Down into the ground
My roots go down

I am a redwood by the forest
My roots go down,
Down into the ground
My roots go down

I am a willow by the water
My roots go down,
Down into the ground
My roots go down

I am an oak tree by a hill
My roots go down,
Down into the ground
My roots go down

—Author unknown

Building more energy
Star after star
Grown to crescendo,
A nova, and more
Toward Father, the Sun,
And kin we do soar
Past Luna to Mother,
Awaiting us nigh
We sparkle, shimmer,
Pass down through Her sky
Go down through Her water,
Go deep through Her ground
Rise into our circle
Breathe deep, hear the sound
Of spirits united, in harmony bound.
    Be here now!
—Rick Johnson, 2001

6. Water and Stone

Solid as a rock
Safe within the harbor
Ancient as a stone
Strong as the sea
Solid as a rock
Set deep within the Mother
And water that flows around me
—Raven Moonshadow

4. Bringing the Family Together

Eyes closed, hands linked,
As family this night
We gather together as
Bright sparks of light
From the sea of forgetfulness,
Which gave us birth
Vast distance we've traveled
To meet here on Earth
Through quasars and galaxies,
Past sun after sun
We've wandered and journeyed
To join here as one
One people, one village,
One clan gone so far

5. Down Down Down

Down, down, down, down
Anchor my soul to the depths of the Earth
Nothing can sweep me off of my feet
Centered and steady I stand
—Author unknown

Circle Castings

7. All-Purpose Circle Casting

Magick! Magick! Everywhere!
In the Earth and in the Air!
Magick seals our Circle round;
In Magick's cords we all are bound.

(alternate variations or additions:)

Magick seals our Circle round;
Within its field all love is found.

Magick seals our Circle round,
And takes us 'neath the barrow mound.

Three times around the Circle's sealed;
What has been riv'n, can now be healed.

Here within this secret place
We gather and form a sacred space.

Between the worlds we wish to go;
Ancient wisdom seek to know.

Full* Moon shines thru silvered tree
And casts the light of Mystery.
(or Waxing, Waning, as appropriate)

To seek the quest for which we came
Our wills are tempered in the flame.

In cavern deep and hidden wells
'Tis there our holy Lady dwells.

To barrow mound and standing stone
Each one comes, all alone.

She bids us enter, as we must,
In perfect Love and perfect Trust.

From where we started, the Circle is sealed;
What is within, now stands revealed.

The Circle is cast;
We are between the worlds!
—*Farida Ka'iwalani Fox*

8. Ostara Circle Casting

I cast the Circle thrice around
From the sky and from the ground
Father, Mother, what is born
A magic charge within the storm
Ancient bridge to future sight
Is what I cast for in this rite.
—*Marylyn Motherbear, 1997*

9. The Circle of Ancient Lore

I cast the circle of ancient lore.
Waves upon a timeless shore.
It has no beginning or an end.
It knows neither foe nor friend.
Ouroboros of legends old.
Rings of power forged in gold.
Wheel of life, circle of stones.
Cycle of creation, birth to bones.
A ring around the silver Moon.
I cast you now oh ancient rune.
—*Mike Fix*

10. The Hands of Time

We are people of the Earth
Come from different places
We are sculpted and formed
By the hands of time

We are circle skin and bone
Come from many nations
We are sculpted and formed
By the hands of time
—*Mz. imani, 1993*

11. One Spirit
(to be sung as a round)

One spirit in the dark
Like a candle wavers.
Many spirits joined as One
Burn with the power of the blazing sun!
There is strength in community;
The Circle empowers you and me.
The Circle binds yet sets us free!
As we will so shall it be!
—*Sean (FireDance 2003)*

12. Circle Invocation

Earth is a circle, wheeling in circles
As She circles the Sun.
Life is a circle, seasons returning in circles
Like a mighty hoop rolling through space-time.
Circles of stone and wood mark the places of stars
Heralding the eight spokes of the year-wheel.
Like a wheel rolling in circles we gather
    momentum
To circle the seasons of our lives.
We are a circle dedicated to each other.
—*Carolyn Clark*

13. Sacred Space

Here we create this sacred space
Here in love adore this place
Together work, together play
And love the only rule we say

The Circle's wide enough for more
Inside the Sun illumes the door
Wider still and then we see
Another Circle merged with me

Shed the flesh that veils the light
Strip away the mirror's blight
Open wide the shine within
Look around, we all are kin.

—Mischa

14. Circle of Power

O Circle of Power, I conjure thee,
That thou may be a boundary,
'Tween realms of flesh and Ancient Ones.
This shield 'gainst bane and harm becomes
A meeting place of Truth, Love, Joy,
Containing the power that we employ.
By God and Goddess, we conjure thee
This is our will, So Mote it Be!

—Crow Dragontree

15. Round Like a Belly

Round like a belly, the womb of rebirth
Round like the planet, our Mother, the Earth
Round like the cycles that ebb and that flow,
Round us a circle from which we shall grow.

Around us the trees fall, the Earth cries for rain;
Within us our souls call, crying with pain.
Around us a world getting lost in despair;
Around us a system that just doesn't care.

But here is a Circle to work and to learn;
Here is a place where we make the world turn.
As magic is made within this sacred ground,
With our hearts and our will shall this Circle
    be bound.

Gods full of wisdom, power and depth,
Our Circle's Your cycle of life and of death.
Give us Your guidance in all that we do;
Give us Your blessings to heal and renew!

—Anodea Judith

16. Out of the Darkness

(Eleusinian Mysteries Circle-casting)

Now out of the Darkness this Circle be cast
To honor the Ancients from out of the past:
The Old Ones and Cold Ones; the High
    and the Bright—
Come join in our working on this sacred night.
To high Mount Olympus, from Ocean and Earth
We cast now a Circle of Death and Rebirth!
We are your children, alone and afraid;
But we come here with magic and love to be made.
Hades, we honor You in these dark halls;
Help us to break down our meaningless walls.
Demeter, Hekaté, Koré and Zeus;
Hermes and Helios, Poet and Muse—
Help us to find the path which is right;
Leave us Your visions, impressed on our sight.
Come to us, come in us, come dance us this night,
That this circle be cast with Your power and might!

—Anodea Judith

17. Cast the Circle Round About

I cast the Circle round and round—
Shadow of Moon upon the ground
I cast the Circle round about—
A world within; a world without.

—Morning Glory

18. Lady Weave Your Circle

(to be sung as a round)

Lady, weave your Circle tight
Spin a web of growing light
Earth and Air and Fire and Water
Bind us to You.

Father, in the coming night
Gather in your ancient might
Sage and Warrior, Hornéd Hunter
Guide us to You.

Lord and Lady guide us,
Be thou here beside us,
Earth and Air and fire and Water,
Bind us to you!

Gracious Goddess Cerridwen,
Lord Cernunnos, Hornéd One,
Help us build a better world;
A new age has begun!

—Author unknown

3. Calling the Quarters

The Four Directions
By Oberon Zell-Ravenheart

After the Circle is cast, the next step in a ritual is "Calling the Quarters." In the HOME Tradition, any member of the Circle may be asked or volunteer to call one of the Quarters, and this is one place where our kids (and newcomers) often take important parts.

The Magick Circle, like a clock face, is also a map of time and space. As such, it has four cardinal points of the compass: North, South, East and West. Each of these points has special associations, or *correspondences,* which we call upon to remind us of where and when we are. Each of the Directions is associated with one of the four Elements: East=Air, South=Fire, West=Water, and North=Earth. The words of the callings (which may be in the form of chants and songs) are based on these correspondences, so familiarize yourself with them (see facing).

The Elements
By Oberon

The four *Elements* of magick are not the same as the 100-plus atomic elements of chemistry. The Elements of magick are Earth, Water, Fire, and Air, known to non-magickal people as *solid, liquid, plasma,* and *gas.* All matter in the universe exists only in those four states, which were first identified as the basis of all life and being by the 5th-century BCE Sicilian philosopher Empedocles. This concept was an essential teaching of Aristotle (384-322 BCE) and the Pythagorean Mysteries of ancient Greece, and has formed the basis of many systems of magick, such as those from the Middle East, Egypt, Greece, and Rome, as well as Hermetics, Alchemy, modern occultism, Ceremonial Magick, Witchcraft, and Wizardry. It is the most widely used conceptual model in the world, and is the foundation of the Enochian magickal system, the Tarot, astrology, the seasons, and the Magick Circle.

The ubiquity of this concept means that the most magickal tool you can have is a simple candle: the hard wax candle itself is solid, or Earth; the flame is plasma, or Fire; the melted wax is liquid, or Water; and the smoke is gas, or Air. Many powerful spells need nothing but a candle and your Will to make them work.

Furthermore, each Element is imbued, as is everything in the universe, with the non-physical essence of the Divine, which we generally call *Spirit.* Just as each person is a unique manifestation of the Divine, so is every animal, every plant, every ecosystem. So Spirit is often considered to be the fifth Element—distinguishing living beings from dead or inanimate objects.

Energy, of course, is neither an Element nor a state of matter, but matter and energy can be converted into each other, as Einstein pointed out in his famous equation: $E=Mc^2$. We'll talk more about energy when we get to the section on "Raising the Power."

There are also magickal creatures or spirits associated with each Element. These are called *Elementals.* The Air Elementals are *Sylphs,* and they look like winged fairies. Fire Elementals are *Salamanders,* and they can take any shape and size, but mostly they appear as flaming lizards or dragons. Water Elementals are *Undines,* and they look like mermaids. And Earth Elementals are *Gnomes,* which are stout, wrinkled little people who live underground. You may visualize these Elementals as you call their respective Quarters.

There are also animals, both mundane and magickal, as well as Archangels, associated with the Quarters. In recent years, however, dragons of different colors and attributes have become

Magick Circle Quarter Correspondences by Oberon

DIRECTION / Wind	East / Eurus	South / Notus	West / Zephyrus	North / Boreas
ELEMENT (State)	Air (Gas) △	Fire (Plasma) △	Water (Liquid) ▽	Earth (Solid) ▽
MUDRA				
ELEMENTALS	Sylphs	Salamanders	Undines	Gnomes
RULERSHIP	Tempest, storms, winds, mind, intellect, learning, wisdom	Flames, lightning, Sun, volcanoes, energy, spirit, will	Ocean, tides, lakes, rivers, springs, love, sorrow, emotions	Mountains, caverns, stones, vegetation, wealth, creativity
COLOR	Yellow	Red	Blue	Green
(Lakota)	Yellow	White	Black	Red
ANIMAL	Eagle	Lion	Serpent, whale	Bull
(Lakota)	Eagle	Mouse	Bear	Bison
(Mythological)	Gryphon	Phoenix	Dragon	Unicorn
ARCHANGEL	Raphael	Michael	Gabriel	Uriel
ALTAR TOOLS	Wand & Censer	Athamé & Candle	Chalice & Water	Pantacle & Salt
TAROT SUITS	Wands (Rods)	Swords (Blades)	Cups (Chalices)	Pentacles (Discs)
COURT CARDS	Knights	Kings	Queens	Pages
PLAYING CARDS	Clubs ♣	Spades ♠	Hearts ♥	Diamonds ♦
CELTIC TREASURE	Spear of Lugh	Sword of Nuada	Cauldron of Dagdha	Stone of Destiny
SABBAT	Ostara	Litha	Mabon	Yule
SOLAR MIDPOINT	Spring Equinox	Summer Solstice	Autumn Equinox	Winter Solstice
ZODIACAL POINT	0° Aries	0° Cancer	0° Libra	0° Capricorn
SEASON / Glyph	Spring	Summer	Autumn	Winter
TIME OF DAY	Dawn	Noon	Dusk	Midnight
WEATHER	Windy	Hot	Rainy	Cold
STAGE OF LIFE	Birth	Growth	Death	Decay
HUMAN AGE	Infancy	Youth	Maturity	Old age
BODY ANALOG	Breath	Spirit (aura)	Blood	Flesh & bones
ATTRIBUTE	Intellectual, joyful	Spiritual, potent	Emotional, fertile	Physical, safe
FUNCTION	Thinking	Feeling	Intuition	Sensation
SENSE	Smell	Sight	Taste	Touch
CARDINAL SIGN	Libra ♎	Aries ♈	Cancer ♋	Capricorn ♑
MUTABLE SIGN	Gemini ♊	Sagittarius ♐	Pisces ♓	Virgo ♍
FIXED	Aquarius ♒	Leo ♌	Scorpio ♏	Taurus ♉
ALCHEM PROCESS	Evaporation	Combustion	Solution	Precipitation
METALS	Mercury, Aluminum	Iron, Gold	Silver	Lead
JEWELS	Topaz, Chalcedony	Fire opal	Aquamarine, Beryl	Quartz, rock salt
INCENSE	Galbanum	Olibanum	Myrrh, Onycha	Storax
PLANTS	Pansy, violet, yarrow, primrose, vervain	Garlic, hibiscus, nettle, pepper, onion, mustard	Lotus, fern, seaweed, water plants, melon	Ivy, comfrey, apples, grains: oats, wheat, etc.
TREES	Aspen	Almond (in flower)	Willow	Oak
GODDESSES	Aradia, Arianrhod, Aditi, Nuit, Ourania	Hestia, Pelé, Vesta, Brigit, Sekhmet	Aphrodite, Amphitrite, Mari, Tiamat, Yemaya	Ceres, Demeter, Mah, Gaea, Rhea, Nepthys
GODS	Enlil, Hermes, Shu, Thoth, Vaya, Zeus	Horus, Hephaestus, Vulcan, Loki, Agni	Poseidon, Llyr, Dylan, Neptune, Ea, Oceanus	Cernunnos, Dionysos, Adonis, Pan, Tammuz
POWER of MAGUS	To Know	To Will	To Dare	To Keep Silent

increasingly popular as guardians of the four Directions. Exquisite figurines of these are becoming widely available, and many Wizards are procuring a set for their Quarter altars.

It is customary to have an object representing each of the Elements on your altar. Many people just use their magickal tools, which have their own Elemental associations. But you may also use a feather, bell, or incense for Air; a candle for Fire; a cup of water or seashell for Water; and a crystal, stone, geode, or bowl of salt for Earth. In the HOME Tradition, we often set up small altars at each of the four Quarters on the outer edge of the Circle area, which are then decorated with appropriate symbols and colors. At nighttime rituals these usually include votive candles in colored glass holders—yellow for Air, red for Fire, blue for Water, and green for Earth.

Invoking the Quarters
By Oberon

If there are enough people in the Circle, we will ask a different person to call each Quarter, but if the Circle is very small (or solitary) one person (or the whole group together) may call all four. As I have said before, in the Northern Hemisphere we generally begin in the East, where the sun rises, and go *deosil*—except at Samhain and Walpurgisnacht (May Eve), when we begin in the West and go *widdershins.* In the Southern Hemisphere, most correspondences of North and South are obviously reversed, but east and west are a bit more complicated. Since the Elemental system of Western magick evolved in Europe, where the Atlantic Ocean was the great western sea, it made perfect sense to associate the Element of Water with the West. This is also true in West Africa, the western half of the Americas, and West Australia. But in those lands where the ocean is to the east, such as the eastern Americas, Asia, and eastern Australia, this association seems incongruous. Therefore, many magickal practitioners and ritualists in these places quite reasonably attribute the traditional correspondences of Water to the East. But this doesn't work for all directional correspondences, because the sun still rises in the east no matter where you are, and the aspects of the Quarters that correlate with the turning Earth have to be separated out from those that correlate with the Elements. Admirably, Australian practitioners have done this, and should be consulted in such workings south of the equator.

Also, some ritualists may, on various occasions, call additional Directions such as Up ("The Great Above"), Down ("The Great Below"), or Center. We suggest that you start with the standard four, and then you may add others when you feel comfortable enough in your ritual work to understand the additional complexity of such symbolism.

In the HOME Tradition, we have special gestures, or *mudras,* in which we hold our arms at each Quarter to identify with the essence of each Element. The powers of each Element are invoked, or called in, at this time. This kind of prayer is thus called an *invocation,* or calling-in. For small Circles, the person doing the calling stands in that direction and faces outward. But for larger Circles, the caller will stand opposite the direction, facing across the Circle, so everyone can see and hear him or her. This is known as "cross-calling."

Invocation and the Power of Sound (1)
By Ruth Barrett

In any ritual where the Elemental powers are invoked, it is vital to identify the specific aspect or aspects of each Element you wish to call upon that align with the ritual's theme and purpose. Within each Element there exist a wide range of aspects. For example, in working with the element of Air, do you wish to invoke hurricane force winds or gentle spring breezes? Consider the range of aspects that may be called upon from the various Elemental powers, and what gifts or blessings might be requested for the specific occasion.

Within your personal memories, you have many paths that can lead you to a deepening relationship with each of the Elements. Discovering and exploring those pathways will make your memories more conscious and available for use in both magick and ritual. Over time, you can consciously develop an Elemental inventory – sort of a "sensory reference library" of personal experiences with each of the Elements. This inventory will help you access your authentic connections to these diverse forces, and can be brought forward in the present and used in invocation. It will give you the knowledge you need to embody and invoke a very specific quality of Elemental power from each direction in order to empower your ritual or magickal working.

Prior to speaking your invocation prepare yourself energetically, and trust that the poetry of the season is alive inside you. Embody the frequency, the resonance, the vibration of the Elemental power you are inviting. Let your words emerge from your center. As each Element is invoked, allow the tone of your voice change in range, pitch, quality of sound, and meter of delivery. Like tuning into the band wave frequency on a radio, dial up each directional "station" to hear the Elemental music clearly. Make an authentic connection to the quality of Elemental energy you seek. For example, Air sounds in the environment tend to be very soft, breathy, and relatively high pitched. Air words are clear, thought provoking, clever, and should give the feeling of expansive open spaces or soaring in their delivery. Fire sounds in the environment are those that are relatively high-pitched, clear, bright, shrill, carry well over distance, and seem to cut through other sounds. Fire sounds grab our attention by irritating our nerves. Fire words are simple but passionate, higher pitched, with a faster-paced delivery; they rise, outburst, or simmer (as seasonally appropriate), with sibilance accentuated. In contrast, Water sounds in the environment are soft but definite, midrange in pitch, and give us the feeling of caressing or stroking. These are sounds that cause us our muscles to relax. Water words flow in a stream of consciousness. They are dreamy and poetic, with connective phrasing and rhythmic undulation in their delivery. Finally, Earth sounds in the environment are definite or heavy, low-pitched, and often "sub-sonic." These are sounds that seem to rattle our bones. Earth words are solid like large stones, simple but carrying much weight. Delivery of an Earth invocation would be slower paced, and with a deeper pitch.

When you are speaking an invocation in a group ritual, remember that you are the conduit between the Elemental energies and the will of the participants in the ritual Circle. You will need to project your voice, speaking out so that everyone present can hear and feel the invocation. This is particularly critical if you are outside where sound can easily be lost. Personal ritual invocations need not be spoken with such projection, but it is still best to speak them aloud. Speaking aloud gives the Elemental forces within you an opportunity to come fully forward. It is a form of self-witnessing. How and what you hear within ritual space may be different than how and what you hear in a state of ordinary consciousness. Try invocation both ways, aloud and silent, in order to hear, see, and feel the differences for yourself. Experiment with the power of your own voice to come into resonance with the power of the Elements. Make lots of magick!

Summoning the Elements—Generic
By Oberon & Crow Dragontree

Here is a generic approach to Quarter calling, with little variation from Quarter to Quarter. Something this simple may be used for many rituals, as it requires very little effort to memorize. This is useful if you are having newcomers or visitors taking part in the ceremony and you want to give them a way to participate that won't be too challenging.

Four people are selected before the ritual begins, and given, respectively, a censer of burning incense, a lit red candle, a chalice of water, and a bowl of salt. The celebrant representing the Eastern Quarter stands in the east, holding the incense. Strongly and confidently call out something like this:

Hail to the Ancients of East and Air!
We call you to our Rite!

> *We call on you to lend your power,*
> *And guard our Circle with your might*
> *Blessed Be!*

And everyone else echoes, *"Blessed Be!"*

Repeat this at each Quarter in turn, going deosil—calling *"South and Fire"* while holding the candle, *"West and Water,"* while holding the chalice, and *"North and Earth"* while holding the bowl of salt.

Calling the Quarters—Specific

By Oberon

Here are more specific and elaborate descriptions of callings for each Quarter, including *mudras* (gestures). Note that the callings should all match up as a set.

East: The person doing the calling faces the East, arms raised and held out like wings, palms up and fingers spread. Everyone else also faces east with the same gesture. The one calling will say something like:

> *O soaring Eagle of the East,*
> *Rider of the winds of change,*
> *Come to us from beyond the sunrise*
> *And bring us inspiration!*
> *Grant us your blessings and spare us your fury!*
> > *Hail and be welcome!*

Everyone else then echoes, *"Hail and be welcome!"*
The yellow East candle or incense may be lit, and a bell may be rung.

South: Then everyone turns to the South, holding hands above our heads, fingertips and thumb tips together in a peak, making a triangle of flame. The South invoker says something like:

> *O golden Lion of the burning South,*
> *Ruler of the flames and lightning,*
> *Come to our Circle from out of the fire*
> *And bring us enlightenment!*
> *Grant us your blessings and spare us your fury!*
> > *Hail and be welcome!*

(If you have read the *Chronicles of Narnia,* or seen the movie, you will certainly be able to visualize the Southern Lion!) The red South candle may be lit.

West: Now we turn to the West, and, still holding our hands in a triangle with fingers and thumb tips together, we bring them down in front of our crotch like a cup. The caller says something like:

> *O great Whale of the Western Sea,*
> *Ruler of the waves and tides,*
> *Come to us from your watery depths*
> *And teach us the lesson of flowing!*
> *Grant us your blessings and spare us your fury!*
> > *Hail and be welcome!*

A cup or shell of water may be splashed on the ground, and the blue West candle may be lit.

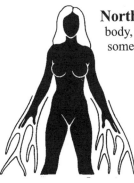

North: Finally we turn to the North. Hands are held low and out from the body, palms down, reaching like roots for the Earth. The caller says something like:

> O mighty Bull of the frozen North,
> Ruler of the stones and caverns,
> Come to us from the icy mountains
> And bring us stability!
> Grant us your blessings and spare us your fury!
> Hail and be welcome!

Salt may be sprinkled on the ground, and the green North candle may be lit.

Center: If it is desired (and not necessarily in all rituals) the priest or priestess may call Spirit by standing before the altar, wand in hand, and calling something like this:

> We stand in the Center of all that is,
> We summon the powers within,
> Earth and Water, Fire and Air,
> And Spirit to bring it all in.
> With Elements four and Spirit as well
> In harmony, playing their part,
> We summon the Spirit that within us dwells,
> And lies at the core of our Art.
> Blessed Be!
> —Crow Dragontree

After all the Quarters have been called, the whole Circle may sing an appropriate Circling song (see following pages), or chant together something like this:

> It's from Water that we come
>> (hands in Water mudra, "swim" them across belly)
> It's to Earth that we will go
>> (stab fingers down towards the Earth like roots)
> We're the Fire of transformation
>> (clap hands loudly above head)
> And the Winds of change that blow!
>> (wave hands in air like winds)
> —Orion Stormcrow

Quarter Callings

Following are a number of Quarter-calling incantations, chants, and songs that can be used for different rituals. Some of them include center as well as the four Cardinal Points. Because many of the selections here were passed on by oral tradition, we have been unable to identify authors for some of them. But we felt it would be remiss to leave them out of this collection, as they are important parts of our liturgical heritage. We apologize for any omissions of credits, and ask anyone who knows such attributions to please contact us.

Incantations
(These are particularly good when having different people call each Quarter. In such case, it is a common practice to print the respective Quarter calls out on small cards that can be held unobtrusively in the palms of the callers.)

19. Invocation of the Watchers

Ye Watchers of the Eastern Tower;
Wings that bear the spirit higher,
Wardens of the Winds of Power,
Creatures of Air, our words inspire!
Hail and be welcome!

Watchers of the South, whose Fire
Fills the heart and hearth with light
And Love to warm the world entire—
In soul and body now burn bright!
Hail and be welcome!

Western Watchers, by whose might
The Moontides cycle through the sea,
Sweet Waters send from cloud and height
To ease our thirst for harmony!
Hail and be welcome!

Ye Watchers of the North, by tree,
By soil and stone, foundation's flower,
The source of all stability,
Uphold us in this sacred hour!
Hail and be welcome!

—Diana Paxson

20. Guardians All

O Guardians of the Airy East,
Attend and sanctify our feast!
At dawn of day, your winds blow free,
Hail and welcome; Blessed be!

O Guardians of the Fiery South,
Plant your hot kisses on our mouth!
By flames and lightning, burning tree,
Hail and welcome; Blessed be!

O Guardians of the Wat'ry West,
Your sacrament imbues our Nest!
By rain and river, lake and sea,
Hail and welcome; Blessed be!

O Guardians of the Earthen North,
We summon, stir and call ye forth!
By bud and branch, by root and tree,
Hail and welcome; Blessed be!

O Guardians of the Quarters all,
Hearken ye unto our call!
Protect our Circle through the night,
And lend your pow'r unto our rite!
Blessed Be!

—Oberon Zell, 1997

21. Endangered Species Callings

In Airy realms the condor's cry
On lordly wings once filled the sky.
Now caged, his call, though muted still,
Inspires our hearts with freedom's will.
Oh spirit of the sightless blue,
From Eastern skies your course pursue,
Attend our rites with echoes strong,
And join your voice in the Mother's song.

On South-sea isles the dragon's hiss
Recalls the sea's and magma's kiss.
And flame-red tongue volcano's fire
From whence rose lands beyond desire.
Komodo Lord, Oh lizard king,
From Southern realms your call will ring.
Attend our rites with echoes strong,
And join your voice in the Mother's song.

The blue whale's call has sounded clear
Around the Earth to one held dear.
Beloved mate is now with calf,
To thwart harpoon that the seas may laugh.
Oh wondrous, giant, breaching whale,
Salute life's hour with lifted tail!
Attend our rites with echoes strong,
And join your voice in the Mother's song.

O'er tundra, steppe and moonlit wood,
A cry of all that's wild and good.
The wolves! The wolves! awake the night
And put both hare and moose to flight.
Oh greycoats free beneath the sky,
We shall not let your voices die.
Attend our rites with echoes strong,
And join your voice in the Mother's song.

—Tom Williams, Samhain 1990

22. Elements of a New Dawn

Winds of the airy heights
Blow soft and pure
Sweeping about me.
Flames of Sun's heat
Burn hot and joyous
Billowing about me.
Waters of the flowing torrents
Flow cool and refreshing
Washing about me.
Hills most dark and mossy
Be peaceful and healing
Encompassing about me.

—Ed Fitch, 1975

23. Immanent Elements

By Air which fills our lungs with breath
And lifts the birds in flight...
By Fire which flames within our souls
And floods our minds with light...
By Water flowing in our blood,
From oceans silver bright...
By Earth of which our flesh is formed,
Through which we find delight!
—Morning Glory Zell

24. The Earth is Our Mother

Chorus: The Earth is our Mother,
We must take care of Her. (2x)

Her sacred ground we walk upon,
With every step we take.
Her sacred ground we walk upon,
With every step we take!
Hey, yona, ho yona, hey yon yon!
Hey, yona, ho yona, hey yon yon!

The Air we breathe renews us,
With every breath we take.
The Air we breathe renews us,
With every breath we take!
Hey, yona, ho yona, hey yon yon!
Hey, yona, ho yona, hey yon yon!

The Fire that can warm us
Is in the love we make.
The Fire that can warm us
Is in the love we make!
Hey, yona, ho yona, hey yon yon!
Hey, yona, ho yona, hey yon yon!

From Water that we drink of
Comes all the life She makes
From Water that we drink of
Comes all the life She makes!
Hey, yona, ho yona, hey yon yon!
Hey, yona, ho yona, hey yon yon!
—1st verse, Hopi chant
—other verses, Morning Glory Zell

25. Hail to the Elements

Hail, Hail! The Wind It Blows;
Hail, Hail! The Fire It Glows;
Hail, Hail! The Water Flows;
Hail, Hail! The Earth It Grows;
Hail, Hail! The Spirit Knows.
—Author unknown

26. The Mill of Magic

Air breathe, Air blow,
Make the mill of magic go.
Work the will for which we pray,
Io Deo Evohe!

Fire flame, Fire burn,
Make the mill of magic turn.
Work the will for which we pray,
Io Deo Evohe!

Water heat, Water boil,
Make the mill of magic toil.
Work the will for which we pray,
Io Deo Evohe!

Earth without, Earth within,
Make the mill of magic spin.
Work the will for which we pray,
Io Deo Evohe!
—William Gray

27. Pentagrams of the Guardians

By pentagram of golden light,
From Eastern realms begin your flight.
By zephyr's breath, on wings of storm,
At our Eastern gate you'll take your form,
O Guardians of the golden East,
Attend, and sanctify our feast!

By pentagram of flaming red,
From Southern realms your course be sped.
By balefire's flame, by candle's light,
At our Southern gate you'll watch this night.
O Guardians of the Southern tower,
Attend, and lend to us your power!

By pentagram of azure hue,
From Western lands your course pursue.
By ocean wave, by river's laugh,
At our Western gate you'll guard the path.
O Guardians of the Western shore,
Attend, where we have gone before!

By pentagram of forest green,
In sylvan glades your forms are seen.
By branch and root, by rock and loam,
Our Northern gate will be your home.
O Guardians of the Northern lights,
Attend, and witness these our rites!
—Tom Williams

Songs & Chants

(HOME is a bardic tradition, and many of our rituals are designed to be sung in whole or in part. Here are our favorite Quarter-calling songs and chants. Unfortunately, we cannot include here the musical scoring for these. Some of them, however, have been recorded on tapes and CDs, and we highly recommend you get these and learn the music—see the Resources section of the Appendix.)

28. Invocation

Soaring Eagle on the wing
From your lair new visions bring
Lift our voices as we sing
Enter us, Powers of the East.

Mighty Lion of the Sun
Burn our heart and will as one
Flaming strength and passion
Enter us, Powers of the South.

Ancient Serpent of the deep
In your waters let us weep
Wave your mysteries here to sleep
Enter us, Powers of the West.

Dark Bull of the Mother Earth
Winter cave that gives us birth
Feed our knowledge of your worth
Enter us, Powers of the North.
    Hear us, Spirit!
      —Moira Ashleigh, 1992

29. Quarter Calling

Winged One, Spirit of Air
Your children invite you here
Come on the winds of the sunrise
Give us your vision so clear
You are the gentle Spring breezes
You are the glory of flight
Winged One, Spirit of Air
Keep us wise through our rite!

Fierce one, Spirit of Fire
Your children invite you here
Come with your blazing noon passion
Banish all sorrow and fear
You are the flickering candle
You are the bonfire bright
Fierce one, Spirit of Fire
Keep us brave through our rite!

Swift One, Spirit of Water
Your children invite you here
Come on the waves of the sunset
Bring to us joy and good cheer
You are the well of deep comfort
You are the crashing waves' height
Swift One, Spirit of Water,
Keep us sure through our rite!

Hooved One, Spirit of Earth
Your children invite you here
Come from the mountains of midnight
With new strength and vigor appear
You are the field of our pleasure
Your are the source of our might
Hooved One, Spirit of Earth
Keep us strong through our rite!
      —Isaac Bonewits, 1992

30. Take Me Down

Ch: Take me down in your embrace,
     Where I see my truest face.
     Take me down into my soul,
     Take me down and make me whole.

Where the Morning Star arises
I can see Her spirit fly
     Take me down, take me down…
Where She spreads the dawning day
Across the crystal sky
     Take me down, take me down…

In childlike trust and innocence
We face the Southern land
     Take me down, take me down…
Where my Lady rides a tiger,
Golden apples in her hand
     Take me down, take me down…

Where the setting sun descends
Behind the belly of the Earth
     Take me down, take me down…
There I look within the Mystery
Of death and rebirth
     Take me down, take me down…

Old Woman of the North,
She rides Her broom across the sky
     Take me down, take me down…
With Her basket full of diamonds
And a twinkle in Her eye.
     Take me down, take me down…
      —Bird Brother

31. Behold, There is Magic All Around Us

Ch: Behold, there is magic all around us
Behold, there is magic all around us
Behold, there is magic all around us
Awaken, rejoice and sing!

I am the Air around you,
I am the breath of life within you,
I am the wind blowing through you,
        I am all that I am.

I am the Fire around you,
I am the spark of life within you,
I am the flame burning through you,
        I am all that I am.

I am the Water around you,
I am the pulse of life within you,
I am the ocean flowing through you,
        I am all that I am.

I am the Earth around you,
I am the heartbeat within you,
I am the ground below you,
        I am all that I am.

I am Spirit around you,
I am divinity within you,
I am the light shining through you,
        I am all that I am.
                    —*Abbi Spinner McBride,* 1993

32. Powers of the Quarters

Powers of the East we call
Bring your wisdom to us all.
Open up our inner sight
And bring us safely through the night

Guardians of the Southern Fire
Protect us as our bodies tire.
Bring us healing in our dreams
And wake us with your bright sunbeams.

Water flowing from the West
Guard and watch us as we rest.
Your love flows over one all
For your children large and small.

Northern watchers come be near
Mother Earth whom we hold dear.
Help us grow both strong and sure
And keep our hearts and spirits pure.
                    —*Rhiannon Bennett*

Circling Songs

(A number of beautiful songs combine casting the Circle with calling the Quarters. These are meant to be sung by the entire Circle. Some of them have been recorded on tapes and CDs, and we highly recommend you get these and learn the music—see the Resources in the Appendix.)

33. We Are a Circle

Ch: We are a Circle within a circle
        With no beginning
        And never ending *(2x)*

You hear us sing, you hear us cry,
Now hear us call to you,
Spirits of Air and sky!

Within our hearts there glows a spark
Love and desire, a burning Fire!

Within our blood, within our tears,
There lies the altar of living Water!

Take our fear, take our pain,
Take our darkness into the Earth again!

The Circle closes between the worlds
To mark this sacred space
Where we come face to face!
                    —*Rick Hamouris*

34. The Witches' Rune

Darksome Night and shining Moon—
East, then South, then West, then North—
Hearken to the Witches' Rune;
Here come I to call thee forth.
Earth and Water, Air and Fire—
Wand, Pentacle, Cup and Sword—
Work ye unto my desire;
Hearken ye unto my word.
Cords and censer, scourge and knife—
Powers of the Witches' blade—
Waken all ye into life;
Come ye as the charm is made.
Queen of Heaven, Earth and Hell—
Horned Hunter of the Night—
Lend your power unto the spell;
Work my will by magick rite.
By all the power of Land and Sea—
By all the might of Moon and Sun—
As I do will, so mote it be;
Chant the Spell and Be It Done!
                    —*Doreen Valiente*

4. Inviting in the Deities

Invocations & Evocations
By Oberon Zell-Ravenheart

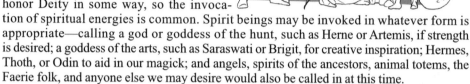

Now, into this Magick Circle where we are gathered, we invite the deities to join us, for our magickal workings are done in their honor, and with their blessings. Many rituals are purely celebrational and specifically designed to honor Deity in some way, so the invocation of spiritual energies is common. Spirit beings may be invoked in whatever form is appropriate—calling a god or goddess of the hunt, such as Herne or Artemis, if strength is desired; a goddess of the arts, such as Saraswati or Brigit, for creative inspiration; Hermes, Thoth, or Odin to aid in our magick; and angels, spirits of the ancestors, animal totems, the Faerie folk, and anyone else we may desire would also be called in at this time.

Some magickal practitioners—especially those of the "New Age" traditions—may regard these spirit beings merely as symbols or Jungian *archetypes,* anthropomorphic personifications representing different aspects of human consciousness (as in Jean Shinoda-Bolen's books, *Goddesses in Every Woman* and *Gods in Every Man*). While there is certainly a degree of validity in such identification with *immanent divinity* (often expressed as "Thou art God" or "Thou art Goddess"), it is not the whole picture. It is our experience that the deities, angels, totems, and other spirit beings of the various cultural *pantheons* (families of deities) are very real personalities, just as we are. Like all living beings, they each have their own stories, histories, attributes, and, perhaps most importantly, their own *agendas*—which may not be the same as ours!

The main difference between Them and the rest of us is that they are *trans-corporeal*—independent of individual bodies and hence immortal. They are not, however, *omniscient* (all-knowing) or *omnipotent* (all-powerful), though they do know things and have influences that we as mortals do not. Just as in dealing with anyone else, we must treat and respect them as real beings if we are to develop a genuine relationship with them. For example, we find it useful to consider that when we call them to enter our circle and attend our rite, the first thing they're going to say is: *"Well?* Why have you called Us? This had better be good!" And it better be!

It is entirely up to you to decide whom you want to invite into your Circle. Whatever works and feels right *is* right. Many rituals will invoke both a goddess and a god, just as you might invite both your mom and your dad to Thanksgiving dinner or to a play or other performance you're in. There are, of course, many different gods, goddesses, and other spirit beings to choose from. Every culture that has existed throughout history has had its own pantheon, and I recommend you study some of these and become familiar with them. (See the lists of deities and their attributes in the Appendix.) But just as one can speak of Woman or Man as an abstract, transcendent idea, without having to name each and every individual man or woman, so we can speak of The Goddess or The God without having to consider all of them individually.

In the HOME Tradition, we usually invite the Goddess in first, and then the God. This order may be reversed at some festivals or Sabbats (such as Lugnnasadh or Mabon), which are particularly dedicated to the God. Some Pagans have the God and Goddess take turns being first as the seasons roll around, while others may call upon only one or the other. Or a particular ritual may call for several deities. If you participate in Circles by various groups, you'll learn how they do it. In such matters, always remember that there is no one true right and only way to worship the Lord and Lady—or any other deities. Some, in fact, are androgynous, hermaphroditic, or transgendered, which will require adaptions. Whatever works and feels right *is* right!

Invoking

There are two ways in which gods and goddesses, spirits, and Elemental Powers may be brought into our Circle: we may call them *in* from outside; or we may call them *out* from inside. The first way, calling in, is called *invoking* or *invocation,* and it is the most common way of inviting their presence.

In traditional magickal practice, "invoking" is the term commonly used for inviting a deity or spirit to enter into us, so that we speak with its voice and/or manifest its attributes in our own person. Conversely, the same term is used to petition or call for help or aid. Morning Glory and I have found it more useful, however, to use these terms in a slightly different manner, which I will explain here…

Of course, beings of spirit are all around us all the time, just like radio waves and TV transmissions. What we are really doing is making *ourselves* receptive to *communion,* or contact with them at a particular time and place. This is much like turning on your TV and choosing the channel you want to watch. This is done by *invocation,* similar to our Quarter callings, in which we address the deity or spirit as we would a friend or relative, in the second person (that is, by saying "you," as in "we invite you to come…"). The simplest invocations run something like this:

> *Oh, most* (gracious, wise, beautiful, powerful, beloved, etc.) (name), (Lord, Lady)
> *of* (attributes…), *I invite you to enter this Circle and join with us in our magick*
> *work. Bring us your* (wisdom, strength, inspiration, courage, etc.) *and your bless-*
> *ings. Hail and be welcome!*

And of course, everyone else echoes, *"Hail and be welcome!"* As the beings of spirit are called, candles may be lit for them on the central altar.

Here is an example of how this may come together in practice:

> *Crescent One of the starry skies,*
> *Flowered One of the fertile plain,*
> *Flowing One of the ocean's sighs,*
> *Blessed One of the gentle rain;*
> *Hear our call 'midst the standing stones,*
> *Full us with your mystic light;*
> *Awaken us to your silver tones,*
> *Join us in our sacred rite!*
> > *Hail and be welcome!*

Evoking

Evoking, or calling out, is done in the first person by saying "I" (as in Doreen Valiente's lovely "Charge of the Goddess"), wherein the priestess, speaking as the Goddess, says: *"I am the beauty of the green Earth, and the white moon among the stars…" Evocations* are usually referred to as "charges." In the solitary practice of Western Ceremonial Magick, this is considered a function of invocation rather than evocation (see above), and "evocation" is the term used for summoning a spirit or deity into visible manifestation outside of ourselves. This appearance may be in a triangle, a crystal, a mirror, or even another person. But the term actually means "calling out," and in our ritual work (which does not include summoning spirits into visible appearance), Morning Glory and I have found it important to distinguish "calling out" from "calling in," so we use these terms with this meaning.

When we *evoke* the God or Goddess, we call them forth from within our own souls, for deep down inside we are one with them. Just as we say we are "one blood" with our human parents, so we are "one soul" with our Divine parents, the Goddess and God. When we call them out with an evocation, we temporarily give over our human identity to allow the God or Goddess to manifest through our body and speak with our voice. True evocation is a very advanced form of calling, and should really be done by a priestess or priest who has been adequately trained and prepared. It calls for the priestess (most often) or the priest (rarely) to enter a trance-like state in which they become a vessel to channel the spirit of the deity, allowing the Goddess, God, or other spirit to speak through them. There is a very beautiful Wiccan rite for evoking the Moon Goddess, called *Drawing Down the Moon*. Variations of it are known from as far back as ancient Thessaly in the 2nd century BCE. It was also recorded by Roman Wizard Lucius Apuleius (123-180 CE) in his bawdy novel, *The Golden Ass* (written in 170 CE); it is believed to have been derived from his initiation into the Mysteries of Isis:

"*I am Nature, the universal Mother, Mistress of all the Elements, primordial Child of Time, Sovereign of all things Spiritual, Queen of the Dead, Queen also of the Immortals, the single manifestation of all Gods and Goddesses that are. My nod governs the shining heights of Heaven, the wholesome sea-breezes, the lamentable silences of the World Below. Though I am worshipped in many aspects, known by countless names, and propitiated with all manner of different rites, yet the whole round Earth venerates me.*

"*The primeval Phrygians call me Pessinuntica, Mother of the gods; the Athenians, sprung from their own soil, call me Cecropian Artemis; for the islanders of Cyprus I am Paphian Aphrodite; for the archers of Crete I am Dictynna; for the trilingual Sicilians, Stygian Proserpine; and for the Eleusinians their ancient Mother of the Corn. Some know me as Juno, some as Bellona of the Battles; others as Hecate, others again as Rhamnubia, but both races of Ethiopians, whose lands the morning sun first shines upon, and the Egyptians who excel in ancient learning and worship me with ceremonies proper to my godhead, call me by my true name, namely, Queen Isis.*"

(*The Golden Ass, XI.5,* Robert Graves translation)

A comparable evocation of the Hindu God Krishna is found in the *Bhagavad-Gita:*

"*I am the Soul dwelling in the heart of everything. I am the Beginning, the Middle and the End. Of the Adityas I am Vishnu. Of the lights I am the Sun. Among the stars I am the Moon. Of the Vedas I am the Sama. Of the senses I am the mind and in the living beings I am the intellect. Of the Rudras I am Sankara. Of the mountains I am Meru. Of words, I am the great AUM. Of the weapons, I am the thunderbolt. Of those that measure I am Time. I am Death that destroys all and I am the origin of things that are yet to be born. The germ of all living beings is Myself. There is nothing moving or unmoving that can exist without Me. Anything endowed with grandeur, with beauty, with strength, has sprung only from a spark of My splendor. I stand pervading the universe with a single fragment of Me.*"

(*The Mahabharata, Bhishma Parva, XLIX.6*)

In the pages following, you will find a number of invocations and evocations of goddesses and gods. These are meant to be read, recited, chanted, or sung in your rituals and ceremonies, as desired.

Invocation and the Power of Sound (2)
By Ruth Barrett

Invocation is the act of inviting a deity or spirits into a specific time and place to witness, to grant a request (as in a petition), to protect, or to praise, thank, or honor her or them. An invocation is spoken in the same way that one utters a prayer: it is a communication from the heart that is spoken with the need to be heard and responded to. Invocations and prayers are different in that prayer calls for the *favor* or *blessing* from a deity in a specific circumstance, while invocation calls for the *presence* of the deity in some form and in a specific time and place. The language of invocation and prayer may be similar if the intention is communion with a deity or when asking for guidance or aid. Invocation is often a prelude to some form of spellcraft or ritual enactment.

Feminist theologian Mary Daly created the word *be-speaking*, and defines it as "bringing about a psychic and/or material change by means of words; speaking into be-ing." To *be-speak* an invocation, you must be fully present with what you are saying. Let the words arise out of the lips of the Divine Spirit who resides within you. *Hear* your own words, your own voice; *listen* to what you are saying. Experience your voice, spoken or sung, as a pathway for the deity to enter. Listen for the echo of your own voice speaking and singing back to you.

The goal of invocation is to speak with such an openness of mind and heart that you come into resonance with Divinity. This can be difficult to do if you are holding a piece of paper and reading your invocation. If you read your invocation, your eyes and mind are on the printed page and not with them. Remember that the purpose of invocation is to *connect* with Spirit. Preparation is most important because it gives you the energetic experience from which your words will emerge. Therefore, writing an invocation prior to the ritual helps to clarify the purpose of your invocation, and can be a part of your energetic preparation. During the actual ritual, however, trust yourself to have a conversation with the God or Goddess. Do you write down exactly what you are going to say before you phone a friend to ask a favor or have a heart-to-heart chat? You might make notes of points to cover if you intend to have a long conversation, but most of the time you just dial the number and talk when the connection goes through. Initially you may want to memorize your invocation or evocation, but with experience you will move beyond this. Once you are experienced with invocation, you will rarely, if ever, need to prepare a script in advance.

A ritual Circle can be a wonderful place to jump into the waters of improvised invocation. Be-speaking does not necessarily have to involve words. Invocation can be communicated entirely with movement, with music, drums, percussion, or breath—or even with silence. Whether in solitary space or in a supportive environment, you can learn to trust yourself to communicate directly with the Deities, unaided by a script or "cheat sheet." As long as you convey the essence of what you are asking for, a simple, concise invocation can be magnificent.

The Mystery of the Gods
By Oberon

Deity manifests in so many ways! Theologically, Morning Glory and I are basically Pantheists. We believe, as Cicero said, that "everything is alive, and everything is interconnected." We also believe in immanent divinity ("Thou art God/dess") and emergent evolution. Just as consciousness arises and develops in an individual person, from infancy through life, so does emerging consciousness arise through the evolution of all life, both individually in each creature and synergistically in the entire planetary biosphere—Gaia, Mother Earth, the Goddess. Thus we are all cells in a greater body, just as we ourselves are composed of tinier cells. We also suspect that the Earth—perhaps the entire solar system—could be just a cell in the larger body of the galaxy, and that galaxies may be cells in the body of the greater universe. And perhaps this universe is but a cell in the vaster complex of "multi-verses" that physicists are now proposing. There's really no end to it, in either direction:

> Great fleas have little fleas upon their backs to bite 'em,
> And little fleas have lesser fleas, and so ad infinitum.
> And the great fleas themselves, in turn, have greater fleas to go on;
> While these again have greater still, and greater still, and so on.
> —De Morgan, "A Budget of Paradoxes"

Coherent consciousness coalescing synergistically at scales and levels greater than ours is what we conceive of as "divinity." This consciousness or divinity seems to be not only immanent, but also transcendent. We share in the greater consciousness of Gaia, for instance, just as the neurons in our brains share in our own minds. But we are legion, and each of us has our own sense of individuality as well.

Princeton research psychologist Julian Jaynes presents a compelling thesis in his 1976 book, *The Origin of Consciousness in the Breakdown of the Bicameral Mind*. Since we have only one organ of vocalization, our cognitive functions are lateralized, with the left hemisphere controlling the mouth and conscious thought. It is in the Wernicke's area of the posterior temporal lobe that our individual conscious identities reside. Jaynes proposes that a completely independent cognitive mentality also developed in the corresponding region of the *right* cerebral hemisphere. And at one time, says Jaynes, the various cognitive functions now displayed only by our left-hemisphere consciousnesses resided in this area as well.

As consciousness is essentially a non-physical state, it may not necessarily be limited to individuals. Given the documentation of telepathy, remote viewing, astral projection, and other kinds of "thought transference," it makes sense to postulate that these right-hemisphere faculties might have made it possible for human societies to share communal awareness of a single trans-corporeal deity, or even entire pantheons of such entities. Communication between the respective "inhabitants" of these bicameral hemispheres (just as in the remnant phenomenon of "multiple personality syndrome") was conveyed through the anterior commissure, in the form of what today we call auditory hallucinations—or, the voices of the gods.

Jaynes states that thousands of years ago, Gaea and all the pantheons of ancient deities had, as an abode and a means of expression, the right cerebral hemispheres of humanity. *"The language of men was involved with only one hemisphere in order to leave the other free for the language of the gods."* As human consciousness was split into two separate manifestations—the human and the divine—Jaynes refers to it as the *bicameral* ("two houses") mind. He also maintains that it was these divine voices that were responsible for the social control that enabled civilization to arise: *"The bicameral mind with its controlling gods was evolved as a final stage of the evolution of language. And in this development lies the origin of civilization."* As collective consciousnesses, these deities were not only omniscient, but omnipresent and immortal as well, and the memories and wisdom that they could impart were those of the people, all the way back to the dawn of time.

Because of this collective consciousness, icons, idols, votive figurines, and other depictions of such deities ubiquitous in those times functioned almost as modern-day Internet access devices. When you had a problem and you sought an answer, you would gaze into the eyes of the image, tracing the lines of the inscribed spirals and whorls. You would invoke the deity, offer a prayer, and the figurine would come to life. And the voice of the deity would be heard as if it was spoken into your left ear.

And for 25,000 years—from their first appearance 30,000 years ago—virtually *all* of these figurines were female. This means that the voices that were being heard, even by the men, were female voices—goddess voices.

Assuming the Positions*
By Oberon

Inviting in the Goddess

In Wicca (and in many other Pagan traditions as well), the Goddess is commonly seen as manifesting in one of three phases (or *aspects*) that reflect the ages of mortal women: Maiden, Mother, and Crone (Wise Old Woman). These aspects are shown in the cycles of the seasons (Spring=Maiden, Summer/Autumn=Mother, Fall/Winter=Crone) as well as in the phases of the moon (new/waxing=Maiden, full=Mother, waning/dark=Crone).

A priestess may take one of two traditional postures when manifesting as the Goddess during an evocation, or when invoking her into the Circle. The first (and oldest) is the *epiphanic*, or "manifestation," position known as "drawing down the moon." It is found in countless Neolithic paintings and sculptures, especially in North Africa and Egypt. In this position, the feet are together and the arms are raised above the head in a wide arc.

The second posture is becoming more common in contemporary Pagan rituals, and is known as the "Goddess-invoking" position. Here, the feet are apart, and the upper arms are held against the sides with the forearms reaching outward from the elbows in a lunar arc:

Inviting in the God

The aspect of the God most commonly invoked in Witchcraft is the Horned God. As Pan, Cernunnos, or Herne, he is ruler of Nature, animals, and wildness. Very fatherly, he is our protector and teacher. He was portrayed quite well in the movie *The 7 Faces of Dr. Lao*, and in the BBC's *Robin of Sherwood* TV series. As Lord of the Dance, he plays the panpipes or *syrinx*, inviting us all to party on! Brother to the Horned God is the Green God, or Jack-in-the-Green. He is the ruler of vegetation who dies every fall, only to be reborn in the spring as the new crop sprouts in garden and field. "Jack in the Green" from Jethro Tull's *Songs from the Wood* is the definitive song about him. Another version of his story is the famous traditional song, "John Barleycorn."

The standard posture for evoking or invoking the God is known as the "Osiris" or "God-invoking" position. The feet are held together and the arms are crossed over the chest, with the hands balled into fists (above left).

1. Goddess Invocations—The Triple Goddess

(NOTE: Because many of the selections here were passed on by oral tradition, we have been unable to identify authors for some of them. But we felt it would be remiss to leave them out of this collection, as they are important parts of our liturgical heritage. We apologize for any omissions of credits, and ask anyone who knows such attributions to please contact us.)

37. Ancient Goddess

Smiling virgin, shining cresent
Waxing fullness luminescent
Sickle of silver, reaper of bone
Maiden, Mother and Crone, wah-ha,
Maiden, Mother and Crone.

Ancient Goddess, Daughter of Moonlight
Ancient Goddess, Mother of Stone
Ancient Goddess, Keeper of Midnight
Maiden, Mother and Crone.
                    —*Abbi Spinner McBride*

36. Invocation to Habondia

By the flowers of the field
Oh, Lady of delight,
By the crops thy blessings yield
Oh, Maiden clear and bright.
We invoke thy presence in kernels and sheaves
We see thy face in the moonlit leaves.
Come to us now, extend thy grace

Come into our circle in this holy place.
Daughter of the Earth, drinking sunlight;
Queen of plants; Sister of night.
By leaf and twig, by root and bough,
By water and earth come to us now.
Bring us your grain, the staff of our lives;
Bring us your fruit wherever it thrives.
Mistress of herbs, unlock your power
And lead us into your leafy bower.
In love and joy we call your name;
With comforting hope you ease our pain.
We see thee in the swelling bud;
We feel thy stirring in our blood.
Oh, Lady clear, we feel thee near!
In Spring a maiden with flowers crowned.
In Summer and Harvest the Mother renowned.
In Fall and Winter the Hag holds sway;
Yet the Maiden remains but months away.
Great Triple Goddess, the seasons flow
And ebb to thy will as you come and go.
                    —*Morning Glory Zell, 1978*

35. To the Triple Goddess

Koré, Corn Maiden
Crescent Moon arise!
Bless us by Your presence,
Silvering the skies!
Demeter, All-Mother,
By Your loving touch
Bless us in Your service,
Whom we love so much!
Grandmother Spider Woman,
Weave the living Web!
Bless the tides that are our lives,
The flowing and the ebb!
—*Morning Glory Zell*

2. Goddess Invocation
–The Maiden

38. Holy Maiden

Oh Holy maiden of the kindling quick
Of merging mist and mazing echo
The innocent bounty of the trees
Bares your faerie flesh of Wildness,
Wonder, Magic, Mirth and Love…
Your beauty seals our bridal with all Life.
The dance of your green pulse unfolds
All bodies from Earth's fragrant form.
        Evoé Koré!
—*Frederick MacLauren Adams, 1968*

3. Goddess Invocations
–The Mother

39. Evocation of the Goddess

in the name of the earth, and the sun,
and the rainbow which bridges them.

1

your counsel is in the cowrie
you engrave sand dollars with your runes
you flower forth in daisies
and teach oaks to twist in the sun
cows learn from you to lick their calves
women to spin flax and clay
the yeasty moon to double
and the sky to turn

2

at dusk, in my kitchen
i strip the onion of its layers
gouge out potatoe's eyes
hack off the carrot's head
forgive me this violence
i am blood of your blood
this is my body, too
and my sister the pomegranate
is the kiss of my mouth

3

lover, sweet lady
couch your love in my mother tongue
speak me the language of mirrors
show me how to maiden you, mother you,
crone you, as you, at my flesh's altar,
do to me

4

mother, i swear by my navel
how i swam like a fish
in your underground lake
sister, our lyric round
of tide, phase, and the womb's atlantis
overlays endlessly
charms the world out of time
daughter, i'd feed you at my veins
if my breasts ran dry
or bury me in the wheatfield
where i'll rot patiently under your breakfast
and my corpuscles will crumble
into vitamins you need

5

architect of the cell's alphabet
navigator of blood's latitudes
keeper of the archives of fire
my heritage unwinds inside me
uncoils like a long galaxy
through the dark nucleoplasm
like a snake gone opaque
she hides in the jungles of the chromosome
she lies at the hydrocarbon's heart
she is the black hole itself
between her thighs
the universe is squeezed from spirit
—*Oothoon, Ostara, 1975*

40. Hymn to Gaia

When o'er your dreaming hills the dawning
    day ignites its fire,
And on your seas the light's caress awakens
    wind and spray,
Your breath bids bud and branch push forth
    to echo your desire,
And in a womb a heart begins your
    rhythmic hymn to play,
The eye that opens upon itself, an eye that's
    opened before,
Seeks knowledge deep with each repeat,
    the better to adore.

    So Yes! Yes! to the beating heart,
    That echoes the surge of the sea,
    And sends blood's course
    With primal force,
    Urged on by the will to be.
    And Yes! Yes! to the pulse that flows,
    The stream of life's rebirth,
    The sacred flame intones your name,
    Oh Gaia, soul of the Earth.

When out of seed and spore and shoot and
    egg your song is raised,
From lovers' bliss your holy kiss awakens
    flesh anew,
To search and feel, and to behold, and find
    a voice for praise,
And then to sing beneath your sky one
    sacred hymn to you.
A song of life begat from death that only
    life may give,
Begins and ends with one refrain that
    heralds the ages—I'll live!

    So Yes! Yes! to the song of life,
    Where all the voices are one,
    The pulse and beat that all repeat,
    What's ended is begun.
    And Yes! Yes! to the quick'ning heart,
    That bids the darkness be spurned,
    A wild tattoo that shouts anew,
    Great Goddess, I have returned!

You dance upon the spiral stair of chromo-
    some and gene,
Oh soft of eye and red of maw, you pare
    and prune the tree.
In many forms I've sung your song,
    through many eyes I've seen,

In many forms I'll wake again, more fully
    yours to be.
Many's the dance I've danced with you,
    one round a pale, cold mask,
The next a glow in a mother's eye as into
    Earth I'm cast.

    So Yes! Yes! to the dance of death,
    Oh Kali, devour me whole,
    Take me home, consume my bones,
    And sing your song to my soul.
    And Yes! Yes! to the wheel of life,
    Oh Isis restore me anew.
    Return my breath to laugh at death,
    And revel, oh Gaia, in you.

When from your warm embrace I'm torn,
    in fields of stars to dwell,
Your voice, a sigh on cosmic dust, calls
    after your lover "return,"
"Embrace my green and loam-filled breast,
    drink of my scented well,
Ignite my fire with love's desire, shout
    through my winds, 'return,'"
Then longing for my lover's arms will call
    me back to you,
And in a cloak of soil-born flesh I'll swear
    my troth anew,

    And Yes! Yes! I will dance with you,
    And forsake the fields of stars,
    And plunge me deep
    In the Earth to keep,
    My vow to Lady and Lord,
    And Yes! Yes! I will live again,
    And ensoul the living Earth,
    At my mother's breast,
    In the hour of death,
    I pledge you my rebirth!

                —*Tom Williams*

41. The Charge of the Star-Goddess

Hear ye the words of the Star Goddess,
The dust of whose feet are the hosts of
    heaven;
She whose body encircles the universe:

I am the beauty of the green Earth,
And the white Moon among the stars,
And the mystery of the waters,
    And the desire of human hearts.

Call unto your soul: Arise and come unto me!

For I am the soul of Nature that gives life
to the universe.
From me all things proceed,
And unto me all things must return.

Before my face, beloved of all,
Let your divine innermost soul be enfolded
In the rapture of the Infinite.

Let my worship be in the heart that rejoices,
For behold: all acts of love and pleasure
are my rituals.
Therefore let there be beauty and strength,
Honor and pride, power and compassion,
Mirth and reverence within you.

And you who think to seek for me—
Know that your seeking and yearning will
avail you naught,
Unless you know the Mystery:
That if that which you seek you find not
within you,
You shall never find it without.
For behold: I have been with you from the
beginning,
And I am that which is attained at the end
of desire!

—*Doreen Valiente*

4. Goddess Invocations –The Crone

42. Hekate

Lady of Tremblings
Sovereign Lady
Mistress of Destruction
Who sets the world in order
She who delivers from destruction
Lady of Heaven
Mistress of the World
Who devours with fire.
Lady of the Altar
To whom abundant offerings are made
She who prevails with knives
Mistress of the World
Destroyer of the foes of women
She who makes the decree for escape of
the needy from evil
Lady of Flames
Who inhales the supplications which are

made to her
She who permits no man to enter at her shrines
Lady of Light
Who is in front
Lady of Fortitude
Who gave birth to all that lives
She whose girth is three hundred and fifty
measures
The likes of her has never been found from
the beginning
Lady of Might
Who dances upon the blood-red ones
She who keeps the Festival of Hekate
On the day of the Hearing of Faults
Terrible One
Lady of Rainstorms
Who plants the ruination of the souls of men
Devourer of dead bodies
Orderer and Producer and Creator of the
slaughtered
Dispenser of Light during her period of life
Watcher of Flames
Lady of the Strength and of Writing
She takes possession of hearts
She has secret plots and councils

—*Morning Glory Zell*

43. Lilith

When shadows steal across the moonlit sky
The sound of silent wings becomes a sigh.
Hyenas prowl the scattered graves of kings,
Their laughter's wailing cry a shiver brings.
When all the waiting world seems drowned
in Fear,
The queen of Darkness, Lilith, will appear.

Her proud head never bent to Adam's rule:
Better freedom, or exile, than serve a fool!
So She feeds upon all Nightmares of denial
Ascetic vows the tool to serve her guile.
Her children, ever outcast, don't belong;
Yet She stands an inspiration to the strong.

Now the Twilight of the Gods and Man is nigh;
In their glory, paid no heed to all the cry
From nature's elder children in dire need;
Now mankind's doomed to die from
poisoned seed.
Yes, it's Lilith who is waiting by the tomb;
Through loving Her we could escape our Doom.

—*Morning Glory Zell, 1978*

44. To the Crone

Hail to Thee
    Dark One
        Wise One
            Crone
Hail to Thee who dares to see
Who draws the knife and severs life
And takes away her children
    To her wintry dark home

Hekate
    Rhiannon
        Wise One
            Come!
And share with us your wisdom
In the darkening sun.
Show us how deep wet darkness
Leads to our rebirth;
Let us see the ancient wisdom
    Buried in the Earth.

Old Woman
    Wise Woman
        Grandmother
            Crone!
Lead us in your meditation
When our work is done
Yet spare us of the knife too soon
Give us time to see
The meaning of your Mysteries
    So Mote It Be!
           —*Anodea Judith*

5. Goddess Invocations –The Moon Goddess

45. Moon-Child

Diana Tana Dana
Artemis Britomartis
Thou art this:
The maiden crescent…
    …growing.

Your naked splendor makes the heavens
Blush lavender.
Deepening to violet blue
Cloaking you in a velvet mantle…
    …flowing.

Bend your slender silver bow
Let fly your arrows

Like shooting stars
Across the early evening sky…
    …falling.

Forever stalking our hearts
Divine Lady of the Beasts
Your cats, hounds, owls and deer
Pursue secrets through dappled shadows…
    …calling

Moon-eyed Mistress of Wilderness
Grant us the thirteen gifts
Which free us from slavery
And reveal thy ancient Mystery…
    …teaching.

Daughter Goddess, Amazon Huntress,
You have captured our imagination
After all this time, now
We turn again to You…
    …beseeching.
        —*Morning Glory Zell, 1978*

46. Charge of the Moon Goddess

I am She who ere the Earth was formed
Was Rhea, Binah, Ge—
I am that soundless, boundless, bitter sea
Out of whose depths life swells eternally.
Astarte, Aphrodite, Ashtoreth—
Giver of Life and Bringer of Death
Hera in heaven, on Earth Persephone,
Diana of the Waves and Hecate
All these I am, and They are seen in me.

The hour of the high full Moon draws near;
I hear the invoking words—
"Shaddai El Chai and Rhea, Binah, Ge."
I come unto the Priest who calleth me.
I am the veiled Isis of the shadows of
    the Sanctuary.
I am She that moveth as a shadow
Beyond the tides of death and birth.
I am She that cometh forth by night
And no man may see my face.
I am older than time and beloved of the Gods.

I am that soundless, boundless, bitter sea,
All things in the end shall come to Me.
Mine is the Kingdom of Persephone—
I am the star that rises from the twilight sea.
I bring men dreams that rule their destiny,
I am the eternal Woman, I am She!

The tides of all men's souls belong to me—
Out of my hands man takes his destiny.
Touch of my hands confers polarity,
These are the moontides, these belong to me.

Hera in heaven, on Earth Persephone,
Diana of the Moon, Star of the sea!
Isis unveiled and Ea, Binah, Ge!

—Dion Fortune

47. Invocation to Arionrhod

Bright regent of the moon, our Triple Queen,
To dwell within your heart this argent night
We pass beyond your gate and stand between
The realms of darkness and returning light.
A silver chalice bears the sacred wine
As silvered is the vessel of your love,
Unemptied as your hands pass it to mine
To share below a vintage from above.
Each heart has warmed another's and rejoiced
To find your blessing passing through the ring.
Each head has lifted and each throat has voiced
The call that through your moonlit halls we sing.
Beyond the earth each loving spirit flies
To bind again the bond that never dies.

—Gwydion Pendderwen

6. Goddess Invocations — The Lover

48. Hymn to Venus

Venus Amathusia!
Laughter-loving Aphrodite!
Come to me with laughing breast,
Come on waves of golden crest,
Come with doves and golden light
Drawn by swans and sparrows bright.
Alight! Alight!
I am thy man, I am thy mate!
Receive me 'til our storm abate!
Thy green glades echo with my calls,
Come to me from emerald halls,
Flanked by maidens winding there
Rose and myrtle in thy golden hair.
Come to me! To me! To me!
And mate with me upon the grass,
Laughing, lusty, of ravishing lass!
Our bodies arch and strain and twine,

I am thine and thou art mine!
Come from heavens of azure hue,
Ocean born and ever new!
Pulsing, laughing, yearning, straining,
Pleasure, lust, all life containing.
Race with me through glades of green,
Exalting, loving, oh rapturous queen!
To me! to me! Oh come to me!
And enter, merge, enfold, unite!
Suffuse desire with golden light!
Never sated in eons of time,
I am thine and thou art mine!

—Tom Williams

49. The Lady of the Dance

I am the Lady of the dance
All Nature feels my emerald glance;
All lovers join me in their magic trance
For I am the Mistress of romance!

> When trees and grasses make pilgrimage
> And fill the glens with life,
> I lead the jingling rout of Nymphs,
> The Faerie Companionage,
> The Faerie Companionage,

I am the Goddess of the Night;
I grant all stars their diamond light;
I let all Worlds unwind their spiral sight
For I am the Enchantress of Delight!

> In the heat of the shimmering days,
> The Sun and Moon shall fuse.
> And in the Ocean of glowing rays,
> My Flesh of Love diffuse,
> My Flesh of Love diffuse!

I am the Lady of the dance
All Nature feels my emerald glance;
All lovers join me in their magic trance
For I am the Mistress of romance!

> From the flickering Grail of Night,
> Seeds of gold I bestow
> On those who Wisdom of Koré sow
> Among the Dreams of Light,
> Among the Dreams of Light!

I am the Goddess of the Night;
I grant all stars their diamond light;
I let all Worlds unwind their spiral sight
For I am the Enchantress of Delight!

Those who lift my skirts of flame
May stairs of stars reveal,
Then mount to the bounds of space surreal
And burst the Seal of Time,
And burst the Seal of Time!

I am the Lady of the dance
All Nature feels my emerald glance;
All lovers join me in their magic trance
For I am the Mistress of romance!
—*Svetlana Butyrin & Frederick Adams*

7. Other Goddess Invocations

50. To the Goddess Bride

Bridget, Bright Regent
Oh, Triple Queen of Brigantia
Rigatona, we call you forth.

Sovereign Goddess of the Waxing Light,
Waken from your snowflake slumber
Appear to us in radiant Glory
Come to us with homely Grace

By Pen and by Poem
By Craft and by Croft
By Wit and by Wisdom
By Fountain and Flame
We know you are among us.

Bright Arrow, warrior Maid
Thou slender as the spear.
Powerful Mother, Busty Brigid
Thou Milk of fertile flocks
Wise Woman, Singer and Healer
Thou Cauldron of Inspiration.

You are: Hammer to our forge
Melody to our harpstrings
Midwife to our fevered dreams

Within the silent Circle of Ancient Stone or
Within the simple cottage of a peasant home
Within the heart of a flickering candle or
Within the heart of a Winter-bitten apple
Dances the Sudden Star
Of your radiant desire.

We kindle your flame of eternal truth
We break your bread of the humble hearth
And we pass your cup of Crimson Wonder

Listen to the voices chanting softly.
Swelling sound of
Nineteen thousand women singing:
Your prayer echoes in the alcove
In your temple, in your abbey,
In your bed of rushes.

Most Holy Bridget, Excellent Woman
Sudden Flame!
May your bright fiery sun
Take us to your lasting Kingdom!
—*Morning Glory Zell, 1/4/90*

51. Morgan Le Fey

Lady of the Apple Trees,
Keeper of the Western Breeze,
Morgan, come to us now!
Guardian of the sacred Well,
Speaker of the healing spell,
Morgan, come to us now!
Mistress of the Dark Moon Night,
Onyx raven, bold in flight,
Morgan, come to us now!
Teacher of warriors, and of sex,
Of spells that cure, and spells that hex,
Morgan, come to us now!
Bean Sidhe by the river ford,
Wielder of the Sacred Sword,
Morgan, come to us now!
Lady of the Sacred Lake,
Where Excalibur, you did make,
Morgan, come to us now!
Ruler of the faerie mound,
Queen of Fey, you are crowned,
Morgan, come to us now!
Goddess of Life, Death, Rebirth,
Ancient One, Oh Mother Earth
Morgan, come to us now!
—*Susa Morgan Black*

52. To the Olympian Goddesses

Athena, grant me wisdom;
Hera, the strength to outlive sorrow;
Artemis, give me courage;
Hestia, take me home!
Aphrodité, please delight me;
Baubo, send me laughter flowing;
Hekaté, guide my decision;
Demeter, make me whole!
—*Susan Arrow*

53. Our Lady of the Beasts

We call your name Fauna:
For truly you are the Sovereign Female
    Spirit of all Creatures.
At once the vixen and the hen you are...
Hawkeyed, deerfooted, cat whiskered Lady
Who floats on silent owl-feathered wings.
Celebrating with the voice of larks; keening
    with the dirge of wolves;
You sing the lonely music of the whale song.
Bitch and sow in the heat of your passion;
Likewise the Great Mother of all Humankind.
You are well pleased with the sound of
    rattles and tympani;
With the voices of birds, the outcries of
    frogs and bright-eyed lions.
        We call your name Anima Animalia:
Tender Huntress, Fierce Mother,
You stalk our hearts amid tangles of primal
    urges...
Down rivers of blood...through vaginal
    tunnels...
We are caught! Devoured! Reborn!
By your Grace...
...By the milk of your breasts we are
    nourished; we are nurtured.
O restless one, forever hungry, in search of
    your Lover
You roam with migrating herds of reindeer,
    elk and bison;
You hide and seek under drifts of fallen
    leaves
Where squirrels hide their winter stores.
        We call your names: Circe, Hathor,
        Artemis Orythia,
Britomartis, Hecate, Sehkmet, Kundalina,
    Medusa.
Mother Nature's hot-blooded daughter;
    cold-blooded killer.
Mistress of both the wild and the tame
You are the Queen of every hive.
Answer our call, o Goddess; let us prey
    with you.
Our throbbing pulse is your drum beat;
Delicious shivers shake your sistrum...
...the growl becomes a purr.
  Outside our Circle of Firelight we see your
    glowing eyes.

                    —*Morning Glory Zell, 1978*

54. Epona

Through warlike stormcloud cumulus
    Epona gallops by.
I see Her on the tumulus,
    Her blazing sword held high.

Black mane the harpers sing of
    Whips in the rising wind;
Her sinews are the string of
    The bow no man can bend.

The Queen of Amazons She is,
    A proud and shining mare,
With courage in Her heart free as
    The hawk who rides the air.

The peace She brings our village
    Has banished fear's dark end;
No rogues would dare to pillage
    The hearth She does defend.

The tides of Fate She must obey
    To breast the swirling flood.
The wine of Life She drinks today
    With laughter dark as blood.

The Omens point a finger:
    Her exile nears its end.
From Shadows where we linger
    She comes to Earth again!
                    —*Morning Glory Zell, 1978*

1. God Invocations -Generic

55. To the Laughing God

What God is this who beckons me
With laughter in his eyes?
Who plays his pipes so hauntingly
With tunes from paradise?

Are you Apollo, radiant Sun,
Or Pan with wild delights?
Or Dionyos, guardian
Of secret mystic rites?

Or are you Hades, Lord of Death,
Or young Adonis fair,
To whom sweet Venus sends her breath
To play upon your hair?

You are them all, yet you are He

Whose name is never known;
Why do you call and beckon me
With every changing tone?

Where do you lead, O tempting One?
Your smile conceals a truth
And ageless wisdom hides beneath
Your fair veneer of youth.

I follow, then for in my soul
The fire has been fanned
And so I meet your trusting gaze
And grasp your outstretched hand.

And I am free, my bonds are shed,
Like dewdrops in the morn.
O God of Joy! O God of Life!
Through you I am reborn!

— *Thera*

56. In Your Eyes

I'm the beat of your heart
In the guise that you wear.
I'm the spark in your eye
For the love that you dare!
I live deep in your breath;
Feel me move, feel me rise,
In your heart, in your soul, in your eyes.

I am Lord, I am Light,
Shining bright on the Earth!
I am Love, and your soul
I will guide to rebirth.
I am strength to be free
From all fear if you're wise
In your heart, in your soul, in your eyes.

I am Death, I touch all,
I will come as I must,
Bringing comfort and rest,
For your souls are my trust.
And reunion, my gift
Beyond death is the prize,
For your heart, for your soul, for your eyes.

I will pulse in your blood,
I will ring from your core,
When the Lady, my Love,
Gives you flesh once more!
You will meet and remember
The loves of your lives;
For your heart and your soul are my eyes.

I am Lord, I am Love,

I'm the beat of your heart!
I am Lord, I am Life,
I'm the seed of your start.
I am Lord, hear me laugh,
Feel me move, feel me rise
In your heart, in your soul, in your eyes.
In your heart, in your soul, in your eyes.

— *Gwendolyn L. Zak*

2. God Invocations – The Horned One

57. Hymn to Pan

Thrill with lissome lust of the light
Oh man! My man!
Come careering out of the night
Of Pan, Io Pan!
Io Pan! Io Pan! Come over the sea
From Sicily and from Arcady!
Roaming as Bacchus with fauns and pards
And nymphs and satyrs for thy guards,
On a milk white ass, come over the sea
To me, to me!
Come with Apollo in bridal dress
(Shepherdess and pythoness)
Come with Artemis, silken shod,
And wash thy white thigh, beautiful God,
In the moon of the woods,
On the marble mount
The dimpled down of the amber fount!
Dip the purple of passionate prayer
In the crimson shrine, the scarlet snare,
The soul that startles in eyes of blue
To watch thy wantonness weeping through
The tangled grove, the gnarled bole
Of the living tree that is spirit and soul
And body and brain—come over the sea,
(Io Pan! Io Pan!)
Devil or god, to me, to me,
My man! My man!
Come with trumpets sounding shrill
Over the hill!
Come with drums low muttering
From the Spring!
Come with flute and come with pipe!
Am I not ripe?
I, who wait and writhe and wrestle
With air that hath no boughs to nestle
My body, wary of empty clasp,

Strong as a lion and sharp as an asp—
Come, O come!
I am numb
With the lonely lust of devildom
Thrust the sword
Through the galling fetter,
All-devourer, all-begetter;
Give me the sign of the Open Eye,
And the token erect of thorny thigh,
And the word of madness and mystery,
O Pan! Io Pan!
Io Pan! Io Pan Pan! Pan Pan! Pan,
I am a man:
Do as thou wilt, as a great god can,
O Pan! Io Pan!
Io Pan! Io Pan Pan! I am awake
In the grip of the snake,
The eagle slashes with beak and claw;
The gods withdraw:
The great beasts come, Io Pan!
I am borne
To death on the horn
Of the Unicorn.
I am Pan! Io Pan! Io Pan Pan! Pan!
I am thy mate, I am thy man,
Goat of thy flock, I am gold, I am god,
Flesh to thy bone, flower to thy rod.
With hooves of steel I race on the rocks
Through solstice stubborn to equinox.
And I rave; and I rape
And I rip and I rend
Everlasting, world without end,
Manikin, maiden, maenad, man,
In the might of Pan.
Io Pan! Io Pan Pan! Pan! Io Pan!

—Aleister Crowley

58. Invocation of the Horned God

By the flame that burneth bright, Oh Horned One!
We call thy name into the night, Oh Ancient One!
Thee we invoke, by the moon-led sea,
By the standing stone and the twisted tree,
Thee we invoke, where gather thine own,
By the nameless shrine, forgotten and lone,
Come where the round of the dance is trod,
Horn and hoof of the goat-Foot God!
By moonlit meadow, on dusky hill,
When the haunted wood is hushed and still.
Come to the charm of the chanted prayer,
As the moon bewitches the midnight air.

Evoke the powers that, potent, bide,
In shining stream and secret tide,
In fiery flame, by starlight pale,
In shadowy host that rides the gale,
And by the fern-brakes, faery-haunted,
Of forests wild and woods enchanted.
Come to us who gather below,
When the broad, white moon is climbing slow
Through the stars to the heaven's height;
We hear thy hooves on the winds of night!
As black tree branches shake and sigh,
By joy and terror, we know thee nigh!
We speak the spell that frees thy power,
Made manifest at this witching hour!
Robin-the-Good, Cernunnos, Pan;
The One-in-All since the world began,
From primal dawn, 'til the end of Time,
Thee we invoke with ancient Rhyme!
Father of Life, Bringer of Fear,
We call thee forth, and thou art here!

—Doreen Valiente

59. The Goat-Foot God

Came the voice of Destiny,
Calling o'er the Ionian Sea:
"The Great God Pan is dead, is dead.
Humbled is the horned head;
Shut the door that hath no key—
Waste the vales of Arcady."

Shackled by the Iron Age,
Lost the woodland heritage,
Heavy goes the heart of man,
Parted from the light-foot Pan;
Wearily he wears the chain
'Til the Goat-God comes again.

Half a man and half a beast,
Pan is greatest, Pan is least.
Pan is all, and all is Pan;
Look for him in every man;
Goat-hoof swift and shaggy thigh—
Follow him to Arcady.

He shall wake the living dead—
Cloven hoof and horned head,
Human heart and human brain,
Pan the Goat-God comes again!
Half a beast and half a man—
Pan is all and all is Pan!
Come, O Goat-God, come again!

—Percy Bysshe Shelly

60. Evocation of Pan

Oh horned one, goat-foot, Great God Pan!
Come to me with eyes of fire,
And with thy pipes awake desire,
Come with wild and lustful grin,
Herald of your flame within,
  Io Pan! Io Pan!
  Io Pan, Pan, Pan!
Shout to me from scented wood,
The call of all that's wild and good,
Come to me with shaggy thighs,
And let the hills return our cries,
Come with satyrs bearing wine,
I am thine and thou art mine!
Come with joyous lusty laugh,
Come with swollen ruddy staff,
Race with me through halls of green,
Thou art my God and I your Queen,
And spend with me a tender hour,
Making love within my bower,
  To me! To me!
  Oh come to me!
And come oh God of stream and wood,
Oh God of life and all that's good,
Never sated in eons of time,
I am thine and thou art mine!
—*Tom Williams*

61. Evocation of Faunus

All wild creatures hear thy call
Upon the haunted wind.
Within thy soul the Horned One
Returns to Earth again.
Together you shall manifest
The magick of the man
And falcons soar from out the sky
To perch upon thy hand.
The serpent's wisdom thou shalt learn
From tip of forked tongue.
The fleetness of the white stag's flight
In starlight or in sun.
Lord of Light and Lord of Shadow;
Keeper of the key
Which unlocks the door of dreams,
Whereby men come to thee.
Cernunnos, Tammuz, Horus, Pan;
By name we set thee free!
O Shepherd of the wild woodland,
May thou be one with he!
—*Morning Glory Zell, 1974*

62. Blessing of the Horned God

Blessed be all in hearth and hold,
Blessed in all worth more than gold.
Blessed be in strength and love,
Blessed be where'er we rove.
Vision fade not from our eyes
Of the Pagan Paradise,
Past the gates of Death and Birth,
Our inheritance on Earth.
From our souls, the Song of Spring,
Fade not in our wandering.
Our life with all life is one,
By blackest night or noonday sun.
Eldest of Gods, on thee we call,
Blessings Be on thy creatures all.
—*Dion Fortune*

63. Horned One

Horned One, Lover, Son,
Leaper in the corn—
Deep within the Mother
Die and be reborn!
—*Buffalo Brownson*

3. Other God Invocations

64. Hades' Song

Oh, Kore,
Hear one who deep within
    the cavern'd world doth long,
To touch the flower'd light,
    to dance with lilted song,
Whose heart is not of stone,
    though stone became his fate,
When lots were cast 'mongst brothers,
    he won the nether gate.
The one received the trident
    and doth rule the perfumed foam,
The other on the heights of proud
    Olympus sits his throne.
They rule their realms as kings
    but all must homage show,
To Her from whom the holy stream
    of life doth ebb and flow.
These rulers are but stewards all

of one great secret deep,
The one the sky, the one the sea,
    the one the caverns keep,
And I alone thought least of all
    among the brothers three,
I guard the utmost mystery
    and this I'll teach to thee.
I sit not on the radiant mount
    nor rule the scented sea,
But lonely in my cloistered halls
    I call the dead to me.
They come with fear and deep despair
    and cry unto the sky,
"Oh why live we and suffer so
    if only now to die?"
My countenance is hard as stone,
    implacable the law,
But oh, my heart would comfort give
    and stay the bloody maw.
Yet all must pass beneath the gate
    to see again the light,
And in the darkness meet their souls
    and seek their paths aright.
And lonely in my somber toil
    I yearn for loving eyes,
A soothing touch, a heart that knows
    how I am moved by cries.
Oh, maiden whom the flowers love,
    who wears the verdant green,
Come with your laughter to my halls
    and rule my realm as Queen.
Let amethyst and azurite
    And radiant tourmaline,
Ignite before the light bestowed
    by Erebos' new Queen.
Let souls who journey through the night
    find comfort in your gaze,
Let those who craven'd in despair
    now find a voice for praise.
To all who walk the spiral path,
    the key of life to gain,
Bestow the token of a glance
    that says all's not in vain,
Unto my realm I beckon you,
    fear not the Stygian gates,
With fullsome heart and outstretched hand—
    thy Dark Lord waits.

                    —*Tom Williams*

65. Invocation of Eros

When all is dark and still,
As it was in the Beginning of Things,
I call to you, Beloved of All,
To stretch your feathered wings.
Born of a windsown egg,
Hatched in Erebos:
Cosmic Attractor, Thou art Eros.
Lover of Chaos, whose golden arrows
Made sweet love bites in the flesh of Gaea,
Rendering Her pregnant with possibility.
Oh, I love you! Yearn for You
Loosener of limbs
Who strikes me down
With bittersweet venom.
Intoxicator of heart and loins
A fever in the blood.
Thou are that and even more
Heart of Hearts that I adore.
Whisper soft wings in the shadows
White stains on my sheets
Sweet pleasure and pain
Sorrow and gain.
All that You are is all whom I love.
For You are the One who caresses
And I confess that I cannot live
Without Your touch upon my senses.
Comforter, Healer who conquers all defenses.
So that even the deathless Gods fear
The havoc that You bring.
I sing Your praise
And raise your hymn
To vaulted Olympus and beyond
To the skies.
Like the rush of blood to cheeks and thighs.
Come here to us drawn by the sighs
Of maid or man
Who would great You as Lover
Or greet You as Lord.
Come in us and through us
Pierce us with your Beauty and Power,
With shafts of Ecstasy: Now!
This hour from Your quiver of Desire.
We walk on fire who call Your name
We know no shame when You inspire.
Aphrodite's Son of Delight,
Come to us now, here in the night!

                —*Morning Glory Zell, Beltane 1996*

66. Invocation to Poseidon

Hail to thee, mighty Poseidon,
    Earth Shaker, Sea Breaker
Come to us from the salty depths,
    from your distant wine-dark
    Aegean home.
Come with your bands of mermaid
    Nereids splashing their tails in
    water ballet.
Ride the white horses of crashing surf
    to our shores.
Bring us the laughter of dolphins,
    the song of whales
    the salt tears of the crying seagulls.

White-bearded, green-eyed Lord of Ocean,
    wake up now and be watchful!
You who bears the trident wand of power;
    protector of the shoals of fishes;
Father of sea horses, jellyfish,
    anemones and starfish.
You nurtured and fed us before ever
we had backbones.
You were our Lord, when our home
    was the sea.
Long have we forgotten you and
    forgotten our watery origins.
Long have we taken your gifts and
    reaped your bounty
Without calling your name in
    simple gratitude.
We are awake, Now! We will remember you,
    Now! We offer respect, Now!

Raise your booming voice, come
    Blow the wreathed horn of Triton
Warn all the creatures of your vastest deeps
    to beware the curse:
Of the driftnet, of the whaling ship,
    of the oil rig,
And of all those who would stripmine
    the very source of life itself.

We join with you, O Ancient One,
    in a prayer, a pact, and a pledge:
We will aid you in your hour of need;
    we will help protect your precious realm,
As long as we have salt water
    in our veins.
Evoé Poseidon! So Mote It Be!
                   —Morning Glory Zell

67. Invocation to the God of Love

Hail to thee, O God as Lover
Over land you gently hover
While caresses heal and cover
Mother Earth with love.
You who come down into Earth to rejoin Her
You who rise up yet again to rejoice with Her
Thou who art wildness, untamed and free
The fire of the sun, the storm of the sea
You who dance to the sound of the flute
Thou who art found in the seed of the fruit
Come to us now by light and by love
Join together below and above
Make the magic union be
Balanced in heart—both tender and free
Bring us your magical, nurturing touch
Healing the Earth who has given so much
Long she awaits you to walk hand in hand
Over the womb of the promised land.
Bellenos, Kernunnos, Osiris, Pan
Bring us the Sacred part that is Man
Father and Lover, helper and mate
Gently weaving your spells of fate
Bring us your light, rekindled anew—
Bring us the joy in love that is You.
                   —Anodea Judith 4/85

68. Invoking the Dark Lord

Darker than a cavern's heart;
Deeper than the blackest hole.
Darker than the Night Wind's breath;
An emptiness that shapes your soul.
Rustle of the ebon wings;
In shadow where He reigns supreme.
The Jewel of Death in time he brings;
Upon a throne of Adamantine.
He holds a chalice filled with blood,
Of hearts that ceased their pulsing flood.

Black leather, Black feather...
Radiant heart of obsidian fire;
Absent light that draws desire.
The silent secret smile of He
Who is the Midnight Sun.
The last thing we shall ever see,
When all our dancing days are done.

The bitter smell of Absinthe
A cord of spider silk
The smoky sound of laughter
A taste of Raven's milk...

In passion or in fiercest rage;
In loneliness or fear
Our darkest dreams and feelings
Are the ones that draw Him here.

He wears a mask of sable hue,
That changes shapes from old to new.
But no One living ever sees
The Face behind the Mask
His Beauty causes blindness
To the One who dares to ask.
In His Power lies Potential;
His potential knows no lies.
His secret lies in history,
The secret is in His eyes.

Fall into them completely;
Shed your final tear.
Name His Holy Mystery;
The Dark Lord now is here!
— *Morning Glory Zell, Samhain 1997*

69. Song for the Dying God

My love—I cry inside the tears you do not shed
And voice for you such words as must be said
To steal through hurts and heal the deepest wounds
Whose pain restrains you as through life
    you've bled.

As Winter comes you're colder by the day
And more and more is taken sorrow's way.
Though Samhain comes to claim your
    world in death
I'll see you rise again with New Year's breath.

If love can reach across the cold abyss
Then take from me this warmth from my
    heart's kiss.
And if you plant the seeds of your heart's wish
This Spring will follow with its hopes of bliss.

You are the God who's married to the land
And with its death and birth you'll understand
The cycles of renewal that doth rule
The spiral that gives hope when life is cruel.

But you and She are one eternal dance
And with Her death your power surely wanes.
But rest sprouts seeds that soon turn into plants
As warmed by your bright rays that soothe
    Her pains.

Do not delay the darkness of the day
For it contains the teaching of the year.

Linger in it though it chills your way
For soon the light returns in Yuletide cheer.

And then the spiral cycles once again
And yet each year we grow to know it more.
And when the dark returns again to men
We shall know it for renewal's door.
— *Anodea Judith, 1986*

4. God & Goddess Combined

70. My Goddess is a Rock

My Goddess is a rock
And She whirls in space
She whirls in space
Oh, she whirls in space
My Goddess is a rock
With a sweet green face
The miracle where I was born.

My God, He is a star,
Burnin' in the sky
He's burnin' in the sky
Oh, he's burnin' 'way up high
My God, he is a star,
Burnin' in the sky
The leaper in the grain and corn.
— *Dragon Singing*

71. Prayer

All wise, gracious Mother of us all;
All powerful Lord, our Father;
Supernal Parents,
Sustain us, Your children, this day.
Give us the wisdom to see Your path
And the strength to prevail in the Darkest Hour.
We thank You for the joys we have
And for the chance You have give us
To prove ourselves in adversity
As well as in happiness. May we thrive.
— *Joseph Wilson, 1974*

72. Invocation of the Lady & Lord

Lady of the Earth, the Oceans and Wind
Mother of the Fire that burns within!
Lord of the Dance, bringer of Light,
Untamed God, give us delight!
— *Ayisha Homolka*

73. Hoof and Horn

Hoof and horn, hoof and horn,
All that die shall be reborn
Vine and grain, vine and grain,
All that fall shall rise again!

Lord and Lady, hoof and horn,
Light revealed, be reborn:
Fire, Water, Air and Earth;
Hunter, hunted, soul's rebirth!

Mother Earth, Mother Earth,
We call on She who gave us birth;
We are Yours, blood and bone,
Kin to tree and standing stone!

She is luminous, She is bright,
She is shining, crowned with light!
He is radiant, He is bright,
He is rising, He takes flight!

Crone and Sage, Crone and Sage,
Wisdom is the gift of age.
Sage and Crone, Sage and Crone,
Wisdom's truth shall be our own!
—*Ian Corrigan*

74. The Lady's Bransle
(to the tune of "Nonesuch")

For She will bring the buds in spring
And laugh among the flowers
In Summer's heat Her kisses are sweet
She sings in leafy bowers
She cuts the cane and gathers the grain
When fruits of fall surround Her
Her bones grow old in wint'ry cold
She wraps Her cloak around Her!
—*Hope Athern*

75. The Lord's Bransle

O, He will call the leaves in the fall
To fly their colors brightly
When warmth is lost He paints with frost
His silver touches lightly
He greets the day of the dance of the May
With ribbons wound about Him
We eat the corn and drink from His horn
We would not be without Him.
—*Artemisia*

76. God & Goddess Immanent

God and Goddess immanent,
We're calling to You!
Join us in our circle now,
And bless what we do.
God and Goddess immanent,
We are divine
As we join with You in spirit,
And body and mind!
—*Anodea Judith*

77. To the Moon & Sun

Holy Maiden Huntress, Artemis, Artemis,
New Moon, come to us!
Silver shining wheel of radiance, radiance,
Full Moon, come to us!
Ancient Queen of Wisdom, Hecaté, Hecaté,
Old One, come to us!
Golden shining Sun of radiance, radiance,
Father, come to us!
—*Peter Soderberg*

78. We Are One

We are one with the Mother
We are one with the Earth
We are one with each other
By our lives, by our birth!

We are one with the Lady
We are one with the Lord
And we pray that our unity
Will this day be restored!
—*1st verse by Ani Heartsong*
—*2nd verse by Oberon Zell*

79. We All Come from Her & Him
(to be sung as a round)

We all come from the Goddess
And to her we shall return
Like a drop of rain
Flowing to the ocean!

We all come from the Sun-God
And to Him we shall return
Like a spark of flame
Rising to the heavens!
—*1st verse by Z Budapest*
—*2nd verse by Oberon Zell*

5. The Working

The Heart of the Ritual
By Oberon Zell-Ravenheart

Now we have reached the heart of the ritual: working the magick! As I said in the introduction to our ritual outline, magick is *the art of coincidence control or probability enhancement.* We work our magick by focusing our individual or group energies in the same direction, like a laser beam, to shift the patterns of possibilities and probabilities so that the things we want to happen are more likely to come about. The power of magick comes from our *will*. When we do magick, we never say, "I *hope* such-and-so will happen," or "I *wish* such-and-so would happen." We say, "It *will* be so!" The ritual words for this are "so be it!" or "so mote it be!" or "make it so!"—which everyone else in the Circle repeats.

There are several steps in doing a magick working in the Circle. Like any good short story or play, a well-designed ritual has an *exposition, characterization, plot development and buildup, climax,* and *denouement, or resolution.* First is the declaration of intent (exposition), in which the purpose of the working is explained and agreed upon by everyone. Then comes the working itself (plot development and buildup)—actually the main part and point of the ritual. This is followed in most rituals by what is usually called "raising the cone of power," in which everyone's energy is combined and built into a powerful force. Next, power is released and sent out to do its work (climax). Finally, centering and meditation (denouement or resolution) enable the participants to recover some of the energy they have just put out.

Declaration of Intent

The purpose of using magick is to change things for the better. Most of our workings are for healing—healing ourselves, healing each other, and healing the planet. Other purposes might be protection, peace, or justice. Finding love, a good job, a home, or an answer to some problem may also be a goal of a magick working. At the beginning of the ritual it is important to decide exactly what the energy you are raising will be used for, and to state this plainly. This is your *declaration of intent.* Often, the declaration of intent is determined and written down before the ritual even starts. This declaration may be subtle or blatant, but should be made clear and unequivocal. In a traditional wedding, for example, this would correspond to, *"Dearly beloved, we are gathered here today to witness the joining of Bob and Connie in the sacred bonds of holy matrimony."* Stating the purpose allows everyone to turn their attention from the preliminaries to the main focus of the ritual, and paves the way for the work that is to follow. (A previous partner, Liza, was really good at stating precise and concise declarations of intent. And she would always conclude with the line, *"This or something better will manifest now in complete harmony, with good for all concerned, and harm to none."*)

Sometimes the declaration of intent may be stated by one person (especially if you are doing a solitary ritual). If you have a priestess and/or priest conducting the rite, this would be their call. A good way to do this is to write down the intent in the form of a brief spell—especially in the form of a little rhyming couplet that will be easy to hold in mind during the power raising. (A simple example could be something like: *"Bring the one I love to me; as I will so mote it be!"*)

At other times everyone in the Circle may be given a turn to state what it is they want to accomplish, or just shout out one- or two-word affirmations, such as *"Peace!" "Love!" "Healing!" "Justice!"* We call this "popcorning." In order to keep the group's energy together, however, it works best if everyone focuses on the same basic goal. If some folks really want to work for different things, these workings should be done in different rituals.

After everyone agrees and the intent is clearly stated out loud, the ritual leader may say, *"As I/we do will, so mote it be!"* and everyone should repeat, *"So mote it be!"*

Working the Magick

This part may be a celebration, or, as the name implies, actual work—be it mental or physical or some combination of the two. This is the heart of the ritual where the purpose is symbolized in the spiritual language, and some form of drama or transformation is enacted upon those symbols. Techniques for this are many and varied, and dependent upon the purpose at hand. Sometimes the real work is figuring out how the problem or purpose can best be symbolized! For example, the work might entail forgiveness between two parties who represent certain opposing forces; or, it might be the burying of a symbol of something unwanted.

In the rites of HOME, especially for the eight seasonal Sabbats, we often conduct a mystery play for this part of the ritual. We will recapitulate and enact an archetypal story, such as The Hero's Quest, The Descent Into the Underworld, The Quest of the Grail, The Journey Into Faerie—or perhaps some myth out of ancient Sumerian, Egyptian, Greek, Celtic, or other source of lore and legend. In performing a mystery play, the entire ritual—including the casting of the Circle, the Quarter callings, and the invocation of the Deities—will be woven into the central theme and story of the mystery.

Other workings that may occur in this part of the ritual might be spellworking, such as healing, house-blessing, tree-planting, protecting, dedication, initiation, etc. Rites of passage in particular, whether they be baby-blessings, puberty rites, handfastings (weddings), or personal transformations, are all conducted as workings in the liturgical sequence of the basic ritual structure. Books II and III in this compilation will provide many examples of actual rites, and workings of many varieties.

Moose Dixon of Ozark Avalon says: "Dry Ice (frozen carbon dioxide) is a very easy way to achieve fog for inspiration. Much information may be gleaned from *http://www.dryiceinfo.com*. It's important to remember that the water bath will cool quickly, thus diminishing the volume of fog. I recommend a heater for the water to prevent the water from cooling so low as to form ice around the chunk of dry ice. Tupperware containers are best—glass and ceramic ones will break and metal ones can make terrible screeching noises as they contract."

Raising & Releasing the Power

Once the working is done, then the microcosm within the Circle needs to be charged so that it will carry itself into the mundane world when the ritual is over. This is basically a matter of providing raw energy in the form of movement, sound, meditation, or passion. Slowly and rhythmically this energy is built to a climax, and then released from each member of the Circle to the focal point, be it an object, person, or concept. If the magick working is to be a healing for someone inside the circle, the energy raised will not be sent out, but rather directed toward the person to be healed. This can be very powerfully done, for example, by everyone laying hands on the person and "pushing" healing energy into them and/or "pulling" pain and illness out. Visualize a warm blue healing light rising in you and spreading out through your hands into the person to be healed, just like you've seen in movies. Use deep rapid breathing to pump up your own energy before you send it out. Then be sure to shake your hands off and ground them into the earth after such workings!

If you are working a solitary ritual, one of the best ways to raise and release energy is through the "Breath of Fire." You sit in a meditative position, and breathe rapidly and deeply in and out as fast as you can. Repeat over and over the words of your intent or spell in your mind, while visualizing the thing you want. Start out slowly and go faster and faster until you feel like you're about to explode. Finally, when you can stand it no more, exhale with a last great rush while shouting out: *"So mote it be!"* Fling your thought and visualization out into the Universe as if you were throwing a spear. Then you should just collapse and lie down until you have the energy to sit up again. *Warning: Don't overdo this! Hyperventilation can be dangerous.*

Most magick is meant to take effect outside the Circle. To raise energy for such purposes, a favorite method is the Circle dance, generally done *deosil* (sunwise for either hemisphere). While you concentrate on the stated objective of intent, everyone holds hands and dances faster and faster around the circle, weaving your steps in and out. Bring your hands gradually up as you dance, until at the climax they are high above your heads. At the same time, visualize a *vortex*, or bright shining cone of energy, forming around the Circle and rising higher and higher, like an upside-down tornado funnel. If the working is to create a spell of protection, for example, you should visualize your combined energy rising up and then spreading over the Circle in a great dome—an umbrella-shaped "deflector shield." Such a shielding dome should have an outside surface like a perfect mirror that will reflect away all negativity. A good focusing device for this is to have a large garden "gazing ball" in the middle of your central altar.

A favorite dance step used in traditional Circle dance as a way to raise energy in a group is called the "grapevine" step, because of the weaving pattern made by the feet of the dancers. At right is a diagram of the grapevine step.

Another very popular Circle dance is the *Spiral Dance* made famous by Starhawk through her book by that name, and her huge public rituals held each Samhain, that have grown to thousands of participants. This dance is also called "Troy Town" after the old maze pattern, which was said to resemble the walls of Troy. The wonderful thing about a spiral dance is that everybody comes face-to-face with everybody else, even if there are hundreds of people.

Here's the way we do a spiral dance: We start out in a circle, all holding hands, and begin moving deosil just as in any other Circle dance. Then the leader breaks contact with the person on her left and starts leading the dance in a spiral towards the center, keeping just inside the outer ring. When she reaches the center, she suddenly turns sharply to her left, leading everyone back out in a reverse spiral until the circle becomes complete again, only this time with everybody facing outward, and releasing the energy out into the world. In the outward part of the spiral, each person passes every other person, and the idea here is to look each one, however briefly, in the eyes. In smaller Circles I've even seen people kiss on the fly, which is really fun! The most important thing in a spiral dance is, *don't let go!* Below is a diagram of a spiral dance.

For the energy-raising Circle dance, a good drumbeat is great (or you can put on a CD with a good heavy beat!), and a Circle dance song will help create the right juice. Here's one of our favorites, which I have found to be very effective:

> Circle 'round the fire
> To raise the cone of power
> To win what we desire
> So mote it be!
> Dance the Circle in the moonlight
> Dance and sing the whole night long
> Dance the Circle in the moonlight
> Dance and sing a Witches' song!
>
> —Selena Fox

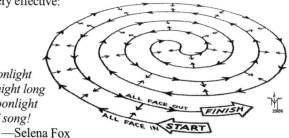

Repeat louder and faster until you can't dance and sing any faster, then on the final "so mote it be," scream that "beeeee!" as loud as you can, breaking loose of each other's hands as you fling your hands to the sky and release all that energy to go and work your will. Visualize the top of the cone erupting like a volcano, sending a beam of power where you want it to go. Immediately afterwards, everybody collapses to the Earth, grounding ourselves and letting the Mother's strength and love flow back into our bodies.

Moose Dixon of Ozark Avalon says: "An easy way to script musical accompaniment for a ritual (background for guided meditation, chants, dance, etc.) is to burn a custom CD. A remote control on the altar can be used to play and stop each piece of music unobtrusively. I've also seen a remote used in this manner and hidden in the sleeves of the HP(s)."

Centering & Meditation

After raising and releasing so much energy, it is important to bring your own energy back to your center with a simple meditation. Come back up to a seated position, legs crossed, with your hands open in your lap. Gaze into the flame of the center candle on the altar, or into the fire if you are doing this outdoors and have a bonfire. Let your mind cut loose of all thoughts, especially of the working you've just done, and just become one with the flame. After a few moments of this, when you feel completely calm and relaxed, you might softly begin to hum *"omm,"* letting your voice merge with everyone else's into a harmonic chant: *"Auu-ommmm...,"* fading away when it has completed its work. Whether a formal time of meditation or a quiet moment of reflection, this centering process finalizes and seals the power raised in the ritual.

Energy and Magick
By Starhawk

The primary principle of magick is connection. The universe is a fluid, ever-changing, and ever-connected energy pattern, not a collection of fixed and separate things. What affects one thing affects, in some way, all things. All is interwoven into the continuous fabric of being. Its warp and weft are energy, which is the essence of magic. Energy is ecstasy. When we drop the barriers and let power pour through, it floods the body, pulsing through every nerve, arousing every artery, coursing like a river that cleanses as it moves. In the eye of the storm, we rise on the winds that roar through mind and body, throbbing a liquid note as the voice pours out shimmering honey in waves of golden light that leave peace as they pass. No drug can take us so high, no thrill pierce us so deep, because we have felt the essence of all delight, the heart of joy, the end of desire. Energy is love, and love is magick.

Of all the disciplines of magick, the art of moving energy is the simplest and most natural. It comes as easily as breathing, as making sound. Picture the power in motion, and it moves. Feel it flowing, and it flows, cleansing, healing, renewing, and revitalizing as it passes. To a trained awareness, the subtle energies are felt as tangible, visible, and malleable. They are, as Dion Fortune says, "more tangible than emotion; less tangible than protoplasm." We can learn to sense them and mold them into form.

The laws of energy are also the laws of ecology. Everything is interconnected, and every action, every movement of forces, changes the universe. You must not change one thing, one pebble, one grain of sand, until you know what good or evil will follow on that act. The world is in balance, in equilibrium, and a Wizard's power of changing and summoning can shake the balance of the world. It is dangerous, that power. It is most perilous. It must follow knowledge and serve need. To light a candle is to cast a shadow.

Yet the equilibrium of the universe is not static, but dynamic. Energy is constantly in motion. It cannot be stopped. Again, using water as our metaphor, when we block its flow it becomes stagnant and foul. When it flows freely, it cleanses and purifies. The rituals, spells, and meditations of the Craft center on aiding energy to flow.

Energy flows in spirals. Its motion is always circular, cyclical, wavelike. The spiral motion is revealed in the shape of galaxies, shells, whirlpools, and DNA. Sound, light, and radiation travel in waves, which themselves are spirals viewed in a flat plane. The moon waxes and wanes, as do the tides, the economy, and our own vitality. The implications of the spiral model are many. Essentially, however, it means that no form of energy can be exerted indefinitely in one direction only. Always, it will reach a peak, a point of climax, and then fall back or turn.

Music & Ritual
By Julie Forest Middleton

The chant started low and slow, and as more of us learned it, we joined in. Someone added a high harmony and someone else started a drum beat on the floor and quickly it gathered steam and became rich and full. Then suddenly it caught fire and we were on our feet and dancing as the fire filled us. The energy snaked around the Circle like braided silver; it rose through us and around us, and when it reached its peak we shouted it off into the universe, sending it out to our chosen destination. We whooped and hollered as we fell to the floor, and as we calmed down, the priestess grounded the remaining energy back into the Earth.

Music and ritual—*how* does it work and *why?* What makes a chant work one time and not the next? What can music do for your rituals? How do you teach songs and use music when your group doesn't like to sing?

What Singing Does and How It Does It

Think about the times you've sung with others around a campfire or at a sing-along during a concert. Remember the feeling of cohesiveness and bonding that happened? When a group sings together, it breathes together, and songs become breathing meditations. Singing together focuses your energy and attention; it gets everyone's energy moving in the same direction and puts all of you in a "groove" together.

In ritual, music can do many things. It can invoke a Greater Being and speak to her or him in prayer. It can also help to raise a cone of power. Music celebrates, grieves, soothes, heals, trances, and connects all the disparate parts of the ritual together. Music also teaches: it carries the word (liturgy) and provides a role model of how to best live our lives.

Has a song ever spoken to you so truly and deeply of your own experience that you cried? Music touches our hearts and dissolves our defenses. It opens us up and allows Spirit to enter. It speaks to the unconscious parts of ourselves (and to the collective unconscious) and brings about healing and change.

When you begin designing a ritual, you first settle on your intention: what do you want this ritual to do? And how do you want it to happen? Each song has a unique tone (which opens us up), unique words (which teach), and a unique energy (which stirs us to change and/or heal). In other words, each song has its own unique *intention*. So when you select songs for your ritual, look at the intention and energy of each part of the ritual and pick songs that will enhance or add to this energy and intention. A song is like a plant: if it's appropriate in its setting it will thrive and grow – and if it doesn't grow there, it's a weed. So ask yourself what you want a song to do at a given point in the ritual. What energy do you want it to bring? How do you want people to feel during and after the song? In short, *what is your intention?*

Chants

In Pagan rituals, chants are the songs most often used, as repetitive sounds awaken the inner world of Spirit. Groups usually sing chants three or four times and then stop. Unfortunately, this gives no chance for the energy of the song to develop and work. A chant is a short song that needs to be sung over and over and over for a long time, until you're totally bored – and then you sing it some more! And it's *then* that the magick happens. If you're using a song to invoke the Goddess, sing it long enough that the Goddess will hear it and come. Don't stop singing it until she *does* come (you'll know when that happens). Likewise, if you're using a chant to raise a cone of power, sing it until it catches fire and takes off, and send it up and out at its highest point. Or sing it until it *doesn't* catch fire, in which case you'll simply bring it to a close and ground the energy. Sometimes it's impossible to raise a cone (people are too tired or wrung out and it just won't happen), and that's okay too. Don't force something that's not going to happen.

Some chants are longer songs that insist on being sung many times—there's something so very satisfying about them that you simply want to keep going. Don't be afraid to sing a song for five or ten minutes – or for thirty. In all times in all cultures, people have sung their sacred songs, and the oldest chants are the devotional ones. Think about Gregorian chant, sung for hours on end in monasteries. Pagans don't have monasteries in which to live and worship; we have living rooms and back yards and parks and, occasionally, dedicated land. So we sing our chants wherever we are.

Zipper Songs

A zipper song is one in which a certain key word or phrase can be replaced to change the meaning. For instance, Starhawk's song "Snake Woman," goes: *"Snake woman shedding her skin / Snake woman shedding her skin / Shedding, shedding, shedding her skin / Shedding, shedding, shedding her skin."* And that's the way you'd teach it – singing it enough times that everyone's familiar with the tune and words. But I might not feel like a snake woman tonight. Maybe I feel more like a worm, in which case I might change it to *"Worm woman burrowing down / Burrowing, burrowing, burrowing down."* And maybe Connie feels like an *"eagle woman flying so high,"* while Jim feels like a *"mountain man feeling so strong."* One way of making these changes while you're singing is to go around the Circle in order and let each one do a verse. Or you may want to let people put up their hands when they've got a verse and you point to them.

Rounds

Rounds are songs like "Row, Row, Row Your Boat," in which you divide up the available singers into groups, and each group begins singing the song at a different time. The trick to learning rounds is to sing the song many times all together as a group so that everyone's thoroughly familiar with it *before you divide into parts.* As a rounds singer you'll learn to listen so you can hear all the parts happening at once. When everyone's comfortable singing it as a round, you can stand up and walk around and sing it, or you can sit in a circle and number off so you're not with the others singing your part.

Call & Response Songs

Call and response songs are fun to teach and easy to learn, and many longer Pagan songs have choruses that are easier for the group to learn than the verses. Try to sing the new song at several different places in the ritual; this will help develop auditory memory. And keep a list of which songs you've taught to your group so you can repeat them at regular intervals. I carry around a small book, listing the songs I have by title under various headings, such as "Earth," "Air," "Healing," and "Winter Solstice." Many songs will be listed under several headings because they fit into several categories.

Healing Songs

Sometimes, during the check-in or during the Circle itself, a person will be so overcome with the emotional muck of life that he or she will im- or explode. This person needs the special attention of an on-the-spot healing. It's best to ask the person what he or she needs: to be rocked, stroked, left alone, listened to. Singing to the person in distress is almost always appropriate. What is the need in this exact situation? Which song you select is important, and here's where having many songs becomes essential.

Trancing Songs

All cultures in all times have had trance songs: Shaker songs, Indian ragas, some Japanese music that expands the mind's frequencies, certain Greek chord changes that alter your consciousness, and various contemporary Pagan chants that spin you out into ecstasy. There are shamanic journeying chants in indigenous tribes all over the Earth, and the didgeridoo's amazingly primal effects on us which are not so much *learned* as *remembered.* Almost any song, however, can be used as a trancing song.

The repetitions of certain sounds are known to facilitate the experience of transcendent realities. The repeated sound patterns stabilize the breath and movements of the mouth and throat, which, along with the volume, all create modifications in the body. Long periods (three minutes or more) of self-produced repetitive sounds bring relaxation, lower brain waves, increased warmth in hands, and a feeling of being centered. When the sounds are long and vowel-centered, the effect is even greater (from Don Campbell, *The Roar of Silence*).

The hard thing to do when you've started a trance-inducing chant is to walk with a foot (or a brain) in both worlds – the trance world and the what-passes-for-reality-at-the-moment world. You *must* keep a foot in the physical space of the Circle in order to shape the energy and eventually to ground it and bring people back. You *must.* You can let yourself go a little bit out, but you must be able to return at will, and you must be able to look at the clock.

Drums & Rattles

Drums help singers connect with the Earth and each other and the songs. Drums keep the pulse of the song going, which also helps you learn the song. Drums add to the energy and help focus it. Rattles draw the energy in and fling it about. Drums provide a sound to trance out on, and are great for dancing! I've been in Circles with many different types of drums, which allows each drum to find its own voice and place in the Circle.

Try "drumming as one drum" to start a Circle and get into entrainment with each other. Try thinking of drums as members of a tribe: the elders, who keep the steady beat; the care-takers, who move about and get things done; and the children, who run all over the place.

Using Music in Ritual

Don't look at music as an add-on to the ritual, but as an integral part of it. Music helps carry the intention of the ritual; helps move, promote, or enhance the energy; and helps bring the teachings to your group. And again, the more songs you have, the more you have to share.

The energy of any given song can be changed in several ways. You can change the tempo of the song – try singing slow songs quickly and singing fast songs in a more prayerful manner. Sing a song louder or softer. Change the style of the song – try swinging it or making it into a gospel song. Add drums. Add rattles. Play with it.

Sometimes you'll get a song started and it will take off for parts unknown, dragging you along like a runaway team of horses. "How on earth am I going to get this stopped?" you'll think. Sometimes if you start singing more softly you'll disperse some of the energy. Sometimes if you repeat the last line or phrase of the song over and over, people will get the hint. Sometimes, if you've got the loudest drum, you can simply beat very loud the last half line of the song and then stop at the end. Sometimes you can put your arms in the air and slowly lower them toward the Earth and people will respond to the visual cue. And sometimes you just have to let the energy wear itself out.

Songs are energy, and when they're combined with your group's energy and the energy of your ritual, you can do magickal things! And music helps it happen.

Magick-Working Chants

Most of the following chants are meant to be sung as a round, over and over, building the energy to a crescendo and then releasing it. Because many of the selections here were passed on by "oral tradition," we have been unable to identify authors for some of them. We apologize for the omission, and ask anyone who knows such credits to please contact us.

80. We are the Flow (round)

We are the flow, and we are the ebb;
We are the weavers, we are the web!
We are the weavers, we are the web;
We are the spiders, we are the thread!
We are the spiders, we are the thread
We are the Witches, back from the dead!
We are the Witches, back from the dead;
We are the flow, and we are the ebb!
—Shekinah Mountainwater

81. Spell of Manifestation

As above me, so below
As outside, so within
The Power's mine, the Light divine
The Magick now begins!
By Fire and Water, Air and Earth
My Magick brings the spell to birth
By light of Star and Moon and Sun
As I do will, so be it done!
—Ian Corrigan

82. Cauldron of Changes

Cauldron of changes, blossom of bone,
Ark of eternity, hole in the stone.
—Oothoon/Morning Glory Zell

83. Well Song (round)

We will never, never lose our way
To the well, of Her memory
And the power, of the living flame,
It will rise, it will rise again!
Like the grasses, through the dark,
Through the storm,
Towards the sunlight, we shall rise again!
We are searching, for the Waters of Life,
We are moving, we shall live again!
—Starhawk, Rose May Dance,
Raven Moonshadow

84. Mystery Chant

Tumble the bones; Cast the stones
Dream the night; Open your sight
She waits within; Now we begin
See the flame; Whisper Her name
Hear Her voice; Remember the choice
Truth She explains; Mystery remains.
—Laura Cates

85. River Song (round)

The river is flowing, flowing and growing,
The river she is flowing, down to the sea
Mother, carry me; your child I'll ever be.
(*or:* A child I will bear for thee)
Mother, carry me, down to the sea.
The Moon she is changing, waxing and waning,
The Moon she is changing, high above me.
Sister, challenge me, your child I'll ever be,
Sister, wait for me, 'til I am free.
—Diana Hildebrand-Hull

86. We Are an Old People

We are an old people,
We are a new people,
We are the same people,
Stronger than before!
We are an old planet
We are a new planet
We are the same planet,
Greener than before!
—1st verse, Morning Feather
—2nd verse, Julie Middleton

87. Fur and Feather

Fur and feather and scale and skin
Different without but the same within.
Many of body but one of Soul;
Through all creatures are the Gods made whole!
—Sable

88. Circle Round

Circle round for freedom
Circle round for peace
For all of us imprisoned
Circle for release
Circle for the planet
Circle for each soul
For the children of our children
Keep the Circle whole
—Linda Hirschhorn

89. When We Are Gone

When we are gone, they will remain
Wind and rock, fire and rain
They will remain, when we return
The wind will blow, and the fire will burn
—Starhawk, Anne Hill

90. She's Been Waiting *(round)*

She's been waiting, waiting,
She's been waiting so long!
She's been waiting for Her children
To remember, to return! (2x)

Blessed be and blessed are
The lovers of the Lady.
Blessed be and blessed are
The maiden, Mother, Crone.
Blessed be and blessed are
The ones who dance together.
Blessed be and blessed are
The ones who dance alone!

—*Paula Walowitz*

91. Children of the Night

We are the children of the Goddess,
We are the children of delight
We are the children of her passion,
We are the Children of the Night!

—*Anodea Judith*

92. Power Raising

We are the power in everyone
We are the dance of the Moon and the Sun
We are the hope that never died
We are the turning of the tide!

—*Starhawk*

93. Circle Dance Round

Circle 'round the fire
To raise the cone of power
To win what we desire
So mote it be!

Dance the Circle in the moonlight
Dance and sing the whole night long
Dance the Circle in the moonlight
Dance and sing a Witches' song!

—*Selena Fox*

94. Power Spot

Make yourself a power spot
Bring you a spoon and a cooking pot
Bring Air, bring Fire,
Bring Water, bring Earth;
You a new universe will birth!

—*Shekinah Mountainwater*

95. Transformation of Energy

Equal dark, equal light
Flow in Circle, deep insight
Blessed be, Blessed be
The transformation of energy!
So it flows, out it goes
Three-fold back it shall be
Blessed be, Blessed be
The transformation of energy!

—*Night An'Fey*

96. We Are Alive

We are alive as the Earth is alive
We have the power to create our future
We have the courage, we are the healers
Like the Sun we shall rise!
We have the courage, we are the healers
Like the Sun we shall rise!

—*Rose May Dance, Starhawk, 1985*

97. Where there is Fear there is Power

Where there is fear there is power
Passion is the healer
Desire cracks open the gate
If you're ready it'll take you through
But nothing lasts forever
Time is the destroyer
The wheel turns again and again
Watch out, or it'll take you through
But nothing dies forever
Nature is the renewer,
The wheel turns again and again
When you're ready it'll take you through

—*Starhawk*

98. Powerful Song

Powerful song of radiant light
Weave us the web that spins the night
Web of stars that holds the dark
Weave us the Earth that feeds the spark

Descant:
Strand by strand, hand over hand
Thread by thread we weave our web

—*Pandora, Starhawk,*
Rose May Dance

6. Communion

Holy Communion
By Oberon Zell-Ravenheart

Blessings

After raising and releasing all that en-
ergy, we now move to the lighter and more joyous part of the ritual. This is a time of celebration, sharing and fellowship, and an easing in the intense focus of energies that characterized
the previous phase of the ritual. In magick, as in life, the balance between gravity (the heavy
stuff) and levity (the light stuff) is very important. For this part of the ritual, there are three
main elements: Consecration, Communion ("sharing") and Hiatus, often called "sacred
bullshit." On the altar you should have an *athamé* (knife), a filled chalice (cup), and a *pantacle*
(or plate) with an uncut round of bread, or uncut fruit, such as apples.

Communion usually begins with the Consecration of the Sacraments. Consecrating means
"blessing for our use." This is much like saying a food blessing before meals, except that
since the God and/or Goddess (or other beings of spirit we've previously invoked) are already with us in the Circle, we don't need to ask them again for their blessings. They are
already blessing us and all we do by their very presence. Instead, we what we do here is
charge our food and drink with Spirit—with the special essence of the Goddess and/or
God—recognizing that our nourishment and refreshment not only come *from* them, but
actually *are part of* them, which we are about to make part of ourselves.

Consecrations-The Chalice & the Blade

The first part of consecrating the sacraments is done with the *Athamé* and the Chalice,
which is filled with water, fruit juice, wine, or mead; all are equally appropriate in any ritual,
depending on your preference. In the HOME Tradition, we always use water, as the concept
that "water shared is life shared" is an important part of our heritage. But we often
have a separate chalice of wine or fruit juice as well.

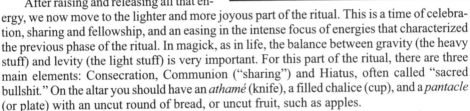

A ritual Chalice should be in the form of a beautiful stemmed goblet. It may be
made of any of a number of materials. Chalices of glass, ceramic, wood, silver (or
silver-plated), pewter, and even horn are all acceptable. But plastic is disdained for
all ceremonial purposes! A ritual Chalice, however, should never be made of brass
or copper, as it can then be used only for water. Fruit juice or wine must not be
used in an unlined brass or copper Chalice, as these metals become poisonous
in reaction with the citric acids in juices or wine. For the same reason, ceramic
Chalices must not have a lead glaze, and pewter Chalices must be nickel-free.

The classical *Consecration of the Chalice and the Blade* is often called the
symbolic *Great Rite,* for it represents the sexual union of the male and female
forces, a union which engenders all life. If you are doing this solitary, you should
hold the Chalice in your left hand, and the Athamé in your right hand, and
speak these lines yourself. If there are a priest and priestess (or any man and
woman) in the Circle, then she should hold up the Chalice with both hands while
he holds the Athamé above it, point down. The priest then lowers it into the
chalice, while saying something like this:

> *As the Athamé is to the male...*

The Priestess continues:

> *So the Chalice is to the female.*

And in unison, they both say:

And conjoined they be one in truth:
For there is no greater Power
In all the worlds
Than that of a man and a woman
Joined in the bonds of love
From which all life comes forth
    Blessed Be!

> ### 99. Great Rite
>
> Now as cup and blade unite,
> Awake the Great and Sacred Rite!
> Weave the dance of perfect love,
> By the horn and by the dove!
>   —*Katlyn Breen*

The second part of the consecration is for the bread. Many options are possible for this (see the following section, "Sacraments & Snackraments"). For the purposes of this model, however, we will assume that you are using a wonderfully aromatic round loaf of fresh-baked bread. *Mmm-MM!* It should be resting on a suitable plate. It is common in magickal rituals for such a plate to have inscribed on it a five-pointed star, or pentagram, inside a circle. Such a plate is called a pantacle, meaning "all angles." But while such a special ritual plate is particularly nice, really any plate will do.

Now, with your previously-consecrated Athamé, you should pierce the bread, releasing its aroma, then break it open while saying something like the following:

We break bread to share in fellowship
As our ancestors have done
Since the dawn of agriculture.
Breathe in the spirit of the Earth,
The Sun, the Rain, and the Fire,
Bound together for our nourishment.

Communion

Grounding excess energy is an important part of any magickal ritual, and eating and drinking before closing the Circle is a very common way of accomplishing this. Though many traditions use other methods of grounding and closing (such as stomping their feet, clapping their hands, singing, etc.), it might be important to note that sharing food and drink is also a cross-cultural ritual of bonding. Sharing a light meal with your fellow celebrants facilitates a comfortable closeness and familiarity with them as well as with the deities. We like to take further advantage of the opportunity to discuss the ritual and its personal meaning to us during this time, as a sort of planning and "debriefing." This not only helps to ground overabundant energy, but carries the necessary magick with us beyond the Circle. (—Crow Dragontree)

According to Webster, to commune is to "communicate intimately with; be in a state of heightened, intimate receptivity," as in "he seemed to commune with nature." Communion is a deep and open sharing at the spiritual level. For those familiar with the term, true communion is *grokking*. (from R.A. Heinlein's *Stranger in a Strange Land;* literally, "drinking")

This is the part of the ritual that modern Wiccans usually call *cakes and wine*. Christians call this Holy Communion, involving the "miracle" of *transubstantiation* in which the communion bread and wine is believed to become literally transformed into the actual physical flesh and blood of Jesus Christ. At the opposite end of the spectrum is the children's rite of "Cookies and Milk"—perfectly appropriate substances for Pagan rituals. But the rite of communion goes far deeper than any modern practice or tradition. It is the primal "feast of fellowship" that is as old as time and a sacred part of nearly every culture in the world. Sharing food and drink in the Circle is a reminder that we share our lives and our purpose. Also, since everything on Earth is part of the body of the Goddess—Mother Earth herself— ritual communion reminds us that everything we eat and drink is sacred, as it really is her flesh and blood we are taking into our bodies to become *our* flesh and blood.

And we also honor the Lord as the Sun God and the Green Man, by remembering that his solar rays provide the energy to ripen all plants, and that he is cut down in the fall to yield the grain for the bread that nourishes us. Thus the bread, cakes, cookies, crackers, fruit, and other foods that we eat are of his body too.

That is why we call the food and drink that we share in Circle *sacraments*. They have been consecrated and so they are *sacred,* or holy, filled with the divine essence. And in the rite of communion, we are reminded that *our* bodies are sacred too; our lives also imbued with the same spark of divinity. In the Church of All Worlds and many other Pagan traditions, we express this by saying *"thou art God"* and *"thou art Goddess"* as we accept the chalice being passed around the Circle. We drink a toast, as it were, to the Lord and Lady, both without and within.

So, after consecrating the sacraments, the priest (most commonly) takes up the plate of bread, holds it aloft, and blesses it, saying something like:

> *The seed of life is roused to grow*
> *By the passionate heat of the Sun's desire.*
> *Thus we're nourished; this we know*
> *By Earth and Sun; Rain, Wind and Fire.*

At this point, if the Circle is being held outdoors, it is customary to crumple a small piece of bread onto the ground as an offering to the Earth. An indoor ritual might have a bowl set out for this purpose. The priest might say something like, *"Mother Divine, take back what is thine."* He then tears off another piece of bread, and offers it to his priestess, saying, *"May you never hunger."* After she does the same for him, the plate is then passed around the Circle, with each person repeating , *"May you never hunger."*

Then the priestess (most commonly) raises and blesses the chalice of drink, saying something like:

> *From the Sea we all were born,*
> *Within the womb our souls ensnared.*
> *Unto the Well we shall return,*
> *Our lives, through Water, ever shared.*

If the Circle is outdoors, the priestess might pour a splash onto the ground as a *libation* (a poured-out liquid offering), saying: *"Mother Divine, take back what is thine."* Indoors, a bowl or even a potted plant might be set out to receive such libations. The priestess then offers the chalice to her priest, saying, *"May you never thirst!"* After he does the same for her, the chalice is then passed around the Circle, with each person repeating, *"May you never thirst!"* to each other.

While the bread and drink are being passed around, you might softly sing or chant something like:

> *Lord of the Sun, Lady of the Earth,*
> *We are one with the energies of the Universe!* (—Ayisha Homulka)

(If you are doing this solitary, simply eat and drink in thoughtful silence.)

NOTE: *Many ritualists prefer to pass the chalice first, and then follow with the bread. But we have learned from much experience that it is far better for the participants to pass around the bread (or other food) first, and then to wash it down with the water or some other drink!*

Hiatus/Sacred Bullshit

After the bread and drink have gone once around the Circle, comes the *hiatus*—the interval that many traditions today refer to as "sacred bullshit" (first called that by the New Reformed Order of the Golden Dawn). As Crow Dragontree says: "At this point, the group takes their ease and chats about the ritual, their plans, and any appropriate coven business that has not yet been discussed. If the group is not terribly conversant after ample time to ground and settle in, the High Priest or Priestess may choose to begin a discussion with a series of open-ended questions, such as those offered in the Sabbat descriptions."

This is the time for sharing personal news, announcements, messages, and other communications; conducting Circle business; teaching, listening to music; a guided meditation; or just quietly sharing the peace that comes from a good Working. This is a space that aids the participants in letting go of the magickal work so that it may travel on. Indeed, if we keep working it, and don't let it go, it never gets sent out. With food, music, and joviality, this break in events restores vitality that may have been drained during the Working. What is said during this period must be related to the magick and the Circle, not stuff like TV shows, movies, outside news, sports, or other mundane bullshit! The time and place of the next meeting may be decided, chants and lore may be shared, and other magickal things discussed. During this phase the plate and chalice may be refilled and continue to be passed as much as is desired. Other food ("snackraments") and beverages may also be brought out and passed around.

If a long evening is planned, this part of the ritual may even become a *bardic*, in which each person in turn around the Circle may sing a song, recite a poem, or tell a story or joke. In a bardic, your turn comes when you receive the chalice and take a drink. If you don't have anything to say, you can just drink and pass the chalice on to the next person.

Sacraments & Snackraments
By Oberon & Liza Gabriel

A "sacrament" is something regarded as holy or sacred. Ordinary acts or substances may be elevated to the status of sacraments in a ritual context, thereby becoming gateways into a greater awareness of the beauty and power of the BIG PICTURE, and our part in it. Such sacraments may be grouped into three categories: actions, rituals, and substances. *No one should ever be compelled or coerced into partaking of any sacrament without their full knowledge and consent.*

The four Elements – Earth, Water, Air, and Fire – are actually the four states of matter: solid, liquid, gas, and plasma (going from lesser to greater energy). These comprise the body, blood, breath, and energy of Gaia. All of material existence is composed of these Elements in varying combination, and so we honor them in our rituals. Many also add Spirit as a fifth Element. Within these broad categories may be grouped all the sacred substances, which are often shared in the communion phase of a ritual as sacraments or "snackraments."

Earth

Food
Some traditions have specially-prepared "holy food" (or *prasad* in Sanskrit), while others just bring home something they like from the grocery store. Because they resemble the crescent moon, almond crescent cookies are quite popular for full moon rituals, or *Esbats*. Fruit is very popular when it is in season—especially apples, which are often cut horizontally to reveal the pentagram formed by the seeds. "White bread" Protestant churches are so named for the tiny cubes of white bread they serve for communion. Roman Catholics use special thin wafers embossed with a cross, while a Jewish ritual might use *matzoth*. And "Redneck Pagans" are said to use *Twinkies*, *Ding-Dongs*, and *Moon Pies!* Of course, other foods (such as the special selection of "underworld foods" eaten in silence at the Samhain "dumb supper") may be shared sacramentally as well. All such foods are considered to be the body of the God and/or Goddess. The most common phrases to accompany the passing of food are "may you never hunger," or "may you always have sufficiency."

Bread
The most universal sacrament shared in communion rites the world over is certainly bread—preferably fresh-baked for the occasion. Often ritual bread is rolled out and then

shaped in symbolically appropriate forms: a Celtic cross; a knotwork design; a "Venus of Willendorf"; astrological sigils; phallic and yonic imagery; etc. Communion bread should always be broken, never cut.

Apples

When an apple is cut in half equatorially, the pattern of a pentagram is revealed in the seeds. This little "mystery" can be utilized to good effect in a communion rite for a small group, as in the Pagan Yule carol, "Gods Rest Ye Merry Pagan Folk:"

Within the blessed apple lies the promise of the Queen
For from this pentacle shall rise the orchards fresh and green
The Earth shall blossom once again, the air be sweet and clean!
O, tidings of comfort and joy, comfort and joy! (—Ellen Reed)

Cheez-Its

The first heresy declared by the Roman Catholic Church was the *Artotyrite* heresy—named for a practice of the Montanist sect, who ate cheese on their communion bread. For over 40 years in the Church of All Worlds we have affirmed the right to diversity in "snackraments" by honoring the Artotyrites with *Sunshine Cheez-Its* (accompanied by an explanation of the symbolism, as well as jokes: "What a friend we have in Cheez-Its," "Cheez-Its saves," etc.).

Water

Water

This is the prime "official" sacrament of the Church of All Worlds; read all about it in *Stranger in a Strange Land*! Water is the essential foundation of all terrestrial life, and comprises 80% of our body mass. Water is the very blood of the Mother; the chemical constituency of the blood in our veins is the same as that of the ancient seawater of four billion years ago, which we assimilated into our bodies as we developed in the oceanic womb of the Mother. We are all one—washed in the blood! Blood, sweat, and tears are the waters of our lives. The physical properties of water – in particular, its ability to manifest as solid, liquid and gas (Earth, Water, and Air) at biologically compatible temperatures—and its unique property of having a solid state that floats in the liquid, are what allow the possibility of life on Earth and throughout the known universe. All CAW rituals include a sharing of water, from a simple communion acknowledging of our water-kinship with all life, to the lifelong commitment of water-brotherhood.

Wine or Juice

Any other liquids, such as wine or fruit juice, may be shared sacramentally as well, as they all partake of the "essence" of Water (and thus are considered to be the blood of the God and/or Goddess). As we offer wine, we may say, "Wine shared is love shared," and with juice we often joke, "May you always be juicy!"

Milk

What could be a more appropriate sacrament of the Mother than milk? "Milk 'n' Cookies" is one of the earliest rituals of childhood. Mother's milk is the very essence of primal nutrient, and is often shared sacramentally in rituals emphasizing birth and motherhood—such as the Festival of *Oimelc* (February 1), the name of which means "in milk." Cow's milk is most common, of course, but goat's milk is often used for the lactose-intolerant—and human milk is the most magickal of all.

Coffee

The "Javacrucian Mysteries" are enacted every morning in countless Pagan households and all Pagan events: facing the rising sun and holding the mug of *brewe*, the celebrant takes a first sip, then elevates the cup and intones, "Gods, I needed that!" And means it. Then begins the daily recapitulation of ontogeny...

Sects of the Javacrucian Tradition vary mainly around additives to the basic brewe:

- The Left-Out Path
- The Path of Delectable Darkness
- The Milky Way
- The Path of Sweetness and Light

Associated cults include Teaosophists, Rastacolians, Matteyanists, and Chocolytes.

Air

Breath

Breath is a rhythm that accompanies every moment. Unlike our heartbeats, we can consciously control breath: holding it, speeding it up, slowing it down, making it shallow or deep, raspy or smooth. Yet when we are asleep or unconscious, our breath continues. Because breath can be controlled both by the conscious and unconscious minds, it is used as a bridge between the two. In many languages the word for spirit and the word for breath are the same: *ruach* in Hebrew, *esprit* in French, *prana* in Sanskrit, and *pneuma* in Greek. Breath has been used since prehistory not only as a bridge between the conscious and unconscious, but also as a bridge between body and spirit. Breath is the foundation of most sacred sex practices. It is used in ritual to raise and focus energy and to bring an experience of full aliveness, embodying the spirit and inspiring the body.

Music

Music plays a central role in almost every religious tradition. Diverse groups of people can grow very close very quickly through an experience of music or singing. Music fills the air around us, embracing everyone present and echoing in our souls. The Pagan community is blessed with many inspired musicians and bards, and these folk contribute to virtually every Pagan ritual and occasion, often inviting everyone to join in. The two most ancient and widespread sacred instruments are the voice and drum. Both are intimately connected to the rhythms of the body—the voice to breath and the drum to heartbeat.

Fire

Campfires

The most ancient and distinctively human experience is that of sitting around a campfire, sharing songs and stories with your clan. A campfire automatically forms the focus of a primal Circle, and scrying into the flames may reveal many things. Firewalking also has been practiced by many as an initiatory and transformative experience.

Candle-Burning

Burning candles of selected colors may be used in spellwork. Some of the most popular color associations are:

- **Red**— Physical work, healing of people and animals, passion, sex
- **Orange**— Pride, courage heroism, attraction
- **Yellow**— Mental work, meditation, intellect
- **Green**— Vegetation, gardening, fertility, prosperity
- **Blue**— Emotional work, love, peace, protection
- **Violet**— Power, wealth, good fortune
- **Black**— Blighting, binding
- **White**— Blessing, or anything you want!

The Fifth Element - Spirit

Chocolate

As a "snackrament," chocolate is widely recognized in Pagan circles as the "Fifth Element." Celebrants are known as "Chocolytes," though those who over-indulge are known as "chocoholics." Chocolate beverages were considered a drink for the gods during the time of the Aztec Empire. In Tantric practices a couple would place a square of dark chocolate between their lips and eat to the middle where they would meet in a long passionate kiss. This not only raises the *kundalini* (among other things) but involves the use of the taste buds in oral satiation. Chocolate has a divine taste that is orgasmic as it melts in your mouth. The theobromine causes a euphoric state which satisfies the deepest of desires and most compelling of cravings.

In Circle, when sharing this snackrament, the most common phrases are "Thou art sweet," "Thou art creamy," and, for the darker time of year, "Thou art bittersweet." When you ingest this snackrament and reach true enlightenment, you achieve the realization that there "s'more than enough for everyone and some to share" *(—Aeona Silversong)*.

Dance

One of the most primal and prevalent scenes in Pagan life is a fire circle with drummers and dancers. Both freeform dancing and circle dancing are essential parts of our rituals and celebrations. Expressing the joy, sorrow, and beauty of our lives through our bodies and through dance affirms our identity as part of the natural world and prevents our rites from becoming mere head trips.

Humor

Pagans in general seem to have an inordinate fondness for humor and jokes, both clever and stupid. Puns especially are virtually a trademark of our sense of humor, and the references from which these are drawn are an affirmation of our common group heritage.

Ceremonial Bread
by Aeona Silversong

I grew up in a Jewish family and I love to cook. I have the medicinal use of chicken soup programmed into me. The sharing of food was an affirmation of family and an extension of love and caring given to friends.

Thus for many years I have baked the breads for our festival rituals. It is a sacred act and I try to infuse the intent and energy of the Circle Magick into the bread. Breads formed into Celtic knots, spirals, and braids weave the energy and give support to the magick when made with intent. I also try to look at the various elements of the ritual for which I'm making the bread. Is it a spring, summer, or fall ritual? If it is, I make a fruit and nut bread, a bread of prosperity. If it's a winter ritual, I make a dark, heavy bread. While kneading the bread, I sing and chant all the songs I know that relate to that particular topic/ritual. I also speak affirmations and words of power into the bread.

The inner artist can manifest with various designs and shapes to be incorporated in the bread. In my opinion, the most beautiful bread I've ever made was for my clergy ordination in 1993: I made a 16-inch Gaiarinth design comprised of the nine circles with Gaia in the center (this was before the Dearinth had been adopted in CAW). For special occasions, I've made a wishing ring cake which gives everyone a wish on their first bite.

I'd like to share with you a fruit and nut bread recipe used for the most special of rituals. I hope you enjoy it. If you've never made bread before, I'd suggest getting a basic bread cookbook. The temperature of the yeast water really does make a difference, as does how long you knead the bread, etc.

Envelop yourself in love and positive thoughts and enjoy this fine art. So mote it be.

Aeona's Ceremonial Bread Recipe

2 packages dry granular yeast
1/3 cup lukewarm water
2 tsp. sugar
2 cups milk
1 stick sweet butter or margarine (¼ lb.)
4 Tbs. golden orange blossom honey

3 egg yolks, beaten
1-1/2 tsp. salt
6 cups unbleached flour
1 egg yolk, beaten with 2 tsp. water
Poppy seeds

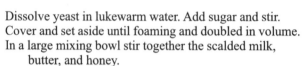

Dissolve yeast in lukewarm water. Add sugar and stir.
Cover and set aside until foaming and doubled in volume.
In a large mixing bowl stir together the scalded milk,
      butter, and honey.
Cool to lukewarm.
Add beaten egg yolks, salt, and 2 cups flour.
Beat vigorously with a wooden spoon until bubbly and well blended.
Add the remaining flour, 1 cup at a time, just enough to make a soft, but firm dough.
Turn out onto a lightly floured board.
Knead for at least 10–15 minutes, occasionally dropping the dough hard onto the board.
Place in a warm greased bowl, turning to grease top.
Cover with a light, clean towel and set in a warm place until doubled in bulk.
Push down with a floured fist and let rise again.
Cut down, turn out into a lightly floured board, and shape into two medium size loaves.
Place in greased and lightly floured 8x 4x 2 1/2-inch bread pans.
Cover and let rise in a warm place until doubled in bulk or until dough reaches top of the pans.
Brush with beaten egg yolks and sprinkle with poppy seeds.
Bake at 400 degrees F for 10 minutes.
Reduce heat to 350 degrees F and continue to bake for 35–40 minutes longer or until the
      loaves are a golden brown and test done (tap the bread—if it sounds hollow the bread
      is done).
Slice 3/4 inch thick and toast lightly for the most fragrant toasts ever!

Variations:
More eggs or just the egg yolks.
Pinch of saffron for exotic color.
Nutmeg for the palate.

Celebratory:
Dried fruits, nuts, and extra honey for
      sweetness.
Nutmeg, cardamom, and/or cinnamon.

Helpful Hints:
Smear bread all over with butter to keep it soft.
Dough should be elastic.
Yeast must be kept 104 degrees F or it will die.
Scald milk and add cold butter and cold honey to bring temperature of milk down.
Turn oven on low and set bread on top to help rising.
Slit bread with knife before rising to tell how much it rises.
Sing songs of the occasion to imbue the bread with love, joy,
      and other wonderful desires!

Consecrations & Communion Blessings

100. Consecration of Chalice & Blade

Priest & Priestess in unison:
    In all things there is an active
    And a receptive force.
P: The active creates power and movement;
Ps: The receptive provides direction and form.
Both: Both are essential for life,
    Growth, and change.
P: The horned God is of life and death;
Ps: The Goddess is of birth and renewal.
Both: There are lessons to be found
    In the spiral of life, leading eternally
    Towards perfection:
    To learn you must suffer;
    To suffer you must live;
    To live you must be born;
    To be born you must die;
    The beginning, the continuation—
    And the end, over and over.
P: The Sun brings forth light;
Ps: And the Moon holds it in darkness.
P: As above
Ps: So below.
P: And as the Athamé is to the male,
Ps: So the Chalice is to the female.
Both: And conjoined they be one in truth:
    For there is no greater Power
    In all the worlds
    Than that of a man and a woman
    Joined in the bonds of love
        Blessed Be!
                    —*Author unknown*

101. Blessing the Sacraments

Blessed be this Bread,
The body of our Lord,
And blessed be this Water,
The blood of our Lady.
As our bodies are nourished
By Their divine energy,
So let Their love ever nurture our spirits.
We are the conscious product
Of Their eternal passion,
And so do we give Them gratitude
In celebration of Life.
    So mote it be!
                    —*Morning Glory Zell*

102. Conjuration of Cakes & Wine

Priestess cups both hands over the cakes as they lie on the pentacle held by the Priest. She says:
    I conjure thee, O Meal! Who art indeed our body, since without thee we could not live, thou who—at first as seed—before becoming flower went into the Earth where all deep secrets hide, and then when flour ground didst dance like dust in the wind, and yet meanwhile didst bear with thee in flitting, secrets strange!
    I conjure thee, O Meal! That as we take part of thee we take part of the wisdom of the Goddess, we learn more of the fields and the forest, and know the ancient lore.
Priestess holds the chalice so it is over the wine bottle, so that all the wine may be consecrated. Priest cups both hands over the chalice and says:
    I conjure thee, O Wine! Thou who didst grow from nothing by light of sun and light of moon, the swelling, ripened grape—the blood of the Earth pressed soon.
    I conjure thee, O Wine! That as we drink of thee, we drink the power of the Goddess— of fire, and lightning, and rain, of things that are wild and free!
                    —*Outer Court Wicca*

103. Passing the Chalice *(round)*

Love, love, love, love.
Pagans, this is our call.
We will love one another as
The Goddess loves us all.
God and Goddess,
Shall I tell you how I feel?
You have shared with me your riches,
Love and joy are real.
Joy, joy, joy, joy.
As we pass the chalice 'round,
Thou art God and thou art Goddess;
Love is abound-ing!
                    —*Hariette, of Coven Vanthi*

104. Blessing & Sharing

The High Priest or High Priestess stands before the altar, wand outstretched over the food in one hand and goblet in the other. Each covener holds their own cup in both hands. The High Priest intones:
Goddess who grows within the fields
God who drives the beasts,
Bless this food our planet yields
And join us at our feast.
We have Food where there is hunger,
Love where there is isolation,
Wisdom where there is doubt,
And Strength where there is fear.
Let us not forget to share our best
With others at their worst
So that the world may someday rest,
Never hunger, never thirst
Blessed Be!
The coveners respond with "Never Hunger, Never Thirst. Blessed Be!" *and all take a sip in salutation. They pour a little bit of the drink into the libation bowl.*

—*Crow Dragontree*

105. Bread & Water Blessing

The seed of life is roused to grow
By the passionate heat of the Sun's desire.
Thus we're nourished; this we know
By Earth and Sun; Rain, Wind and Fire.
          May you never hunger.

From the Sea we all were born,
Within the womb our souls ensnared.
Unto the Well we shall return,
Our lives, through Water, ever shared.
          May you never thirst!

—*Oberon Zell*

106. Bread Blessing

The seed of life itself
Is roused by the heat of the Sun's desire
Fills the womb of the Earth's belly
Is kissed by the Air's breath
And caressed by Her flowing Waters.
From these do we come
By these are we nourished
To these we return
          Blessed Be

—*Avilynn Pwyll, 1992*

107. Autumn & Winter Bread Blessing

Together we break bread.
Our Lord died
          for when the grain was cut in the field
          it was His body sacrificed
          that we might be sustained by bread.
Our Lord is living still in this loaf.
Our Mother has created Him,
          sacrificed Him,
          now gifted him with new life in the loaf,
          gifted us with life through this loaf.
We break bread together.
Thus are we sustained,
          filled with His joy and power.
We break bread together.
Thus are we sustained
          not only by the bread
          but by each other's company.
          So be it.

—*Francesca de Grandis*

108. Bread Blessing

Grain ripened by the Summer Sun
Baked in the belly of the oven;
The bread of life is the body of our Lord;
May you always have sufficiency!

—*Oberon Zell*

109. What a Friend We Have...

What a friend we have in Cheez-Its;
Saffron wafer of delight!
Golden squares with central vision,
Guiding us to clearer sight!
If you hold your wafer
To the bright and shining Sun,
You can see the light beams shining through;
What a friend we have in Cheez-Its,
Snackrament we love to chew!
Long past, in the Days of Legend,
When Star Trek newly had its birth,
Our ancestors met to honor
Sacred Fridays with sweet mirth!
And the precious snackraments
Were passed around the Circle:
Strange popcorn and the tasty yellow squares;
What a friend we have in Cheez-Its;
Pass on what the Ancients started there!

—*Maerian Morris*

7. Ending the Ritual

All Good Things
By Oberon Zell-Ravenheart

All good things must come to an end—at least until the next Circle. Attention is now refocused after the communion to send our magick out of the Circle and into the world to do its work. Now it is time to thank the deities and spirits, and bid farewell to the Elementals, all in reverse order of their invocation. There are several different terms for this. Some call this "banishing," but that sounds rather unfriendly to us, so we prefer to consider this as "releasing" or "dismissing" the Elements. After this the Circle itself is released or opened, and with it all the power created by the ritual.

Thanking the Deities
This enchanted evening we have been blessed by the presence of our beloved God and Goddess, and/or other deities. They have been our special guests, and we must now thank them for coming, and say goodnight. If different people invoked them, those same individuals should now step forward to bid them farewell, and in reverse of the order in which they were first called.

A farewell to the God, for example, might go something like this:

> Radiant Lord of Light and Laughter,
> Thank you for your blessings here.
> We are yours forever after—
> One with oak and sun and deer!
>> Blessed Be! (all repeat, "Blessed Be!")

And then to the Triple Moon Goddess we might say:

> Lady of the Silv'ry Wheel,
> Maiden, Mother, ancient Crone,
> We bear within your mystic seal—
> We thank you, for we are your own!
>> Blessed Be! (all repeat, "Blessed Be!")

Of course, if we are using chants or songs to call them in or say goodnight, everybody will join in together. Here's a little chant we often use at HOME to thank both the God and Goddess together at the end of our ritual:

> Give thanks to the Mother Goddess;
> Give thanks to the Father Sun!
> Give thanks to the children in the garden where
> The Mother and the Father are one!
> (repeat at least three times; on the last, sing:)
> ...The Mother and the Father have fun!

If candles have been lit for the God and Goddess on the central altar, they should be put out now—rather than blowing them out they should either be pinched out with your fingers (lick them first!), snapped out (practice this!), or snuffed with a candle snuffer. The person putting out the candles might say something like:

> As these flames of the material world are darkened,
> They shall ever burn in the worlds beyond.
> The rite is ended; Blessed Be! (all repeat, "Blessed Be!")

Dismissing the Elements

Thanking and dismissing the Elements is also done in reverse order. If the Quarters were cast as they normally are in the Northern Hemisphere (except at Samhain), beginning in the East and going *deosil* (clockwise),then they will be dismissed starting in the North, and then going *widdershins* (counterclockwise) to the West, South, and finally East. This sequence, of course, should be adapted to the season or hemisphere; the important thing is that it be the reverse of the original callings. These dismissals should also be done by the same people who called them before. If they were done in turn by different people, then those individuals should now move to the appropriate quarters and make the appropriate *mudras* (gestures), while everyone else turns toward that direction and makes the same gestures. If Quarter candles have been lit, then each caller in turn concludes their dismissal by snuffing that candle as described above.

If five or more Directions have been cast (such as Center, Above, and Below), or ancestors, Faeries, etc. have also been invoked, then these also need to be dismissed at this time—again, in reverse order of their invocation.

Many of the more poetic Quarter-calling invocations given in Chapter 3 have matching dismissals, which should be used now if the Quarters were called in that fashion. But if the Quarters were called more simply, or spontaneously, then here is a very common generic model for dismissing them:

> *O Guardians of the Watchtower of the frozen North,*
>   *(watery West; fiery South; windy East),*
> *We thank you for attending our rites.*
> *Go if you must; stay if you will.*
> *And ere you depart to your fair and lovely realms,*
> *We bid you hail and farewell!*
>   (all repeat, *"Hail and farewell!"*)

After each of the Elements has been dismissed in this way, we may turn again to the center of the Circle, hold hands, and chant:

> *The Earth, the Water, the Fire, the Air*
> *Returns, returns!*
>   (repeat over and over as a round, with different people
>   starting in different places)

Sometimes we will add another verse to this round that goes:

> *The owls, the wolves, the foxes and bears*
> *Return, return!*

Opening the Circle

When we cast the Magick Circle at the beginning of this ritual, we closed off a little bubble of sacred space between the worlds. The last thing we do now to undo that Circle is burst that bubble and return this space to the mundane world. We call this "releasing" or "opening" the Circle rather than "closing" it, because we are now opening the door to leave.

The person who cast the Circle in the first place now goes back to the East, where it all began (again, depending on hemisphere and season). Pointing your wand, sword, or *athamé* (knife) at the ground, walk widdershins around the outside of the Circle (i.e. in the opposite direction of the casting), unwinding it and drawing back into the implement the power of the blue fire, while saying something like:

> *Circle of magick, Circle of art—*
> *The rite is ended; now we part.*
> *This Circle drawn between the worlds*
> *Begone! as Time and Space unfurls...*

Returning once more to the East, fling your arms wide to the outside, saying,

> *The rite is ended. Blessed Be!*
> (and all repeat, *"Blessed Be!"*)

It is customary in many traditions for everyone to add,

> *Merry meet and merry part,*
> *And merry meet again!*

In the HOME Tradition, we usually release our Circles with Gwydion's Faerie release:

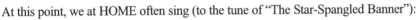

> *All from air, into air*
> *Let the misty curtains part.*
> *All is ended, all is done,*
> *What has been, must now be gone!*
> *What is done by ancient art,*
> *Must merry meet and merry part*
>   *And merry meet again! (—*Gwydion Pendderwen)

At this point, we at HOME often sing (to the tune of "The Star-Spangled Banner"):

> *The Cir-cle is open*
> *But sha-all never be bro-ken.*
> *Merry meet and merry pa-rt—*
> *And merry meet again!*

However, it should be noted that these are particularly Wiccan closings. Other traditions have different ones. For instance, Christians conclude their rites with *"Amen,"* the Vodoun version is *"Ache"* or *"Ashay,"* and some Native American ones are *"Aho!"* or *"Mitakuye Oyasin"* (Lakota for "all my relations").

Sometimes a ritual may be concluded with a final blessing or *benediction* ("well speech") upon the participants. This is especially common in various rites of passage—particularly handfastings and weddings. This sends everyone forth from the Circle blessed and empowered. A favorite of these is "I Bid You Goodnight," which the Grateful Dead always used to sing at the end of their concerts. Pagan verses are given below.

Moose Dixon of Ozark Avalon says: "Here is a particularly energetic way to end a circle with a large number of participants. The ritual team ends the rite and starts a chant. As the chant continues, each member of the ritual team dances out to the Circle of participants and randomly chooses a dance partner. After ten seconds or so, instruct them to also choose a dance partner at random from the remaining circle of participants, then do the same yourself. After a very small number of iterations, the entire group will be dancing and the energy of the Circle is physically spread to the audience. I have used this as the end of an opening ceremony for a large public event. Be sure to honor the wishes of those who do not want to dance."

And now everybody helps pick up and put away all the stuff so the ritual area is clean. Group hugs and kisses are given all around, and we bid our farewells to each other before heading home to our own beds and magickal dreams.

Merry Meet Again!
By Estara T'shirai

You may have wondered, what is the origin of the expression, "Merry Meet"?

Well, of course you know the longer phrase it comes from. I found a marvelous thing in the *Annotated Mother Goose* that contains the wording my tradition actually uses...let me see if I can dig it up for you, here...ah yes, here it is, and its introduction:

"Young Father Goose"

His name was James Orchard Halliwell-Phillips, although he preferred to shorten it, as a by-line, to James O. Halliwell.

He was born in 1820, and so precocious an antiquary did he soon prove himself to be that he was made a Fellow of the Royal Society at the age of 18.

At the tender age of 22, Halliwell produced perhaps his greatest book. *The Nursery Rhymes of England* was published in 1842; it was revised and enlarged five times—in 1843, 1844, 1846, 1853, and c.1860. And in 1849 Halliwell was also to produce a substantial "sequel," which he called *Popular Rhymes and Nursery Tales.*

In these volumes, Halliwell collected much that had gone before, but he also added much that was new to print. He writes that his rhymes are gathered "principally from oral tradition," but it is apparent that he also did much research in libraries; again and again he states that he was able to trace one rhyme or another to a 15th- to 18th-century manuscript.

More than any other man, James O. Halliwell deserved to be called—if he chose to claim the title—"Father Goose."

Here is the poem:

> *Merry are the bells, and merry would they ring,*
> *Merry was myself, and merry would I sing;*
> *With a merry ding-dong, happy, gay and free,*
> *And a merry sing-song, happy let us be!*
>
> *Waddle goes your gait, and hollow are your hose,*
> *Noddle goes your pate, and purple is your nose;*
> *Merry is your sing-song, happy, gay, and free,*
> *With a merry ding-dong, happy let us be!*
>
> *Merry have we met, and merry have we been,*
> *Merry let us part, and merry meet again;*
> *With our merry sing-song, happy, gay, and free,*
> *And a merry ding-dong, happy let us be!*

Deity & Element Dismissals

110. Quarters Farewell

Wise One…
Brave One…
Sure One…
Strong One…
We bid you now hail and farewell!
Go by the powers that brought you,
Go by the unweaving spell.
As the bright pentagrams fade,
Depart as the Circle is gone—
Winged One…
Fierce One…
Swift One…
As we say, so be it done!
   —*Deborah Lipp & Isaac Bonewits, 1992*

111. May We Walk in Beauty

May we walk in beauty in a sacred way
May we walk in beauty each and every day
May we walk in beauty in a sacred way
May we walk in beauty each and every day

N: May the beauty of the Earth
Fill our hearts with mirth.

W: May the beauty of the Rain
Wash away our pain.

S: May the beauty of the fire
Lift our spirits higher.

E: May the beauty of the Sky
Teach our minds to fly.
   —*Author unknown*

112. Unorthodoxology

Praise Her from whom all blessings flow.
For Waters deep and Fire's glow.
For Life and Breath and Earth our Home.
Praise Mother, Maid, and Ancient Crone.
    Blessed Be.
—Anie Heartsong

113. Song of Thanksgiving

Thank you Mother Earth
Thank you Sister Water
Thank you for our birth
From your sons and daughters!

Thank you father Sun
Thank you Air in motion
Thank you everyone—
Earth, Sun, Air and Ocean!
—Susan Arrow, 1985

114. Dismissal of the Watchers

Northern Watchers, strong and sure,
Our thanks for your support today.
If you must go, power to endure
Leave with us as your gift, we pray.
    Hail and Farewell!

Ye Watchers of the West, ye may
Depart with blessings if you will;
But let your rhythms with us stay,
For to your tides we answer still.
    Hail and Farewell!

O Southern Watchers, you who fill
Us with the sacred Flame, now go
Your ways, yet leave your warmth until
The grace to face your fires we know.
    Hail and Farewell!

O Watchers of the East, whose pure
Air we've breathed, your blessings blow—
Though you depart—to be our cure,
For as above, so 'tis below.
    Hail and Farewell!
—Diana Paxson

115. Endangered Species Dismissals

The song of wolves has filled our heart,
And lingers though your forms depart.
You've watched our rite and blessed our spell
We bid you now hail and farewell!

A whale song has this night been sung,
And echoes in the chimes we've rung.
You've watched our rite and blessed our spell
We bid you now hail and farewell!

The dragon's cry did split this night,
And called our ancient roots to light.
You've watched our rite and blessed our spell
We bid you now hail and farewell!

The condor lord above the storm,
Our dreams rise with your soaring form.
You've watched our rite and blessed our spell
We bid you now hail and farewell!
—Tom Williams

116. The Earth, She is our Mother
(a dismissal of the Elements; Traditional Native American, with three additional verses by Morning Glory Zell)

The Earth, She is our Mother,
We must take care of Her;
The Earth, She is our Mother,
We must take care of Her!

Ch: Hey, yonna, hey yonna, hey yon yon!
    Hey, yonna, hey yonna, hey yon yon!

N: Her sacred Ground we walk upon
    With every step we take;
    Her sacred Ground we walk upon
    With every step we take!

W: From Water that we drink of
    Comes all the life She makes;
    From Water that we drink of
    Comes all the life She makes!

S: The Fire that can warm us
    Is in the love we make!
    The Fire that can warm us
    Is in the love we make!

E: The Air we breathe renews us
    With every breath we take;
    The Air we breathe renews us
    With every breath we take!

The Earth, She is our Mother,
We must take care of Her;
The Earth, She is our Mother,
We must take care of Her!
—Morning Glory Zell, 1989

117. Circle Banishing

Like the Sun at day's end
Pass into the Earth our friend.
Fade now like the waning Moon
Or a whirlwind on a shifting dune.

Banished be thou sacred space
As the Circle's edge I trace.
Let your power sundered be
Flowing back to Earth and sea.
As we emerge from your embrace
Return us now to time and space.

—*Mike Fix*

118. Circle Release

A Circle is cast upon the ground
When in our hearts true love is found
When we open the Circle,
The love isn't gone.
It lives in our hearts
As the Dance goes on.

—*Mike Fix*

119. Turn the World Around

(North)
We come from the Mountains,
Living in the Mountains;
Go back to the Mountains,
Turn the world around! *(spin)*
We come from the Mountains;
Go back to the Mountains,
Turn the world around! *(spin)*

(West)
We come from the Water,
Swimming in the Water;
Go back to the Water,
Turn the world around! *(spin)*
We come from the Water;
Go back to the Water,
Turn the world around! *(spin)*

(South)
We come from the Fire,
Sitting round the Fire;
Go back to the Fire,
Turn the world around! *(spin)*
We come from the Fire;
Walk upon the Fire,
Turn the world around! *(spin)*

(East)
We come from the Sky-yi,
Flying in the Sky-yi;
Go back to the Sky-yi,
Turn the world around! *(spin)*
We come from the Sky-yi;
Go back to the Sky-yi,
Turn the world around! *(spin)*

(Center)
We come from the Circle,
Dancing round the Circle;
Go back to the Circle,
Turn the world around! *(spin)*
We come from the Circle;
Go back to the Circle,
Turn the world around! *(spin)*

(to all)
I am but a Monkey,
You are but a Monkey;
Be the Hundredth Monkey,
Turn the world around! *(spin)*
We are all but Monkeys;
Be the Hundredth Monkey,
Turn the world around! *(spin)*
Be the Hundredth Monkey,
Turn the world around! *(spin)*
Be the Hundredth Monkey,
Turn the world around! *(spin)*

—*Author unknown;*
Popularized by Harry Belafonte

120. The Circle is Open

The Circle is open, but unbroken
May the peace of the Goddess
Be ever in your heart!
Merry meet, and merry part,
And merry meet again!
—*Author unknown*

121. Merry Meet & Merry Part

Merry meet, and merry part,
And merry meet again!
From Earth and from Water,
From Fire and from Wind.
In the Circle of Life,
The dance never ends,
So merry meet, and merry part,
And merry meet again!

—*Author unknown*

122. Alexandrian Release

The Gods have been worshipped,
The Work has been done,
The Dances are danced,
And the old Songs sung.
Keepers of Wisdom,
Hold love in your hearts
For merry we meet,
And merry we part!

—Alex Sanders

123. Air I Am

Ch: Air I am; Fire I am;
Water, Earth, and Spirit I am!

N: Dark bull of the Mother Earth
In the cave that gives us birth.

W: Ancient serpent of the deep
In your waters let us weep

S: Mighty lion of the sun
Burn my heart and will as one.

E: Soaring Eagle on the wing
From your lair new visions bring.

—Andras Corban Arthen, 1992

124. May the Circle be Unbroken

Ch: May the Circle be unbroken
Through the seasons of rebirth.
May Her love bind us together,
All the children of the Earth.

And the Lady in the Springtime,
Wears a robe of living green.
And renews us with Her waters,
Ever living, cool and clean.

And the Lady, in the Summer,
Wears a robe of shining gold.
And She cools us with Her breezes
Breathing love for young and old.

And the lady, in the Autumn,
Wears a robe of ruby red.
Earth, her body, overflowing,
With her gifts of wine and bread.

And the Lady, in the Winter,
Wears a robe of silver white.
And She warms us with her fire,
With her spirit, and Her light.

—Roz Tognoli

125. Star-Spangled Pagan
(to tune of "The Star-Spangled Banner")

This night we partook
Of fellowship bright
In the manner of ancients
Beneath the clear starlight
Our fair Lady and Lord,
Their patronage giv'n,
The dance of their union
We danced once again.
'Neath the star-spangled sky,
Ah, the wine, how it flowed!
Hear now our most ancient
Of blessings bestowed:
The Circle is open
But shall never be broken
Merry meet and merry part
And merry meet again!

—Laurie Olson & Cynthia Lee

126. Back, Back, Back

Back, back, back
Through the tunnel of my birth,
Back, back, back
Through the middle of the hourglass
Back, back, back
Rooted deep within the Earth
I am dreaming in the darkness,
Dreaming in the light
Dreaming possibilities,
Opening my life.

—Franklin Abbott

127. Bountiful Blessings

Bountiful blessings of the elements.
Bountiful blessings of the moment.
Bountiful blessings of the ancestors.
Bountiful blessings of ourselves.
Bountiful blessings of each other.
Bountiful blessings of our association.
Bountiful blessings of our affection.
Bountiful blessings of our experience.
Bountiful blessings of our emotions.
Bountiful blessings of our intentions.
Bountiful blessings of our effort.
Bountiful blessings of our attention.
Bountiful blessings of our action.
Bountiful blessings of our effect.

—Donna Henes

128. No End to the Circle

Chorus:
There is no end to the Circle, no end
There is no end to Life, there is no end
There is no end to the Circle, no end
There is no end to Life, there is no end

For you can see me in your eyes
When they are mirrored by a friend
There is no end to the Circle, no end
There is no end to Life, there is no end

For I am the power to begin
I dream and bring to birth what's never been
There is no end to freedom, no end
There is no end to Life, there is no end

For you can hear be in your voice
And feel me in each breath that you breathe in
There is no end to the Circle, no end
There is no end to Life, there is no end

For I am the power to sustain
I am the ripened fruit and growing grain
There is no end to my abundance, no end
There is no end to Life, there is no end

And you can feel me in your heart
When it beats with the heart of a friend
There is no end to the Circle, no end
There is no end to Life, there is no end

And I am the power to end
I am the Crone who cuts the cord I spin
Though all things that are born must die again
There is no end to Life, there is no end

For all proceeds from me and all returns
All that returns to me comes forth again
There is no end to the Circle, no end
There is no end to Life, there is no end

And you touch me with your hand
Reach out and take the hand of a friend
There is no end to the Circle, no end
There is no end to Life, there is no end
—*Starhawk & Lauren Gale*

129. I Bid You Goodnight

Traditional [Sarah Doudney]
Sung a capella *by the Grateful Dead to close many of their concerts in the late 60s and early 70s, and revived in 1989-91.*

Lay down, my dear children,
Won't you come and take your rest
Lay your weary head upon your Mother's breast
Oh I love you, but the Goddess loves you the best
So I bid you goodnight, goodnight, goodnight
And I bid you goodnight!

Goodnight fair Witches
Lay down your head and rest
Lay your body down and be the mountain's guest
The stars will guide you; your dreams will do the rest
So I bid you goodnight, goodnight, goodnight
And I bid you goodnight!
—*1st verse adapted by Oberon Zell*
—*2nd verse Author unknown*

130. Benediction of Peace

Deep peace of the running wave to you.
Deep peace of the flowing air to you.
Deep peace of the quiet earth to you.
Deep peace of the shining stars to you.
Deep peace of the gentle night to you.
Moon and stars pour their healing light on you.
Deep peace of the Light of the World to you.
—*Author unknown*

131. Within the Circle
(to the tune of "Wayfaring Stranger")

I wandered lost, with no direction
And every turn I took was wrong.
Until I stood within the Circle,
And found the place where I belong.
I found the Moon to light the darkest night,
I found the Sun to warm the day.
I saw the Lady and Her mighty Lord,
And found their love to guide my way.

So now I know where I am going,
And I know what I'm going for,
For I have been within the Circle,
And I'll go wandering no more.
I found my brothers and my sisters,
And here I'll stay, no more to roam.
I found my place within the Circle;
Within the Circle, I came Home.
—*Elexa of Sothistar*

Book II: Rites & Rituals
Table of Contents

Pagan's Way

Not for me the mage's high golden road;
My heart is set in silver: wind in the trees,
Green grass beneath my feet, and the moonlit grove.
Content with the power in the deep bones of the
Earth Mother, I would not command the heavens.
I have trod the solitary path, and shall again.
I have hard the Lady's laughter at moonrise,
And suffered Her tender scourge in my heart;
I have eaten with the Lord of Shadows,
And been reborn.
I have spied shy horned faces peering golden-eyed
From the rocks at the Circle's edge.
I have called to the Watchers at the World's
Four Quarters, and from their Gates
They answered; I have watched the salamanders
In the chortling stream. All this I know,
And more... I have no need of the passionate cold
Of the celestial vault, or the comet's fire.
So I will walk my quiet road in peace,
And conjure spiral wonders—for the morning sun
Is gold enough for me.

—Gale Perrigo, 1984

Preface: Types of Ritual Workings
By Oberon Zell-Ravenheart

132. Children of the Goddess

Let no man dare to ride the wind as Mother's children do.
Let no man dare to tempt the fire their way.
Let no man think the waters will obey him and be true.
Nor order up the earthquake in his day.

For the Children of the Goddess walk a very special road,
And to speak the truth, it's not an easy way.
But to one who hears Her calling and has felt the gentle goad,
There is no other path and he is fey.

So filled with joy he follows Her, and though the road is long
He hums an ancient ley, or merry tune;
And his burdens grow much lighter, for he knows he is not wrong,
And his children's children's children sing the ancient witches' rune.

He's the one to ride the wind that answers his command.
And he'll tame the fire that others say is wild;
And the waters will obey him and the earthquake seek his hand;
And he smiles, for he knows he's Mother's Child.
—Author unknown

The "Working" is the core, heart, and purpose of a magick ritual. There are many types of workings that may be done—indeed, this phase of the ritual may be as varied as your own purposes and imagination may conceive. Various examples of such rituals will be presented in this section, but here I would like to give a brief explanation of a few basic types of ritual workings and how they may be conducted.

Worship & Celebration
Worship and celebration is a perfectly good purpose for a ritual. This basically means throwing a party and inviting the Gods to attend! Such a rite should include lots of drumming, singing, dancing, music, feasting, and general merrymaking. Full moons, birthdays, special events (such as an eclipse) and seasonal *Sabbats* are generally celebrated in this manner (see Book III: "Wheel of the Year").

One of our favorite such rites is a "Convocation of the Gods," wherein everyone comes prepared to *aspect* (take on the persona of) their favorite Divinity, with appropriate costumes, masks, and associated accoutrements. It is important to remember, however, that if you invite the Gods to attend a really good party, They will most likely show up! And Their first response is going to be: "This had better be good!" So make sure it is!

Anodea Judith says: "When you take on a Deity role in a ritual, it's of the utmost importance that you *know/become* that Deity. You must have ample resources and time available to immerse yourself in that energy. I suggest you build and dedicate an Altar to the Deity and that every day you devote some time getting to know that persona."

Consecration & Blessing
Every new venture—moving into a new home, establishing a business, opening an office, starting a family, founding an enterprise, beginning a major project—is a perfect opportunity

for rituals of consecration and blessing. If it's a new place to be occupied, the space may first need to be cleared and cleaned—physically and ritually (as with a *banishing*). Then it will be consecrated for its new use, and new people, with a ritual of blessing.

New tools (such as artist's tools, musical instruments, magickal implements, etc.) should be ritually consecrated as well, and blessed for their new use.

And of course, blessings may be bestowed upon people, places, creatures, and things of all nature. As Rabbi Tuckman says in Mel Brooks' *Robin Hood: Men in Tights:* "Bless 'em all!"

Shielding & Protection

Shielding and protection may be done for an individual, a group, or a place. Such rites involve throwing up a protective field around the target which will repel unwanted energies. The perfect metaphor is the energy fields/shields used to protect *Star Trek*'s Starship Enterprise from phaser fire and photon torpedoes. Shielding is done by taking the basic barrier of the Circle itself, and strengthening it into an impenetrable shell, reflectively mirrored on the outside. Use visualization as well as actual hand-held round mirrors as you circle around the person or place to be protected, holding your hands up as if against an invisible wall.

Healing & Transformation

Healing may be done for someone actually present in the Circle, or for someone far away who is known to one or more of the participants, who can link with them and relay the energy. A common method is for the person(s) to be healed (or their surrogates) to sit or lie in the center of the Circle while everyone else directs healing energy into them through their hands, which may be laid on the person's body, particularly over any specific areas that may need healing. Then everyone breathes together, deeper and faster, making sounds with each breath, until finally reaching a crescendo, simultaneously pumping out the combined Chi of the group into the center person(s) with the release of the last total exhalation.

Another method involves the person to be healed remaining linked in the Circle, with everyone holding hands and facing to their right. A current is created and built by each person in a wave snapping their head around to catch the eyes of the person on their left and blowing out with a "whoosh!" while simultaneously squeezing the hand of that person. At the same time, that person inhales the breath, then repeats these actions towards their left. After a few times around the Circle, this wave can gather tremendous power. When the one to be healed feels it is strong enough, all they have to do is break their link with the next person on their left, thereby collecting the full force of the energy wave without passing it on.

Healings may also be done for animals, a community, an ecosystem, and the planet. Except for animals, which can be brought into or passed around the Circle, these greater healings require symbolic "object links," such as photos, models, or a globe.

Transformation rituals can use these same techniques imbedded in a more complex psychodrama, which may be physically enacted, or played out through a guided meditation.

Elemental Rituals

Elemental rituals involve attunement with the four Elemental Principles of Nature: Earth, Water, Fire, and Air. These usually entail some actual physical involvement with that particular Element. Here are some examples:

Earth—Rituals may be conducted around gardening, tree-planting, hiking, rock- and mountain-climbing, spelunking (cave exploring), and pilgrimages to natural wonders. These invariably include "grounding" exercises and meditations, visualizing "putting your roots down deep into the Earth."

Water—Rituals are commonly performed around sacred wells, waterfalls, pools, hot springs, at the beach, and any place where the Element of Water appears naturally. Often shrines may be set up at such places, adorned with shells and other representations of Water.

Swimming, wading, diving, splashing, soaking, bathing, showering, SCUBA-diving, and sharing water may all be incorporated into Water rituals. Even standing outside in a soaking warm Summer rain can be a magickal experience!

Fire—Fire rituals are very basic, and a part of all outdoor Pagan gatherings. Elaine Hirt says: "The Fire has a profound way of opening up parts of your spirit, soul or energy." Most cultures honor and venerate fire, often in connection with the Sun. The first hymn of the Hindu Rig-Veda is devoted to Agni, the divine fire. There are also the old Persian Mithras-cult, the comprehensive Vedic Agni-rituals, Buddhist Goma/Homa fire rituals, Egyptian Earth/Star fire-worship, Irish Brigit, the Slavic Kupalo solstice, and the Aztec and Mayan New Fire ceremony every 52 years, the Phoenix and Promethean myths, the volcanic Pele-worship of Hawaii, the Celtic Beltaine and Samhain, the middle column of the Qabalah as the pathway of fire… (from "The Fire-Ritual: Heaven's URL," by Luc Sala).

Some of the most popular fire rituals have always been drumming and dancing around a blazing bonfire. Frequently, these go on all night at Pagan festivals, where the fire may be built as big as a house! Other fire-rituals may involve walking barefoot on hot coals, fire-spinning, a cozy fire in the fireplace, or even simple candle magick.

Air—Special breathing exercises are often incorporated into rituals—especially for raising energy. Smudging and burning incense are also part of many rites. Smoke-weaving and cloud-busting may be developed as psychic skills. Flying kites from a windy hilltop can be a true mystical experience if you ritualize it. And of course, there are the many ambitious aerial sports, such as wind-surfing, parasailing, hang-gliding, parachute jumping, and hot air ballooning; all of these can be ritualized.

Rites of Passage

A major purpose for community rituals in all cultures is to conduct "Rites of Passage," marking the transition from one phase or stage of life into another. These are rituals of honoring and empowerment, and unlike most rituals, they often include an audience of witnesses. Such passages include the following:

Being Born—Rite of *seining* (baby blessing) or Christening, in which infants are presented to the community, given their names, assigned God- & Goddess-parents, and receive blessing gifts—verbal, symbolic, and actual.

Entering Puberty (attaining fertility)—ceremonies heralding girls' "first blood" or menarche; boys' "first seed."

Coming of Age (attaining legal or social maturity)—Being of legal age to get a driver's license, vote, join the military, drink alcohol, sign contracts—in other words, becoming a recognized and responsible adult in one's society. This is also the "age of consent" in sexual matters. And these may not all be the same age, as laws in different countries and states vary widely regarding each of these adult rights.

Taking a Mate—Rites of *handfasting* (marriage). Probably the most universal and public of all Rites of Passage, binding people as committed life partners, usually to begin a family.

Giving Birth—Rites of delivery, motherhood, and fatherhood. These will be repeated for the birth of each child.

Attaining Elderhood—Menopausal rite, or "croning," for women to mark the end of their fertility. Rite of "saging" for men becoming "senior citizens."

Dying—"Last rites" include "passing," wakes, funerals, and burials or other dispositions of the body, such as cremation and the scattering of ashes.

Bardic Circles

The most quintessential ritual in the HOME Tradition, a Bardic is a wonderful experience that can easily be done by anyone in a small group. This is a ritual of sharing, in which each person in the Circle gets a turn to offer something to the rest of the group—usually a song, poem or story. The typical way a Bardic is conducted is by having a large chalice of fruit juice, wine, or mead ("Bard Oil") passed around the Circle. As it comes to each person, that one may take a drink and offer their piece, taking another drink before passing it on. If they do not wish to contribute anything at this time, they may just take a drink and pass the chalice.

Web-Weaving

Web-weaving is a particularly delightful type of magickal working, the purpose of which is to create magickal links among previously dissociated elements of the physical or spiritual world. Here's a typical example of such rituals as we have created and participated in:

A ball of twine is passed around the Circle, and each person takes their own "measure" by stretching a length of twine from middle fingertip to middle fingertip of their outstretched hands, then cutting off that piece. Then, while everyone holds one end of their measure, the free ends are gathered together and tied into a knot in the center, along with the end of the remaining ball of twine. When the knot is tied, everyone pulls taut on their ends of twine, raising the entire array high enough above the ground so that someone can sit comfortably beneath it.

Then, while everyone sings a Web-Weaving chant (usually: *"We are the flow and we are the ebb; We are the weavers, we are the Web..."*), one person sits under the Web and ties the string from the ball into an expanding spiral, one strand at a time outward along the measures. As the knots are tied in each person's measure, that person may call out the name of something they wish to link into the Web.

Once made, such a Web may continue to be used in subsequent rituals. Morning Glory and I now have several that we helped weave, and have added to over the years: one originally from Australia, one from Peru, and another from Texas. Each time such a Web is deployed, everyone holding an end may tie another knot into it to link whatever they wish into the collected energy field. Also, other items, such as crystals, ribbons, talismans, etc. may be tied into the Web as people wish to make their personal connections.

The Great Rite

The Great Rite is sex magick done in the Circle, usually between a Priest and Priestess. This rite is normally performed as a private ritual, where the entire rite is a two-person affair from beginning to end. Of course, it may also be performed by a small group of lovers as a ritual orgy. In some cases the Great Rite may be conducted in a regular Circle, while all the other people simply turn their backs on the couple performing it in the center; or even watch and chant while the rite is being performed. This need not be as exhibitionistic as it sounds; a common (and modest) position involves the man either sitting or lying on his back (or even tied to the Maypole!) while the woman, wearing a full skirt, straddles him, as in the *Yab-Yum* position.

The magick of the Great Rite is done by the couple holding the thought of the ritual intent firmly in their minds through a mutual orgasm, and releasing it with the full power of that charge. This can take a bit of practice!

Initiations & Mysteries

Throughout the 1940s and 50s, most Wiccan rituals, as well as those of the Masons, Rosicrucians, and other secret societies (all of which were similarly structured), consisted almost entirely of Initiations. First entry into the Circle, as well as passage into each successive grade or degree, has always been conducted in the form of an Initiation, in which the Initiate is blindfolded, bound, brought to the threshold of the Circle, and challenged ominously. Passwords are required, and an ordeal—symbolic or actual—must be endured and passed. Initiations may include welcoming of new members to the community, dedications to a path or course of study, or ordination as a Priest or Priestess of an Order or Tradition. Often such initiations are elaborated in the form of dramatic Mysteries, of which no more will be said here, as these cannot be described, but only experienced.

1. Rituals for Recurrent Occasions

Introduction
By Oberon Zell-Ravenheart

Of the many possible rituals, the most commonly practiced are those for recurrent occasions, when people get together at some regular intervals, be they weekly (such as church services), monthly (such as full moons), or annually (such as birthdays and holidays). There are also events that occur sporadically but predictably, such as lunar and solar eclipses. In this chapter we will explore varieties of recurrent rituals.

Full Moons
Full moons have been occasions for night-time ceremonies since the dawn of time. Even animals are more active on nights when the strange colorless moonlight floods the fields and forests. Wolves and dogs howl their eerie pack songs over valleys and hilltops, and it is said that werewolves transform into beasts during the three nights of the full moon.

Indeed, our four-week time periods, or *months,* as well as the *menstrual* cycles of women, are named for the moon. There are thirteen full moons in each solar year, although some years have only twelve, because a lunar month is actually about 29 and one-half days. A "blue moon" is popularly defined as the second full moon in a calendar month, although some define it as the second full moon while the sun is in one sign of the Zodiac.

In most cultures, the moon is considered to be feminine—the female counterpart and mate of the masculine sun. In classical Greece, the Moon Goddess was worshipped as Artemis, huntress of the night, whose bow was the thin crescent of the new moon. To the Romans she was known as Diana—the second most popular name for a girl in the Western world (the first being Mary, meaning "beloved"). Artemis (and later Diana) was the center of cults of women who would hold night-time revels at the times of the full moon, from which men were banished upon pain of death. These Women's Mysteries eventually became associated with Witchcraft, and full moon gatherings of Witches became known as *Esbats.*

The term *esbat* is probably a recent adoption among modern Wiccans, dating to the writings in the 1930s of anthropologist Margaret Murray (1863-1963). This term was used during the European Witch trials to describe the supposed monthly meetings of wicked Witches. It is derived from French *esbat,* meaning roughly "frolic or romp," with sexual connotations.

In C.G. Leland's *Aradia: The Gospel of Witches,* the Goddess, Diana speaks to her followers thus:

"Whenever you have need of anything, once in the month, and better it be when the Moon is full, you shall assemble in some secret place and adore the spirit of Me who is Queen of all Witches."

Dark Moons
In recent years, in addition to celebrating full moons, some women's Circles have begun celebrating dark moons. As full moons have become primarily celebratory occasions, dark moons are more commonly focused on deep inner working, healing, protection, and Women's Mysteries. But men can also gain much wisdom by going deeply within and embracing their Shadow, so we are including a dark moon ritual that can be used for men as well as women.

Weekly Worship Meetings
Many religious groups, regardless of their faith, hold some sort of weekly worship service or meeting. The most common day for this is the first day of the week: the day of the sun

in all calendars used in the Western world throughout history. But in Judaism and traditional Christianity, worship is held on the seventh day of the week, dedicated in the Western Gregorian calendar to Saturn, God of Time and the Harvest. Because the Biblical Fourth Commandment specifically orders the followers of Jahveh to "remember the seventh *(Sabbath)* day to keep it holy" (Exodus 20:8-11), many are confused as to why most Christian churches hold worship on Sunday rather than Saturday, and this is a matter of considerable dispute between various denominations. This is because the foundations of the Roman Catholic Church were laid by Emperor Constantine (285-337 CE), who declared Christianity to be the official religion of the Roman Empire at the Council of Nicea in 335 CE. Traditional days of worship in the Roman religion—including holy Sundays—were then converted to Christian use. And an interesting side note of this debate is that some calendars produced today for use in predominantly fundamentalist Christian regions of the United States. actually begin on Monday, and show Sunday as the seventh day!

So to accommodate everybody, our civil calendars designate both Saturday and Sunday as the "weekend," and many businesses, schools, etc. take these days off. Therefore, most modern Pagan groups who meet weekly also schedule their meetings on weekends. Such local meeting groups may be known as *covens* (Wicca), *hearths* (Norse), *groves* (Druid), *nests* (Church of All Worlds), or—more simply and commonly—*circles*. Rituals at these weekly gatherings tend to be focused primarily on community-building, teaching, spellwork, healing, divinations, or just plain fun. For participants, such anticipated get-togethers are the high point of the week.

Deity Feast Days

In a number of traditions, the gods and goddesses of their respective pantheons may be assigned a specific birthday, to be celebrated with feasting and honoring by those of their faith. These are identical to the feast days of the saints in the liturgical calendar of the Catholic Church, and such commemorations are often distinct from lunar, solar, and weekly rituals. Such are particularly observed in Egyptian (Khemitic) religion, Hinduism, Buddhism, and the Afro-Caribbean traditions. And various special festivals in honor of selected deities also appear in Greco-Roman and Celtic calendars. (See the "Pantheons" in the Appendix for listings of some of these dates.) Think of these occasions as special birthday parties held in their honor, and celebrate accordingly. Put out their pictures, statues, and associated objects. Many have favorite foods, drinks, and incense. Gifts may be given and exchanged—all in their names:

As the Moon Goddess Diana says in Leland's *Aradia: "Sing, feast, dance, make music and love, all in My presence, for Mine is the ecstasy of the spirit and Mine also is joy on Earth."*

Holidays

Every culture has its own cycle of public holidays. Some of these are local, some religious, and some national. Most of them commemorate significant events in the history of that culture. What we call "holiday customs and traditions" are the rituals associated with these occasions: sitting down together at the family table with a traditional feast (ham? turkey? goose? roast beast? pork and beans? corned beef and cabbage?), attending some special religious service, decorating the house for the holidays, or reading aloud a traditional story ("Why is this day different from all others?").

In most of the modern Pagan traditions, eight seasonal celebrations, spread evenly around the year at six-week intervals, comprise the ritual cycle known as the *Wheel of the Year*. Book III of this compilation will be devoted to these.

Birthdays

Just as the births and deaths of gods, prophets, saints, and presidents may be commemorated annually by religious and national observances, each individual's nativity is certainly the most important day in their life! Birthday parties can become much-anticipated annual events for each of us and our friends, and may be celebrated quite lavishly—especially at the culmination of each decade, with "the big 0." And these are also excellent opportunities for rituals of transition and transformation: celebrating another trip around the sun, looking back over the past journey that has brought us this far, and envisioning our hopes for the future. "What a long, strange trip it's been!"

New Year's Celebrations

Since 1582, when the Roman Julian calendar was switched over to the Gregorian, the Western world has become used to celebrating January 1 as New Year's Day, with December 31 as New Year's Eve. (January is named for the Etruscan *Janus,* god of all beginnings, portals, doorways, and thresholds.) However, other cultures and religions designate the turning of the year on different dates, calculated in different ways. The most common of these is Winter Solstice, which occurs around December 20–22, and began the Roman Saturnalia—a week of intercalary revelry "outside of time" before the onset of the new year. This is why the common representation of the passing old year is Saturn, the Roman god of time, as the Grim Reaper, with scythe and hourglass. Winter Solstice is most widely known as *Yule,* from the Norse word for "wheel." Among the Pueblo Indians of the Southwestern United States, this time is known as *Soyal.*

April Fool's Day originated with a pre-Gregorian New Year celebration that was held from Spring Equinox to April 1. When the new calendar, starting on January 1, replaced it, people who continued to celebrate the traditional new year were, apparently, mocked and teased and the subject of various humorous harassment.

Many peoples divided the solar year into two parts: winter and summer. The transitions between these would then provide two "new years." Among modern Pagans, the most commonly-observed example of this custom is from the Celts, who marked the two "hinges" of the year at *Samhain* (Hallowe'en) and *Beltaine* (May Day). As with all new year celebrations, festivities begin on the evening before the first day of the new year, with nocturnal rituals culminating at midnight, in which the "gate between the worlds" stands ajar, and spirits may pass from one realm to another. Spirits of the ancestors and beloved dead are welcomed and invited to the feast, but malicious spirits must be kept at bay.

But by far the majority of ancient calendars were not solar, but were (and are) based on a combination of lunar and solar movements. The lunar cycle, as I mentioned above, is about 29 and one-half days. In order to catch up with the solar calendar, peoples using a lunar calendar have to insert the equivalent of an extra month every seven years in a nineteen-year cycle. This is the same as solar calendars adding an extra day on leap year. And this is why the Chinese, Jewish, Moslem, Hindu, and many other new year celebrations fall on a different date each solar year. Here are a few of these:

Chinese New Year starts with the new moon on the first day of the new year and ends on the full moon fifteen days later. The exact date can fall anytime between January 21 and February 21. The 15th day of the new year is called the Lantern Festival, celebrated at night with lantern displays and children carrying lanterns in a parade. New Year's Eve and New Year's Day are celebrated as a family affair, a time of reunion and thanksgiving. Traditionally, the celebration is highlighted with a religious ceremony given in honor of heaven and Earth, the gods of the household and the family ancestors.

Jewish New Year is called *Rosh Hashanah* ("Head of the Year"). This celebration occurs 163 days following *Pesach* (Passover). It begins the month of Tishri, and falls between the Gregorian dates of September 5 and October 5. Rosh Hashanah commemorates the anniversary of Creation, when Jahveh opens the Book of Life and decides the fate of his creatures for the coming year. On the eve of Rosh Hashanah, celebrants prepare for this judgment by bathing, receiving haircuts, donning special clothes, and giving treats to children.

The **Islamic New Year** (*Maal Hijra*) is celebrated on the first day of Muharram, the first Islamic month. Compared to Western calendars, the Islamic year goes 11 days backwards every year. Unlike most other new year celebrations, Maal Hijra is usually quiet. Muslims gather in mosques for special prayers and readings, reflecting on the passing of time and their own mortality. A major component is the telling of the *hegira*, Muhammed's flight from Medina to Mecca.

Here are some other dates for new year celebrations in different cultures:

- In the **Eastern Orthodox Church**, **New Year's Day** (also a celebration of the infant Jesus' circumcision) is on January 14 (January 1 in the Julian Calendar). Many predominantly Eastern Orthodox countries celebrate both the Gregorian and Julian New Year holidays, with the Gregorian day celebrated as a civic holiday and the Julian date as a religious holiday.
- The **Vietnamese New Year**—the *Tet Nguyên Ðán*—is usually the same day as the Chinese New Year.
- The **Tibetan New Year**, called *Losar*, is celebrated from January through March.
- The **Iranian New Year**, called *Norouz*, is the day of the Vernal Equinox, commencing the Spring season.
- In the **Bahá'í** calendar, the new year occurs on the Vernal Equinox and is called *Naw-Rúz.*
- The **Teluga New Year** generally falls in the months of March or April, when the people of Andhra Pradesh, India, celebrate the advent of lunar year.
- The **Thai, Cambodian,** and **Laos New Years** are celebrated from April 13-15 by throwing water.
- The **Bengali New Year**, *Poila Baisakh*, is celebrated on April 14 or 15 in a festive manner in both Bangladesh and West Bengal.
- The **Ethiopian New Year**, *Enkutatash*, is celebrated on September 11.
- The **Gujarati New Year** is usually celebrated two days after the festival of *Diwali* (held in mid-November).
- The **Assyrian New Year**, or *Rish Nissanu*, occurs on the Vernal Equinox on March 21, commencing Spring.
- The **Punjabi New Year**, *Vaisakhi*, is celebrated on April 13 and celebrates the harvest.
- *Hola Mohalla,* **New Year's Day** in the **Sikh Nanakshahi** calendar, is on March 14.

Lunar & Solar Eclipses

Lunar eclipses occur when the moon in orbit passes through the shadow of the Earth cast by the sun. Similarly, a solar eclipse occurs when the moon passes between the Earth and the sun, and the shadow of the moon falls across the Earth in a narrow swath from west to east. Eclipses may be *partial* (the Earth's shadow only covering part of the moon, or the moon only covering part of the sun), *annular* (in the case of a solar eclipse when the moon is farther away from Earth, and a ring of sunlight shows around it) or *total* (when the moon passes completely within the shadow of the Earth, or completely covers the face of the sun). Eclipses, of course, can only be viewed from certain places—from the facing hemisphere of the Earth for a lunar eclipse, or along the narrow band of the Earth across which the Lunar shadow passes in the case of a solar eclipse. For exact times and viewing locations, see NASA's eclipse page: http://sunearth.gsfc.nasa.gov/eclipse/eclipse.html

Eclipses are amazing experiences, and perfect opportunities for powerful rituals. Of course, given the physics of the situation, lunar eclipses occur only at the full moon, and solar eclipses only at the new moon, so these naturally lend themselves well to being utilized for power-raising at full and dark moon Esbats. There is a palpable force in these alignments that can energize a well-constructed Circle like charging a battery—especially one held within a consecrated henge of wood or stone.

The most powerful ritual I ever engaged in was during a total eclipse of the sun. The ritual took place at a full-scale replica of Stonehenge, restored on the bleak and barren bluffs above the Columbia River in the State of Washington, on February 26, 1979. I will include this particular ritual later in this chapter.

I. Full Moon Rituals

Here is a lovely and evocative description of a full-moon Esbat:

133. Esbat

The clouding incense makes the room grow dim;
The candle flames with unfelt air do stir;
The tools with sudden beauty flashing forth;
The cup with wine and blessings to the brim;

The solemn stillness of the magic sphere;
The rolling words, the ringing chants of power;
The graceful dance—the step that binds the spell,
And builds the cone that brings our Lady nearer.

The shining forms that on the air are seen;
The Mighty Ones who guard our tower gates;
The Hornéd Hunter in His splendor comes;
All bow before our gracious Silver Queen.

The frenzy of the dance now beckons all
To join their spirits to the Gods they love,
And laugh as merry children at a game
Until with weariness they start to fall.

At last the faithful, fresh with wine and love;
Their strength regained, and standing hand in hand
Renew their oath of love and friendship fast;
And thanks and love are offered those above.

The shimmered forms of thought-bent force-on-air
Disperse before the steel now held on high;
The Circle from that other world returns
Though the thoughts, and love, will linger there.
—*Diane Kirkland, 3/74*

And here is the most beloved of all Esbat songs, by renowned Bard Ian Corrigan:

134. Question Song

The Moon is high above the hill,
And we are come to work our will.
What is your will, O children wise-o?
To call our Queen down from the skies-o;
Our silver Queen who rides the skies!

Oh is she dark or is she light?
How will you know her in the night?
What is her token to her own-o,
That she among you might be known-o?
That she among you might be known?

Oh she is bright as starlight clear;
Yet in the dark, we know her near.
The three-fold Moon is her own sign-o,
That we may know her as divine-o;
That we may know her as divine!

How will you call her from the stars?
How will she hear you from afar?
And if she comes unto this place-o,
How will you call her three-fold grace-o?
What name shall you call her ancient grace?

We'll dance the Circle nine times nine;
We'll bow before her holy shrine;
Draw down the Moon upon the green-o—
And hail Diana as our Queen-o;
We'll hail Diana, our bright Queen!
—*Ian Corrigan*

Drawing Down the Moon
By Susan "Moonwriter" Pesznecker

The ritual known as "Drawing Down the Moon" is extremely important to many Pagan and Wiccan traditions. During the ritual, the Goddess—symbolized by the full moon—is invoked and becomes present, a powerful force that touches all who are present and blesses them with her spiritual powers. The ritual is conducted within a Circle, which becomes a sacred place through its casting, a place between worlds. The Circle is held outdoors at the full moon—an Esbat—and usually in a private location. Within the Circle the participants use music, chanting, and dancing to raise what is called a "cone of power."

After the power is raised, the actual "drawing down" begins with the recital of the "Charge of the Goddess" (see page 59, #41), a lyrical address written by Gardnerian Wiccan High Priestess Doreen Valiente (1922-1999). The coven's High Priestess then extends her arms skyward, beckoning to the moon and drawing down its energy. If a High Priest is also present, he assists in drawing the Goddess into the High Priestess. She enters a trance-state and becomes a vessel for the Goddess, a transformation that allows the energy of the Goddess to affect everyone in the circle. Once evoked, the lunar energy can be further directed toward a particular purpose, such as healing, or those present can simply bask in the energy until the ritual ends.

Communing with the Moon

Although the ritual of Drawing Down the Moon is traditionally done with a group, you can conduct your own version all by yourself, or with one or two others. Your moon ritual should take place outdoors on a night when the moon is full.

Purify yourself by bathing or showering (a bar of frankincense soap is a nice touch for purification), then don clean clothing. If you have magickal robes or garb—particularly if they are silver or white—these are ideal attire. If you have privacy, total nudity is even better. You may also wish to wear magickal jewelry, particularly anything that includes moons or moonstones. Ground and center yourself, then spend some time meditating on what it is that you plan to do. You may wish to play soft background music on a portable CD player— drumming, soft chants, Celtic harp music, Native American flutes, etc. Set up your altar as desired, then cleanse and consecrate your space and cast a Magick Circle. Call the Quarters and invite the presence of the God and Goddess.

Now, stand at the center of your Circle and raise your arms above your head, facing the full moon. Speak to the Goddess that is the moon, asking her to fill you. Feel the energy as it flows down your arms and fills your soul. Many report feeling a tingling sensation, or a feeling of warmth. Most people feel very emotional at this time, and may laugh or weep.

After drawing down the moon's energy, you may wish to dance, or just walk the inside perimeter of your Circle in a *deosil* (clockwise) fashion. If you choose to direct the energy towards another purpose, this is the time to do it. Otherwise, simply enjoy feeling the energy move through you, and be aware of being blessed and enriched by its presence.

While still under the full moon, celebrate with "wine and cakes," or some variation thereof (see pp. 82-83). Finally, spend some time meditating on what you have accomplished. When you're ready, release the Quarters, close the Circle, then kneel and place your hands on the Earth, sending the excess energy back to the Mother.

And finally, here is a tasty recipe for Esbat Cookies:

Jam or Chocolate Stuffed Cookies for Esbats
By Lezlie Kinyon

All one wants in a cookie: soft, buttery, and rich. Use a star-shaped tip or form into crescent moon shapes for Esbats and other Circles. Children love to make these and everyone loves to eat them!

1 stick unsalted butter	1/2 cup unbleached white flour
1/2 cup sugar	Clean out 1/2 tsp. of vanilla seeds from
1 tsp. vanilla extract or almond flavoring	the inside of a vanilla bean with a sharp
1/2 tsp. salt	knife to add interest to the cookies
1 egg, at room temperature	

Mix all ingredients in a food processor on pulse until they form a ball. Cover a cookie sheet with cooking parchment and pipe the mix onto the sheet with the star tip—make little stars and space an inch or so apart. Top with chocolate chips and bake at 350 degrees F for 15 minutes. Cool on a rack.

When cookies are cool, take two cookies, spread the bottom of one with your favorite jam, and "sandwich" it with a second cookie. Arrange them on a pretty platter and serve.

135. Three Faces of the Moon
By Melanie F. Stoehrer (Redwood Shadowtree)

(To be spoken by three priestesses in a "Drawing Down the Moon" ritual. Cut an apple in half equatorially, and pass it around as these lines are being recited.)

Maiden's Glory
I am Maiden, Call to me!
Sister, daughter, huntress!

I am the beauty of innocent youth.
I am freedom, power and poetry.
I am the Lady of untried potential.

I choose white to represent my power,
The white of the apple's flesh,
It is the color of a cloud floating free and
    unburdened through an endless sky,
It is the color of an artist's canvas, or a
    poet's page,
A blank space,
Untapped
Unknown
A color of inspiration, a place of beginnings.
I am the light of all colors before they are
    split by Nature.

Think of Me when the Moon is waxing,
And my bow is silver in the sky.
And know me always by the color white
The color of innocence and potential.

Mother's Radiance
I am Mother to the Maiden,
And I will always heed your call.
I am the lover, the parent, and spouse.

I am the lush ripeness of maturity.
I am protection, commitment and fulfillment.
I am the Lady of motherhood.

To represent my power, I choose the color red.
I am the color of a ripened apple.
The color of blood that drops from the
    wounds I heal,
That runs from the womb that brings forth life,
The color of the fluid which nourishes a child
Before it ever opens its eyes to the world.
The color of womanhood and perpetuation.
I am the rind that protects the flesh and seeds
    of all I create.

Call to me when the Moon is full,
Pregnant in the sky.

Know me by the color red,
The color of maturity, protection and love.

Crone's Reflections
I am the Grandmother Crone,
And your calls to me will echo in silence.

I am a friend, a wise-woman, a guardian of
    the cauldron.
I am reflection, withdrawal and wisdom.
I am the culmination of life with death.

Black is the color of my power.
For black is the absorption of all colors,
And none may escape it.
It is the color of the seed that will be planted
    again,
The color of the cold winter earth,
It is the color of decay and dissolution.
It is the color of endings and beginnings.

When the moon wanes in the darkening sky,
And the earth echoes with the stillness of the
    night,
Know me by the blackness that awaits you
    after your last breath is gone.

Joined as One
We are the three known as one.
We are the Fates, the Morrigan, the aspects
    of the Triple Moon.

To be balanced and complete we are joined,
A triad, unbreakable and intertwined.

Know us not by any moon phase, but by all of
    them together.
Know us by the apple we chose for our power.
The white flesh of crisp youth is the power of
    the Maiden,
The red rind, the protection and blessing of
    the Mother,
The Crone's black seeds, deadly, and yet a
    hope for the next life.

We choose to be joined always,
Watch for Us as the month rolls by,
In the faces of the moon.
And know that we are always One.

II. Dark Moon Ritual

Crone Moon
By Julie Forest Middleton, 2006

In the darkest period of the Wheel of the Year after Samhain comes the holy day of Crone Moon. Falling on the dark of the moon just before the returning of the light at Winter Solstice, Crone Moon is the darkest of the dark times, and has been taken by Crones as their own.

In age order, we enter the hall in nearly total darkness, lit only by enough candles or *luminaria* to see our way to our chairs.

The altar is set in honor of the Crone goddess. Hecate is the patroness of our Circle. She is invoked and invited into our midst.

We sit in silence in the dim light, contemplating the darkness: the quiet, gentle darkness of winter's death, and the larger, more disturbing darkness that has crept into our world.

The senior Crone breaks the quiet with a question that asks for Crone wisdom: *"How has the darkness changed in the last year?"* or *"What new qualities are apparent in the darkness?"* We speak, slowly, with long spaces between thoughts, until the answers run out.

Another question: *"What has seemed to work at keeping the darkness at bay?"* and again we speak.

A third question: *"What powers does each have to offer?"* We make our pledges, lighting candles on the altar, and the room brightens.

"Who," the senior Crone asks, *"has made the long journey to the Summerland since last we met?"* Names are given, contemplated, honored, and more candles are lit in reverence.

A song is started, slowly and quietly, which then grows in intensity as we claim our power and our place in the scheme of things. When the energy subsides, we ask Hecate for blessings on ourselves and on our group, and we each offer prayers. We sit, then, in silence, just as we began, and the secret cronish handshake is passed around the group.

Then, at last, we break for gossip, goodies, and the good-humored laughter and cackling that define our group.

III. Birthday
By Ruth Barrett

Here is a witchy alternative to the traditional cake and candle ritual. At your party, instead of lighting the birthday candles and *then* making a wish, bring out the cake and hand out birthday candles to all the guests. Offer a variety of colors to choose from so that the color of the candle selected by each person has personal significance. One by one, each of the guests puts his or her candle on the cake and speaks a blessing or a wish for the honored one, and then lights the candle for the wish. This is a wonderful and loving experience for the honoree to hear from friends and family. It also creates a warm feeling of intimacy among everyone because something real and heartfelt is happening.

After the candles have been lit (and yes, the wishes must be brief in order for the cake not to go up in flames!), the honoree also lights a candle for herself for the year. Then sing the "Happy Birthday" song if you wish. The honoree takes a bite of cake first, with the consciousness of taking the wishes literally and symbolically into herself and into her new year of life. This activity restores the proper sequence of a spell. (Dianic priestess Pat Devin first introduced the author to this new birthday custom in the early 1980s.) To allow the candles to burn down all the way, the blessing candles can be placed in a bowl filled with earth, salt, or sand, instead of on the cake. In order to energize the spell, the candles will have to burn all the way down, so the bowl or salt or sand is magickally the best option.

136. Birthday Candles

Here's what to say before blowing out the candles on your birthday cake:

A year has come; a year has passed.
I make my birthday wish at last!
Magick powers, old and new,
Make my birthday wish come true!

(Make your wish, then blow out all the candles with one breath!)
—Morning Glory Zell

10. New Year Rituals

Chinese New Year's Customs

House Cleaning

In China, the entire house should be cleaned before New Year's Day. On New Year's Eve, all brooms, brushes, dusters, dust pans and other cleaning equipment are put away. Sweeping or dusting should not be done on New Year's Day for fear that good fortune will be swept away. After New Year's Day, the floors may be swept. Beginning at the door, the dust and rubbish are swept to the middle of the parlor, then placed in the corners and not taken or thrown out until the fifth day. At no time should the rubbish in the corners be trampled upon. In sweeping, there is a superstition that if you sweep the dirt out over the threshold, you will sweep one of the family away. Also, to sweep the dust and dirt out of your house by the front entrance is to sweep away the good fortune of the family; it must always be swept inward and then carried out, then no harm will follow. All dirt and rubbish must be taken out the back door.

Bringing in the New Year and Expelling the Old

Shooting off firecrackers on New Year's Eve is the Chinese way of sending out the old year and welcoming in the New Year. On the stroke of midnight on New Year's Eve, every door in the house, and even windows, have to be open to allow the old year to go out.

Feast for the Ancestors

In China, the sacrifice to the ancestors, the most vital of all the rituals, unites the living members with those who have passed away. Departed relatives are remembered with great respect because they were responsible for laying the foundations for the fortune and glory of the family. The presence of the ancestors is acknowledged on New Year's Eve with a dinner arranged for them at the family banquet table. The spirits of the ancestors, together with the living, celebrate the onset of the New Year as one great community. The communal feast is called *weilu,* meaning "surrounding the stove." It symbolizes family unity and honors the past and present generations

New Year's Spell

By Adella DragonStar

(To be done on either Samhain or January 1)

Materials needed: 12 month-stones, index card, pen or pencil, lighter, candle, flame-proof bowl (preferably cauldron) with water either in it or handy, lighter, candle (preferably white), and stone necklace with a stone for focus, energy, protection, etc.

Before you begin, write the most regretted thoughts of the previous year on the index card.

Set up the mini-altar in a safe place away from flammable objects. As you set up, think about what you desire for the coming year. Place the candle on the mini-altar, the 12 month-stones surrounding it in a circle. Cast the Circle as usual and light the candle. Pass the cleansed stone of the necklace over the fire, saying:

As the new year progresses, may this stone give me _____.

Fold the card in fours before burning it in the bowl. For safety, you can set the bowl in the sink before you burn it. That way, you can drown the fire with water.

> *By flame of the fire,*
> *The year past is gone.*
> *Bring me what I desire,*
> *As the new year carries on.*

Close the Circle as usual, and clean up the mess.

New Year's Box - A Tradition from Scotland or Ireland

From Lady Pythia
(A yearly reminder from a third-generation priestess of my line—wonderful spellwork in this!)

This is for anyone who would like to participate in my family's New Year tradition. It's about the ONLY tradition we have!

As far back as my mom can remember, my dad's family made a box (shoebox, whatever) to be put out sometime before midnight on New Year's Eve. Then it is brought back in any time *after* midnight. Traditionally, it is brought back inside by the first person to visit your house after midnight. It is used as a blessing for every aspect of your family and life. Items placed in the box represent food (nonperishable), money, religion, pets, jobs and/or income, and anything else you want to bring into your life over the coming year.

It is so simple that everyone in your household—young or old—can participate!

Important: Put the box in a safe, dry place outside or even in a plastic bag if the weather is bad. And it's totally acceptable to bring it back in yourself, since people don't visit the way they did years ago. You can even decorate your box if you so desire!

Both my parents are one-half Scottish and one-half Irish, so I'm unsure whether this is an Irish or Scottish tradition.

New Year's Prosperity Spell

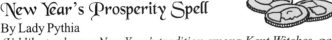

By Lady Pythia
(I'd like to share a New Year's tradition among Kent Witches, garnered from a very ancient Mediterranean spell, which we adapted for modern usage. Many of our sister covens know this Working, but we've spread it by word of mouth only for the last 20 years.)

Gather three pennies dated with the outgoing year. In the ancient Mediterranean, the coins weren't pennies—as always, we work with what we have!

Place on a table or altar a longish piece of new aluminum foil.

Take the pennies. The head faces out on one side, and the tail out on the other. The third is sandwiched in between. Place on foil and wrap, folding foil lengthwise only.

Holding the lengthwise-wrapped spell, rub your thumbnail over the head and tail so that you can make out the outline through the foil. Do not wrap them all the way up, as it is important that the outline of the coins is visible to incoming light.

Place on windowsill before midnight (if you're going out, place there before you leave). Let the spell spend three days and three nights where it is—it will be charged by alternate lunar and solar energies.

On the morning of the fourth day of the new year, take the spell and wrap it up the rest of the way to protect the coins. In order to protect foil from getting shredded over the next year, you may place it in a small mojo bag if you wish. Put in purse or wallet with the money that you carry, and keep it with you during entire year.

On the next new year, unwrap and spend one penny each day in three different places, so that all that you have reaped will return to the abundant universe. You will spend three days giving back, literally, and then have your spell for the new year.

In addition, if you want to increase potency, you may combine it with any other prosperity spell, such as a buckeye wrapped in a dollar bill and bound by 9-fold knot magick with green yarn, and anointed with appropriate oils and powders if you wish.

The coin spell is not only meant to work in the realm of finance. Copper is ruled by Venus, and connected also with Mercury. Venus energies will bring prosperity to the heart, to hearth and home, where the heart feels most rooted, with Taurean growth energies. And her Libra dominion also augments, with this, healthy relationships and communication, partnerships, etc., as well as creativity

Wearing gold of some sort on New Year's Eve in order to bring prosperity into all areas of life is also an old custom. "Shiny" colors, such as red, are also worn for reinforcement of one's life energies.

V. Solar Eclipse at Stonehenge, USA
By Otter G'Zell (March 1979)

The Prophecies will come
When Shadow mates with Sun.
Be There. You know Where... 2/26/79

I received this message and image in a vision in July, 1978, at the Oregon Country Faire. I circulated it widely throughout the Pagan community, and on the morning of February 26, 1979, over 3,000 people were gathered at a full-scale replica of Stonehenge—restored to the grandeur of its original design of over 3,600 years ago. "We knew where, and we were there" to experience the last total eclipse of the sun to be visible in North America until the year 2017.

The great road and railway baron, Sam Hill, built the Stonehenge replica near Maryhill, Washington, on a bluff overlooking the gorge of the Columbia River. As a Quaker, he had intended the monument as a "sermon in stone"—a prominent reminder that human sacrifice was still being offered to the gods of war. As such, it was the first WWI memorial in the United States.

On June 8, 1918, upon the day of a total solar eclipse, the altar stone was laid and dedicated. An astronomer planned the layout so that the rising sun at the Summer and Winter Solstices would cast shadows on the altar as they do at the original Stonehenge in England. The natural stone of the area proved inadequate for the project, so it was built with 1,000 tons of concrete. What took ancient engineers centuries to create, Sam Hill erected in a decade, and his Stonehenge II was rededicated upon completion in 1929.

In his 1965 book, *Stonehenge Decoded*, astronomer Gerald Hawkins explained his theory of Stonehenge as a calendrical and astronomical computer whose functions included the prediction of eclipses. Sam Hill's interpretation of Stonehenge as a sacrificial temple to the Druidic gods of war has proven erroneous in the light of recent archaeology. But the vision of Stonehenge as an observatory and calculator of eclipse cycles attained a new significance on that chilly morning in 1979, as Sam's restored replica was for the second time (actually, the first time since it was completed) directly in the path of a Solar eclipse.

The ceremony was created by members of the New Reformed Druids of North America, the Covenant of the Goddess, the Church of All Worlds, Madrakara, the New Reformed Orthodox Order of the Golden Dawn, Pentalpha, and a number of Witchcraft covens. After each group had made its contributions, a number of us went back out to Stonehenge, where Stephen was conducting an all-night vigil. We spent the night in chanting, dancing by firelight, and weatherworking to clear the skies for morning. It had been raining and cloudy for weeks, and the weather reports were very discouraging for the day of the eclipse. We were asked a number of times by the media and museum people if we had any magick to clear away the clouds, and we had replied with confidence. That night, as we sang to them, one by one the stars came out.

There is an incredibly mythic quality to the spectacle of hundreds of robed and costumed figures chanting, singing, dancing to flutes and drums, intoning invocations and prayers, and enacting ancient rites within a vast Circle of standing stones and lintel-capped trilithons. When the occasion for such a gathering is a total eclipse of the sun, the myths and legends materialize from the dreamworld into a living reality that simply defies description.

As we gathered in full regalia in the pearly pre-dawn light, the sky was thinly overcast. From tents and campers, and from cars that had been rolling in all night, thousands were stirring and gravitating from the surrounding hills and fields towards that great megalith high on the bluff above Sam Hill's tomb. At sunrise, with Priestess Morning Glory and Archdruid Isaac Bonewits attending the altar, Selene Kumin and I led the procession from the heelstone into the henge: *"We come, we come, with the rising of the Sun...O rise, my spirit, rise!"*

The Elements were invoked, candles and incense lit, and an ancient Egyptian myth of the battle between Ra, the Sun God, and Apep, the cosmic serpent, was recounted. Lila and Tom invoked the Moon Goddess and Sun God, and Selene and Danaan embodied them in a dance of passion, embrace, and withdrawal. Morning Glory's "Prayer for the Healing of the Earth" was raised, followed by specific prayers for endangered species such as whales, condors, and redwoods. A thousand voices joined in the responses: *"Wolf and Tiger proud; raise your voices loud!"* (Later, we heard on the news that the wolves in the Portland zoo had all turned towards the eclipse, laid their ears back and howled.) Other songs, chants, and prayers were led by different priests and priestesses, including Morning Glory with her powerful eclipse litany.

Finally, through the light haze still veiling the eastern sky, the sun appeared...with a small bite out of its right side! A cheer went up, and Isaac called for all present to join in the most ancient and effective magickal banishment known: *"Rain, rain, go away! Come again some other day!"* It quickly changed to *"Clouds, clouds, go away!"* And sure enough, as that powerful wave of psychic energy hurtled forth from a thousand minds and throats within that awesome Circle, the clouds parted to reveal clear skies for the entire eclipse!

The Circle was then opened so everyone could find good places for viewing the celestial light and shadow show. As the moon shadow crept across the solar disk, there seemed little change in the light for a long time. Finally, in the last moments before totality, rippling shadow bands appeared across the faces of the trilithons, and the shadow came racing towards us out of the west at 2,000 mph. At 8:16 a.m., as if a cloak had been pulled over our heads, we were suddenly enveloped in unearthly darkness. A brass gong was sounded, lights came on in the little town below, a few skyrockets trailed red streamers across the heavens, and cows on nearby hillsides stampeded. Strange golden clouds boiled on the southern horizon, but within that ancient temple of the cosmos, the spectacle of the corona radiating in all directions from behind that dark circle in the clear starry heavens erased all other thoughts from our minds. Under the gaze of that eye in the sky, a few children cried in the eerie un-dark, but most of us just wept with rapture as we stood awestruck and speechless, tears streaming down our uplifted faces as we were bathed in the aetheric aura of the sun's outer atmosphere. 3,600 years dropped away from our souls, and we were all together once again on the ancient Plain of Salisbury. We remembered...

All too soon it was over. The "diamond ring" effect appeared with dazzling brightness and we once again had to look through filters. Someone shouted *"Encore!"* But it was not to be. To be at Stonehenge as it was in its days of glory, for a total eclipse of the sun, was an experience for which we had waited a hundred lifetimes. As the clouds returned to the skies, we turned and saw the image of the eclipse in each other's eyes. We had stood together under the shadow of the moon, and we emerged from that shadow blessed and baptized.

As the waxing sun grew, people came to the altar to receive back the objects they had earlier placed to be charged: jewelry, talismans, ritual tools, magick mushrooms, wine, bread, seeds, fruit. A couple who had placed a deer skin on the altar with two rings told us that this had been their wedding rite. A young boy had placed a lion figure on the "stone table": "This is Aslan," he solemnly informed us. Then we poured a libation of wine over Sam Hill's remains, with thanks.

And what of the prophecies that were to come? Oh, they came, they came. 3,000 people went forth from that Circle of stone under the shadow of the moon, and we have all been changed. 3,000 pilgrims have gone forth as prophets, and new tales will be told, new songs sung, new visions painted, danced, and played. We are coming to a new beginning, and we have been sanctified together. Great beginnings require great endings of what has been before, and the Wheel is turning. This eclipse signaled to many of us the closing of the Age of Pisces (in which sign it occurred), but there must yet be an interval of purification and healing of the Earth before the book opens again on the Age of Aquarius.

> *When Shadow mates with Sun.*
> *Be there. You know where.*

Addendum: Twenty years later, on August 11, 1999, I led a similar ritual for the total eclipse of the sun in the ancient stone circle of Boskawen-un in Cornwall, England. Thus was this 20-year ritual cycle completed. Of the 3,000 people who had stood together in Stonehenge II in 1979, only one other woman also showed up at the concluding rite in 1999.

We suffused the lunar shadow with these intentions to carry across the face of the Earth:
1. We are all one—all children of the same Mother (Gaia), flesh of her flesh and blood of her blood;
2. We want an end to human conflict (especially religious wars!);
3. We want healing and restoration of the Earth;
4. We want a return to the reverence of nature, the seasonal cycles, and the ancient ways, including the preservation and restoration of sacred sites, temples, stone circles, and groves;
5. We want an awakening of the planetary consciousness of Gaia;
6. We desire the ushering in of a new millennium—the Aquarian Age, with all that signifies.

The next total solar eclipses to pass across the United States will be on August 21, 2017, and April 8, 2024. Don't miss them! (For dates and maps of solar eclipses through history, see the NASA Eclipse home page: *http://sunearth.gsfc.nasa.gov/eclipse/eclipse.html*.)

The Stonehenge Eclipse Ceremony
(Unless otherwise indicated, all poetry and songs were written by the people who performed them in this ceremony.)

Procession from the east, Otter carrying stang with medicine skull (eclipse painted on in black on red), Selene carrying Venus of Willendorf replica, Cyndie carrying chalice, Danaan carrying broadsword, leading a line of Pagans into the henge. All sing:

We come, we come, with the rising of the sun,
To the East of East where morning lies.
And we bring the sun with us
On the wings of the wind,
Oh rise, my spirit, rise.

                    (—Frodo Okulam)

The Elements are invoked. A reading from the Egyptian Book of Apep is recited. Lila invokes the Moon Goddess:

O moon, O lovely one of a thousand names,
As you approach the moment of meeting
We watch, and wait, and honor you.
As you approach your moment of fullness,
May we realize, male and female,

The power of you,
And the power of the feminine within us.
May your blessing be upon all of us.

Selene Kumin appears as Moon Goddess in long grey velvet cape, dances while all sing:

She is bountiful, She is beautiful,
She loves her children,
Her daughters and sons.
She won't forget us,
She speaks within us,
Open your heart, let her come.

                    (—Susan Arrow)

Tom Williams invokes the Sun God:

We've come to the edge of morning,
Cold and lonely, and we wait.
We call the Sun – Oh light of night!
We call the Sun God, bright.
Your face is piercing brightness
And your heart the soul of flame.
We call you Ra and Bellenos,

You go beyond the name.
Oh hark to your children calling!
Rise up shining, banish night!
Now hear the solar lion's roar
And see – now comes his light.

*Danaan appears as Sun God in black robe
with embroidered sun on back. Moon Goddess covers Sun God with robe. Sun God
takes off black sun robe and emerges in shiny
golden robe. All sing:*

May the longtime sun shine upon you
All love surround you
And the pure love within you
Guide your way on.
                    (—Incredible String Band)

*Morning Glory leads her Prayer for Heal-
ing of the Earth:*

From the flesh of this planet we grew,
    She is our Mother;
    Let Her be Healed.
    People and Trees
    Dolphins and Bees
We are the children of Earth
    Let the Earth be Healed.
We are the cause and we are the effect
    For good or for ill
Our prayers create Reality…so:
    Let the soil be unpoisoned,
    Let the winds blow fresh,
    Let the waters flow clear,
    Let the fires burn clean,
Let the Earth be Healed!
    However it must happen…
        …Let it Be.

*Isaac sings David Geller's "Now Do We with
Songs and Rejoicing"; Morning Glory re-
cites Oothoon's "Evocation of the Goddess."
Other songs are sung: "Will Ye Not Come
Back Again?" "Turn to the Sun," and "Here
Comes the Sun." To focus the eclipse energy
on endangered species, the following poems
were chanted (written by Isaac; Anodea and
Morning Glory changed theirs slightly).*

Otter chants:
    Children of the sea
    Whale and dolphin free
    Friendly manatee
    White fur seal baby

All repeat several times.

Morning Glory chants:
    Children of the land
    Oak and redwood grand
    Wolf & tiger proud
    Raise your voices loud
All repeat several times.

Anodea chants:
    Children of the sky
    May you forever fly
    Eagle, crane & condor
    May your spirits always wander
All repeat several times.

Isaac chants:
    Children of the sea
    May you live strong and free
    Children of the land
    We join you in your stand.
    Children of the sky
    Listen to our cry:

All chant several times:
    Sea and Land and Sky
    We will not let you die!
    Sky and Land and Sea
    You shall all be free!

All chant:
    Rain, Rain, go away,
    Come again some other day!
    Clouds, Clouds, go away,
    Come again some other day!

Morning Glory leads her Eclipse Litany:

Magickal Mirror of Darkness,
Golden Creator of Light,
Your embrace for a moment surrounds us;
We share in your perfect delight, delight;
    We share in your perfect delight.

Magickal Mirror of Darkness,
Golden Creator of Light,
Your embrace for a moment surrounds us;
In shadow we search of insight, insight;
    In shadow we search for insight.

All chant Otter's words:
    The Prophecies will come
    When Shadow mates with Sun.

*Circle is dissolved and everyone finds a place
to view the spectacle.*

2. Blessings, Dedications, & Consecrations

Introduction
By Oberon Zell-Ravenheart

Some of the most important rituals to be conducted by one or a few people are *blessings, dedications,* and *consecrations.* Blessings are generally very simple, and often done without the casting of formal Circles—though they may always be performed as the "working" in any rite. A *blessing* is simply the ritual bestowing of benevolent wishes on a person, creature, group, project, place, thing, or enterprise. Blessings can be done to welcome people, and to send them on their way. We bless people when they sneeze or hiccup. And modern Witches, Wizards, and many other magickal people commonly conclude their rituals, letters, and partings with the ritual phrase, *"Blessed Be!"* Indeed, blessings can be for any purpose imaginable!

When something is being created for a specific purpose, when something old is being given a new use, when a space is being occupied by new tenants, a new building is being opened for business, or any time something is being devoted for a new goal or purpose, it is appropriate to have a ceremony of *dedication,* which is a special kind of blessing. Dedication ceremonies can be quite formal and elaborate—as in the dedication of a public building or the office of a newly-elected politician. Every new venture—moving into a new home, establishing a business, opening an office, founding an enterprise, beginning a major project—is a perfect opportunity for a ritual of dedication and blessing.

Consecration is a type of blessing more commonly used for special objects, particularly magickal tools. This is done when a hand-made tool is completed and ready to be used, and when a new or used tool is purchased or found. A ritual of consecration is usually done just by one person—the proud creator or owner of the item to be consecrated. It may include invoking Spirit or deities as witness, and even applications of the Elements—such as dipping the object into a cup of Water and a bowl of salt (Earth), and passing it through a candle (Fire) and incense smoke (Air). Consecrations may be included within larger ritual Circles, but are more often done without any such formalities.

I. Blessings

Self-Blessings
This most basic and widely-used blessing was created in 1970 by Ed Fitch, for inclusion in Susan Roberts' 1971 book, *Witches USA.* Over the years, it has been adopted and adapted by many, many people, and has been incorporated in many rituals. While originally designed to be done by an individual standing naked before a full-length mirror, it can also be done for another, just by changing first-person pronouns to second. Here is one version, adapted by Morning Glory:

Ingredients: salt, wine or juice, water, candle. Sprinkle the salt on the ground and stand on it. Light the candle. Mix the water and wine together. Meditate on the reason for performing the self-blessing. Say:
Bless me, Mother for I am thy child.
Anoint eyes with water/wine mixture. Say:
Blessed be my eyes, that I may see thy beauty in the world around me.
Anoint nose. Say:
Blessed be my nostrils, that I may breathe thy sacred essence.
Anoint ears. Say:
Blessed be my ears, that I may hear thy words of wisdom.
Anoint mouth. Say:
Blessed be my mouth, that I may speak thy holy names.
Anoint breast. Say:
Blessed be my heart, that I may be true

and faithful in thy service.

Anoint arms. Say:

Blessed be my arms, that I may be strong and skillful in thy work.

Anoint genitals. Say:

Blessed be my loins, givers and receivers of pleasure.

(*Alternate for a woman:* Blessed be my womb, which brings forth the life of humanity as thou hast brought forth all creation.)

Anoint knees. Say:

Blessed be my knees, that I may kneel at thy holy altar.

Anoint feet. Say:

Blessed be my feet, that I may walk in thy ways to the end of my days.

Meditate for a little while before leaving.

Goddess in the Mirror/Sexy Witch Anointing Ritual
By LaSara FireFox

I. Coming Present to Sacred Space

Cast Circle as you will, or focus on breath and recognize sacred space, which exists everywhere. It is only our attention that wanders.

II. Devotion/Invocation:

Oh, She of a Thousand Names,
Ishtar, Babalon, Isis, Namaah, Inanna, Aphrodite
Be with us now, and bless this rite with your lush and bountiful gifts.
Sacred Lover, Sacred Mother, Sacred Whore
Keeper of time and bringer of seasons,
Keeper of rites and bringer of pleasures,
May we see ourselves in you. May we see you in ourselves
More love, more joy, more delicious and delightful worship
Our senses are yours. Our joy is yours. Our love is yours.

III. Dedication

I consecrate these works to the unfolding of self-awareness.
May this act serve me, and may it serve all beings through the revelation of awareness. May my increasing awareness and presence serve to bring awareness of presence to all beings everywhere throughout space and time. So it is. May this rite be dedicated to a renewal of the relationship of humanity with her senses. May we all become more aware of feeling, and thereby, of being. May compassion lead to love, and may love lead to the enlightenment of all.

IV. Sacred Play

All ritual participants couple up, triple up, or otherwise group together, and feed one another, massage one another, kiss, love, feel, touch, guide, and play with one another.

V: God/dess in the Mirror

Priest/ess stands by the mirror, and each participant comes towards the mirror. Priest/ess anoints each, or the anointing can spread: as each is anointed, they may anoint. The person performing the anointing says the following, or whatever they are moved to say, as they anoint:

1. Wet finger and anoint the feet. Say: *"Blessed are your feet that walk the Sacred Path."*
2. Wet finger and anoint the knees. Say: *"Blessed are your knees which touch the Earth in humility and gratitude."*
3. Wet finger and anoint the pubis or the genitals (if you are intimate enough with the initiate). Say: *"Blessed is your sex, which brings the gifts of pleasure and of creation."*
4. Wet finger and anoint the womb. Say: *"Blessed is your womb, seat of life."*
5. Wet finger and anoint the solar plexus (stomach region). Say: *"Blessed is your power and presence."*

6. Wet finger and anoint the heart chakra (sternum). Say: *"Blessed is your heart which loves with strength and beauty."*

7. Wet finger and anoint the throat. Say: *"Blessed is your voice which says what must be heard."*

8. Wet finger and anoint the lips. Say: *"Blessed are your lips which speak the words of power."*

9. Wet finger and anoint the third eye (center of forehead, just above the brow line). Say: *"Blessed be your vision which sees the way things are, and the way things may be."*

10. Wet finger and anoint the crown (top of the head). Say: *"Blessed be your crown, where you and all of creation are one."*

11. Step back and say: *"Blessed are you, and blessed is your presence on the Earth. Blessed is your body, your soul, and your spirit. Blessed is the world that you create, and blessed your path in that world."*

VI. As each stands in front of the mirror, all participants offer compliments and worship to the God/dess in the mirror.

VII. After each has had his/her turn, priest/ess says:
This magick is your magick. Steward it as you will. Use it wisely and playfully, with joy for all. When you are ready to let this magick find grounding, do so. But remember that we are always in sacred space. It is our attention that wanders. All space is sacred space, and every moment a sacred opportunity to experience our connection with the Divine.

Empress Blessing Spell
By Jessica Rabbit

This blessing spell calls on the Lady to help your goals bloom to their fullest. Place a 7-day candle on your altar in the color of whatever you wish to manifest: green for money, pink for love, blue for inner peace, brown for security in the home, yellow for joy, etc. In front of the candle, place the Empress tarot card, or else a Queen of Hearts from a regular deck of cards. Sprinkle a combination of meadowsweet, clover, and rose petals around the arrangement. On a slip of paper write the following incantation and place it under the candle. Light the candle and repeat the incantation for at least three rounds each day for seven days leading up to the full moon.

The Universe is blessing me
Abundantly
Every day in every way
With good toward all and harm to none
So mote it be!

Chant this invocation three times each day for the duration of the candle. On the day of the full moon, gather the herbs and strew them outside your front door. When the candle burns out, recycle the glass jar and keep the Empress card someplace where you will pass her each day until you receive what you asked for. Then, either return her to your deck permanently, or save her for your summer altar. Recycle any supplies or items that you can, and keep the incantation in your wallet or purse until that which you desire has appeared.

137. The Great Blessing

I offer my thanks to the Mother of All,
I offer my thanks to the Gods, Dead and Spirits.
May the Three Sacred Kins
Bring joy to all beings, and renew the ancient wisdom.
To the Fire, Well and Tree I offer my thanks.
May Wisdom, Love and Power
Kindle in all beings and renew the ancient wisdom.
To the Earth, Sea and Sky I offer my thanks.
May the ancient wisdom be renewed, and may all beings
Know peace, joy and happiness
In all the worlds.
So be it.

—Ian Corrigan

138. Daily Affirmations

(Stand before your mirror as you say these affirmations)

I am a divine and beautiful being.
I choose to live each moment with
appreciation and complete acceptance
of my own divinity and beauty.
I choose to appreciate and accept the
beauty in all beings and the perfect
divinity in each moment.
I open my heart to the possibility of love and
benefit from every being and each moment.
I purge myself of all doubt, negativity,
judgmental tendencies, guilt, panic,
and fearful thinking.
I always seek that which I need to grow, to bud,
to bloom, to blossom, to fruit, to bear seed.
I dare to draw into myself the positive
manifestation of each trial and difficulty, the rightness of every lesson.
I breathe deeply and savor the love and
benefit that surrounds and embraces
my life as I live it each moment.
I forgive myself with each breath I take and
renew my transformative intentions
with every beat of my heart.
I glory in the goodness and rightness of all
that I encounter and all that I am.
I am a divine and beautiful being.
                                    —*Donna Henes*

139. Ancient Scottish Blessing

Bless ourselves and our children,
Bless every one who shall come from our loins,
Bless him whose name we bear,
Bless her from whose womb we came.

Every holiness, blessing and power,
Be yielded to us every time and every hour,
In the name of the Holy Threefold above,
Maiden, Mother, and Crone eternal.

Be the Foundations of Earth to shield us
downward,
Be the Lights of Heaven to shield us upward,
Be the Breath of Spirit to shield us outward,
Be the Waters of Life to shield us inward.

Accepting our sacred blessing from us,
Accepting our sacred blessing from us.
                        —*Traditional; adapted by Oberon*

140. The Morning Song

Blessèd is this morning,
Washed awake with dew and light.
Blessèd is this day, all that lives—lives true!
Blessèd are the gods in their lands—
Blessèd are the men.
Blessèd are all things that breathe,
Or sleep no more!
Blessèd is this day!
Goddess threefold Goddess!
Blessèd is this day!
                                    —*Mark Will, 1974*

141. A Blessing of Spirit

(to be spoken to the one being blessed by a priestess, speaking for the Goddess)

I will always love you.
I guarantee that nothing will ever happen to
cause me to stop loving you.
I love you for who you are, not what you
do or don't do.
I accept you for who you are at this moment, and
I welcome the changes your growth brings.
I accept the person you have been and I
accept the person you will be—
unconditionally.
I will protect you and keep you safe;
No harm will come to you because it would
have to come through me
And I am powerful enough to keep you safe.
I will meet all of your needs that I can,
And I will support you meeting your needs
the way you see fit.
I am neither jealous nor possessive, but I
am faithful.
I love you. I am devoted to you.
I am always here for you; whenever you think of
me or look for me or call me, I am with you.
I always have enough time and energy and
attention for you.
Turn toward me and I will envelop you in my
light and my wings will comfort you
And soothe your fear and your pain.
I am your shield and your strength,
Your shade-tree in the summer and your
campfire at night,
Your food, water and air.
I am all around you always, in all ways.
                                —*Abbi Spinner McBride*

142. A Valentine Blessing for Love

May you be loved well and truly
May your spirit be held yet not too tightly
May your soul be appreciated in its
    darkness and light
May you be told the truth with love and
    compassion
May your body be worshipped and
    pleasured and adored
May your feelings be honored and given
    space to breathe
May the love you give be received ever more fully
May your dreams be listened to and encouraged
May you be given promises which are kept
May you be inspired to grow and laugh and
    open your heart—again
May love grow within you, through you
    and around you
May you be loved well and truly!
    —*Francesca Gentille, February 1999*

143. Blessing of the Meal

Holy Mother Earth, Yours is the power
To grow, to destroy, to give birth.
We conjure You now by seed and by shoot,
By flower and fruit, by light and by love,
From below and above, in Your ancient names:
Koré, Demeter, Persephoné.
Grant us the blessings of Your body;
Thank you for the blessings of Your body!
    —*Moonrose*

144. Grace

Thanks and blessing be
To the Sun and the Earth
For this bread and this wine, this fruit,
This meat, this salt, this food;
Thanks be and blessing to them
Who prepare it, who serve it;
Thanks and blessing to them who share it
And also the absent and the dead.
Thanks and blessing to them who bring it
May they not want;
To them who plant and tend it,
Harvest and gather it
May they not want;
Thanks and blessing to them who work
And blessing to them who cannot;
May they not want—

For their hunger sours the wine
And robs the taste from the salt.
Thanks be for the sustenance and strength
For our dance and the work of justice, of peace.
    —*Rafael Jesús González, 2002*

145. Dream Blessing

Dreams to you and dreams so fine
Find the gates inside your mind
Open up and open wide
As you journey deep inside
And love the safety, bliss and blooms
In your mind of many rooms
Know you're loved and dream so well
And that's all I've got to tell!
    —*Jack Phoenix, 2/27/04*

146. Sleep Blessing from the Goddess

Sleep now, beloved daughter of Mine.
Rest your mind and let Me heal your body.
Come to Me and I will give you strength and
    courage.
When My eye shines on you, look in, and be
    healed by Light.
Listen for My voice in your dreams, beloved.
I love you. I bless you. You are safe and well.
Good night, dear heart.
    —*Abigail Spinner McBride, 2002*

147. 'Puter Blessing

Blessings on this fine machine,
May its data all be clean.
Let the files stay where they're put,
Away from disk drives keep all soot.
From its screen shall come no whines,
Let in no spikes on power lines.
As Oaks were sacred to the Druids,
Let not the keyboard suffer fluids.
Disk Full shall be no more than rarity,
The memory shall not miss its parity.
From the modem shall come wonders,
Without line noise making blunders.
May it never catch a virus,
And all its software stay desirous.
Oh let the printer never jam,
And turn my output into spam.
I ask of Eris, Noble Queen,
Keep Murphy far from this machine!
    —*Author unknown*

II. Dedications

Congressional Office Dedication Ritual
By Diane Darling

The Green Party of California's gubernatorial candidate was former U.S. Congressman Dan Hamburg. He and his wife live in Ukiah. Our kids went to school together and I've worked on some of Dan's other political campaigns, including defeating a recall vote which had been incited against Dan when he was a county supervisor, for being too "green" for the liking of local developers and law-and-order types. After that he was elected to Congress as a Democrat.

In 1993, when he first opened his congressional office in Ukiah, Dan and his staff invited Sister Jane, the local activist nun, and me to bless the place and the work they would be doing there. I accepted gladly and contemplated what this meant. For me, it meant coming out to the entire liberal community of Mendocino County as a Pagan priestess. And it meant Dan recognized us Pagans as important constituents. Dan and his staff valued the blessings of our gods sufficiently to request a public rite, in front of the mayor, the county supervisors, and everyone!

On the appointed day, I arrived with Oberon, with votive figures of Athena and Gaia, and a special elixir made of spring water, *eau de vie*, powdered unicorn horn, and *yohimbe*. I set up a small altar on Dan's desk and waited nervously while a wide assortment of folks arrived to hobnob. It was a very inclusive crowd: silver-buckle cowboys, long-haired attorneys, most of the local liberals and activists, ranchers, grape growers, pot growers, winemakers, and therapists. And there was me in my blazing tie-dye, Oberon with his old-growth hair, and Dan in a suit.

Dan said a few words about his new job in D.C., and then invited Sister Jane to say a prayer. To my great astonishment, she began with *"Heavenly Mother, Heavenly Father…"* The Goddess was invoked before the Pagan stuff ever began! Then I introduced myself as a lay priestess from the Church of All Worlds, a green, Earth-centered religion. I explained that, as polytheists, we regarded our gods as specialists, and for this occasion I would invoke Athena, matron of justice and sovereignty, in whose name we would banish all ill and bless this space. I showed them the little statues of Athena and Gaia, and then began:

> Hail Athene, wise warrioress
> Loyal protectress of hearth and sovereign state,
> Sea-washed daughter of Metis and Olympos' king.
> Nike stands on Your right hand
> Her victory laurels offered up.
> We invite you to bless this office and its staff
> In the names of Freedom, Justice and Wise Council,
> In the name of the people served
> Through the office of our champion in Congress,
> Dan Hamburg.

With an owl feather, turning widdershins:

> First banish doubt — let our work be just and compassionate
> Next banish fear — for this work is right and our time is now
> Banished be the small view — for thousands of hearts are with us
> Lastly banish weary despair — for Earth's heroes are massing
> In our lifetimes the Sun rises on a new, green era.

Taking up a blooming laurel twig and the elixir, asperging the celebrants and especially the congressman, turning deosil:

> Let the Sun shine here in every corner, in every heart
> Let the sweet Winds bring change, laughter, lively speech and Motherwit.
> Let the Waters of Life spring forth to cleanse and quicken and refresh

And let the Will of the People and the work done here
Be rooted in the Earth
In the name of Gaia, we will prevail.

Then we invoked Gaia, whom I identified as the Great Mother and First cause, the sine qua non, for which I used the lovely Homeric Hymn, with all its images of bountiful harvests, fine children, heavy-laden vineyards, and noble rulers.

Taking up a chalice of spring water, I explained water sharing and offered water to Dan, saying: *Water shared is Life shared...never thirst!* Smiling and misty-eyed, he drank.

I thanked Athena that she might depart, but since Gaia is always with us, the very ground is her bosom, the wind her breath, the waters her blood, Gaia's votive figure and her presence would remain here always. Blessing Dan again, I concluded the rite.

I realized as I got into my priestess groove that *they were all with me*, paying close attention, respectful, and smiling. Later, during the munching and wine tasting part of the celebration, several very disparate people thanked me and remarked on how moved and uplifted they felt during my ritual. For months afterward, every now and then I would encounter someone who would stop me right there in the Safeway or at the courthouse to tell me similar things. It was most gratifying.

I left a non-denominational altar, with Gaia, in the center of the offices. I encouraged people to put a token of themselves and their gods on the altar. Today, below a poster of Dan giving the peace/victory sign (just before he went to get arrested at a Headwaters rally) is a relief globe of Mother Earth. Under her is a round mirror, placed so that a person standing in front of the planet can see his or her own face. Objects representing the four Elements are arrayed around, as well as a pot of honey for sweetness and a lump of sugalite for sanity.

It is a formidable act to vote from the heart *for* someone or something good, rather than succumbing to fear and voting *against* the scarier of the "Tweedle-dum and Tweedle-dee" mainstream candidates. Pagans and political and environmental activists who see themselves as champions of the Earth face this choice at every election, and other choices like it every day. We walk our talk by recycling, simple living, personal health and social hygiene, kindness and authenticity. In our Magick Circles, we ask our gods in our prayers and invocations to help us manifest a green and living future for our children and our future incarnations. We vote with our magickal and mundane energy for the health of our Mother and her biosphere, our home. We can vote with our ballots for a healthy, fully representative political future. We can make the mundane act of going to the polls a journey of Earth magic, a sacred act of speaking out for what is good. Politically, it's the least we can do.

The Druid on the battlefield manifests today as the Pagan in the campaign office, at the rally, and on the front lines of civil disobedience actions. Most modern political combat takes place in offices, in the media, at rallies, and over the phone. We can do that and we can do more and, if we're really good, Momma will reward us with cheesecake and victory.

148. City Council Invocation
By Bryan Lankford, Interfaith Director, Betwixt & Between
Delivered in Texas before the Dallas City Council on Wednesday, October 4, 2000

Mother Goddess, Father God: we thank you for life and the world we share.
We ask that you bless this council and the mayor with the wisdom to lead this city into our
*   tomorrows, that it may flourish in harmony and prosperity.*
We ask this city be transformed with the harmony and balance that faith in a greater power brings.
Just as the ancient alchemists felt the elements of life were Air, Fire, Water, and Earth, the
*   elements of spiritual alchemy are Honesty, Love, Compassion, and Faith.*
We pray that our words and deeds be open and honest, without malice or deceit, so others will always
*   be able to trust our actions, believe our words, and see that our motivations are pure.*

For honesty breeds trust, and without trust all our actions are suspect.
May our souls be lit with the light of love which shines into the dark corners of our being, removing the darkness of hatred, anger and prejudice, so no one ever need fear for their safety or be made to feel shame for their race, religion or lifestyle.
For where love shines, darkness cannot find hold.
May we show compassion for those whose lives are not as easy as our own.
Let our hearts see that the spirit inside each of us comes from the same divine source and is, therefore, deserving of dignity and respect no matter what the body's present condition.
For only with self-respect can one find the strength to improve their condition.
We pray that our lives are grounded in faith because faith in something greater than ourselves gives us the power to aspire to be more than we are, reaching beyond our human limitations to propel the human spirit to new levels.
Faith brings us the comfort of divine planning, letting us understand all that happens, happens for a reason, a purpose which we, from our limited perspective, may have trouble seeing. But the Divine sees the outcome of every event and knows why each event must occur.
We pray for Honesty, Love, Compassion, and Faith, that our spirits be transformed into golden spirits, shining with the light of the Divine.
We ask this of deity in whatever form each of us perceives it.
So may it be.

III. Consecrations

Cleansing Your Space (an Elemental Consecration)

By Moonwriter

This ritual can be a part of seasonal cleaning, such as spring cleaning, or can be done anytime a place needs to be "sweetened." Prepare by washing (bathing or showering, if possible, with a dab of rosemary oil added for auric purification) and putting on clean clothes or magickal garb. Watches and jewelry should be removed, but magickal jewelry may be added.

Arrange a simple altar in in the room, representing the four Directions and the Elements. On the altar, place a sprig of protective herbs, tied with a ribbon or piece of yarn in a meaningful color correspondence (your choice). (Some common plants and herbs that are very good for removing—and preventing—negative energy are: aloe, anise, barley, basil, bay leaf, cactus, carnation, cedar, chamomile, cinnamon, clove, cumin, curry, dill, dragon's blood, eucalyptus, fennel, fern, flax, frankincense, garlic, ginseng, ivy, lavender, myrrh, onion, parsley, pepper, peppermint, rosemary, sage, thyme, and violet.) Begin by spending a few moments at the altar, centering and connecting with the center of the home. Using a broom (besom), create a circle by sweeping deosil around the room, starting and ending in the North. At the altar, combine water and salt in a chalice or ritual bowl. Walk deosil around the room, starting at the North; sprinkle droplets of the salt water (symbolizing the Elements Water and Earth) throughout the room.

At the altar, ignite a smudge stick or a small pile of dried herbs in a thurible or other fireproof container. Blow out the flame and, starting at the North, walk deosil around the room and waft the smoke (symbolizing the Elements Fire and Air) throughout the room with your fingers or a feather.

Place the sprig of herbs above the door to the room. You may also wish to leave your besom or broom standing just inside the door.

At the altar again, close your eyes and breathe slowly, connecting with the home's center. Do this for as long as you wish. Offer a simple blessing of thanks.

Sweep the circle closed (widdershins).

Take the herbal sprig from the altar and mount it above the door as a protective amulet.

Consecrations of Magickal Tools
By Oberon

In working magick, magicians, Witches, and Wizards summon the subtle forces of the Elements and their guardian spirits, the Elementals. We consecrate our tools and ritual objects with the Elements by touching or passing them through each substance—salt, soil, or crystals for Earth; a cup of Water; the smoke of burning incense for Air; and a candle flame for Fire. When a Magick Circle is cast, each Element or its symbol is placed at the corresponding Quarter, and its guardian spirit is invoked.

If you have purchased or made a set of magickal tools, you should consecrate them for use in something like the following manner:

Wand

The wand is a phallic symbol, associated with divine wisdom. As an Elemental tool, it represents the Element of either Air or Fire. To a magician, his wand is an extension of himself—a measure of his ability, wisdom, and imagination. Personalized in size, shape, and design, this tool is valued above all others. In ritual, the wand serves to unite our body, mind, and soul with that of universal consciousness to bring into manifestation our magickal desires.

To consecrate your wand for magickal use, burn some Mercurial incense, such as cinnamon. Pass your wand through the smoke, saying:

I consecrate thee, Rod of Skill
To focalize my Truest Will.
May my power flow through thee,
As I do will, so mote it be!

When you are finished, wrap it in linen or silk.

Chalice

The magickal cup, or chalice, represents the ancient cauldron of Cerridwen, which granted poetic inspiration, rebirth, and immortality. The Holy Grail of the legends of King Arthur is another version of the chalice. Containing the mysteries of life and death, the cauldron, bowl, or cup symbolizes the womb of the Goddess from which all life comes forth. The chalice, therefore, is seen as female in nature (as the wand is male), and the water that it contains is the sacred Elemental Water of life. As the wand is the tool of the mind or intellect, the chalice is the tool of the emotions—especially love.

To consecrate your chalice, wait until the moon is almost full. It is also best to do this on a Monday—the day of the moon. Mix up some of the following herbs in a bowl of salt water: basil, fennel, hyssop, lavender, mint, rosemary, sage, valerian, and/or verbena. For a lunar incense, sprinkle some lavender, jasmine, white rose, honeysuckle, and/or mugwort on a burning charcoal block. If you'd rather consecrate your chalice to Venus (for love), do it on Friday and use an incense made of sandalwood, orris root, rose, and/or rosemary. Sprinkle your cup with the herb "tea," then pass it through the smoking incense, visualizing a blue purifying light surrounding it and chanting:

By Water and Fire be purified
No adverse will within thee hide.
Be clear in service unto me;
As I do will, so mote it be!

Panticle

The *panticle paten* is a disc engraved with a five-pointed star, or *pentagram*. It represents the forces of nature and physical manifestation. The pentagram on it represents the Element of Earth and forms a shield of protection to guard you from hostile forces. In ritual the panticle will provide you with the ability to ground and center your intentions. The panticle may be made of stone, clay, wood, or metal. Consecrate it during the waxing moon by sprinkling salted water over it, and passing it through the smoke of burning incense compounded of rosemary, cedar, sandalwood, pine resin, and lavender oil.

An Earthly Star before me rests
A vessel strong to manifest.
All things that I would conjure here,
Or banish forth the things I fear.
So mote it be!

Athamé

The *athamé*, or magickal dagger, represents power, action, and domination. The first iron blades were made from meteoric nickel-iron—practically the same as stainless steel—and were rightly considered to be the thunderbolts of the gods. Thus, the athamé symbolizes the Element of Fire. Here is the quintessence of masculinity, corresponding to the positive and creative forces of nature. Such magickal blades have been used in every culture throughout the world over the past 3,500 years.

On a Tuesday (the day of Mars) when the moon is waning, compound an incense of Martial herbs, such as dragon's blood resin, powdered rue, ground peppercorns, ginger, and sulfur. Prick your finger or the heel of your hand with the point of your blade, and mix in a few drops of your own blood. Set half of this mixture aside, and burn the rest in your thurible (see page 32). Purify the blade by sprinkling it with distilled water from your chalice, dry it off, and then pass it through the incense smoke.

Now take the remainder of your Martial herb compound and stir it into your chalice. Heat the blade of your athamé on the thurible coals until it gets as hot as possible. When it is good and hot, plunge it into the mixture in the chalice, chanting these words:

Blade of steel I conjure thee
To ban such things as named by me.
Cut cleanly through adversity,
As I do will, so mote it be!

Do this three times to temper the steel, and visualize the blade glowing with power after each immersion.

In ancient times, such blades were always magnetized, giving them a truly magickal power. To magnetize your athamé, stroke the blade repeatedly with a lodestone or bar magnet. Hold your athamé in your dominant hand, the magnet in your other, and beginning at the handle end, draw the magnet down the whole length of the blade to the very point. Do this over and over again for at least five minutes, always stroking in the same direction, and chant these words at every stroke:

Blade of steel I conjure thee
Attract such things as named by me.
Draw tight the circle 'round the tree,
As I do will, so mote it be!

After you have finished, wrap your athamé in linen or silk, declaring: *"So mote it be!"*

Thurible or Censer

The *thurible* or *censer* is a container in which incense is safely burned to represent the Element of Air. It can be anything from a simple incense burner or chafing dish, to an ornate swinging brass censer on a chain. In magickal terminology, a thurible is an open dish, usually set upon three legs, while a censer has a cover with little holes in it to let the smoke out. Censers are often fitted out with chains so they can be hung or swung, like those used in the Catholic Church. Such censers are almost always made of brass.

When the moon is waxing, consecrate your thurible by burning a little dragon's blood incense in it, saying *"Blessed be thou Censer of Air."*

3. Rituals for Protection & Healing

I. Protection Spells & Rituals
By Oberon Zell-Ravenheart

When doing defensive spells against psychic attacks, set them to send any negative energy right back to where it came from. The best kinds of protection and defense magick are mirrored wards and shields. These involve throwing up a protective field around yourself and your space, which will repel unwanted energies. The perfect metaphor is the energy fields/shields used to protect the Starship Enterprise from phaser fire and photon torpedoes.

"Harden" the outer shell of your auric field into a psychic shield. Stand strong, feet apart, and close your eyes. Center yourself with a *grounding* (see pages 36-39). Then, with palms flattened and fingers spread wide, move your hands up, down, and all around your body at arm's length, while visualizing that you are shaping and pressing against the inside of a Teflon-coated shell all around yourself.

Now open your eyes and expand that shield around your entire room, apartment, or house, strengthening it into an impenetrable shell that is reflectively mirrored on the outside. Use visualization as well as an actual hand-held round mirror as you circle around each room, holding your hands up as if against an invisible wall. That's a shield.

Tape small mirrors to the insides of your windows, reflecting side out. If you can't use mirrors, make balls of aluminum foil and leave them on your window sills. A small box, completely lined with aluminum foil (shiny side in), with your picture and a lock of your hair in the box, makes for an inexpensive mirror-box. Cover the outside with foil as well, shiny side out.

In addition, hang fresh garlic cloves around your home, and place cut halves of onions on the windowsills. When they no longer make your eyes water, slice off another section to keep the surface fresh. A small saucer of vinegar (which can hold an onion half) can be placed somewhere out of sight and still absorb negativity, replacing it as often as necessary.

> NOTE: Don't just throw spell items that are done into the trash! Take your garlic to a crossroads after it's done its work (Hekate will just love it!).

Finally, drive a few large iron nails into the ground in front of each doorway into your house, and, if you can get one, hang a horseshoe or hex sign over the door.

Witch Bottle

"Witch bottles" were very popular in England in the 17th–8th centuries to create protective fields around houses and everything within them. Think of it as a psychic field generator throwing up a repulsion barrier that no enemies may cross. To make one, take a large glass jar with a screw-on lid, and fill it with sharp objects: pins, nails, tacks, broken glass (*especially shards of a broken mirror!*), thorns, urine, salt, etc. Add leaves of rosemary, basil, and bay. Screw the lid tight, and seal it with melted wax from a black candle, saying:

> Witches' Bottle, herbs and charms,
> Banish evil, ward off harm.
> Protect me from all enemies
> As my will, so mote it be!
> (—Gerina Dunwich)

Hide the bottle in the back of the cupboard under the kitchen sink, or bury it at the farthest corner of your property when the moon is waning. A Witch bottle protects its owner from harm, and makes a great housewarming gift!

Mirror Spell Ritual

Here is a classic protective mirror spell that Morning Glory and I have been using, with appropriate variations, for decades. We have found it to be quite effective.

I recommend creating your protective Circle not with a blade, but with a hand-held round mirror. One with a handle would be ideal for this. Use lipstick or a dry-erase marker to draw a protective pentagram (one point up) upon the face of the mirror. You can capture moonlight in your mirror at night if you do the spell as soon as the moon has risen. If you cannot see the moon from any of your windows, take the mirror outside and catch moonlight reflected in it to charge it. Do this by holding the mirror in such a way that you can see the moon in it, and chant:

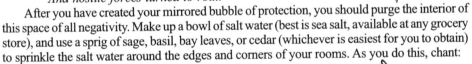

> *Silv'ry Moon, reflected light,*
> *Flow into my mirror bright.*
> *In the darkness of the night,*
> *Protection grant by magick's might.*

Face the mirror outward and walk around a Circle to encompass your space, as you visualize a reflective circle forming around that space. It's best if you can walk around the outside of your entire building, but if you only want to protect your own apartment, walk around the inside of each room, facing the mirror towards the outside walls. With palms flattened and fingers spread wide, move your hands up, down, and all around your body at arm's length, while visualizing that you are shaping and pressing against the inside of a "Teflon-coated" shell all around your space. Expand the reflective Circle upwards and downwards in your visualization until it becomes a mirrored band, and finally a sphere or bubble, completely surrounding your entire apartment and strengthening it into an impenetrable shell, reflecting and deflecting all negative energy back to its source.

As you create your protective Circle, chant:

> *I cast the Circle round about,*
> *A world within, a world without.*
> *Let all within the aerie wheel*
> *Bear witness to the mystic seal.*
> *Let all without be turned about*
> *And hostile forces turned to rout.*

After you have created your mirrored bubble of protection, you should purge the interior of this space of all negativity. Make up a bowl of salt water (best is sea salt, available at any grocery store), and use a sprig of sage, basil, bay leaves, or cedar (whichever is easiest for you to obtain) to sprinkle the salt water around the edges and corners of your rooms. As you do this, chant:

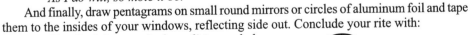

> *Water and salt, where you are cast,*
> *No spell or adverse purpose last*
> *That is not in accord with me.*
> *As I do will, so mote it be!*

And finally, draw pentagrams on small round mirrors or circles of aluminum foil and tape them to the insides of your windows, reflecting side out. Conclude your rite with:

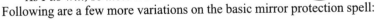

> *The Circle's cast; the bound'ries sealed.*
> *All ills at last may now be healed.*
> *By all the might of Moon and Sea,*
> *As I do will, so mote it be!*

Following are a few more variations on the basic mirror protection spell:

Mirror Shield Charm
By Rev. Ahriana Platten

Here is a method I use for creating a "mirrored wall" as a shield for you or your home. Remember that this energy must be worked from a place of love and universal connection, and that there should be no negativity of your own attached to it. The mirrored wall is a sphere that surrounds you and your home—and, once set in place, will reflect only what is sent to you back to the originator. This is in line with the "harm none" lifestyle most of us lead.

1. Select a mirror, preferably small and round, with flat edges.
2. Wash it in mugwort (an herb that clears any pre-existing energy). Mix the mugwort with water, strain, and use the water to bathe the mirror.
3. Charge the mirror under the full moon. Place it outside at dark and take it in before dawn. This creates a "battery" to hold the mirrored sphere around your home so that you are not the energy source. Recharge as often as you are called to do so. The mirror will call you when it needs more "juice." There is no specific time measurement as it depends on how much "reflecting" the mirror is doing. You cannot over-charge it.
4. Place the mirror flat and facing the ceiling in an area where it will not be disturbed.
5. Visualize a mirrored sphere around you—above, below, and all around. Inhale universal energy as you breathe, and use that energy to expand your sphere when you exhale. Keep expanding it until it surrounds your home or the area you wish to protect. You may also simply keep the sphere around you. Know that any energy sent your way that does not serve you will be returned to the person who sent it your way to begin with.
6. Speak the following charge:

> *No more, no less, do I return*
> *Venom, anger, words that burn.*
> *Nothing enters mirrored wall.*
> *No more, no less, return it all.*
> *By law of three, so mote it be!*

Warding, Blessing, or Protection Ritual
By Katlyn Breene

Purpose: To protect, charge, or bless anything you hold dear, whether that be a person or an object.
Needed: A hand-held mirror, acrylic paint, a candle, and a dimly lit room.

1. Write down your exact intent before you begin.
2. Create sacred space and cast a Circle.
3. Call the gods whom you wish to witness the work and lend their aid to the ritual (your own words, straight from the heart, are probably the best way of doing so).
4. Paint the pentagram (or magick symbol) upon the mirror's face.
5. Light the candle and hold the mirror before it so that the light reflects on the glass. Direct the light onto the person or object that you wish to be protected or blessed and see how the shadow of the pentagram is emblazoned on it.
6. State that the person, place, or thing is now blessed or protected. Not that you *wish* it to be protected, but that it *is* protected. In your mind, it should already be done. Again, your own words here are probably best.
7. Thank the gods for being there and helping with the working and release the Circle. *(NOTE: This can also be done outdoors on a sunny day, reflecting the light of the Sun onto what- or whomever you wish to protect.)*

One Heart Container Spell
By Ellen Evert Hopman

This is a ceremony that I learned from a Hopi elder that he asked be shared with all people.

The heart is the balance point of the body and the central star, and feelings of oneness and love for all creation find their origin there. As a way of affirming and ritualizing this concept, buy or make a round or oval ceramic container, with a hole at the top big enough to put in some soil. Have as many people with good hearts as possible blow their prayers for peace and freedom into the ceramic egg. At the day of each full moon, deposit the "one heart" container at a location that is sacred to you, preferably a mountaintop or the highest point you can reach. Inspire others to do the same. In the meantime, purify yourself as best you can and honor all life. (You can also place a feather in the top of the ceramic egg so that your prayers will waft to the winds.)

149. Invocation of Protection

This is the Day, This is the Hour
Cry aloud the Word of Power
By blazing moon or black midnight
It is my will to seek the light
Be far hence, all things profane
From the portals of this fane
Eleven-fold the right I claim
By the virtue of this name
Faring forth adventurous
By the pathway perilous
Fend me from the fear of fear
By the voice of the chief Seer
Show within the darkest night
The extension of the light
Great Ones who have gone before
Speak the blessing evermore
here between two worlds am I
Child of the earth and sky
Deeply do I dare assay
One step on the mystic way
Aid me from the Realms above
Powers of life and light and love.
—*Author unknown*

Protection Against Nightmares

Anti-Nightmare Spell
By Oberon

Hang a "dream catcher" or a small wreath of gray feathers over your bed to prevent nightmares and bring restful sleep. A pyramid-shaped crystal under your bed will protect you from psychic attack in your sleep. Hang up a red onion and place mugwort under your pillow to keep away evil spirits. Then set a Magick Circle of protection around your bed each night before you go to sleep, like this:

Stand in the middle of your bed and hold up a small mirror, like a makeup mirror, facing outwards, so that the walls of your bedroom are reflected. Turn around *deosil* (clockwise) in a complete circle, and visualize a circular reflective wall spreading outward from the mirror in your hand, as if you are on the inside of a mirror ballt. As you do this, say:

> *Circles of Light surround my bed;*
> *All fears of night gone from my head.*
> *May peaceful dreams come unto me;*
> *As I do will, so mote it be!*

Another charm against nightmares goes like this:

> *Thou evil thing of darkness born*
> *Of tail and wing and snout and horn,*
> *Fly from me from now till morn!*
> —Valerie Worth

Anti-Nightmare Chant
By Vi (Grey School student)

Whenever I have a rough night, with nightmares and all sorts of "nasties" jumping out at me, I chant a little saying three times or so, and it all goes away. Normally I use this chant at night, or when I'm about to go to sleep and my mind will not allow me to (sometimes my mind gets too active, and scary random images pop in). But this chant can be used for many occasions by just changing a couple of words:

Great God, Great Goddess,
Protect me with your love and light,
Great God, Great Goddess,
Let no nightmares touch me this night.

While I say this, I imagine a white light spreading from my core outwards throughout my entire body, pulsing with love and protection. The chant is very effective! You can also substitute evil and negative energy for nightmares—basically, you could substitute in there anything you wanted to keep away.!

150. The Unicorn Visionary Spell

I am the watcher of the night
Protector of your dream
I am the one to comfort you
Silencing your screams

I am Magick, I am love
I am a wish come true
I'm anything you want me to be
I live inside of you

I am playful, I am bright,
I'm magickal and fair
I am like a ray of sunshine
Blinding rain's discouraging glare

I am the watcher of the night
Soother of your screams
I am the mighty unicorn
Guardian of your dreams
        —Adella DragonStar

151. Dragon Visualization Spell

I am the protector of the weak
With magick in my eyes
A simple breath of fire from me
Would be a big surprise

I will guide your given path
When you need a hand
Just call upon your inner self
To help you understand

When times of life are sad for you
And nothing at all goes right
Call upon me to get you through
I'll help you in the night

My job is to protect and guide
Teaching rights from wrongs
Helping you to harness powers
Steering you all along

I am the mighty dragon
So magickal and true
Whenever you need a dragon
I'll always be there for you.
        —Adella DragonStar

A Witch's Banishing Ritual
By LaSara FireFox

This lesser banishing is a simple and profoundly effective way to clear ritual space, cast the Circle, and call on the guardians of the gates in one fell swoop. It is a beautiful piece of ritual when executed well, and can be modified to encompass your group's orientation.

This modification of the lesser banishing ritual was created by myself and assorted ritual partners over the years. Throughout the instructions, I give you options that will allow you to modify it further, and ideally to make it your own.

A Witch's Banishing
1) Practitioner enters Circle.
2) Other participants follow in a clockwise flow, creating a loose circle around the practitioner.
3) **The Tree of Life,** performed at the center of the Circle:
   a) Practitioner points index and middle fingers of right hand, folding other fingers.
   b) Touching her forehead with the extended fingers, she says, *"I am I."*

   c) Pointing to the sky she says, *"in harmony with the heavens."*

   d) Pointing to the ground she says, *"with the Earth."*

   e) Touching her right shoulder she says, *"with the sun."*

   f) Circling to her left shoulder she says, *"and with the moon."*

   g) Bringing her hands to the prayer position she says, *"for ever and ever."*

   h) Lying left hand palm down on top of right hand, palm up, she says, *"So it is."*

   i) All participants say, *"So it is."*

4) **The Banishing**

   a) For the banishing, you can use whatever words make you feel that the guardian, entity, energy, or intention of a Direction has been made present. This can be done by assigning a goddess to each Quarter (e.g., Aurora in the East, Pele in the South, Oshun in the West, and Kali in the North), or by saying the Direction or an idea that the Direction represents (e.g., inspiration in the East, passion in the South, regeneration in the West, wisdom in the North), or you can use any of the words that have been used by any ceremonialists. There are many, and you can easily find them by doing a web search on the lesser banishing ritual.

   b) Practitioner walks to the eastern edge of the Circle and draws a pentagram in the air with her finger or her wand. In drawing the pentagram, start at the left lower corner. This is basic invoking pentagram.

   c) Starting with her arms at her sides, she slowly raises them, focusing intently on the pentagram she has drawn in front of her, and the word she will use to invoke the Direction.

   d) Once her arms are pointing out from her shoulders parallel to the ground, the practitioner will bring her hands to the sides of her face, with palms facing back.

   e) Next, she steps forward with her right foot, and while forcefully thrusting the energy with her hands towards the direction she is facing, she says the word out loud.

   f) She will then step forward with her left foot meeting the right, and bring the index and middle fingers of her right hand to her lips in the sign of *"shh…"* (This is the sign of the initiate. For more information on the significance of this sign, do your research.)

   g) Next, the practitioner will go to the South, and do the same, using whatever word she has chosen for the South.

   h) The same in the West.

   i) And in the North

   j) And she completes the Circle at the East.

5) **The Center**

   a) Again the practitioner stands in the center of the Circle, facing East. She stands with her arms outstretched at her sides, parallel to the ground.

   b) All participants face East and stand the same way.

   c) All say: *"Before me the rushing wind, behind me the raging sea, to my right hand the leaping fire, and to my left hand the cool and trembling Earth. For about me is the omnipresence of her body, and within me is the consciousness of the continuity of existence."*

6) **The Tree** (the practitioner performs the cross again as in step 3)

7) Practitioner joins Circle, all face the center and sit or stand.

Simple Home Rituals and Ceremonies
By Moonwriter

- While showering, make a ceremony of stepping under the shower and out again four separate times, making a quarter turn each time (for the four Directions). During the first two dips say, "I am being purified. Misfortune is being washed from me." During the second two, say, "I am being purified. I am being washed clean."

o Variation: To envision strengthening, change these statements to, "Weakness is being washed from me" and "I am being robed in strength."

o For even more effect, "dress" the shower stall or bathtub with a few drops of essential
   oil, chosen for a specific purpose, or wash with a specific scented soap. For example,
   frankincense and lavender are excellent for purification, sandalwood for balancing
   emotion, lemon for clearing and enhancing energy, rosemary for stimulating the mental processes, and juniper for protection.

• When putting on lotion, powder, or cosmetics, be mindful and thoughtful of the ways in
  which you are nurturing and blessing yourself.

• When leaving the house in the morning, say, *"Another morning, here for me, greet the
  morning, blessed be."*
Substitute other words for "morning," e.g., sunrise, Tuesday, rainstorm, etc. The point is to
be thankful for the new day and its opportunities.

• If you are a computer user, create folders of seasonal images for display as your computer
  desktop/wallpaper. Change these on the equinoxes and solstices.

• Change things around your home to honor the seasons. For instance, at the Spring Equinox you may wish to change the bed linens, towels, and tablecloths from a "winter set" to
  a "spring set." Changing from dark jewel tone colors and patterns to lighter, sunnier patterns helps make the seasonal change obvious. Keeping a seasonal indoor wreath is another way to honor the changing months.

• Meditating at work and/or school is a good way to relax and feel less stressed. If you can't
  meditate while at work or school, try sitting quietly with eyes closed. Ground and center,
  then work to put your mind at peace, relaxing as fully as you can for even 3-5 minutes.
  When you finish, have a drink of water, tea, or fruit juice and say, "I am at peace."

• When you get home each day, remove your shoes as soon as you cross the threshold. This
  represents leaving the travails of the world at the door, so that they do not violate the
  sanctity of your home. Pause for a moment, close you eyes, and take a slow, deep breath.
  Feel gratitude at returning home. Murmur a "thank you," and bask in the feeling of returning to your haven.

• When you climb into your bed at night, settle in and luxuriate in how good it feels.
  Think about how the day has gone and what the next day will hold. Starting with your
  feet, move slowly up your body to your head, taking stock of each part and how it feels,
  and consciously relaxing yourself in preparation for sleep. When you finish, murmur
  "Blessed Be," or a blessing of your own choice.

Altar Spaces

A home altar is usually in the main living space. Ideally it should be as close to the
home's center or "heart" as possible. Devote a home altar to two things: 1) showcasing
family successes or celebrations, and 2) honoring the seasonal wheel.

Many people keep a magickal altar in their home's sacred space. This will have all of the
usual items: representations of the four Elements, candles, magickal tools, representations of
Deity, a small cast iron cauldron/thurible, dried herbs, etc.

People involved in a committed relationship may keep a sweetheart altar in the bedroom. This might include candles, oil lamps, an abalone shell for burning incense, a candle
snuffer, personal memorabilia and photographs, etc. Pink and red—the colors of love and
passion—are good choices here.

Another important type of altar is the ancestor altar, which honors the departed ones.
This could be a "traditional" magickal altar, with pictures or objects representing the ancestors, or it could be a much more casual display of family memorabilia. Items referencing time
and the four Elementals are always appropriate on an ancestral altar.

II. Healings
By Oberon

We live in a world of far too much wounding, pain, and suffering. From personal injuries and accidents; mental illness and instability; new plagues and epidemics of incurable diseases; rampant mental, physical, and sexual abuse in families; "holy wars" (an oxymoron if ever there was one!) and jihads; terrorism and rioting; to hurricanes, floods, earthquakes, tsunamis, and other natural disasters—much healing is needed. A popular bumper sticker among Wiccans states: "WITCHES HEAL."

When Circles are convened for rituals, the most common requests for the Workings are healings. If it is a member of the group who needs healing of some sort, they may be seated in the middle of the Circle, and the energy raised focused on them in some way. Morning Glory and I are great advocates of the healing power of "laying on of hands"—a common practice in many religions.

If a healing is to be done for someone at a distance, a photo of them may be placed on the healing altar. Other object links may be personal items, pieces of clothing, a handwritten letter with their signature, a lock of their hair, etc.

If healings are to be done for others, things such as animal species, the Earth, devastated regions, etc., photos, models, newsclippings, and the like may be used as object links for focusing the group's intention.

Appropriate deities of healing include Aesculapius, Kwan-Yin, Brigit, Hygeia, Freya, Serapis, Imhotep, and Rudra. An image or replica of a medical caduceus is also an excellent item to have on your healing altar...or the sacred snakes of Aesculapius.

Rituals and spells of protection, such as the ones given above, are the preventative province of magick. Healings are the curative rites. Here are a few rituals, spells, and chants we can use to heal each other and the world around us:

Psychic Self Defense & Distant Healing
By Diane DesRochers

If you fear you may be under psychic attack, your first line of defense is to build a healthy sense of self-esteem. There are plenty of books on the subject, so I won't belabor this issue. Valerie Worth's *Psychic Self-Defense* is the classic.

In responding to attacks of any sort, there are karmic repercussions to be considered (Newton's third law of motion: for every action there is an equal and opposite reaction). You can't attack someone just because you suspect—even if you are convinced—they have put you under psychic attack. For one thing, what if you are accusing the wrong person? Moreover, what if you are imagining the whole thing? It isn't always the fault of a fellow being, the gods or even fate. Shit happens.

Often too, "psychic attacks" may be nothing more than people whose negative feelings toward another person (or persons) may be so intense that they are unconsciously projecting that negativity without realizing what they are doing. After all, we are all interconnected through the "universal unconscious" (Carl Jung) or our "species consciousness" (from Rupert Sheldrake's theory of formative causation).

There is an old saying: The best way to fight the devil is NOT to fight the devil. The more we fight an enemy, be it a bad habit, a phobia, or a person, the more we give it power over us. *To fear a thing is to empower it.* Conversely, laughter can be a potent ally. So surround yourself with life-affirming, inspirational activities: Spend time where children are playing, or go for walks where you can strengthen your links with the Great Earth Mother and Sky Father. While you're out there, pick flowers or gather brightly colored stones and bring them home with you to help retain that connection. Rent comedy videos or CDs. Llisten to music that makes you laugh or is inspirational. Paint your living area in bright, cheerful colors.

Cleansing Bath for Body and Spirit:

Mix together equal amounts of parsley, sage, rosemary, thyme, and either sea salt or kosher salt. Stir several teaspoons full into boiling water. Cool 'til comfortably warm, then strain.

Take a shower or bath. After rinsing off the soap suds, pour the warm, strained liqueur all over your head and body, making sure that all bodily orifices are washed in the mixture. Rinse again in warm water, then you're done. Repeat this for the next eight consecutive days.

Healing the Shadow Self

By Bonessa Cezanne (*astrologer and writer of trash romances*), 2002

First you need an altar with something to represent the elements (Earth, Water, Air, Fire), an obsidian or black stone, and a crystal. You also need music of your choice.

Start out by visualizing yourself in a bubble of perfect love and trust. Light a candle to the Deity or deities of your choice. Let the music begin.

Holding the black stone, face the direction of Air. Visualize any intellectual, educational, and/or male-related issues/problems that you feel need to be transformed in your life. Visualize it all going into the stone. Dance as long as you are able to.

Turn to face the Direction of Fire. Visualize any problematic issues pertaining to creativity, passion, and/or children that need to be transformed. Visualize it all going into the stone. Dance as long as you are able to.

Face the Direction of Water. Visualize any problematic issues pertaining to the emotions, the soul, and/or women that need to be transformed. Visualize it all going into the stone. Dance as long as you are able to.

Finally, face the Direction of Earth. Visualize issues of the body, workplace, finances, and elders that are problematic and need to be transformed. Visualize it all going into the stone. Dance as long as you are able to.

Drop the black stone into a cup of salted water.

Hold the crystal and dance the Directions again. Only this time visualize the crystal sending out the transforming changes that you desire.

Offer incense of your choice to the Deity or deities of your choice as thanks for the healing changes that will soon be.

Pour the water onto the Earth and hold the crystal to the sun.

The ceremony is completed.

Healing Chants & Spells

152. Healing Spell

By the strong forces of Earth, Air, Water and Fire,
With the highest intents aide our desire.
Breathe with the air, awaken the Spring.
Bring healing clarity deep within.
Dance with the fire, allow play to heal—
And like a child, laugh with full-bodied zeal!
Flow with the water, cleanse heartaches and loss,
With grace and beauty release all dross.
Root with the Earth, nurtured and complete,
A miraculous healing, that is yours to keep.
With strength of the Male and grace from the Female,
Turn a time of darkness into a magic-filled tale.
A healing so deep and a magic so true—
That it's hard to believe any sickness knew you.
With harm to none and blessings to all—
May this magic be fulfilled or even better called!
—*Debi LaFaye, 4/14/06*
Academy of Ancient Arts

153. Healing Circle (round)

I am a circle, I am healing you;
You are a circle, you are healing me.
Unite us; be one; unite us, be as one!

The Earth is a circle, She is healing us;
We are a circle, we are healing her.
Unite us; be one; unite us, be as one!

You are my family and you are loving me
You are my family and you are loving me
You are my people; we are one, we are one!
—Sun Bear

154. Healing Song

How could anyone ever tell you
You were anything less than beautiful?
How could anyone ever tell you
You were less than whole?
How could anyone fail to notice
That your loving is a Miracle?
How deeply you're connected to my soul!
—Libby Roderick

155. Healing Chant (round)

All shall be well; all shall be well;
All manner of things shall be well!
(name) shall be well;
(name) shall be well;
All manner of things shall be well!
—Author unknown

156. Healing Tea Chant

(Since the herbs in tea have healing proper-
ties, I wrote a tea chant which I use to heal
colds. I use visualizations with it, and stir with
a spoon or move my hand over it clockwise.)
Sacred magick of the tea,
Come and help to heal me.
The cold I have is out of hand.
From here on forth it shall be banned.
—Gero, Grey School student

157. 9/11 Prayer for Peace

Where there is hate, may there be Love.
Where there is anger, may there be Wisdom.
Where there is sorrow, may there be Comfort.
Where there is injury, may there be Healing.
Where there is loss, may there be Renewal.

May this great tragedy be an occasion
To connect with the Divine each in our own way,
To strengthen our bonds of support for each other
And to re-kindle our resolve to bring about
A world of greater peace, harmony, & well-being.
    Blessed Be.
        —Selena Fox, September 12, 2001
(Permission to pass on to others is granted –
        please include this note if you do.)

Orphic Hymns for Healing

158. To Aesculapius (67)

Great Aesculapius, skilled to heal mankind,
All-ruling Paean, and physician kind;
Whose arts medic'nal, can alone assuage
Diseases dire, and stop their dreadful rage:
Strong lenient God, regard my suppliant prayer,
Bring gentle Health, adorned with lovely hair;
Convey the means of mitigating pain,
And raging, deadly pestilence restrain.
O power all-flourishing, abundant, bright,
Apollo's honored offspring, God of light;
Husband of blameless Health, the constant foe
Of dread Disease the minister of woe:
Come, blessed saviour, and my health defend,
And to my life afford a prosp'rous end.

159. To Hygeia (68)

O much-desired, prolific, gen'ral queen,
Hear me, life-bearing Hygeia, of beauteous mien,
Mother of all; by thee disease dire,
Of bliss destructive, from our life retire;
And every house is flourishing and fair,
If with rejoicing aspect thou art there:
Each daedal art, thy vig'rous force inspires,
And all the world thy helping hand desires;
Pluto life's bane alone resists thy will,
And ever hates thy all-preserving skill.
O fertile queen, from thee forever flows
To mortal life from agony repose;
And men without thy all-sustaining ease,
Find nothing useful, nothing formed to please;
Without thy aid, not Pluto's self can thrive,
Nor man to much afflicted age arrive;
For thou alone of countenance serene,
Dost govern all things, universal queen.
Assist thy mystics with propitious mind,
And far avert disease of every kind.

4. Elemental Rituals

Introduction: The Elements of Magick
By Oberon Zell-Ravenheart

Credited to the fifth-century BCE Sicilian philosopher Empedocles, the concept of four (or five) Elements as the basis of all life and being in the universe was an essential teaching of Aristotle (384-322 BCE) and the Pythagorean Mysteries of ancient Greece. This system has figured prominently in the magicks of all Western systems (such as those finding their origins in ancient Greece and Rome) as well as in Hermetics, alchemy, modern occultism, Witchcraft, and Wizardry. Magickal traditions from the Middle East and Egypt were influenced by this teaching as well. It is the most widely-used conceptual model in the world, and is the foundation of the Tarot, astrology, and the Magick Circle. Simply stated, the Four Elements are Earth, Water, Fire, and Air, and each Element is imbued (as is everything in the universe) with the non-physical essence of the Divine, which we generally call *Spirit*. Just as each person is a unique manifestation of the Divine, so is every rock, every tree, every mountain, every river. Thus Spirit is often considered to be the Fifth Element—distinguishing living beings from inanimate objects.

Although modern chemists have adopted the word "elements" to refer to the 100-plus different kinds of atoms, that was not the original meaning or intention of this term. Rather, the Elements as the ancients (and magickal folk throughout history) have understood them are what mundanes call the *states* of matter. Everything in the universe is composed of matter and energy, or some combination of the two. Anything made of matter can exist in any of four states—*solid*, *liquid*, *gas*, and *plasma*—and with the addition or subtraction of energy by various means (such as adding or reducing heat or pressure), they can transition from one state to another. We usually think of water, for instance, in its liquid state. But when energy (in the form of heat) is removed from it, it can be frozen solid into ice. Alternatively, the liquid can be boiled away into gaseous vapor if heat is added. Its component atoms of hydrogen and oxygen can also be ionized (stripped of electrons) as fiery plasma, such as we see in the auroras.

This is why a simple burning candle is the most perfect of all magickal tools—it contains all four Elements simultaneously: the solid waxen candle itself is Earth, the liquid melted wax is Water, the gaseous smoke is Air, and of course the glowing flame is Fire.

The ancient Mithraic Mysteries held that a person must master all of the four Elements before he can attain spiritual enlightenment and wisdom. He must successfully undergo initiations of Earth, Water, Air, and Fire—each of which challenges a different aspect of one's nature. Here are a series of such rituals for connecting with the Elements.

Declaration of the Four Sacred Things
By Starhawk

The Earth is a living, conscious being, so in company with cultures of many different times and places we name these things as sacred: Air, Fire, Water, and Earth. Whether we see them as the breath, energy, blood, and body of the Mother, or as the blessed gifts of a Creator, or as symbols of the interconnected systems that sustain life, we know that nothing can live without them

To call these things sacred is to say that they have a value beyond their usefulness for human ends, that they themselves become the standards by which our acts, our economics, our laws, and our purposes must be judged. No one has the right to appropriate them or profit from them at the expense of others, and any government that fails to protect them forfeits its legitimacy. For it is everyone's responsibility to sustain, heal, and preserve the soil, the air, the fresh and salt waters, and the energy resources that can support diverse and flourishing life.

All people, all living things, are part of the Earth-life, and so sacred. No one of us stands higher or lower than any other. Only justice can assure balance, and only ecological balance can sustain freedom. Only in freedom can that fifth sacred thing we call Spirit flourish in its full diversity.

To honor the sacred is to create conditions in which nourishment, sustenance, habitat, knowledge, freedom, and beauty can thrive. To honor the sacred is to make love possible.

To this we dedicate our curiosity, our will, our courage, our silences, and our voices. To this we dedicate our lives.

160. Elemental Call to Power

I raise my hands, my heart, my voice
To call upon the forces of life.
Earth, Air, Fire, Water and Spirit
The five Elements combine to become one
Triple Goddess, hear the calls

I call the Maiden for a new beginning
Mother for life
Crone for experience
Goddess bless, Blessed be
Triple Goddess, I call for thee.
Mystic power, so mote it be.
—*Adella Moon DragonStar*

I. Earth

Attunement with the Earth
By Farida Ka'iwalani Fox

Let us start with the Earth. Go outside somewhere where it is quiet and you can be undisturbed. Find a comfortable spot and take a moment to stand there. Feel the contact your feet make with the ground. Be aware of your weight as it is supported by the Earth and feel the force of gravity that is a reality of our physical existence.

Now focus your attention on your breathing. As you exhale, visualize openings in the soles of your feet and imagine that you are sending roots down into the cool and nourishing Earth. With each exhalation, let those roots sink deeper until it seems as if you cannot move from the spot. As you are becoming more firmly established in the Earth, imagine that you are releasing the tensions and stresses of your life—simply breathe them out and visualize them running down your body, into your roots and out into the Earth.

As you breathe in again, begin to draw up into yourself the nutrients that are in the Earth herself. Think of such qualities as steadfastness, endurance, stability. In this simple exercise you are reconnecting with the foundation of your life. You are grounding yourself. Let yourself enjoy this connection. You may actually feel something like an electrical current running into your feet and legs. This would be a good time to reflect upon the graciousness of our planet who receives not only our personal toxins but the excessive pollution of our modern life. Our gratitude for the purification work of the Earth is helpful.

You can end this little exercise by taking a walk on the Earth, being very aware of each step you take. Imagine an interchange between you and the Earth, and as you make contact with each step, you bless one another. This activity of consciously walking and breathing becomes a very real relationship between you and the planet who is our Mother and our physical home.

Standing on Holy Ground
By Ikari Segawa

Many Pagans feel that a formal ritual to cast a Circle for sacred space is not always appropriate when you are in nature, as it can feel a bit artificial. So here is a very simple ritual that is suitable for outdoor working:

Hold a cup of water (if you are working near a river, ocean, pond, etc., take water from there) in both hands. Ground and center.

Imagine that the water in the cup is beginning to glow in light—and also realize that you are actually standing on a very big Circle—the Earth. Expand your awareness around you until you can visualize the whole Earth as a sacred Circle. Become one with it. Then, sprinkle the water around you, saying, *"I am standing on holy ground. I call the sacred Earth to attend this ritual. Blessed Be!"*

It's very simple, but an effective form of creating sacred space for outdoor rituals. It really helps you to become one with the Earth and nature.

When you've finished the main ritual, just thank the Earth, ground the excess energy, and slowly return to your normal consciousness.

As you can see, this is not exactly a "Circle casting," but more of a way to increase awareness of the sacredness of the Earth for the purpose of the main ritual.

161. Blessed is the Earth

Blesséd is the Earth—
Our Mother and our Home.
Blesséd is She whose spirits dance
In the forests and grasslands
And in all living places.
Blesséd is She who brings forth all things
Living and non-living;
Our sustenance, our comfort, our shelter,
To Whom we return when our living ceases,
With Whom we are One always
In the perpetual cycle of taking and giving back.
Blesséd are we for we are Her
With all creatures and plants—
With all of Life.

—Julie Carter, 1974

Plant a Tree - Blessed Be!
By Dawnwalker

"Plant a Tree," sung to the tune of "Let it Be," was the unofficial theme song for Forever Forest's 12th annual New Year's tree planting, held this year at Harbin Hot Springs, California. Attended by more than 100 people from Forever Forests and the Church of All Worlds' extended family, the Earth Stewards Network, and residents of Harbin, this was the best-organized and most enjoyable of Forever Forest's annual treeplantings. It was a true celebration of renewal and hope in the darkest and coldest time of the year.

We began Friday morning with an opening invocation and the creation of a sacred space for the entire weekend. Just before the first group of planters left the warmth and comfort of Harbin's conference center, the rain stopped, leaving the Earth soft and moist for the new seedlings. That evening's variety show gave us a wonderful opportunity to get to know each other through music, poetry, and theatre, all followed by a midnight global peace meditation.

Saturday was the peak planting day with five crews going out both morning and afternoon. Saturday night was New Year's Eve, which was celebrated with a powerful ritual journey. We met three ancient Crones who warned us that the threads of the tapestry of life were very thin at this time. And we met the Green God of life and growth, who sent us into the devic realm of the tree spirits to hear their messages and feel our connectedness. This was followed at midnight, the "witching hour," by flowing champagne, drumming, dancing, and music – along with much hugging, kissing, and merry-making.

Sunday was a delightful sunny day for the planting of the last of the weekend's 2,000 trees, as well as the completion of an erosion control project by the Pan Trans road crew, and the building and dedication of a medicine wheel. In the afternoon, slides were shown of previous years' plantings, featuring Gwydion, the departed founder of Forever Forests, and a colorful collection of Faeries, elves, and various and assorted ents.

It was a time of true Earth magick—realizing that the healing of the planet and our personal healing are one and the same; visualizing our hopes and dreams for the world that will be when the seedlings we planted have grown to maturity; releasing our tensions and fears into the healing waters of Harbin's hot springs; nourishing our bodies with the delicious food prepared by Pagan Plates; and seeing old friends and meeting new ones. We are reclaiming the future by planting the seeds of a world, with honor and respect for life and for the mysteries of nature. We feel the pain and suffering of the Earth Mother and her green trees, as well as their joy at knowing that at least some of humankind hears the call, does care, and is doing what it can to restore the balance.

> *Blessed be, little Tree,*
> *Long may you live*
> *And tall may you grow.*
> *And blessed are we*
> *To be among those who know.*

II. Water

Prayer/Blessing to Use With Water
By Kari Lynn Eckholt

Place a goblet before you, one made of deep indigo blue, turquoise, or aqua blue-green glass, or of pure clean-cut crystal—preferably something that fills you with a sense of wonder and beauty. Fill a pitcher with pure clean water, and add a small pinch of sea-salt to the water to best mirror our true and ancient relationship to water.

Center yourself, and if there are others present, silently pass the pitcher so that all may say their own name—introducing themselves and the water that each carries in their own body to the water in the pitcher, with each pouring some of the water into their own goblet or glass. An alternate possibility is for the pitcher to be in the center of the group, with all taking turns introducing themselves and passing the pitcher so each may have some in their glass for the start of the actual blessing.

If you are solo, simply introduce yourself and pour a glass.

All participants should contemplate the waters running through their veins and through the Earth, and contemplate that the salinity of the blood plasma of our bodies, the salinity of the cerebral-spinal fluid bathing our nervous systems, and the salinity of our Great Mother Ocean is nearly identical. If you are in a group, the leader should pick up the goblet/glass and speak, for sound in water creates an incredibly powerful vibration (all others should simply cradle their goblets and look into the water):

In this moment, we are holding a glass of
*   pure water, H_2O, the lifeblood of our*
*   Mother Earth and our very selves.*
In this moment, we remember we are ONE
*   with all the waters of the universe,*
*   always connected to all.*
Each droplet of our water has traveled
*   over, under, and thru our world and*
*   our universe endlessly, as part of an*
*   ever-changing journey.*
We remember we have been in the dirty
*   snowballs called comets, and in oceans*
*   and seas, in rivers, lakes and streams.*

We remember we live in the great glaciers,
*   and the snow on the mountain tops.*
We remember we have been to the bottom
*   of the deepest ocean.*
We remember we have risen as steam,
*   evaporated into clouds, fallen as rain,*
*   snow, sleet, hail.*
We remember we have both formed rocks,
*   and broken great mountains of*
*   boulders, and carved riverbeds.*
We remember we have risen as sap,
*   carrying the lifeblood of trees to their*
*   joyful leaves and flowers.*

We flow in the blood of every living crea-
ture, remember walking, burrowing,
crawling, soaring.
We remember we have flowed in every
living creature before them.
We have flowed in the blood of all our
human ancestors, and we carry their
memories. We remember.
We remember that our water will one day
flow in the bodies of our children, our
grandchildren.
We remember to honor every drop of the
living water, for it is Who We Are.
And so we mingle the water carried in our
current physical vessel with the water
of life in our goblets. We drink of the
waters of the Earth.
(Drink deep. The ritual is complete.)

Pool Watersharing Ritual
By Oberon & Liza Gabriel

This ritual is held in a swimming pool or natural body of water. The air and water temperature should be comfortable for standing still in the water for a considerable period, say forty minutes. In a swimming pool this means 78°F or warmer. At one end (preferably in the west) an altar is built with a large chalice on it, plus an appropriate goddess image, sea shells, and other water items and smudging items. At night, candles are set at intervals alone the edge of the water.

Before the ritual, locate four volunteers to call the Quarters, and fill four large chalices with water and set them around the pool edge at the quarters. Tell each Quarter caller to end their calling with *"Hail and be welcome!"* And at the end, for dismissals, they will conclude by saying, *"Hail and farewell!"* The Quarter callers will also be responsible for passing a chalice to the participants in their respective quadrants.

When it's time to begin, people are asked to disrobe as they enter the sacred space. Participants stand in a circle around the pool, while the priest and priestess stand (or tread water) in the middle of the pool. Explain that this will be vigorous, and everyone must be able to swim! Small children (if there are any) must be carried by parents. It's best to leave off eyeglasses and jewelry that could come off or get caught in someone's hair. Participants are shown our *mudras* (gestures) for the Quarters—arms raised, fingers spread like wings for East; "A" flame with hands arched high for South; "V" cup with hands below belly for West; and hands down, fingers spread, and reaching downward like roots for North.

Then a gate keeper tells the people to enter one by one silently. If silence is not a realistic possibility, you could play canned music, have musicians playing, or ask people to chant. Everyone enters the water two by two, with the priest and priestess standing at either side of the stairs into the pool. Either with their hands or with large shells, the priest and priestess pour water onto the people as they enter, hugging them and saying , *"Welcome to the Pool of Living Waters."* They should also help anyone who needs it to enter safely. The participants are motioned to circle clockwise around the pool, creating a Circle along its edge, with the Quarter callers taking their proper positions. (For such circles, where it can be hard to hear someone speaking away from the Circle, we like to do cross-callings, where a person calls East from the West side, etc. That way, everyone can hear clearly.)

When all are in position, the priest goes to the center, faces East, and slowly turns with his hand in salute to cast the Circle. A chant is started, one that people will be familiar with, such as *"We are a Circle Within a Circle"* by Rick Hamouris. While this chant is happening, someone smudges around the edge of the water. Then an athamé is taken from the altar and the Circle is cast by the priest or priestess (Morning Glory cast the Circle with bubbles!). Then both should nod towards each of the Quarter callers to call the directions/Elements.

When this is done, the priest and priestess move to opposite ends of the pool to invoke the Goddess and God. First, the priest invokes Amphitrite (or *"Queen of the Sea,"* *"ocean mama,"* *"tide mover,"* etc). At the conclusion of the invocation, the priestess dives under the water and swims towards center of pool, where she leaps high from the water like a dolphin.

Then the priestess invokes Poseidon (or *"King of the Sea," "wave crasher," "surf rider,"* etc). Then the priest dives under the water and swims towards center of pool, where he leaps high from the water to embrace the priestess. They spin around together, splashing and laughing, holding out their free arms to the wider circle as they repeat to each other, then to everyone, "Thou art God; thou art Goddess!"

Each person then gives a little "rap" about the sacred nature of water: how it is in our bodies and in the Earth; how all of space is a snowfall of water, falling upon all the worlds; how comets, the surfaces of moons, and the rings of Saturn, are all of frozen water; and how frozen oceans lie beneath the dry sands of Mars and liquid seas surge beneath the ice of Europa, Ganymede, Callisto, and Enceladas—the frozen moons of Jupiter and Saturn.

Everyone should ponder how all water is one, indivisible, flowing through all barriers of cell membranes to cycle and recycle in the great "round river" through evaporation and precipitation; how all water is always flowing to the sea, as consciousness always flows towards Spirit; how the composition of our blood retains the composition of the water from the ancient seas of our origins, 500 million years ago; how the water we drink today was once drunk and pissed out by dinosaurs; and how this water in which we now stand will continue to circulate through all time and space, carrying with it our magick and our intentions imprinted in its quantum field.

Thus the sharing of water is a profound and sacred act, avowing our kinship at many levels: first, with those with whom we wish to bond deeply and intimately; second, with those in our greater circle, tribe, and community; and finally, with all living beings on earth, and ultimately throughout the cosmos. For water shared is life shared.

During the Working, people are told to take hands and begin moving deosil, bouncing up from the bottom with each step in a circular wave. Everyone should be told that this will form a great whirlpool of energy, and that they are to imbue it with all the love and sense of communion that the whole idea of water sharing imparts to them. Doing so hastens the awakening of Gaia, and enacts and affirms a kinship with all of the beings that will come into contact with these molecules of water, down through the aeons. At the crescendo of the vortex, everyone should release all this energy by jumping and splashing as high as they can to get those droplets into the air.

As the people are motioned into a clockwise spin, the priest and priestess join hands in the circle, and the Circle begins turning – slowly at first, building faster and faster, until everyone is laughing and filled with energy and the water is carrying everyone around in a great rushing maelstrom. The water in the pool quickly becomes a powerful vortex and care must be taken that no one is hurt. An appropriate water chant is repeated while the vortex is spinning, such as *"we all come from the Goddess,"* or *"water rushing, water flowing, ever moving, ever growing..."*

In a few minutes a completely chaotic scene will emerge. And at an auspicious moment, the priest and priestess let go their hands from the Circle, move to the center of the pool, and start splashing and laughing like crazy as everyone else joins in. Then, the priest and priestess and their assistants guide people back into the Circle.

When things calm down, the Quarter callers each take a chalice of water, and bring it around to the people in their respective quadrants (extra water in pitchers should be positioned along the side), sharing with each one and saying, *"May you never thirst."* As the chalice is passed, people are led in a chant: *"Drink deep, drink deep from the waters of life, water shared is life shared."* This chant can be done in a round.

The Elements, Goddess, and God are thanked and the Circle opened, and people are invited to continue playing in the water or schmoozing.

162. Water Sharing Chant

I open up my body
To receive the Living Waters
That spring from the heart of life

That spring from the heart of life
The Earth is guiding me clear and true
To the living source of Love
To the living source of Love
—*Liza Gabriel, 1995*

163. Love Like a River *(round)*

Love like a river,
Flowing from my heart,
Flowing from my heart.
Love like the waves of the sea,
Washing over you, and
Washing over me.
                    —*Loren Lightbeam*

164. Water Song

Water rushing, water flowing,
Ever moving, ever changing!
Water rushing, water flowing,
Ever moving, ever changing!
                    —*Miriam Arachne*

165. Litany to Water

Thanks to thee, O Mother for water
Without which we would not be.
Man is born of water,
The body is full of water,
Life would not be long,
Were it not for water.
O Thanks unto thee!
For salty seas, cascading glaciers,
Silent streams, brittle icicles,
And singing rivulets—
Water is the source of life,
Whether it be ocean, or blood, or issue,
Water is our source of being—
All hail unto Water!
                    —*Mark Will, 1974*

III. Air

The Invisible Sword
By Farida

Air is the Element we are most immediately and vitally dependant upon. One may survive up to forty days without food (Earth) and perhaps several days without Water. Body temperature (Fire) may fall for several hours before life is threatened. But how many *minutes* can one exist without Air? It is impossible to consider our relationship to Air without considering our breath, the taking in of oxygen and releasing of the toxic by-products of the living processes.

Take a normal but full breath, in and out, through your nose. Does the inhalation seem rough, hurried, or shallow? When you exhale, do you have a tendency to blow it out, sigh deeply, or release in a shaky or broken way? Notice that when you are upset or agitated your breath is more rapid and noisy. When you are calm and peaceful, your breath is also. It is possible to control, to some extent, the emotional atmosphere around you through controlling your breath. This simple fact was a secret of the ancients and is still taught today in spiritual communities, most notably Zen, Yoga, and Sufi.

The breathing process is with us from the beginning to the end. As taught by slower cultures, breathing is meant to be enjoyed. Let us begin with our conscious connection with the Element Air by learning to enjoy breathing and learning to notice what effect different types of breathing may produce in our emotional state.

Here is a breathing practice given by the Lord Buddha to his disciples:

Breathe in a noisy breath, and know you are breathing in a noisy breath. Breathe out a noisy breath, and know you are breathing out a noisy breath. Noisy breath in, noisy breath out.

Breathe in a quiet breath, and know you are breathing in a quiet breath. Breathe out a quiet breath, and know you are breathing out a quiet breath. Quiet breath in, quiet breath out.

Breathe in a deep breath... (and so on, repeating the above form, moving through *shallow* breath and bringing awareness to a number of different kinds of breath—always through the nose—and ending with *refined* breath, refined by lengthening and quieting it).

With this refined breath, breathe in all the joy you can. Joy in and joy out, fill the room, fill the town, fill the country, the world...

Then breathe in all the love you can, and breathe out all the love you can. Love in and love out. Fill yourself, the room, the town...

Lastly, breathe in all the peace you can. Breathe out all the peace you can. Peace in and peace out. Fill your heart, fill the room, fill the town, the state, the world, the universe. Peace in and peace out...

Surrounded by the peaceful, pass into bliss. OM SHANTI, SHANTI, SHANTI.

Orphic Hymns to the Winds

166. To the South Wind (#82)

Wide coursing gales, whose lightly leaping feet
With rapid wings the air's wet bosom beat,
Approach benevolent, swift-whirling powers,
With humid clouds the principles of showers:
For showery clouds are portioned to your care,
To send on earth from all surrounding air.
Hear, blessed powers, these holy rites attend,
And fruitful rains on earth all-parent send.

167. To the West Wind (#81)

Sea-born, Aerial, blowing from the west,
Sweet gales, who give to wearyed labour rest:
Vernal and grassy, and of gentle sound,
To ships delightful, thro' the sea profound;
For these, impelled by you with gentle force,
Pursue with prosp'rous Fate their destined
    course.
With blameless gales regard my suppliant prayer,
Zephyrs unseen, light-wing'd, and formed
    from air.

IV. Fire

What Is To Give Light Must Endure Burning
By Farida

If you have access to a fireplace or open fire pit, make an appointment with the spirit of Fire. Lay in your tinder and wood for burning with care. This fuel is the nourishment you provide for feeding the Fire. You would do the same for any other creature committed to your care.

When you are ready to ignite the materials, think for a moment of the miracle that is about to happen. With the strike of a match, the flame will spring into being. You may want to greet the flame with a blessing, such as "Blessed Be, thou creature of Fire."

Watch, as the little Salamanders eagerly lick the meal you have prepared for them. Observe the nature of Fire as it gains strength and crackles merrily—or snaps angrily. Imagine that the popping and snapping is a form of communication. What might Fire be saying to you? Tell the Fire your deepest secrets, your hidden desires, and passionate longings. Watch the directions of the dancing flames. As time passes and the Fire matures, gaze into the glowing coal caverns. What shapes do you see there in that fantastic Fire world?

Allow yourself to view your own passions: Do they consume you with rage and fury or do they radiate warmth and light that sustains you and others around you? Does this trait tell the truth about who you really are at the center of your being? Does it reflect the divine light within you? Or is it a lie and a pretense, reflecting what you or someone else might *think* you are? Would you be willing to sacrifice that which holds you back? Would you be willing to throw your fear into the Fire? Or your jealousy, distrust, or self-hatred?

Write on a slip of paper a quality that you believe you would be better off without and ask the Fire to take it and burn away the pain and unhappiness it has caused you. Or, even more powerful, choose an item from among your personal possessions that symbolizes the quality you wish to transform, and give it to the Fire. But be sure to visualize what will come in its place. As the old jealousies, angers, and hidden shame are consumed, the true self, compassionate and forgiving and radiant, is able to shine brightly, a beacon light for all to see.

The Universal Fire Circle
by Jeff Magnus McBride and Abigail Spinner McBride

Alchemy is the gentle acceleration of growth through the use of the fire of nature.
—Paracelsus (1493-1541)

Fire Circle alchemy is a ritual composition conducted with a fluidity copious enough to embrace, encourage, and inspirit spontaneous expression. As such it is also an unbounded and eternal experiment, one in which mutual creation is delivered from the celebration and discovery of each other. What emerges from this venture is a ceremonial union of opposites, a mélange of formal structure, artful improvisation, and inspired spiritual offerings. Although the lineage of the alchemical Fire Circle can be traced back to Pagan gatherings, it has evolved beyond the conventions of its origin, for it welcomes all modes of life-affirming spirituality.

In order to maximize the elegant flow of the experiment, there are a number of fundamental details that must be addressed, starting with set-up of the ritual container and gathering of materials. This work is comprised of: gathering wood for the fire, assembling and positioning benches for the musicians, ensconcing tiki torches for illumination, supplying water bottles to facilitate hydration, preparing a food area for sustenance, constructing a welcome portal or gate to encourage conscious entry to the vessel, and organizing a rattle altar (upon which shakers and other small percussion instruments are made available to all celebrants for use for the duration of the rite). In addition, there are often symbols or circles marked out in flour or chalk on the ground, as part of the preparation for the ceremony.

The ceremony begins with connection, elicted by the physical linking of hands, the emotional meeting of eyes, the mental contact of naming both ourselves and our places of origin, and, periodically, by the spiritual correspondence of invocation through expression of ritual intentions. This initial interlacing of essence is attentively followed by a Circle casting.

Our magic Circle, or alchemical vessel, is formulated from a conglomeration of hands, hearts, minds, and spirits, all interwoven through music, chant, spoken word, and movement. There is no pre-scribed liturgy or pre-rehearsed form.

Every alchemical Fire Circle is unique and inimitable. Because the process unfolds extemporaneously, it is never exactly the same, although there are some similarities in the pattern. For instance, a fire-lighting ceremony of some nature invariably occurs, along with an opening ritual that consistently stimulates and fuels a thematically appropriate chant. Another chant will, in all probability, ripen into a related but divergent theme. And on and on the Circle turns, all the way to illumination. When we attend to what is actually happening in the Circle, finding our inspiration and improvisational directions from each other while staying mindfully engaged in the process, we deepen the discovery of ourselves, our relationships, and our community.

Alchemical Fire Circle rituals include:
1) **A Beginning:** This is a time when the entire group of celebrants unites in a collaborative effort to ensure the mindful creation of the ritual/alchemical container in which the ensuing magical Work will soon transpire. Most often, this is a task with multiple layers, accomplished in part by asking community members to create "prayer flags," strips of fabric which they have the opportunity to adorn with their intentions or invocations in whichever way they find most appropriate (e.g. language, symbols, etc.). These prayer flags are then tied onto a cord that has been affixed to long torches secured to stakes, encircling the ritual area and thereby forming the boundary of the vessel.
2) **A Middle:** This period is defined by an amalgam of multi-faceted symbiotic relationships, in the midst of which there is a collective awareness of the planetary influences on the actions and reactions of the people in the Circle—a veritable embodiment of

the alchemical metals in solution. These interactions are based around the offerings of drum, dance, voice, spontaneous ritual, and service.

3) **An Ending:** As the solar disk begins to rise, there is a concomitant rising of the energetic vibration of the group, followed by an interlude of stillness and an intimate pause for reflection, both internal and external, juxtaposed with reverence. It is in this space of conscious group connection that the sun's ascendance is celebrated, a cosmological mirroring of the "gold" that has been created during the ritual process, and a symbolic ending of the ceremony.

Walking the Fire
By Francesca Gentille

(There are folks going around in the magickal community creating special "fire-walking ceremonies." After a big log fire has burned down to coals, a thick bed of red-hot, glowing coals is raked out into a long, wide carpet, and people who have been properly prepared walk the length of this flaming pit in their bare feet. This is truly an amazing experience! But NEVER try this on your own, without qualified guidance, preparation, and supervision!)

I have always loved fire, and I came to the Fire that night, as I had so many times before, in awe, in wonder, in friendship. Looking at the leaping multi-colored flames I could feel the answering heat in my own body. I felt myself to be the flame of truth that purifies, the light of insight that illuminates, the dance of ideas and inspiration that ignites new creations, the deep burn of passion (whether for a person, a project, or life itself) that always destroys and transforms who I think I am.

Our evening firewalk had been skillfully prepared with a presentation and exercises on learning how to know and focus our intentions. Our inner rhythms had been attuned with drumming and with chanting. Only after the hot cedar bonfire had been combed into coals were we to be allowed to cross its six-foot expanse. We learned that night that cultures around the world have worshipped the Fire, leaped the Fire, and walked the Fire as a delving into the truth, power, and focus of their spirits.

As a priestess I had spent years facing my deepest truths, sharing my insights, and creating from my passions. And now, as I faced the Fire, I felt myself to be the Fire; I knew I would be safe. As I watched person after person come to the edge of the Fire and walk, stroll, or dance across, I noticed I did not move forward. I wondered why my body and spirit were waiting to cross the Fire. I knew my intention—to commit my life to the Fire—to truth, to transformation, to being a catalyst and a healer. I felt at peace, yet inexplicably I did not step forward. Then a woman came and stood next to me. She appeared shy and hesitant. I turned to her and smiled. She said, "I am frightened, I wish I had someone to walk across the Fire with me." I held out my hand.

That night I learned that the flame of my spirit is sparked, is moved, by compassion. I always learn something at the Fire, if I will listen. We walked to the edge of the flickering wind-whipped coals and paused, gathering our focus and words. As our naked feet purposefully strode the five paces across the coals, we each spoke our sacred intent to the Fire, to one another, and to the surrounding circle of witnesses. I said, "I dedicate myself to the Fire." The heat was intense, and periodically it felt as if it was nipping (or "kissing," as it is called amongst firewalkers) my soles. As we walked off our flaming carpet we joyfully embraced and breathed in that we had no burns, only the sweet rush of success.

168. Fire, Fire, Fire

Fire, fire, fire
Kindle my spirit higher
In your flames, naught remains
But fire, fire fire!

—*Cynthia R. Crossen*

169. Rise With the Fire

O we can rise with the fires of freedom!
Truth is the fire that will burn our chains!
And we will stop the fires of destruction!
Healing is the fire running through our veins!

—*Starhawk*

170. Nine Woods for the Fire

Nine woods in the cauldron go,
Burn them fast and burn them slow.
Birch into the fire goes,
To represent what the Lady knows.
Oak gives the forest might,
The fire brings the God's insight.
Rowan is the tree of power,
Causing life and magic to flower.
Willows at the waterfront stand,
To aid the journey to the Summerland.
Hawthorne is burned to purify,
And draw faery to your eye.
Hazel, the tree of wisdom and learning,
Add its strength to the bright fire burning.
White are the flowers of the apple tree,
That brings us the fruits of fertility.
Grapes that grow upon the vine,
Giving us both joy and wine.
Fir does mark the evergreen,
To represent immortality unseen.
Elder is the Lady's tree,
Burn it not, or cursed you'll be.

—Ellen Dugan

171. Burn Bright *(for lighting the fire)*

Burn bright, flame within me:
Kindled of eternal fire.
Of the people I do be:
And the people part of me,
All one in many parts:
A single fire of flaming hearts!

—Skye Ranger Nick (Nicholas Sea) 1982

A Flashy Spell for Any Occasion
By Crow Dragontree

Writing down a magickal intent and burning it in a fire is a magickal practice that appears to have endured for centuries. My personal preference is to write my intent upon flash paper with a colored felt-tip pen and ignite it in the flames of a colored candle. Flash paper is chemically-treated paper often used by stage magicians to create a large, flaring glow when ignited. Of course, this creates a rather remarkable impression during spellcasting, but the real reason I enjoy using this is a bit more mundane: Flash paper gives off no smoke or smell, so you can cast your spell in the house without annoying anyone else. In addition, flash paper ignites and burns almost instantaneously and leaves no ashes, so there's no need for a special fireproof bowl, and no cleanup of messy ashes afterward. Nonetheless, it would still be helpful to have a supply of water handy in the unlikely event that anything needs extinguishing.

To cast a flash-paper spell, you'll probably want to have the associated colors in felt-tip and candle handy. There are many, many tables of correspondences available that will provide you with the various colors that are associated with a given intent (see pages 43, 266).

Although you may choose the candle and felt-tip of the same color, it might be more effective to use two colors, emphasizing two different aspects of your intent. For example, if you wanted to cast a healing spell, you may wish to use a green candle to represent healing, but write upon the flash paper in red ink to represent strength and vitality.

Once you've chosen your colors and are set to cast the spell, light your candle, chanting something to the effect of:

> *Here, I summon Fire's light,*
> *To aid me in my spell tonight!*

Now, in the candlelight, write your intent in a clear, concise manner. This may be in verse form, but flash paper pads generally give you pretty small pieces upon which to write, so brevity may be very helpful here! Focusing on your intent, carefully place one corner of the flash paper into the candle. As you do this, be prepared for a large flare as the paper vanishes in a burst of flame. As it does so, call out something like:

> *I call upon the strength of Fire*
> *To bring me that which I desire!*

You should see some very vivid results rather quickly with this spell!

5. Rites of Passage

Introduction: Rites of Passage
By Luke Moonoak & Oberon Zell-Ravenheart

Rituals of transition and life changes, called "rites of passage," mark significant periods in life, movement between life stages, and personal transformations. These are rituals of honoring and empowerment. They are a public acknowledgment and recognition of growth. Just as the seasons pass in order, so do the stages of life. The inner and outer worlds mirror each other, so rites of passage provide a further link with the Earth and the cosmos. Rites of passage include coming of age, marriage or handfasting, pregnancy and birth, passage into elderhood, handpartings, and death and rebirth.

Birth

When a child is born it is a remarkable event, and when a child who is loved by many and nurtured by a whole community is born, it is a miracle. When we gather to name and honor a new baby, we honor life itself. Other terms for this rite are *seining,* or baby blessing. At this time those who will nurture the child are identified: goddessmothers, godfathers, parents, siblings, and other loved ones who may have a part in the baby's life are recognized before all. We pass the new baby around the Circle, with magickal gifts and blessings for long life, health, and happiness: "Live long and prosper…"

Puberty

Centuries ago, the phrase "coming of age" meant "of age to marry," but these days we no longer expect people to marry so young. Normally held between the ages of 11-13, modern puberty ceremonies celebrate the onset of adolescence in one's body and mind. From this point begins the exploration of our new and changing bodies. Adolescents must learn their own boundaries, likes and dislikes, and about their right to say yes or no when it comes to *their* bodies. Usually this rite is performed by adult members of the child's own sex, and may involve an initiatory ordeal and the giving of a magickal name.

Adulthood

This rite can occur anytime between the ages of 16-21, depending on the person and local laws concerning "legal maturity." This ceremony heralds the beginning of the journey into adulthood, and entails adding adult attitudes, abilities, responsibilities, and maturity to our best youthful attributes. The rite usually involves a sacred/special place, a "vision quest," and a "rebirth" into the community of adult men and women. A symbol is gifted to the new adult and he/she is honored before all—often with a new magickal name.

Handfasting (Marriage)

Choosing to live with a mate or partner is a commitment to that person, a joining of two independent beings because they are *greater* together than they are apart. Handfastings are made "for as long as love shall last" because a couple may stay together for the rest of their lives or they may not, and both choices are honorable. This rite sends them off on a joint adventure, with as much joy and passion as possible! And if they should someday decide to part, a ceremony of handparting will allow them to do so with honor and goodwill. (This will be covered more in depth in the following chapter.)

Parenthood

While birth rites are centered on the baby, parenthood is a ceremony for the new parents. It is a time for honoring the mother and father whose life journey has brought them to this place. We bless the new parents with a "baby shower" and a Circle of love and support.

This is a celebration and a party, a time for giving gifts and saying: "We're here if you need us—you don't have to raise this kid alone!"

Elderhood (Crones & Sages)

Elders, like children, are priceless treasures of our community. After the age of 50 or so, we may formally acknowledge and honor our elder folk for their wisdom, knowledge, skills, or whatever they have gained from their years on Earth. Often they are the ones who settle disputes, bless babies, and speak with greatest authority in councils. At this rite, another symbol may be gifted to them in recognition of their value.

Death & Rebirth

Near or at the time of death, we give comfort and compassion in a rite of passing. Beloveds gather to say goodbye, and to send the spirit out through the Circle. We ask that they be blessed with peace, a time of rest, and then a new journey and a new birth. After death, we remember them with a gathering called a wake. This is a farewell party where we share treasured memories and stories. A funeral may follow, in which a few chosen speakers may deliver a *eulogy* ("good words")—speaking of the impact of the departed person's life on their own, and on the world.

A time of death is a sad time, but also one filled with hope and joy, for death is part of life, and just as the seasons turn, so we also will be reborn and continue. It is a time to let go and move on. When a loved one dies, it's a comfort to know that we may have inherited a guardian angel in our lives, whom we can petition for aid ("may your spirit continue to guide us").

The great cycle, the spiral leading ever forward, continues: the moments of a day, the seasons of our lives, our lives themselves, generations, planets, stars, galaxies, and universes—all turning in the great circle of life, one within the other. I am proud to be a part of this circle, because fun, adventure, and growth are the greatest treasures I can imagine!

I. Birth Rites

Blessing Way
By Cheryl Reynolds, 2002

This is a blessing rite for a to-be-mommy. This can be done before a baby shower or as the shower itself, with gifting later. Here are the items needed:

- Large green pillar candle for the mother-to-be.
- Something with which to inscribe names on the candle.
- Small table and cozy chair for the mother-to-be, plus earth cloth (this will be gifted to mommy after rite).
- A very long piece of twine, preferably red to symbolize the mother element.
- Matching small white or green tapers with candle hand protectors for each person present at the rite.

Before mommy arrives, have all present inscribe just their first name on her green pillar candle. When she arrives, set the candle on the table in front of her with some matches; place her chair in the *middle* of the circle (we made an elaborate chair fit for a pregnant mommy!).

All participants should gather around her and hold hands. Have one women tie her hand around to the women on the left with one loop...keep the string loose so the women can lift her arms up and then go to the next women. One woman should go around entire room and link the circle of women together hand to hand with the string, making sure that there is enough room for the women to lift up their arms. The mother-to-be should link the last loop of the two women together (do not tie the string—just loop.). All should be linked together, with mommy in center.

Through our Great Mother, you have linked us all together and created a circle around you.

<pause> *A circle is a continuous reminder of life. Life created by generations of women. Through each of us, knowledge has been passed through by our mothers, grandmothers, ancestors and our Great Mother Earth. Our ultimate teacher! We are a representation of the ultimate gift.* <Pause> *Life.*

I want you to look at these women. (You may have to move the circle around so mommy can see everyone at least once.) <Pause> *We are the reminder of your womanhood, your ability to nurture and to continue the circle of life. We are your circle of wisdom, hope and strength. As we stand before you, we stand bound together in truth, trust and love to help support and guide you through your gift of love.*

<Pause> *We are your sisters, mothers and friends!*

Each woman states who she is a clockwise fashion—for example: *"I am your sister and your friend," "I am a mother and your friend,"* etc. At the end all should shout together *"We are one!"*

We have inscribed our names in your candle as a reminder of our strength to you. This string that I want you to unwind and wrap around your candle is your spiritual umbilical cord to us. If you need additional strength as a mother in need, please light the green candle. Remember, the string may be untwined now, but it will always *remain unbroken in our hearts and mind.*

Have the mother-to-be unwind the string from around each woman and then wrap it around the candle (only go halfway up the candle). Have her light her green candle.

Now from this candle that is embraced and encircled with our energy of love, we bestow upon you our wisdom of the ancestors. We light our candle from your divine pillar of strength, to guide you upon your childbirth journey.

Going clockwise, the first girl will go up and light her taper off the "mommy candle," saying: *"The blessings I bestow from my ancestry, strength, and wisdom are:"* (Other participants can give blessings or advice at this time.)

After each participant has lit her candle, give mommy a few minutes to look around at all the members holding the candles.

Now, we will put our candles out (snuff out candle).

Remember…our light will always *remain a divine guide and beacon for you to travel through your journey of childbirth. We will relight this candle the moment we get news of your upcoming labor!*

Mommy can make a statement if she wishes.

Wrap up the candle in a very Earth-like cloth for mommy to bring home. At this time you can do the standard baby shower, or if you are a bit more Earth-oriented you can do a belly cast (or for a shy mommy, you can give her a cast of the baby's and mommy's hands). In the future, when the hand cast is set, mommy can wrap a piece of the red string around the wrist of this cast as a reminder of this special rite. These casts can be purchased at any large baby outlet store.

Gypsy Birth Ceremony
By Lewis Spence

Prior to the birth of a child, the Gypsies light a fire before the mother's tent, and this fire is not allowed to go out until the rite of baptism has been performed. As they light and feed the fire, the women croon the following chant:

Burn ye, burn ye fast, O Fire!
And guard the babe from wrathful ire
Of Earthy Gnome and Water-Sprite,
Whom with thy dark smoke banish quite!
Kindly Fairies, hither fare,
And let the babe good fortune share,
Let luck attend him ever here,

Throughout his life be luck aye near!
Twigs and branches now in store,
And still of branches many more,
Give we to thy flame, O Fire!
Bless the mother; bless the sire.
Burn ye, burn ye, fast and high,
Hear the little baby cry!

Baby Blessing Ceremony
By Morning Glory Zell

A rite of baby blessing, called *seining,* should be conducted within the first lunation after birth. It should be a very simple ceremony, so as not to put a strain on the baby. The assembled guests should include god- and goddess-parents. The ceremony should take place within a traditionally cast and consecrated Circle. Small altars should be set up at each of the quarters, holding burning sage and bird's wing fan (East), a lit red candle (South), a chalice or shell of water (West), and a small dish or half geode of salt (North). The Quarters should be called by individuals stationed at those points. Parents are stationed in the East, and god- and goddess-parents in the West. After invoking the God and Goddess (who should be particularly parental deities, such as Isis & Horus, etc.), there are traditionally four phases of a seining:

1. Presentation & naming of the baby
2. Presentation of god- and goddess-parents
3. Anointing
4. Offering of blessings

Presentation & Naming

The parents, standing in the East and holding the baby, turn it to face the Circle, saying: *"We are greatly blessed this day. A new life has entered our Circle. Let us give joyous welcome to (baby's name)."*

Everyone responds with something like *"welcome, (baby's name), into our Circle of life!"*

Presentation of God- & Goddess-Parents

The parents ask, *"Who will come forward now to be god- and goddess-parents to (baby's name)?"*

From their places in the West, the god- and goddess-parents step forward into the center of the Circle, saying, "We do."

The parents pass the baby over to them, saying: *"May your love and support nourish (baby's name) through good times and bad as (s)he grows in strength, wisdom, and beauty. May you always be there for him/her in times of need. Do you accept this charge?"*

The god- and goddess-parents reply, *"We do."*

Anointing

God- and goddess-parents carry the baby around the Circle. At each Quarter they stop, and the person who originally called that Quarter conveys the blessing of that Element, thusly:

- East— smoke from the burning sage is wafted around the baby using the bird's wing fan: *"By the Air which is Her breath, may you live long and prosper!"*
- South— the baby is passed over the candle flame: *"By the Fire which is Her radiant spirit, may you live long and prosper!"*
- West— water is sprinkled over the baby: *"By the Water which is Her blood, may you live long and prosper!"*
- North— salt is sprinkled over the baby: *"By the Earth which is Her body, may you live long and prosper!"*

Offering of Blessings

This is just like the baby blessing in the beginning of Disney's *Sleeping Beauty.* The parents begin the offering of blessings by saying something like: *"(Baby's name), I offer you the gift (or blessing) of (music, dance, fine speech, good health, love of reading, insight, compassion, creativity, many friends, beauty, love, intelligence, coordination, etc.). May this gift serve you well."*

Then they pass the baby to the person on their left, who says: *"(Baby's name), I offer you the gift (or blessing) of (whatever),"* and then passes the baby on around the Circle, with each person taking the baby and offering their own special blessing.

When the baby has been passed around the full Circle, and is returned to the parents, they say, *"Thank you all, friends and family. We are all blessed this day."*

172. Scribing the Circle-Seining

This sacred knife today we take in hand
To cut the cord of newborn memory
Of sorrows; cut the fears and birthing pains.
You'll start anew with newborn wings set free.

We scribe this holy Circle; sacred space
Within the holy temple blessed with mirth.
Come forth in babyhood, my sweet, to learn
Of Air and Water, Fire and holy Earth.

We set the stage, oh little one, today's
The day to come and meet the universe.
This blade doth circle and these words do make
A temple sweet and fine as any verse.
—Rev. Paul V. Beyerl

173. Preparing to Visit the Elements

Oh come with me, my child, and we will see
The secrets found within the Mystery.
For untold ages all have known the lore:
The Mystery of life within the Four
Some people know the four as winds above
While others call them Unicorns, with love.
No matter how they're seen nor by what name
For Four are Universal, just the same.
Oh come with me, my friend, as we will see
The secrets found within the Mystery.
—Rev. Paul V. Beyerl

174. We've All Come to Welcome You

We've all come to welcome you...
To welcome you to Earth.
We've all come to welcome you...
To celebrate your birth.

And we are here to love you...
We are here to love you,
We are here to love you...
To love you on this Earth!
—Author unknown

175. Forever Young

Goddess bless and keep you always,
May your wishes all come true,
May you always do for others
And let others do for you.
May you build a ladder to the stars,
And climb on every rung,
And may you stay forever young!
    Forever young, forever young,
    May you stay forever young!

May you grow up to be righteous,
May you grow up to be true,
May you always know the truth
And see the light surrounding you.
May you always be courageous,
Stand upright and be strong,
And may you stay forever young!
    Forever young, forever young,
    May you stay forever young!

May your hands always be busy,
May your feet always be swift,
May you have a strong foundation
When the winds of changes shift.
May your heart always be joyful,
May your song always be sung,
And may you stay forever young!
    Forever young, forever young,
    May you stay forever young!
—Bob Dylan

II. Puberty Rites

Rite of Passage, Boys
By Oberon

Traditionally, a boy's rite of passage from childhood into adolescence occurs at puberty, when he becomes sexually mature. This time, usually around 12-14 years of age, is marked most visibly by the development of pubic hair, though technically it is said to be indicated by "first seed," or the production of semen.

According to Joseph Campbell, a boy's rite of passage has several phases:

1. Separation from the mother
2. Isolation and disorientation
3. Vision quest
4. The ordeal
5. Joining the company of men
6. The return

Separation from the Mother

In some tribal societies, this was accomplished by a nighttime "kidnapping," in which several men of the boy's family would sneak into his abode at night, bundle him up roughly in his bedding, and carry him off. This would all be conducted in silence on the part of the men, but if the boy cried out, the mother (who of course would be in on the whole thing) would come out wailing something scripted like, *"My baby! My baby! Don't take my baby!"*

Isolation and Disorientation

Following the "capture," the boy is typically isolated from human contact for a time, while remaining deprived of his normal senses. Sometimes a boy would be placed in a dark room, blindfolded, and just left there for awhile, while some tribes would place the boy in a small hole or cave for a period of time, covered over and in total darkness. Some modern magickal groups will use a coffin for this purpose. The idea is to create a sense of both fear and disorientation—and a symbolic brush with death.

Vision Quest

If time and circumstances permit, many tribal societies send a boy out on a vision quest or "walkabout" during this phase. He is taken to some isolated spot, given a few basic tools, such as a knife and fire-making tools, instructed to avoid human contact, and left alone for a period of time (which may be as short as a few days or as long as a full lunation). He may be expected to fast entirely, or to eat only what he can find in the wild. His assigned mission on this quest is to make contact with his inner spirit, totems, and allies.

The Ordeal

There is often also a challenge and a "life-or-death" ordeal of some kind, requiring the candidate to undertake a "leap of faith." The ordeal typically entails something that is really scary to the boy, but is carefully structured by the men so that it presents no real physical danger. Such "leap of faith" ordeals might entail bungee jumping or leaping off a tall cliff blindfolded. Of course, if a person is blindfolded, he has no way of knowing whether the cliff he is jumping from is 30 feet high or only three feet. A "leap of faith" can be just as effective from a small height as a great one, provided it is done convincingly and involves a long climb upwards and voices coming from far below.

Other and perhaps less dramatic types of ordeals may, of course, be equally effective. Emrys had to drum all night, without stopping or losing the beat, for a Walpurgisnacht ritual.

Joining the Company of Men

After successfully passing his ordeal, the candidate is then welcomed into the men's circle. This might include a sweat lodge ritual or other formal men's ceremony. It might happen as a part of a "Wild Men Weekend," or a fire dance. For my son Zack, we held a sweat and then brought him into a campfire circle where all the men were masked. We each told stories of how we first became men—our own various "rites of passage." For most of us, it was our first sexual experience that was the threshold. This is a time when the young man might be given a new name—a "man name" to replace his "boy name."

In some tribes, if he's old enough, the new initiate might at this time even be sent off to a private hut where an experienced and willing young woman waited to give him a sexual initiation. He might be blindfolded for this experience, or she might be masked. Or the hut might just be totally dark, replete with with furs and cushions.

The Return

In the morning the young man is returned to his mother. He is proudly introduced to her by his new name, and she is told that *"We took from you a boy, and we return to you a man."*

176. Boy's Rite of Passage Blessing

You have grown but there is more growing to do.
You have planted seeds of your future self
That germinate at different times and under
    different conditions.
Some seeds need love; some seeds need fertilizer
(We all know what fertilizer is made of)
And all that some seeds need is a kick in the ass.
As long as you are on the planet (and
    perhaps even after)
You will always have work to do.
You might as well get used to it and start
    enjoying it.

So sit back, enjoy and feel the breeze
Don't be afraid to turn on cruise control at times,
Just don't forget to keep steering, because
    you are in control.
If by chance you get into a rut or an unfortu-
    nate happening,
Don't be afraid to ask for help from me
Or any travelers who happen to come along.
Then after you get out of your fix
Just keep driving and let the road lead you.
Make your choices when they come to you,
As long as you follow your heart
They will be the correct ones and then the
    road continues on.

—*Wheeler Stone*

Rites of First Blood
by Marylyn Motherbear Scott

Blood rites for girls are bloody hard! Periods in general are embarrassing to some, if not most, girls. Many primitive cultures, however, acknowledged and honored the first blood as sacred, with a profound respect for the process of becoming a woman and a vessel for bringing in life. A glimpse of this can be seen in the movie *Where the Spirit Lives*.

For the Neo-Pagan community, these rites are relatively new, and it's important that we don't presume what should be done. Out of half a dozen blood rites I attended, I recall only one where the girl seemed to feel relaxed. Every effort should be made to find out what the girl will enjoy and what will make her feel comfortable.

I recall one ritual of first blood in which a lovely circle of females gathered—women of all ages, including some of the girl's peer group. Red, of course, was featured in candles, scarves, and food. As we went around the circle, everyone who cared to share a story told of their first blood, what happened, how they felt about it, how their mother treated it.

Rites of passage are important and will be carried out whether or not the parents and community take part. Creating rites consciously, with sensitivity, honoring our children's steps into the mysteries of living, is a way of telling them they are valued and loved; it helps to create an awareness of who they are for themselves and others so that a positive self-image can emerge.

177. Daughter

My dear Daughter, Daughter of mine
And Daughter of all Daughters before

I bow to you
The Goddess who you are
And have always been
Let me hold your hand, guide, support
And behold your Rite of Passage
Your Menarche

You are heralded Girl and Woman
You walk our ancient path walked before you
Know thy Power, thy Beauty, thy Blood
It is a Moon River of pleasure, fecundity,
Of Goddess continuity

Relish its floral fragrance, pungent sweetness
In all its forms, colours, sensations
Know its unguent use,
And wield wisely

You are with your sisters, mother, grandmothers
And daughters and on
You are connected, supported
Yet unique and free

Let your ruby essence come forth
You embody the Red Goddess & Scarlet Woman
Let us celebrate your Divinity
I love you, embrace you, kiss you
Sanguine blessings, dear Daughter.

—*Kitty J. Shaw, 2005*

178. Maiden Blessing

I bless your mind that you may know the
  wisdom of the Goddess.
I bless your eyes that you will see your true
  beauty, within and without.
I bless your mouth to praise life.
I bless your heart to love and be loved.
I bless your breasts to nurture yourself and
  those you love.
I bless your womb and yoni that you may
  know creativity and pleasure as a
  divine gift to share in sacred ways.

I bless your hands to make the world a holy place.
I bless your feet that you may walk paths of
  wisdom and understanding.

—Ruth Barrett

179. Sacred Blood

Sacred blood of the Mother runs through
  my veins,
And with each lunation, scarlet She rains.
Mother to daughter passes this gift.
Blessed be the Mother, within us She lives.

—Ruth Barrett

III. Passage to Adulthood

Sean's Rite of Passage- FireDance 2001
By Bob Gratrix and the men of FireDance

(I was a participant in this rite of welcoming a young man into adulthood, into the Circle of men during a night at FireDance. We men formed a Circle within a tight ring of redwood trees, lit by candles, and the young man was brought to us blindfolded. When he was admitted to the Circle, and the blindfold removed, the following is what we said to him. —Oberon)

This tribe of spirit-men has followed the path of the sun from the beginning of the new dawn.
This tribe of spirit-men has followed shadows and light and shadows without end—
Into the night, into the life that now flows through your veins.
Now this night has come to you like a spear thrown by the Father of all—
It has pierced the veil of time, it has pierced every mystery, and it has found its way to you.
This power, this shining, now rests upon your brow.
It is the light that you must bear into this world of humanity—
This world supported by the child, supported by the woman, supported by the man.
And the light is the source of the pillar upon your shoulder.
By this power you shall nurture the world.
And into this world shall you lovingly sacrifice the essence of your life.
For this power requires you to transform yourself into the source,
To transform yourself into the bravest kind of love, pure beyond measure.
We are a tribe of spirit-men who welcome you into the light by which we gather.
We honor the God who now breathes through you.
In this moment, and in this place, we trust you with the sacred duties of life.
Be thou wise, like the breeze in the leaves.
Be thou courageous, like the lion in the sun.
Be thou kind, like the healing rain.
Be thou present in all things— in the stars and in the stones.
Into this brotherhood of this tribe of spirit-men you are summoned.
And this weight that is borne by us, we now share with you, for it takes all of us to carry
  this weight forward.
This is your portion, this is your measure. Accept now the symbols of your bliss, your
  duty, and your sacrifice.
May love prevail.

Each spirit-man in turn opened his hand to show a stone he has previously selected to
   Sean, saying, "I have found sacredness in this world. It exists."
He then tosses the stone outside of the Circle into the darkness saying, "I now charge
   you to find sacredness in this world."
Jeff presented antlers to Sean, and Sean drove the fire all night.

LaSara's Coming of Age
by Marylyn Motherbear Scott

She was born a child of Faerie, raised on the land. She spent her early years toddling around on the high hills of Triple Tree Holt, Greenfield Ranch. Homeschooled from start to finish, her teachers were the trees and grasses and the dark earth, the starry night sky, the moon through her cycles, the sun as it rose and sat on the near hill, the animals wild and domestic, insects and birds, birth and death. Now she was crossing another line into a scary place known as adulthood, and I wanted to honor this lovely young woman I am privileged to call daughter.

Turning age 18 in America is a juncture unlike any of the models in primitive culture. It was not a passage connected with a particular body change, like "first blood": It was a socio-political and cultural event. At agen 17 she was still my legal responsibility, she could not vote, and sexually was still considered "jail bait." Suddenly at 18, she was legally responsible for herself, could vote, and the sexual approaches of men more than a few years older than her no longer put them at legal risk. That's what I mean: sca-a-ary!

Of course the primary intent of the rite was to celebrate LaSara. On another level, I wanted to manifest continued protection on the part of the whole community. (In this way, we see that a rite is not only for the one whose passage is being acknowledged, but also a passage for the whole family, the community, etc.) I also wanted the community to acknowl-edge that LaSara had co-created herself as woman out of child within this circle, and that on some level she would always continue to be our child.

It was Beltane at Annfwn, 1989. Although there were rituals upon rituals that long, warm weekend, still, a large Circle formed. LaSara stepped into it, with long red hair like flames licking off her head and a radiance that surrounded her crown chakra—a powerful and lovely Faerie goddess. From the center, she spoke her heart. Then stories of her childhood came forth to honor her, telling of the gifts that she had brought to the tribe simply by being.

As we approached the time for her to be birthed into her new relationship with the world, I invited the respective animal totems of all who were in the Circle to attend and bring a gift of their medicine. "*All My Relations*"—this was the protection. And each came forth, some with story, song, poem, or dance, and some bearing magical tools and trinkets. Her gratitude and humility shone into the heart of the Circle.

I gave great consideration to the next round, and whether it was okay for men and children to be part of the birthing. I decided that the circle of our lives and each of its passages was co-created by the whole. And I decided that there was a necessity for commu-nal healing, so that men would take conscious responsibility for what they birthed, that children would grow up conscious and aware of what they were becoming, and that women would accept help and healing when offered.

The Circle re-formed, each facing the back of the person before them. LaSara removed her clothes (we are all born naked) and laid herself down. The whole circle "gave birth" to LaSara as she made her way upon the Earth and through the open legs of each man, woman, and child. The labored moaning that day made its own music, a song that became a story that is told and retold.

Return again, return again, return to the land of your soul. Return to what you are, return to who you are, return to where you are born and reborn again. A radiant goddess was born and reborn that day out of the overarching womb of the grown-up world, ready to take her place.

10. Croning Rituals
By Ruth Barrett

The word *crone* is a reclaimed word that describes a woman whose womb bloods have stopped for a minimum of a year, and who has reached, in astrological terms, her second Saturn return. This is the return of the planet Saturn to the point where it was at the women's birth for the second time. The first Saturn return occurs between the ages of 27-30, and is a maturing cycle. The second Saturn return signifies the receiving of wisdom and occurs between the ages of 56-60. The combination of these two passages signifies the passage of a woman into elder status, as a young wise woman or "Earth Crone." It is a convergence of physical, psychological, and psychic changes that bring a woman to this threshold as Earth Crone. Crossing this threshold is an occasion for ritual. Her later transition from Earth Crone to "Stone Crone," or "Hag," at age 86-90 is another passage to honor through another ritual.

The words "hag" and "crone" are both words that, in recent years, have begun to be proudly reclaimed and restored to their original ancient and honored meanings. Hags and crones are the magick makers and transition-easers, the healers and distributors of age-old sacraments. "Hag" comes from the Greek *hagios*, meaning holy, especially as applied to the principle of female wisdom, Hagia Sophia. Hagios is also a cognate of the Egyptian *heg*, a pre-dynastic matriarchal ruler who knew the words of power, or *hekau*. In Greece, this hag goddess aspect became *Hecate*, or Queen of the Dead. These terms are being used again to denote respect for elder women in the Dianic community.

Women entering their 50s, and sometimes even much younger, experience great fear and anxiety about aging. In patriarchy, once a woman is past her reproductive or sexual prime, she becomes valueless and invisible. A croning ritual can be an important rite of passage that helps women transition into this next phase of their lives, which is otherwise experienced in isolation. The ritual of croning acknowledges a woman's value as a woman of wisdom, and as a person to be cherished and respected. Each woman's needs are different, and in the creation of her ritual, it may be important for a woman to first acknowledge the negative attitudes about aging that she has internalized from the dominant culture. Once these negative attitudes are spoken aloud, she may not feel the need to address them during her ritual in any great detail, if at all.

A Croning Ritual

The invited guests arrive to the heartbeat of a drum. A Circle forms as women begin to sing a chant whose words praise the sacred Crone, the Goddess in her third aspect of maturity and deepening wisdom, as well as the woman being honored tonight as she crosses the threshold into her elderhood.

> *She is changing, she is changing, her river now runs underground*
> *Time of deepening, time of deepening, the years of bleeding are all done*
> *Inward journey, inward journey, final secrets to be sung*
> *Name her river "Wise Blood" in celebration.*
>
> —Ila Suzanne

Led by a procession of singing women, Kay enters the room dressed in colorful robes. She invokes her ancestors, calling the spirits who have guided her in her life as a woman and musician. The facilitating priestess explains to the guests how, in women's rituals, every age is honored and each transition marked as one passes into another stage of being. This ritual tonight honors Kay as an elder who formally enters a new stage of life as a Wise Woman.

Kay lights seven of the eight candles that represent the Fibonacci series, sharing a memory, an image, or some wisdom from every stage of her life. Her daughter presents her with a symbol of her mother-line, linking the generations one to another. Kay plays her flute, improvising from Spirit, letting divine inspiration come through her music. While speaking aloud her future visions and wishes for the Fates to weave, Kay lifts two chalices in her hands, pouring water back and forth between them, symbolizing the flow between her manifested art and creativity. She speaks her commitment to herself as an elder, and to the aspects of Cronehood she will celebrate. Lifting the full chalice to her lips, Kay drinks in her commitments, making the magick a part of her internally. She then punctuates the magick externally by lighting the eighth candle, symbolizing the manifestation of creativity in her next stage of life. As another chant begins, Kay gives thanks for the many gifts of her life.

180. Crone and Sage

Crone and sage,
Crone and Sage
Wisdom is a gift of age.
Sage and crone
Sage and crone
Wisdom's gift shall be our own.
—*Author unknown*

V. Rites of Death & Rebirth
By Oberon

"Last Rites" are generally conducted for someone on their deathbed to prepare them for their final journey from this life into the next one. This is all very well if the person is dying predictably, as at the end of a long illness, and there is time to make all the necessary arrangements. But very often people die unexpectedly, and there will have been no opportunity to prepare them, or their family and friends. Even so, it is appropriate to conduct a final rite of passing to facilitate their transition to the "unknown country." Many departed spirits seem bewildered, not realizing that they have actually died. Rather than moving on, their ghosts hover about the places and people they knew in life. They are held as much by the emotional anguish, love, grief, and guilt of those left behind as by their own unfinished business. So a magickal sense of closure is needed when someone dies—to liberate their spirit, as well as the spirits of all who loved them.

Rites of passing include a laying-out of the body—bathing them, brushing their hair, making them up, and dressing them in their funerary finest. These proceedings have traditionally been conducted by women. Fresh flowers may be arranged around the body or even covering it like a blanket. And as they lie in state, friends may come to pay their last respects. Their favorite songs should be sung or played—especially those they may have said they'd have liked played at their funeral.

There are many funerary customs in different cultures for disposal of the body. Simple burial has been the most common from the dawn of time, often involving little more then laying the body in a deep hole, filling in the hole, and setting up a marker of some sort upon the grave. The body may be placed in a coffin, and grave gifts may be interred as offerings. Important figures such as royalty were generally entombed in crypts or mausoleums, which could be astonishingly elaborate—think of King Tut's tomb! Mummification was an important practice in many cultures (as embalming still is today) in an attempt to preserve the semblance of life. Parsis, Incas, and some North American tribes exposed their dead in high places to be consumed by vultures—returning later to collect the bones. Today, cremation is becoming increasingly popular, as it leaves ashes that may later be kept in an urn, scattered in some favorite place, or even shot into space!

Any of these customs and practices are to be conducted in a ritual manner.

My personal favorite—which I would choose for my own disposition—is the old Celtic custom of burying the dead before the next sunrise, without embalming or coffin, and not too deep. According to this custom, they would be dressed in their favorite clothes, accompanied by a few favorite items as grave goods. A winding sheet would enshroud the body. A sapling fruit tree (generally apple) would be planted upon the grave, and as the tree grew, its questing roots would draw sustenance from the decaying corpse, recycling what was once human into a thriving memorial tree. And eventually that tree would put forth its fruit to be eaten by the people, and the cycle of life would come full circle. (See song by Oscar Brown, Jr., "A Tree and Me.")

As an extension of this custom, a couple desiring a child would make love on the fresh grave on the nights following the interment, ritually inviting the spirit of the beloved dead to incarnate into the new life being conceived. The child, if there was one, would be given the name of the departed, and the afterbirth would be planted beneath the grave-tree, which would then become the child's own sacred totem tree. Apple trees normally live about as long as humans, so the fate of the child and his/her tree would be intertwined.

In addition to rites and practices involving the disposition of the body, there are two other very important ceremonies of passing that are as much for the living as the dead. These are wakes and funerals.

Wakes are best held as soon after the death as possible. All those who knew the deceased are invited to a big party in their honor. In former times, the corpse would also be present on a bier. Whiskey and other intoxicants would be passed liberally around the circle, as people took turns telling increasingly outrageous stories of their departed friend, laughing, singing songs, and generally having enough fun and making enough noise to "wake the dead." Conducted ritually, a wake is very similar to a bardic.

Funerals are generally more formal affairs. These days, they are usually held in churches or funeral parlors, which are set up with the coffin or urn on a platform or altar at the front of the room, and seating arranged as if for a lecture presentation. There will likely be a prescribed order of service, starting with a *eulogy* ("good word") presented by the deceased's closest kin. One at a time, selected people may be invited forward to tell their stories, as in the wake. And according to the deceased's spiritual beliefs, selected inspirational hymns of passage to the afterlife will be sung (our current favorite of these is "Into the West," sung by Annie Lennox at the end of the movie, "The Return of the King").

And finally, an ancestor altar should be established in the west side of the family's temple room, with images and mementos—including ashes—of the deceased.

181. Ritual of my Death

This is the Ritual of my Death.
It is a feast of Joy,
For I will dance among the stars.

Do not grieve my passing,
For we shall meet again,
And dance again, and love again,
For such is the Law and the Promise.

For now, let me take leave
And hold me no longer,
For I must be free...

I am the voice of the Beloved.
Find me within the Universe...
Remember me with as many names
As there are stars in the sky...

—*Frank Cordeiro*

182. A Tree Has Been Cut Down

The giant trees stand in a circle
Silently communing with the One
Who lies felled on the forest floor.
"One of us has been cut down".

The form but not the Being within the form.
Your freedom is our loss, beloved friend.
No longer do you stand with us on the Earth path,
Your precious, beautiful, human form destroyed
But You, Immortal Soul, dancing freely now,
Moving as lightning, or wind, or winged Spirit,
Communing with us in our earth-body sleep.

Farewell, dear friend.
As you depart for that unknown country,
We can remember
The Oneness of all Being.

—*Ralph Metzner, June 2003*

183. I'll Be Reborn

When I grow old, my time is near
And all my friends have gathered 'round,
O don't you weep, and don't you mourn,
'Cause you can't keep a good man down!

And in the Spring, yeah, I'll be back
Like the grass in yonder field.
I'll be reborn into this world
When the Lady's will is revealed.

Now when my body is in the ground
Well, there ain't nothing can keep me down;
I'll come with the blossoms and the growing grain
And then you'll know I'm back again.

Now I've had freedom, and joy and tears;
I'm proud I've learned each lesson well,
So when I come back in the Springtime
I won't repeat this lifetime's hell.

When I come back, I may be a baby
Or a bird high in a tree,
But you will know me if you still love me
'Cause I'll be born both wild and free!

Well, life's a burden, but death's a lie
And there ain't no reward up in the sky;
Just let me cast off this robe of mortal pain
And pick up where I left off again.

Now I ain't perfect, my soul ain't clean:
I done some things I ain't put right.
But all that karma will be forgotten
In a blaze of eternal light!

Now put my body beneath the ground
Don't plant no headstone on my grave;
Just plant an acorn and pass the whisky
And then you'll know that I've been saved.

Now seal the Circle, and dance and sing,
And let my spirit pass through the ring;
But don't you worry, and don't you weep
and mourn
'Cause I been promised, I'll be reborn!
I'll be reborn, I'll be reborn...
—Gwydion Pendderwen, 1979

184. Blood of the Ancients

It's the blood of the Ancients
That flows through our veins,
And the forms pass,
But the Circle of Life remains.
—Ellen Klaver

185. A Tree and Me

Please carve no cold headstone for me,
But rather plant a sapling tree;
And lay my ashes 'neath its foot,
So through my body it takes root.
Then as the seasons come and go,
My monument and I will grow;
Wave bright green flags at Summer's sky,
And harbor birds who happen by.
We'll bronze each Autumn, bloom with Spring,
And wear the white coat Winters bring.
The tree I marry with my dust,
Will husband me with rooted thrusts.
Our seed will scatter far and wide,
Across the fertile countryside;
And soon an arbor family
Will share our immortality,
A tree and me,
A tree and me.
—Oscar Brown, Jr.

186. Do Not Stand at My Grave and Weep

Do not stand at my grave and weep
I am not there. I do not sleep.
I am a thousand winds that blow.
I am the diamond glints on snow.
I am the sunlight on ripened grain.
I am the gentle autumn rain.
When you wake in the morning hush,
I am the swift, uplifting rush
Of quiet birds in circling flight.
I am the soft starlight at night.
Do not stand by my grave and mourn.
I am not there, I am reborn!
—Mary Frye, 1942

187. Well Song (round)

We will never, never lose our way
To the well, of Her memory
And the power, of the living flame,
It will rise, it will rise again!
Like the grasses, through the dark,
Through the storm,
Towards the sunlight, we shall rise again!
We are searching, for the Waters of Life,
We are moving, we shall live again!
—Starhawk, Rose May Dance,
Raven Moonshadow

6. Handfasting

Introduction: Handfasting
By Oberon

I first began performing weddings in the summer of 1968, for Neo-Pagans and hippies who wanted a ceremony other than those offered by established churches. Since the Church of All Worlds was one of the very first legally-incorporated Pagan churches (March 4, 1968), and I had been legally ordained by Life Science Ministries the previous year, I may have been the first person in the new Pagan Renaissance to have been legally qualified to perform such rites. Indeed, I have checked with the founders and elders of the few other Pagan groups around in the 60s, and none of them had any marriage rituals in their liturgies at that time. But CAW came out in a very public way, with a big temple, interviews in the paper and on TV, and active participation in various events—such as the first Earth Day in 1970. Many starry-eyed couples came to me to marry them.

In response to these requests, I cobbled together our first CAW marriage rituals from various sources: the Unitarian Church, my studies in anthropology and medieval history, science fiction novels, and romantic movies. When I began to study Ceremonial Magick and Witchcraft in 1970, I added elements such as casting the Circle, calling the Quarters, and invocations. And as the ritual evolved through numerous unions, I published some of this material in *Green Egg* magazine, which was widely read throughout the early Pagan community. In the early 70s, Ed Fitch created a set of rituals he constituted as "The Pagan Way," with a basic "handfasting" ritual largely derived from my materials.

> We get the term *handfasting* from Old Irish common law that existed before current forms of legislation. To hold something fast means to make it secure. It is a sailing term and literally implies being tied in place, hence the hand-fasting cord. It was not exclusively used for love relationships, as leaders of nations could be handfasted in battle. A handfasting involved a public statement of a commitment for a set period of time in order to accomplish some task so that both parties could be secure. Some of the most common reasons were marriage, whether or not the couple lived together, the raising of children even from rape, and property mergers. (—Dr. S. D'Montford, 2003)

In the spring of 1974, Morning Glory and I were married at Llewellyn Publications' Spring Witchmoot in Minneapolis, in the most spectacular Pagan wedding up to that time. Isaac Bonewits and Carolyn Clark officiated as priest and priestess, and Margot Adler was the minstrel. Hundreds of people attended, and the event was covered by all local media—as well as a TV crew from Japan! The entire ritual was later published in *Green Egg*, and it is also reproduced below. Subsequently, this ceremony was picked up and adapted (often with much simplification!) by many other Pagan groups. Morning Glory and I have, upon occasion, been courteously invited to take a small part in handfastings at Pagan festivals around the country. I recall one such ceremony during which the priestess handed Morning Glory the Tradition's hoary Book of Shadows, asking her if she could memorize one of the ancient invocations. Morning Glory laughed, saying, "I think so; I wrote it!"

Here is a basic outline of the now-"traditional" handfasting ritual Morning Glory and I developed and refined over the past 38 years, including advance preparations:

Planning

Parties to wed should meet with priest and priestess several months before the wedding date to consult regarding the ritual, vows, venue, guests, dress, music, reception, and other details. Set the date, work up a script for your ceremony, and prepare for the handfasting. Is it going to be a legal wedding as well as a magickal rite? If so, a marriage license will need to be obtained, and the priest and priestess may need to be ordained clergy of an incorporated church (check in your state). If the ritual is to be photographed or videotaped, who will do it? What customs are to be incorporated into the ceremony? What special objects are to be on the altar? What is the color theme? What flowers are to be worn, or used as decorations?

Morning Glory and I also insist on a "couples (or whatever) counseling" session beforehand, to ensure that all parties are on the same page regarding their convictions and expectations—especially concerning aspects of married life that few people seem to think of during courtship. Among other things, we ask: "Why do you each want to be handfasted? What does getting handfasted mean to you? What do you hope that getting handfasted will do for you and your relationship?" (Incidentally, while most of this discussion refers to "couples," the CAW sanctions marriages for same-sex couples as well as multiple partnerships.)

The Ritual

Rehearsal and Site Preparation: At least 24 hours prior to the ceremony, and often again just a few hours before "showtime," it is important to do a walk-through of the ritual with all parties. Set up the altar, and hold a final briefing with everyone who has a role in the ceremony.

Arrivals: Ushers or other helpers direct the guests to their seats as they enter. Music may be played. Priest and priestess take their positions at the altar.

Processional: When it is time to begin the rite, the attendants process up to the altar, and to the sides, followed by the groom(s) and finally, the bride(s).

Welcoming: This is the *"Dearly beloved, we are gathered together to witness the union of..."* part. At this time, if they wish, the parties may now acknowledge their families and special guests.

Circle Casting: While most magickal Circle castings are intended to isolate the Circle from the mundane world, handfasting Circle castings are intended to be more inclusive, and are usually unique to this rite.

Elemental Invocations: Here the emphasis is on Elemental blessings, rather than guardianship. Again, these are usually unique for handfastings.

Deity Invocations: In a handfasting, it is common for the God to be invoked into the groom, and the Goddess to be invoked into the bride. Of course, standard invocations may also be used, asking for divine blessings.

Exchange of Vows: These are usually written by the bride and groom themselves. They may be read from little scrolls, or from the Book of Rituals, as few couples can be expected to recite memorized pieces under these circumstances!

Exchange of Rings: The rings are acknowledged and exchanged, and each partner slips the ring onto the other's finger. Other tokens may be used as well, such as necklaces.

Handfasting: This is the central act of a handfasting rite. The couple clasp hands while priest and priestess wrap and tie a cord around their wrists, binding them together.

Pronouncement of Marriage: If this is to be a legal marriage, the priest and priestess pronounce that the couple is now married, by the power vested in them. The couple kiss.

Sharing: As their first act of hospitality, the couple offer a communion of food and drink to each other and the guests.

Benedictions: The priest or priestess offers a final benediction upon the newlyweds.

Jumping the Broom: Two attendants take up either end of a broom, holding it about a foot above the ground. The broom symbolizes the threshold of the bride and groom's new abode. With clasped hands, they jump over it and run out the exit.

Thanks & Dismissals: The deities and Elements are thanked and bid farewell.

Opening the Circle: Merry meet and merry part, and merry meet again!

Merry-Making: On to the reception area for gift-opening, cake-cutting, feasting, photography, music, dancing, and general merriment.

ꞔ. A Common Rite of Handfasting

By Morning Glory & Oberon

(This rite has evolved over 38 years, and has been used as a basis for countless handfastings! It is infinitely adaptable, as any element may be replaced or expanded upon. The vows are not stated here at all, as these are individually composed by the couple.)

Circle Casting *(all participants holding hands)*:

A Circle spun of living Love,
a Circle of the Heart;
A Circle of the silver Moon,
and each of us a part;
A Circle made of passion's fire,
Uniting all as One;
A Circle of the greening Earth,
A Circle of the Sun.
A Circle to be cast by day,
So love be made at night
A Circle of the ancient way,
A Circle of delight!

(—Anodea Judith)

Calling the Quarters:

E: I call the Eastern powers of Air,
You whose breath of life we share,
Bring understanding, kindness, care,
And loving words, both clear and fair,
Come bless this day our rite of love,
    As below then so above.

S: I call the Southern powers of Fire,
Whose light doth stir the poet's lyre,
With love's bright spark our hearts inspire,
Bring passion's flame, bring sweet desire,
Come bless this day our rite of love,
    As below then so above.

W: Oh powers of the Western sea,
Oh water's flowing unity,
Bring feeling, warmth and empathy,
That all our lives may blessed be,
Come bless this day our rite of love,
    As below then so above.

N: Oh Northern powers of living Earth,
Charge our souls from death to birth,
On solid ground of rock and loam,
Bring forth our food and build our home,
Come bless this day our rite of love,
    As below then so above.

(—Tom Williams)

HPs: Brothers and sisters, we are gathered together today to celebrate the sacred rites of handfasting between [BRIDE] and [GROOM]. We are their friends and family, and we join hands together in a circle to create this sacred space to honor their perfect love and trust. There is magick to be done here today; the magick of love.

*(**Processional:** Bride & groom enter with best man, maid of honor, and parents. Bride, groom, best man & maid of honor stand before altar, with bride opposite HPs, and the groom opposite HP. Parents return to Circle.)*

HP: We call upon the power of the God and Goddess within us all to manifest their presence here in this sacred space and to be present in the bodies of [BRIDE] and [GROOM] that they may look at each other with the eyes of love and always see the divinity of their beloved.

HPs: *(to bride)*
Thou shalt be the star that rises
From the twilight sea.
Thou shalt bring a man dreams
To rule his destiny.
Thou shalt bring the moon-tides
To the soul of a man,
The tides that flow and ebb, and flow again;
The magic that moves
In the moon and the sea;
These are thy secret, and they belong to thee.
Thou art the eternal woman, thou art she...
The tides of all men's souls belong to thee.
Danu in heaven, on Earth, Persephone,
Diana of the moon and Hecate,
Veiled Isis, Aphrodite from the sea,
All these thou art and they are seen in thee.

HP: *(to groom)*
All wild creatures hear thy call
Upon the haunted wind.
Within thy soul the Horned One
Returns to Earth again.
Together you shall manifest

The magick of the man,
And falcons soar from out the sky
To perch upon thy hand.
The serpent's wisdom thou shalt learn
From tip of forkèd tongue.
The fleetness of the white stag's flight
In starlight or in sun.
Lord of Light and Lord of Shadow –
Keeper of the key
Which unlocks the door of dreams
Whereby men come to thee.
Cernunnos, Tammuz, Horus, Pan –
By name we set thee free!
O shepherd of the wild woodland,
May you be one with he.

HP & HPs: *(Bowing to the bride & groom and speaking in unison)* The Lord and the Lady are with us.

HPs: Marriage is a real experience and not a fairytale romance, and as such it must be considered carefully. Do you, [BRIDE], take this man to be your lawful wedded husband? To love, honor, cherish, and respect him? To care for him always in sickness and health, poverty and wealth, when happy or sad, through good times and bad, for as long as love shall last?

BRIDE: I do.

HP: Marriage is a binding promise not to be undertaken lightly nor discarded conveniently. Do you, [GROOM], take this woman to be your lawful wedded wife? To love, honor, cherish, and respect her? To care for her always in sickness and health, poverty and wealth, when happy or sad, through good times and bad, for as long as love shall last?

GROOM: I do.

HPs: Have you considered the gravity of your commitment?

BRIDE & GROOM: We have.

HP: Have you considered the levity of your commitment?

BRIDE & GROOM: We have!

HPs: Then offer now your vows to one another. *(They do so)*

HP: What do you give to one another as a token of your vows?

BRIDE or GROOM: We give these rings as a symbol of our love.
(Best man brings rings from the altar and offers them to bride & groom, who take and place them on each other's hands.)

HP: *(Maid of honor takes cord from altar and hands it to HP & HPs)* Clasp your hands together. *(They do so)* With this cord we do bind your hands together, in token that you are now one. *(HP & HPs bind their clasped hands together)*

HPs: Let this binding be a link but not a chain; that your love will draw you closer but not enslave you.

HP: In the name of the Goddess and the God, you are bound together, hand to hand, and life to life.

HPs: And now, by the power vested in me by the Goddess and by the Church of All Worlds...

HP: And by the power vested in me by the God and by the Church of All Worlds...

HP & HPs: *(in unison)* We now pronounce you husband and wife.

BRIDE & GROOM: *(THE KISS......!)*

HPs: *(Taking chalice of water from altar and holding it up)* We consecrate this sacrament of pure water that it be a reminder of the bonds of life on Earth. For water shared is life shared. *(HPs holds chalice while HP consecrates with wand.)*

HP & HPs: *(in unison)* As above, so below.

HP: *(Taking plate of bread from altar and holding it up)* We bless this hearty bread—the staff of life—that it be a token of our bonds of fellowship. For bread broken and shared together both nourishes and heals. *(Offers bread to bride & groom)* May you never hunger!

HPs: *(Offers water to bride & groom)* May you never thirst! This will be your first act of hospitality as a married couple—to share this pure water and this hearty bread with your family and friends.

BRIDE & GROOM: *(Offer bread and water to best man & maid of honor, saying to each, "May you never hunger; may you never thirst." Then best man & maid* *of honor take water round the Circle and share with all. During this sharing, HPs sings "Give Yourself to Love." Finally chalice and plate are returned to altar.)*

HP: *(Benediction, to Circle, with hands outstretched in blessing to the couple)* Out of the billions on Earth, these two have come, have looked into each other's eyes, and are now made one. Their ways have converged and shall now be together. In our deepest being we hope that their path may be pleasant and the sky fair where they reside. But if sorrow comes, as it can surely come to all, may the pressure of the trial only bring them more closely together. With clasped hands and united hearts, may they bear life's trouble together and share its joy together.

HPs: Leaping the broom is the ancient traditional way of signifying that you are establishing a joint household together.

[BRIDE] and [GROOM], prepare to go forth now in perfect love and perfect trust.

(Best man & maid of honor clear a space, kneel down at the edge of the circle, and each hold one end of the broom. Bride & groom jump the broomstick and exit. All assembled cheer as they leave the room.)

HP: Will you all rejoin hands for one more moment? A Circle of sacred space was created for this ceremony. It is time to conclude by releasing that energy and returning this space to its normal state. We will do so with these magick words:

HP & HPs: *(in unison.)*
All from Air into Air,
Let the misty curtains part.
All is ended, all is done,
What has been, now must be gone.
What is done by ancient art,
Must merry meet and merry part,
And merry meet again!

188. Handfasting Quarter Calls & Circle Casting

(Written for the handfasting & legal marriage of two friends, this could easily be adapted to fit any commitment ceremony for two or more people. Instructions are given because the attendees in the original rite came from a variety of religious backgrounds.)

Let us begin in the East—the Land of new beginnings.
Here we ask for the blessings of the element Air:
Which brings truth, communication, wisdom and vision.
May the Air of the East
Join us to bless [couple's names] on this Sacred Day
And throughout their lives together.
Blessed Be!

Now we turn to the South,
Where we ask the blessings of the element Fire
Home of passion, pleasure, joy, and happiness.
May the Fire of the South
Join us to bless [couple's names] on this Sacred Day
And throughout their lives together.
Blessed Be!

Now let us turn to the West,
Where the element Water flows forth...
Bringing tranquility, peace, deep emotion and serenity.

May the Water of the West
Join us to bless [couple's names] on this Sacred Day
And throughout their lives together.
Blessed Be!

Now we turn to the North,
Where the element Earth resides
Deeply grounded in strength, comfort and support
May the Earth of the North
Join us to bless [couple's names] on this Sacred Day
And throughout their lives together.
Blessed Be!

And in the Center and all around us,
Above and Below,
Resides the Spirit...
Who brings blessings of love, magic, friendship and community.
May the Spirit of all things Divine
Join us to bless [couple's names] on this Sacred Day

And throughout their lives together.
Blessed Be!

From heart to heart, hand to hand
Flows the energy of our loving friendship
and support.
Creating a Circle of Sacred Space:
A glowing sphere of love and light.
It is a safe place filled with our hopes and
blessings
To support this wonderful couple
As they affirm their love for each other
On this special day.
Blessed Be!
—*Lady Moondance*

189. In Humble Thanks

Holy Isis, you who are all things
The Earth and the Sky, the Cup and the Blade
You are the space where the future brings
All of the todays that our dreams have made.
Deep in my heart, your sacred voice sings.
I've heeded your call, your commands obeyed

I give you thanks for this love I've won
Sacred Ones, Ancient Ones, I honor you
Mother and Father, Daughter and Son
Mother Isis, I pledge myself anew
My service to you is never done.
I follow your path, it's always been true.
—*Avilynn Pwyll*

190. Blessing of Mead & Cakes

MEAD: We consecrate this sacrament of living alchemy, of pure water, honey, yeast, and the fire of life, to the gods as an emblem of their lifegiving blessing. Drink deep of the intoxication of being alive and in love!

CAKES: The grain is the fruit of the Earth, kindled and ripened by the sun. Each day, we are blessed with the offered lives of other children of this rich Earth, so that we may live. Eat this, knowing the sweetness of living, the fleetingness of the rich passing taste.
—*Dragon Singing & Nemea Arborvitae*

II. Soliloquy on Multiple Marriages
By Morning Glory, for her handfasting with Oberon & Wolf

To be delivered by officiating Clergy:
Marriage is a very unique state of being. It defies the law of nature that moves the individual to struggle against all others to achieve his goal. Instead it calls forth an even greater evolutionary purpose: the union with others to achieve goals inaccessible to the individual. The driving force that makes this union possible is love that dissolves all boundaries. And yet for a marriage to be successful, its partners must retain the boundaries necessary to a high degree of individuality. This harmonious balance is all about unique and individual beings choosing to merge their lives and work together. The primary purpose of marriage is to create a family; families create communities, communities create tribes, and so goes the human adventure toward unity through diversity.

In nature there are many ways to find a mate and create a family. Human beings have had many models in the past. However, we live in a time when the single pattern of the monogamous nuclear family has come to be the only form of marriage allowed in this part of the world. But evolution may not be outlawed or only outlaws will evolve, so there will always be those who choose to live lives of adventure and experiment beyond the comfortable beaten track. Such is the path of those who choose to open their hearts and lives to more than one lifemate at a time.

A multiple marriage is a wild adventure into unknown territory; it is a bold challenge to those who deny that such a thing can ever exist. It is a rare creature like a unicorn—composed of dreams and vision, but also of flesh and blood. Like any other marriage it has its highs and lows, agonies and ecstasies. A multiple marriage calls for greater levels of commitment to communication, to tolerance, to trust, and to creativity. The more mates in a marriage, the more complexity increases, and the more effort that is called forth to answer the various challenges.

When a multiple marriage is successful, its fruits are bountiful: higher energy levels, pooled resources, ecstatic sexual union, and most precious of all, a sense of freedom. This freedom grows from the glad knowledge that no single partner has to meet all the needs of another. Your mates are your allies in the pursuit of a joyous life. There are more hands to do the work together, more shoulders to cry on, and more points of view with which to examine the universe. When a multiple marriage is in difficulty, there are more systems to go wrong, more lives at stake, and more hearts to be broken. In general the stakes are higher both ways; the risks are greater but so are the rewards.

Multiple mates are pioneers on a road that leads to a new future in human community. They must jettison all unnecessary cargo that holds them back: jealousy, possessiveness, shame, righteousness, unhealthy addictions, antagonism, pettiness, and revenge are all poisonous burdens that they cannot afford to bear. There will be bandits along the way who will attack them for what they are, and sneak thieves in the night who will try to poison their well or rob them of their bliss. They must hold onto each other as well as their resolve to reach their goal.

Such a family will have a personality of its own. Oberon, Morning Glory, and Wolf are a different energy dynamic than any of them separately or paired as two. The larger community must learn to recognize and respect this group personality. And as this family grows, each new person will change the group dynamic so that its collective persona will alter in a fluid changing harmony – like a chorus that increases in power and beauty with each added voice. This marriage will have to evolve systems to honor the smaller patterns within the relationship as well as to embrace larger changes, for this will be a family of strong individuals as well as powerful shifting magickal relationships.

Our community welcomes this marriage of bold pioneers and we honor their courage and their efforts to give birth to a new entity that will grow and mature, and hopefully live far beyond the span of years of its original creators; for such a family is a human creature with immortal potential.

Poly Handfasting Components

(Here are but a few of the components that went into our triad handfasting ten years ago; the entire rite is far too long to include here. —OZ)

HP: Dearly beloved, we are gathered together today to celebrate the sacred rites of handfasting among Oberon, Morning Glory, and Wolf. They have been joined in love and life and they have learned to work together in partnership, and to envision and create new ways of living in harmony. We are their friends and family, and we have joined hands together to create this sacred space to honor their perfect love and trust. Here be magick; here be love!

OZ *(enters Circle to stand before altar):*
One man alone is like a cripple bound to his pillow, ennobled/humbled by the daily discipline of conquering trivial detail, even the lacing of boots a major challenge. When does the one achieve more?

MG *(enters Circle to stand at left of Oberon, taking his hand):*
Two may love serenely, with occasional storms of high happiness, if the weather and the times are with them, and chance smiles on them, and death does not halve them. When expectations are small, and life benevolent, a two works well enough.

WOLF: *(enters Circle to stand with Oberon & Morning Glory, taking their hands):*
Three restlessly seeks another mate like water seeks the sea. But a triumvirate is the freest of all marriages from conflict. A chair with three legs does not wobble.

(—from Courtship Rite, *by Donald Kingsbury)*

191. Begin To Weave: A Poly Handfasting Song

Written September, 1996, for the handfasting of Morning Glory, Oberon, & Wolf
by Liza Gabriel, with love and affection

Leaping Lord and laughing Goddess;
With all our wounds and follies can you tell us,
With all our fears and rages do we have it in us,
To weave together in your ever expanding love?

Begin to weave and the thread will be given
Commit your hearts and watch them spin
Give and receive beloved children
Weave you tapestry of love again and again

Weave around the silvery moon
Embroider passion's rune
Weave the many weave the one
Weave a circle round the sun
Weave with air weave with fire
A fabric of desire
Weave with water weave with earth
Weave with death and rebirth
Weave by night weave by day
The Holy Mother's way
Weave by day weave by night
A circle of delight

Begin to weave and the thread shall be given
Commit your hearts and watch them spin
Give and receive, beloved children
Weave your tapestry of love again and again

Weave together weave apart
With your guts and with your heart
Weave with darkness and with light
With divine inner sight
Weave with silence weave with song
Through the seasons short and long
Weave below weave above
With a thread of living love
Weave below weave above
With a thread of living love
Weave below weave above
With a thread of living love

Begin to weave and the thread shall be given
Commit your hearts and watch them spin
Give and receive, beloved children
Weave your tapestry of love again and again

192. Handparting

By Oberon

Sadly, even with the best of intentions, not all relationships last forever. Sometimes it is necessary to dissolve a union begun in love, but no longer desired. Thus there is a modern Pagan tradition of "handparting," done as a kind of reversal of the rite of handfasting. It involves making statements to the Circle that explain the reasons for this parting, and essentially undo the original vows taken. Then the original handfasting cord (or an acceptable substitute, if the original is not available) is held by both parties at opposite ends, and ceremonially cut with the athamé, after which the severed pieces are burned in the ritual fire. Finally, a chalice of vinegar may be ceremonially passed, and then poured onto the ground. Afterwards, each party departs the Circle in opposite directions.

In old Irish Common Law the handfasting contract was considered finished at the end of the agreed upon period and simply could not be broken before that time. Their magickal word was their bond. After that period of time had elapsed there was often a celebration by means of a "Feast of Completion."

The whole village attended the Feast of Completion and both partners were required to attend. If both partners could not attend, the feast was rescheduled until they could. Before the feast began both praised the other and wished each other well in future endeavors. Then there was much feasting and drinking. It was a happy time. This allowed both partners to maintain open friendships with all in the village. This would allow them to not have to choose one person over the other. The community could still function and could get on with business as usual. (—Dr. S. D'Montford, 2003)

Separation Ritual to Begin a Feast of Completion
By Dr. S. D'Montford, 2003

(An open Circle is cast that includes the whole affected group. On the altar are any remaining tokens of the handfasting if the couple were handfasted. If not you will still need a cord, a cup, and a candle.)

HIGH PRIESTESS:

As the seasons turn in their cycle and their planets in their orbits so we return to our beginning.

Spring has become Winter; the circle of the cup is drained to be filled again.

(Adapt to current season)

You have completed the period of your vow to each other and now turning in your unbroken course you diverge.

Ho! You elemental forces of the West and winter, help us complete here today what was begun long ago

HIGH PRIEST/ESS *(hands them the cup, with each repeating)*:

As the cup was filled it is now drained to be filled again.

ALL *(With both of their hands on the cup, the couple pour some mead or wine onto the ground. High Priest/ess hands them the cord. Each helps untie the knot and then repeats)*:

Our wills, wishes, and desires were bound together for a purpose. That purpose has now ended to begin again elsewhere. The circle of the cord is open but unbroken.

(As mentioned above don't cut the cord or do anything destructive to it, especially if it was used at a handfasting, as all present took a vow based on the tying of the knot.)

ALL *(High Priest/ess gestures to the candle, while couple places one hand on the candle snuffer)*:

The fires of love and the light of purpose that was lit by (insert name of personal love Deity or Dieties here) and has burnt so brightly in our breast is now extinguished to be re-lit again elsewhere.

(The former couple extinguishes the flame.)

HIGH PRIEST/ESS:

Do you have a blessing for each other?

FORMER COUPLE *(saying loudly)*:

We do!

(A short blessing is given by each to the other:)

I thank you (name) for having been my partner for (period of time). The wheel has turned, the cycle is complete. The winter has arrived, the road diverges and it is now that we must walk our separate paths into the west. My blessings to you on your journey. May the road rise up to meet you and may the winter wind be ever at your back, moving you forward to the east where you will walk in the pleasant fields of spring again soon.

(Something more individual, spontaneous, or personal may be stated, but remember to keep it very neutral. More blessings may be added by members of the group. After the exchange of blessings there can be a short reading or invocation. I often use the verse from "Desiderata":)

"...Be yourself. Do not feign affection, neither be cynical about love, for in the face of all aridity and disenchantment it is as perennial as the grass..."

FORMER COUPLE:

I thank our friends seen and unseen who witnessed our vows made within the sacred space of a Circle, and who helped us to keep our magickal word. This day you are witness to its successful completion. Eat, drink, dance, and celebrate with me on this night for tomorrow my journeys begin again.

(all cheer)

A grapevine dance is lead by the former couple. The Quarters are dismissed. Then everyone feasts and parties.

7. Meditations, Initiations, & Mysteries

I. Meditations
By Nova Love

Grounding Journey

Imagine if you could take a moment and stop, knowing that the process of life continues to move on around you, over you, under you, to each side, and through you. Allowing the current of time to run its course, you simply stay put and rest. For three mindful breaths, see the circumstances you are involved in that are asking for your attention flash to mind. Now acknowledge them gratefully and inform yourself that you may return to them later if you then choose. Taking three more breaths, each deeper than the last, settle into the position you choose to hold during your grounding. Wiggle into a place of stillness, and then be set. Feel the weight of your body as you release the muscles in your face and mouth. Feel the expansion of your lungs as you settle your eyes either comfortably open or closed.

Imagine that you're sitting on a mirror and that there is a reflection – another you – within the realm below the surface. The image of your appearance is clearly your body in complete reflection, and as you inhale a few more breaths, shift your consciousness into the other you of the mirror's reflection. Notice the difference in the surroundings beginning to emerge around you. The walls of an earthen room are there; you are in a simple hut. As your inner eye opens to the calm filtered light, you see a pail near you. Moving to get the pail you find it is holding liquid…pigment. Begin painting yourself – if you can smell, the pigment is earthy and you know what to do with it. Seeing your work, you recognize that you are ready to travel down the stairway you now see in the room. You can walk down it and through a hallway into a court-way that opens up. A throne-like seat awaits you here; you observe the look and feel of it.

Finding your way into the seat, you settle in. Vibrations of peace and healing concentrate here, in you. (*pause*) Awareness opens and you realize there is a mirror-like surface above you and the throne. You see yourself as the mirror person above and begin to move up, completely entering yourself through the surface in a few breaths, bringing peace and a grounded sense. Returning fully now into your body here in this room, breathing all of your-self deeply into your body, moving some, remembering, and integrating as you open your eyes, wholly return – calm, safe, gratefully grounded.

Centering Journey

After creating sacred space and completing grounding, get into a comfortable posture that can be held for some time without effort. Breathe in, consciously feeling the air pass through your nose and relaxing the muscles of your body as it enters and exits your lungs. Envision the particles of the air as though they were clearly visible, being drawn into you, intermingling and exchanging with the particles of your body, and exiting into a great sea of similar stuff. Take several rounds of breaths and continue this visualization. Now looking down as though from above, create a mental picture of your body peacefully breathing. Slowly begin expanding this perspective of the self and start to include the room or surroundings about you. Your peripheral vision is gaining increased perspective as you rise up safely. Now see the shelter you were in from above the roof, as though you have just floated above the upper reaches of where you came from. The outside sky welcomes you as you float on, seeing everything below you begin to open in an ever more expansive panorama. As you float still further, it may help you if you see the neighborhood or area beneath, and then the city or surrounding countryside all visible now. The landmass begins to become distinguishable, and as your pace quickens now, you rise high into the sky. This far above the low atmosphere, the details of the Earth begin to recede. Beyond the atmosphere and into near space you continue traveling: now at amazing speed the solar system passes, the arm of our galaxy – our entire galaxy – many, many galaxies, and finally eternal space. Quietly remain here for a time that feels right to you. Retrace your travel, returning toward Earth as you are ready. Return to the room your body occupies, and back above your body. Breathe yourself into your nostrils now as the particles you know are here. Fill your body with your consciousness in every cell, now enlivened with the breath and completely within the body. Gradually awaken your muscles by some small movement until you are ready to rise. Stand up as you are called to and stretch—with your arms in the air reach the farthest places as they all touch you.

¶¶. Initiations

Arcana Encounter: The Fool's Journey
By Oberon

Here is an initiatory ritual we created on January 22, 1998, for the British TV show, "Desperately Seeking Something." "The Fool" in this case was Peter, the host of the show, who was traveling the world seeking out all kinds of religious and mystical groups in search of something truly meaningful. Somehow he found us, and brought along the whole crew to do the show. After a few days with us, his producer said, "Well, that's it, then. We don't have to look any further!"

But this little rite would work very well for an initiation into any metaphysical group. I am omitting the usual Circle casting, invocations, dismissals, etc. and only giving the Working itself:

Ten people have previously selected 10 Tarot Trumps, and designed a "Celtic cross reading" using them. Everyone sits in a circle, with the 10 seated in sequence of the reading, holding their cards and a small token of that card's message:

No.	Trump	Position	Trumper	Token
0	The Fool	Significator	Peter	Rose
1	The Magician	Covering	Imiri	Wand
2	High Priestess	Crossing	Morning Glory	Winged Isis necklace
3	The Empress	Root	Maerian	Barley
6	The Lovers	Crown	Liza	Heart
7	The Chariot	Past	Wolf	Motorcycle model
8	Strength	Future	Sunny	Lion figurine
13	Death	Self	Wynter	Tiny skull on necklace
16	The Tower	Family & Friends	Starwhite	Chess rook
17	The Star	Hopes & Fears	LaSara	Star
21	The World	Final Outcome	Oberon	Earth globe

Magician places the Fool card in the center of the altar, gives rap, and puts fool's cap on Fool, also giving him a bindlestaff and a rose. Fool is then sent around the Circle to "encounter the Arcana." As he comes to each of the cardholders, that person stands, saying, *"You have now reached the House of _____. The chosen card is _____."* They place the card into position in the reading. Then the cardholder delivers the message, blessing, etc. of that Trump, concluding by giving the Fool a small token of that Trump to place in his bindle.

After the whole Circle has been traversed, the Fool is blindfolded by Empress, and led up onto a kitchen stepstool (while people speaking gradually lower themselves to the ground, behind him), and told he must make "a leap of faith" by falling backwards into the Circle.

When he does, he is caught in the arms of all the people, his blindfold is removed, and he is lifted high while people sing "We sing for Mother Earth..." (led by High Priestess). Then he is slowly lowered to the ground as everyone comes to a sitting place. All wait until Fool sits up. Then we cheer, and serve communion feast, sacred bullshit, etc.

Coven Nemorensis Oath of Fealty
By Anath Stryx

The coven is Earth. I plant my feet firmly in the soil of the coven. I am a seed in the coven. My roots will seek nourishment in the coven, and my fruits are offerings to the coven. I place my Earth upon the altar of the coven with Perfect Love and Perfect Trust.

The coven is Water. In this Water I am cleansed and refreshed. My body, mind, and spirit may drink deeply of the coven and be purged and enlightened. My tears, blood, and sweat run into and merge with the river formed by my sisters and brothers of the coven. Our river is swept into the Sea of Greater Consciousness. I place my Water upon the altar of the coven with Perfect Love and Perfect Trust.

The coven is Fire. I immerse the passion of my faith into the coven. My heart is a sacred altar, upon which the flame of my devotion and desire is kindled. I am warmed, cheered, and guided by the coven. My fears are burned away, my ignorance dispatched, and my will to act is ignited by Fire. My love becomes one with the Fire of the coven. Love is the beacon of the coven. I place my Fire upon the altar of the coven with Perfect Love and Perfect Trust.

The coven is Air. The breath of Divinity rushes through the body of the coven and invigorates it. Let my breath be one with the coven. I will utter the power of words with the Air, and my will shall be manifest. I place my Air upon the altar of the coven, so that the coven will rise upon the wings of wind. I do this with Perfect Love and Perfect Trust.

The coven is Akasha. Akasha is the life of the coven. Let no act be performed without Spirit, let no intent be designed without Spirit. The coven offers the communion with Spirit as a blessing. Let my offering of Spirit to the coven be accepted at the heart of the coven with Perfect Love and Perfect Trust.

It is with these five Elemental offerings placed upon the altar that I seal my oath of fealty to the coven.

III. Mysteries

Reflection of the Mysteries
By Melanie Stoehrer (Redwood Shadowtree)

Preparation before ritual:
- Find individual, pocket-size mirrors for all participants. You can find these in craft stores.
- You will need at least 3 boxes that "nest" within each other. The smallest will contain the mirrors, so plan size accordingly. Put the mirrors inside the smallest box and wrap it with paper. Put this small box in the next largest box, and wrap. Do the same with the final box.
- Ritual leaders may wish to teach the group the chant prior to doing this ritual, as well as explain how the energy raised will be "swallowed" back into each person.

Ritual:
Deity invocations:

Isis, Goddess of hope and intuition, Lady of the Stars, heighten our intuition so we may find what we seek!

Thoth, God of wisdom and magick, Lord of the Mysteries, give us the wisdom to know what we are looking for!

The group should sit comfortably with the wrapped boxes in the center of the Circle.

Ritual Leader: Look up at the sky for a moment…in such a sky it is easy to lose oneself. The whole universe surrounds us. And it is made up of many layers. Far above us, beyond distances we cannot comprehend, are other worlds, other stars, other suns, each creating a layer to the universe.

Look around you at all you see…trees, grass, animals, even the voices of the wind surround you, creating the comfortable layers of our lives. The sounds and smells are familiar—even commonplace. Because we are human, this is what we sense and know. These layers are tightly wrapped around us—they are the universe we are familiar with.

But if you close your eyes and listen to the music of your soul, of your spirit, of the spirits of those around you, you can just barely hear what is a whole other universe—one which exists beyond your mundane senses.

The ancient Egyptians believed the onion to be a sacred plant because it contained the universe within its many layers. To reach the mysteries of the universe, we must strip away the layers…removing the tangible and familiar until all that is left is the universe within, and the key to all its mysteries

But how do we unlock them? How can we close our eyes on the world we live in and see BEYOND what our senses tell us? Those mysteries are well guarded…guarded and locked by layers we create. To reach that universe, those Great Mysteries, we must remove those layers.

This box will be our onion, a representation of the universe, and in the center lay the key to the Mysteries. To reach that key, to find what we seek, we must remove the layers of the onion to get to the core.

I ask you all to come and kneel around this box. The layer you see before you is the first one we must remove. It represents all the problems, all the barriers, all the garbage we face everyday. Close your eyes and think about those problems. Feel the emotions associated with them…experience every part of those barriers that surround you.

Now, lay your hand upon this box and rip the barriers away *(participants should rip up wrappings on the box)*. Rip it into tiny bits…crumple it up and throw them away. Get rid of that which prevents you from reaching the Mysteries.

Leader should remove second box from larger one. Take the first "layer" out of the way so that everyone can see the next layer.

Leader: Once we throw away the problems that face us everyday, we are left with the barriers in our minds; inhibitions, fears, and restraints that block us from the Mysteries. Now is the time to look honestly at yourself and reflect upon the past turning of the Wheel. What are your barriers? Your fears? Your restraints? Your inhibitions? See them, feel them, and know them. Lay your hand upon this box and with all your strength, rip this layer away! Tear it to tiny pieces and throw them in the air, letting the wind blow them away!

Ritual leader should open the box and remove smallest box. Put it in the center where everyone can see it. Take the second "layer" out of the way so that everyone can see the next layer.

Leader: Ahhh—now we are but a step from the center *(ritual leader should come forward and cut away the paper, exposing the box)*. The universe and its secrets lie within this core—as does the key for reaching them. *(Cut tape holding box shut)* Move closer. *(Open box flap)* Close your eyes. *(Open box flap)* Open your consciousness. *(Open box flap)* Expand your mind. *(Open final flap)* Join hands and open your eyes and gaze upon the Mysteries…and discover the key to unlocking them!

Group should look into box. The mirrors should be placed reflective side up.

Leader: Yes…the key to this Mystery and all the others are found within you! YOU are the key to unlocking them.

Have each person reach in and take a mirror.

Leader: Look at your reflection. Study your face. *(Pause for a few moments of contemplation.)* The face you look upon is the face of a Goddess or God. *(Pause for a few moments.)* That face is the key to the mysteries…and your body is simply a vessel to contain the Mysteries. When seeking the mysteries, you must reflect upon yourself.
While group is still looking at their reflection, ritual leader should begin the chant:
When I seek the Mysteries,
The key is found inside of me.
Group should join in. Continue the chant until the energy has reached its peak. At that time the ritual leader should yell:
NOW!
Each participant should take energy back into them, and relax with their eyes closed.

Leader: Hear the words of the Goddess…*
*During this ritual, the traditional "Charge of the Goddess" was read. But ritual leaders should feel free to substitute any reading they feel appropriate

Leader: Always remember the key to all the mysteries of the universe, as the Mysteries themselves are found within you. Look within and know yourself in order to unlock them.
Ritual leaders should anoint participants foreheads at this time.

Leader: *May you always be able to find the Mysteries. So mote it be!*

Awakening Gaia
by Oberon & Morning Glory (with much material by Anodea Judith & others)
Main Ritual for Summerland Festival 2003

PROPS & COSTUMES:
Central altar (round)
   Magick refilling ewer
   Inflatable Earth ball
   Central altar cloth
   Gong or bell
   Small chalice
4 Quarter altars
   4 large chalices
   4 round mirrors
   4 statues of Millennial Gaia
   Elemental-colored altar cloths
Elementals: Appropriately-colored tabards
Priestess: Green robes, tabard, and veil
Fauna: Animal mask, horns, furry costume, etc.
Florus: "Green Man" mask, leaves, green tunic, etc.

GROUNDING *(Priest):*
We come into the Circle today and we stand alone—each of us apart and unique, like a cell or a seed.
We come from our small circles of separation into this larger Circle of cooperation. We come with a common purpose: to heal the pain of separation and transform the world by awakening our planet—our beloved Mother Gaia—into consciousness.

But before we can transform the world we must be willing to make some changes in ourselves. The magick we need to work for awareness is the ability of keeping our focus. So take a breath and release it.

Focus on the face you accept and acknowledge as you:
Your eyes and nose and laughing mouth.
Claim your face. Take a breath and release it.

Focus on your own heart beating, beating and never stopping.
Your heart that has courage and love, passion and hope, and desires unique only to you.
Love your heart and claim it. Take a breath and release it.

Focus on your body. Your physical vessel:
Your spine. Your chest. Your hands. Your feet on the earth. Your hips. Your sex, and the wonderment of your living self.

Cherish it and claim it. Take a breath and release it.

Focus on those you stand among. Your brothers and sisters. Your kin, who wonder and worry if they are loved, if they'll keep their job, if maybe that lump is cancer, wonder if you even see them. Claim your humanity with them. Take a breath and release it.

Focus on the Earth and the Elements; the plants and animals, rocks and seasons, the sun and the stars and beyond where your mind can conceivably grasp, where it dissolves in wonder and terror. Take a breath and release it.

From the stars to Earth to our tribe gathered here, from your face and your eyes, into your shadows—

We are one. We are one. We are one. Everyone breathe one last breath, hold it and release it altogether with a sound.

CIRCLE CASTING *(Priestess):*
Round like a belly, the womb of rebirth
Round like the planet, our Mother, the Earth
Round like the cycles that ebb and that flow,
Round us a circle from which we shall grow.

Around us the trees fall, the Earth cries for rain;
Within us our souls call, crying with pain.
Around us a world getting lost in despair;
Around us a system that just doesn't care.

But here is a Circle to work and to learn;
Here is a place where we make the world turn.
As magic is made within this sacred ground,
With our hearts and our will shall this
  Circle be bound.

Gods full of wisdom, power and depth,
Our Circle's Your cycle of life and of death.
Give us Your guidance in all that we do;
Give us Your blessings to heal and renew!

CHANT (Ps):
Round and round the Earth is turning
Turning always round to morning
And from morning round to night. (x3)

CALLING THE DIRECTIONS

PRIEST: We call forth now the Elemental
  Children of Gaia…
PRIESTESS: *(Chants)*
  Children of Gaia, Come to us now,
  We claim you as our own! *(Gestures to all)*

ALL: Children of Gaia, Come to us now,
  We claim you as our own!

EAST: *(Steps forward)* I am the Air of
  Gaia:
The winds, the hurricanes and breezes,
The scent of flowers,
The vibrations of birdsong and drums.
I am Gaia's breath, echoed in your own.
(Steps back into Circle)

ALL: Children of Gaia, Come to us now,
  We claim you as our own!

SOUTH: *(Steps forward)* I am the Fires of Gaia:
  The volcanoes and geysers, the hot fluid core,
  Alive and changing, the lightning, the sparks,
  The slow smoldering chemistry of life.

ALL: Children of Gaia, Come to us now,
  We claim you as our own!

WEST: *(Steps forth)* I am the Waters of Gaia:
The rain and rivers, the seas and the snows.
We are the fluid in Gaia's veins—
Feel us in your blood and tears.

ALL: Children of Gaia, Come to us now,
  We claim you as our own!

NORTH: *(Steps out)* I am the Earthwork of Gaia:
  Mountains and caverns, beaches and canyons,
  Crystals, metals, and gems.
  We are Gaia's flesh and bones.
  (Steps back into Circle)

ALL: Children of Gaia, Come to us now,
  We claim you as our own!

Ps: The Elemental Forces are here and it is good.
  Now let us call forth the living beings:
  Children of Gaia.

ALL: Children of Gaia, Come to us now,
  We claim you as our own!

FAUNA: *(Steps forward)* I am Fauna;
  I stand for the animals.
  Finned, furred, feathered, scaled and skinned.
  We are Gaia's Children.
  We call to the humans to see us as your kin.
  (Steps back into Circle)

ALL: Children of Gaia, Come to us now,
  We claim you as our own!

FLORUS: *(Steps forward)* I am Florus;
  I stand for vegetation.

The canopy of forests, the healing herbs,
The flowers and fruits, vegetables and grains.
We are Gaia's Children.
We call to the humans to see us as your kin.
(Steps back into Circle)

ALL: CHILDREN OF GAIA, COME TO US NOW,
WE CLAIM YOU AS OUR OWN!!

P: Welcome, Children of Gaia!
We too are Children of the Mother.
We are your brothers and sisters.
You are part of us, as we are of you.

CHANT (Ps): She's been waiting, waiting,
She's been waiting so long!
She's been waiting for her Children
To remember, to return… (x3)

P: Now, please, everyone be seated.

ELEMENTALS: *(Begin circulating round
hand mirrors from each Quarter, deosil…)*

Ps: Consciousness—what a concept! How
did it come to be? Let's imagine how it might
have been. How it was for us.

In a time before there was memory, we
lived in our Mother's belly. We were embedded in creation, held in her womb, woven
together in the fabric of life.

We were a part of the Earth and Waters,
and the Fires and the Air, one with trees and
beasts and rocks and seasons—a web of
teeming life, merging, connecting all in our
unconsciousness deep within the Mother.

Our Mother's love was great and her desire kept us held to her breast, and we suckled for millennia—cycles of time spiraling
around and around and around.

And then—

In one moment of time, within one millennium, we reached out of the darkness, and
emerged into the light.

And a dazzle of brightness that was the I,
the Me, the Ego, burst into glory. Our eyes
opened—*my* eyes opened, and I saw my image in the waters.

For the first time I knew myself—ME.
You looked and saw yourself—YOU.

I AM ME! YOU ARE YOU! WE ARE
DIFFERENT!

It's incredible. I know who I am. I can
think about me and my world. I can analyze,

categorize, name things. This is that and
that's this, and I've named everything in the
world and it's mine to change.

Our egos were a glorious gift. We made
great changes. We learned to speak and to
dance and tell stories and build shelters and
temples and to count and sing songs and track
the stars and to cook and make wine and to
heal the sick and to follow in our hearts where
our life went when it left us.

And it was good. It was very good.

Can you each remember back to your own
childhood or infancy to your own first individual moment of epiphany? Try to remember the exact moment when you knew who
you were. The blazing instant you understood
that you were not your Mommy or Daddy,
or the kitty or the TV set. You were your
very own person. *(Pause)*

And that person had a name. Consciousness is inextricably interwoven with the
magick of naming. We have names. They say
that cats and dogs and other animals as well
have a secret name that only they know. We
are who we are when we can name ourselves.
And now we will use that power and speak
the name we wish to claim for ourselves—
starting with YOU! *(Points to someone. Then
everyone goes quickly deosil around the
circle and says their name.)*

CHANT (Ps): Blessed am I, freedom am I
I am the infinite within myself
I can find no beginning,
I can find no end
All this I am. (Great Goddess…) (x3)

P: Consciousness has come forth on this
planet at various times and in various guises.
It is the product of an inexorable force greater
than plants and animals. Greater than the Elements; even greater than time and space.

That is the mysterious force of evolution
to which all these things are subject. No matter what the public schools in Georgia and
Mississippi teach, when evolution is outlawed, only outlaws will evolve! *(Pause for
laughs)*

Now we will call upon that force to aid us
in our working today.

FAUNA & FLORUS: *(Step forward and read
alternating passages.)*

FAUNA: We call upon the spirit of evolution, the miraculous force that inspires rocks and dust to weave themselves into biology. You have stood by us for millions and billions of years— do not forsake us now. Empower us and awaken in us pure and dazzling creativity.

FLORUS: You who can turn scales into feathers, seawater to blood, caterpillars to butterflies, metamorphose our species, awaken in us the powers that we need to survive the present crisis and evolve into more aeons of our solar journey.

FAUNA: Awaken in us a sense of who we truly are: tiny ephemeral blossoms on the Tree of Life. Make the purposes and destiny of that tree our own purpose and destiny.

FLORUS: Fill each of us with love for our true self, which includes all of the creatures and plants and landscapes of the world. Fill us with a powerful urge for the wellbeing and continual unfolding of this self.

FAUNA: May we speak in all human councils on behalf of the animals and plants and landscapes of the Earth.

FLORUS: May we shine with a pure inner passion that will spread rapidly through these leaden times.

FAUNA: May we all awaken to our true and only nature—none other than the nature of Gaia, this living planet Earth.

FLORUS: We call upon the power that sustains the planets in their orbits, that wheels our Milky Way in its 200-million-year spiral, to imbue our personalities and our relationships with harmony, endurance, and joy.

FAUNA: Fill us with a sense of immense time so that our brief, flickering lives may truly reflect the work of vast ages past and also the millions of years of evolution whose potential lies in our trembling hands.

FLORUS: O stars, lend us your burning passion.

FAUNA: O silence, give weight to our voice.
(BOTH): We ask for the presence of the spirit of Gaia to be with us here, for our own highest good and for the highest good of all.
(—John Seed)

CHANT (Ps): Gaia! Mama Gaia!
          Mama Gaia, can you hear?
          Gaia! Mama Gaia!
          We're askin' you to draw near.
          'Cause we're gonna sing a song
          An' dance around the Fire
          Gonna dance all night long,
          Raising the energy higher! (x3)

GUIDED MEDITATION

P: There is power in the name of Gaia. It is an ancient name, from an ancient land. She has in turn given her name to science: to geology, geography, geophysics. Our Mother has a name and now, thanks to science, she has a face that we have all seen. Almost all humanity has seen the lovely image of our home planet spinning in her blue and white majesty—all alone in the diamond-dusted blackness of space. We are going to conjure up the face of Gaia here today. We will do it as an act of will and magickal focus. We want to visualize that image floating here, in the center of our Circle. All of us together beaming our intent into that single tightly focused image. Let us close our eyes.

Imagine you are lying back and gazing up at the night sky. Hold your hand up against the stars, moving your fingers together and apart, and watch the auras stretch thinner and separate. And let this image morph into one of cell division, as the dividing cell stretches slowly apart until it separates into two.

From this image, let your imagination "rewind the film" backwards, within your body, so the two cells become one, merging with others, over and over, until all of the cells in your body become the one original zygote.

And realize that all those trillions of cells were just multiple subdivisions of the first one, still comprised of the same protoplasm, the same DNA. And that's why you are a singular being, rather than a colony of separate cells.

But don't stop there. Continue to follow the thread of your own DNA back through your parents, your ancestors, apes, monkeys, lemurs, tree shrews, reptiles, amphibians, fish—swimming upstream like a salmon, tracing the river of life back to its original source— back to the first cell that ever was.

And then, running the film forward again, watch it dividing and replicating back up the entire evolutionary Tree of Life until you feel your own presence in all life, and the presence of all life within you.

Now let your consciousness rise high above the Earth as you watch teeming life spread across its surface—all one vast planetary organism. See that beautiful blue and white sphere floating in space, and realize how much it resembles a single cell on a cosmic scale. Look at the cloudy swirls veiling the continents, the shape of mountains ranges reduced to fine textured lines. See it resolve into the face of the Mother Goddess. And now see her eyes open to penetrate deep into your soul. She smiles at you and says, "Now you know me."

Now, open your eyes and behold her…

FOUR ELEMENTALS: *(Take up statues of Millennial Gaia and pass them deosil around the Circle from each Quarter.)*

Ps: *(Standing, veiled in green, with green crushed velvet tabard, holding aloft a large inflated Earth ball. She sings or plays recording of "Gaia's Voice," by D.J. Hamouris:)*

Sacred land, sacred place
Sacred people, I have come
We are one, all in one.

Through my tears I saw you birthed
Little ones, sacred ones.
Birthed with me in tears of joy.
You have grown.
We have grown.

Move with me and make my will
Be my will, we are one.
I see through your eyes,
I act through your hands,
Your hands are mine,
Our will is one,
Thy will be done.

Children of my womb
Live in me, live through me
We are one, all in one.

I heard your call
I felt your call
Bringing me to your sacred place.
But I have always been here,

Will always be with you, where you are
Till you return into me.

Sacred land, sacred place
Sacred people, we are One.

FOUR ELEMENTALS: *(Receive back and replace statues of Gaia. Then take up half-full chalices of water and bring them to PRIESTESS in center. Take positions around her, go down on one knee, holding chalices aloft for her to bless and fill.)*

Ps: *(Pouring water from pitcher into each chalice.)* My children, I give you the Waters of Life. For Water shared is life shared. (After filling Quarter chalices, she fills one on central altar, which PRIEST holds. They share water at the same time as Elementals take sips.)*

FOUR ELEMENTALS: *(Each take a sip from their chalice, then take chalices back to their Quarter and pass them into the Circle during following chant. When the chalice reaches the following Quarter, that ELEMENTAL receives it and places it on Quarter altar.)*

CHANT (Ps): We all come from the Goddess
And to her we shall return
Like a drop of rain
Flowing to the ocean… (x3)

CIRCLE DANCE: *(ELEMENTALS help position people.)*

P: Now every other person take two steps forward into the Circle. Now, the inside ring of people turn around and face the outside ring. Take the hands of those on either side of you. The inside ring will move *deosil* (sunwise), while the outer ring moves *widdershins* (counter-sunwise). That is, everyone move to your right!

CHANT (Ps): Mother, I feel you under my feet;
Mother, I feel your heart beat! (x9)

Ps: *(Ends dance with gong or bell.)* Without leaving your spot in the Circle, stand opposite a partner—they don't have to be the opposite sex! If there is someone left without a partner, please raise your hand. *(PRIEST joins with them.)*

Now, hold both your partner's hands and stand close to them. Gaze into each other's eyes. See how unique and special that person is. Just give the person a smile that honors how special they are. Now realize that you are looking at a person who embodies part of the soul of Gaia. You are looking at one of the many faces of Gaia.

Take a moment to think of an action that you can take in the next three months that will support the awakening of Gaia. It can be an environmental project, a research project, a political decision, a personal goal.

When you have decided on your action, take turns speaking it to each other. Look the other person in the eye and speak to them as though you are making a promise. You are in the living presence of Gaia. *(Pause.)*

Now all please form once again into one large Circle. *(Pause while they do so.)*

Now reach down and touch the Earth. Touch Gaia. Reach out and touch your own face. Touch Gaia. Reach out and take the hand of the person next to you. Touch Gaia.

P: *(Leaves the Circle, if he is in it, and comes to stand beside PRIESTESS.)* We thank Gaia for her presence. And we thank the children of Gaia for their presence.

Ps: Thank you Mother Earth,
         Thank you Sister Water
         Thank you for our birth,
         From your sons and daughters!
         Thank you Father Sun,
         thank you Air in motion;
         Thank you every one—
         Earth, Sun, Air, and Ocean!

P: The Circle will open in a moment and we will go where we will go. But ere we depart to our fair and lovely realms, we must remember, my friends. We must remember to be conscious and to act consciously. Remember your promise.

For we are Gaia, and we have changed the world. As you walk away, look for what is changed. For the newness that has awakened. For what you want this world to be. That is the Real World. That is the spirit of Gaia smiling at you.

Try to notice at least one new thing every day. Accept that as reality. Whatever else that you encounter, invoke the power of evolution and know that change is inevitable.

We are going to close with a chant to turn the world around. When you finish this chant, if you believe in what we have done, turn around and embrace the people around you. Embrace Gaia.

DISMISSAL CHANT:
     "We come from the mountains, etc."

192. The Witches' Ballad

Oh, I have been beyond the town
Where nightshade black and mandrake grow
And I have heard and I have seen
What righteous folk would fear to know

For I have heard, at still midnight
Upon the hilltop far, forlorn
With note that echoed through the dark
The winding of the heathen horn

And I have seen the fire aglow
And glinting from the magic sword
And with the inner eye beheld
The Horned One, the Sabbat's Lord

We drank the wine, and broke the bread
And ate it in the Old Ones' name
We linked our hands to make the ring
And laughed and leaped the Sabbat game

Oh, little do the townfolk reck
When dull they lie within their bed
Beyond the streets, beneath the stars
A merry round the Witches tread

And round and round the circle spun
Until the gates swung wide ajar
That bar the boundaries of earth
From Faery realms that shine afar

Oh, I have been and I have seen
In magic worlds of Otherwhere
For all this world may praise or blame
For ban or blessing naught I care

For I have been beyond the town
Where meadowsweet and roses grow
And there such music did I hear
As worldly-righteous never know
         —*Doreen Valiente*

8. Other Rituals

Introduction: Ritual Magick
By Oberon Zell-Ravenheart

As I hope you've come to understand by now, rituals may be created for any conceivable purpose. Virtually any human activity can be conceived and structured as ritual, simply by conducting it in a ceremonial framework. Rituals may be elaborately formal, or quite simple and informal. Most fall somewhere in between. Saying a simple prayer before bedtime, or an affirmation into the mirror each morning, counts as ritual. Sitting down to dinner with your family, holding hands in a circle around the table, and offering a blessing for the food about to be eaten and a thanks to those who prepared it, is a ritual. Lighting a candle before a photo of a friend or loved one who could use some healing blessings; walking around your car while envisioning it enclosed within a protective bubble before you drive off to commute to work each day; making a wish and blowing out the candles on your birthday cake; family customs around holidays, such as opening presents together on Christmas morning—all these things qualify as rituals.

The defining factor in all these cases is *intention*. This is where the magick comes in, transforming a mere mindless routine into a ritual act to make a difference. As Anodea Judith says, magick is the art of *probability enhancement.*

This definition offers us a real key as to what we're doing when we practice magick. We are shifting the *probabilities* (or "odds") from one outcome to another. All events that have not yet come to pass have some degree of probability that they may or may not occur. We can express such probabilities in terms of percentages, as when we say, "There's a 50% chance of rain tomorrow," or "The odds against that happening are ten to one." In such a statement, there are two factors: the *probability* and the *improbability*. If the odds are ten to one against, the *probability* is one and the *improbability* is ten. But the thing is, in such a case, if you do it ten times, then the improbability drops to one, and the probability goes up to ten. Once more, and the improbability becomes a *virtual certainty.*

In this context, doing magick as "probability enhancement" consists of increasing the odds (probabilities) in favor of our desired outcome. It's like piling rocks on the high end of a seesaw (lever) until the balance shifts, and the other end goes up. Every bit helps—not only large boulders, but even small pebbles and grains of sand; it just takes more of them. When both ends of the seesaw are off the ground and level, the balance is 50:50, and it hinges on the *fulcrum* (balance point). At that point, it doesn't take much to tip the balance one way or another—or even to pivot the whole thing into a different alignment entirely.

The trick is to find the *cusp*. A cusp is an intersection between fields of alternative probability. At such places, the potential as to which of these alternatives the probability wave will collapse into is in delicate balance—things could easily go either way. At a cusp, it takes little energy to move between the intersecting states, and the intentional "probability enhancement" of a focused ritual can have very large impact because of a "domino effect" of probabilities shifting outwards through space and time like ripples in a pond.

Following are an assortment of rituals for various purposes.

The Conspiracy of Heart's Desire
Liza Gabriel Ravenheart, May 1999

The "conspiracy of heart's desire" is a magickal "garden" in which heart's desires are planted and tended. This activity serves as a focus for the people in the conspiracy. The garden takes the form of a Celtic cross, a prehistoric symbol of wholeness. All "legs" of the cross are balanced and equal in length, and the cross itself is situated within a circle. The "conspiracy of heart's desire" uses the cross to harmonize the five Elements – Earth, Air, Fire, Water, and Spirit. The paths connecting them are the paths of desire that embrace all the Elements.

Practical application: Sometimes we can't give a person what they want, even someone we are close to and love, a mate for example. If we are in a large conspiracy, we can help that person find what they need without feeling we have to provide it personally. Of course if you are polyamorous, this is especially helpful.

This ritual is an invitation to embrace human desire without judgment. It is an invitation to take any desire – our own or someone else's – and follow the thread of that desire back to a "heart's desire," one that serves our essential nature and the whole.

What we do:
1. We chant the rhyme, and ask the questions.
2. Each person shares their name and a desire. The group responds by making a hand over hand motion, inhaling, and following the thread back to heart's desire. On the exhale they place their hands over their hearts and accept the heart's desire into their heart.
3. We chant the rhyme again.
4. In silent meditation, we follow our thread of desire back to our heart's desire.
5. We write our heart's desire on a heart-shaped peice of paper.
6. We do a milling through the Elements, in a childlike wandering, gathering the energy of each Element and asking its aid in the fulfillment of our heart's desire. This is also a time to invoke any special guides, guardians, devas, or deities and ask their aid.
7. When we have milled enough, we "plant" our heart's desire in the soil in the center of the circle.
8. After planting the desire in the garden, we walk around the cross three times.

9. Then we chant: *"This or something better will manifest now in complete harmony with good for all concerned."*
10. We share our experience.

A chant of heart's desire to open up energy:
Pleasure, love, desire, need—
Grow this garden; plant this seed.
Blood, passion, spirit, breath—
Give our heart's desires flesh!
Open pleasure like a bud,
In perfect trust and perfect love.

Questions to stir the pot:
Do you trust your desires?
Do you trust other people's desires?
When you feel a strong desire, do you feel alone?
Does the experience of sacrifice and pain bring you closer to your essential nature?
Does the experience of fulfilling a deeply felt desire bring you closer to your essential nature?
What does the phrase "all acts of love and pleasure are my rituals" mean to you?

Ritual for Abundance
By Moose Dixon

This abundance ritual is a full ritual involving the blessing of quarters (coins). In this particular instance, the coins were supplied by HP and HPS, blessed, then donated to the group supplying the venue.

1. **Ritual Prep**. HP and HPS discuss flow of ritual with participants.
2. **Enter the Circle**. HP and HPS cleanse participants by brushing third eye or crown with fresh-cut sage dipped in pure well water. Hand out four quarters (coins) to each participant. Chant "Unknown Blessings" until everyone is in Circle. Make sure the drummers stand together. *"I give thanks for unknown blessings already on their way."*
3. **Invocation**. End chant. HPS grounds and centers the group. Callers invoke Directions:

E: *Bring into our Circle abundance of spirit, learning, and growth. Be with us now. Be us. Blessed Be.*

S: *Bring into our Circle abundance of energy, good health, and motivation. Be with us now. Be us. Blessed Be.*

W: *Bring into our Circle abundance of love, community, and relationships. Be with us now. Be us. Blessed Be.*

N: *Bring into our Circle abundance of wealth, right and gainful employment, and enough money to reach our goals. Be with us now. Be us. Blessed Be.*

HP and HPS invoke Deity.

4. **Ground and Vision**. HP does free-form guided meditation to discover areas of life in which to increase abundance. Leave participants in total silence for at least 3 min.

5. **Asking for Abundance**. Drummers begin and maintain a barely audible back beat (use fingertips). Each participant comes to the altar and leaves their quarters (coins) in an offering bowl. As they do so, they say aloud (or silently if they wish) the specific area of their lives in which they will increase abundance.

6. **Charging the Quarters**. Drummers increase volume and tempo. Ritual team encourages ecstatic dancing among participants to raise energy. HP anchors the drummers and directs the energy.

7. **Cakes and Ale**. HPS grounds the participants. Ritual team ensures all participants get food (cubed honeydew, cantaloupe, and watermelon).

8. **Devocation**. HP and HPS release Deity. Quarter callers release Directions. HP announces Circle is open. End with "The Circle is Open" chant.

9. **Object Lesson**. HP and HPS donate charged quarters to host group. Direct them to spend their abundance on current projects and watch it return threefold.

Nature-Timed Rituals
By Mike Nichols

Although I have spent much of my life studying the genuine folk traditions associated with our fixed-calendar holidays (which I have presented in my book, *The Witches' Sabbats*), I am no less intrigued by rituals that have no specific calendar-date associations. In fact, it can be almost guaranteed that their placement in the cycle of the year will vary widely, because it is Mother Nature herself who dictates the timing for them.

This is important for a couple of reasons. First, it underscores our dependence on nature, something which is undeniably at the very heart of our ancient religious tradition. Second, it introduces an element of spontaneity often lacking in fixed-date rituals. You don't have time for elaborate preparations. Indeed, the very essence of these celebrations is that they invite you to drop your regularly scheduled activities and day-planner priorities, and instead make a quick response to certain beautiful, yet ephemeral, moments in nature.

I have chosen two such rituals as examples. The first is an elaboration of a traditional children's activity that usually occurs in early summer. The second is more of a meditation exercise for early winter. Indeed, its focus actually *defines* the beginning of winter for many people, more so than any calendar date.

Firefly Blessing

Think back to when you were a kid. Happily, this is not too difficult for most Pagans. Don't you remember playing outdoors on a warm summer evening, when suddenly your attention was arrested by a tiny point of light that appeared across the yard? It grew bright, then dimmed, seeming to disappear, fairy-like. Remember your reaction? Eyes suddenly wide, you *ran* with all your heart to the spot where you saw it, hoping to catch another, closer glimpse. Nope, the little creature has eluded you. But now you stand rooted to the spot, all your senses on high alert, scanning the yard and the adjoining ones. Suddenly, you spot another at the far side of a neighbor's yard, and you launch yourself at full speed towards it. But before you cover half the distance, you stumble in mid-careen, as another tiny light blinks on just to one side. Oh my gosh! The lightning bugs have come! The first of the year! This is magick, pure and simple, and as good as it gets!

Now if you were a sensible kid, the ritual has begun. Step one is to head to the house or garage in search of an empty, clear jar, with a screw-on metal lid soft enough to poke little holes in for air to pass through. (Because this involves using something sharp, like an ice pick, it's best to have an adult supervise or perform this step.) Next, pull up some fresh grass and drop it into the bottom of your jar, then lightly sprinkle the grass with droplets of water. With your jar ready, it's time to catch as many lightning bugs as possible. Since we are good Pagan children and deeply respect all life, we take great care not to hurt them as we snatch them from the air and transfer them to the jar. (Remember how gently Gandalf caught the moth?)

When your jar is full enough to be all a-twinkle, carry it back into your house and turn off all the lights. Carry the jar to each of the main rooms of your house, and sit in silence in each room until the lightning bugs begin their patterned blinking. As they do, say:

Blessings be upon thee, oh creatures of light! Tiny lanterns of the Goddess! Please bestow upon our house the fairy-light glow of your blessings. Just as your tiny lanterns invite love and health and regeneration, let that same invitation reside within our house this whole year through.

When all the main rooms have been similarly blessed, take the jar back outside and put it in some undisturbed spot, removing the lid to allow the lightning bugs to fly away home. Be sure to check the jar the following morning. For each living lightning bug that has remained, you may be granted an additional wish for the year. Gently shake any remaining lightning bugs into some undisturbed tall grass, and save the jar for next year.

The First Snowflake of Winter

The waning months of the year are often very busy ones. There never seems to be enough time to get everything accomplished, from winterizing your car and house to preparing for the holidays, getting ready to host friend and family gatherings, buying gifts, while juggling all the usual responsibilities of business and domestic life. Yet sometime in the middle of it, unheralded by anything but the weatherman's dubious report of a "slight possibility," you will see it! It will come wafting down out of the leaden-grey sky, falling through space in utter silence and solitude. The first snowflake of the year! You may then glance around and notice other flakes dancing on the air, but that first one is the special one. It is your own personal beginning of winter and it belongs to no one else. That means it should be celebrated.

As quickly as you are able, finish whatever you were doing and retire to your favorite spot for meditation, perhaps at the little altar in your bedroom. There, turn out all the lights and light some candles and incense, and meditate on the coming of winter. If you keep a diary or journal, you may want to note the date for this first snowflake of the year and highlight it so you can compare it to other years. You may also want to jot down other impressions as they come to you. The role of winter in the great Wheel of the Year. What it means to you and your family and friends. What it means to the furry and feathered creatures of the forest and plains. The hardships it may bring to them and the little things that you might be able to do to help them through this time of hardship (perhaps a well-stocked bird-feeder for your yard?). Meditate on winter's majesty. Think of a virgin snowfall and how it seems to unify the land, the single white mantle erasing curb lines and sidewalks and streets, yards and fields, turning it all into a single, unsullied oneness, bringing out the connectedness that lies hidden there on most other days. And finally, think once more upon that first snowflake of winter, so tiny and yet the harbinger of it all.

When you have finished your meditation, extinguish your candles and incense, and continue with your day's planned activities. But as you do, know that you have taken the time to honor that first snowflake, and so have grounded yourself more completely into the rhythm of the year's turning.

Campfire Ritual
By Moonwriter

Preparation:

Pre-lay a council fire. Erect a small tee-pee arrangement around a set of sure-catch fire starters. Then, build a log cabin structure around the teepee (be sure to leave openings at the base for lighting the fire starters).

For safety purposes, have buckets of water and one to two shovels concealed nearby.

For best effect, conduct this ritual after dark.

The Event:

Have participants assemble at the Fire Circle. A ritual procession and entry may be used, with a ritual call and response if desired. Once in the Circle, silence should be kept.

The firelighters enter the Fire Circle from the four Cardinal Directions. They should be robed in ceremonial garb and carrying a light stick, lighted wand, or enrobed flashlight (the idea is to cast a soft light over their chests and faces, while not illuminating them clearly).

They each take position around the fire, standing at their Cardinal Points and facing each other across the still-unlit fire. They raise their arms to the sky and speak, one at a time, beginning with the West and going deosil:

Spirits of the West, place of water,
Cauldron of the greatest ocean, hear us!
Spirits of the North, place of Earth,
Panticle of stone, hear us!
Spirits of the East, place of Air,
Hall of winds, hear us!
Spirits of the South, place of Fire,
Crucible of the rising sun, hear us!

The four then lower their arms and take three backwards steps, then remain still. A voice comes out of the darkness:

Kneel always when you light a fire.
Kneel reverently, and thankfully,
For earth's unfailing charity.
And on the ascending flame we share
A little prayer that shall upbear
The incense of our thankfulness,
That this great gift of warmth and light
Is given again for our delight.
              (—John Oxenham)

The firelighters stand and move to the edge of the fire, where they kneel. With as much uniformity as possible, they use "strike anywhere" matches to light the fire from the four Directions simultaneously.

When the fire lights, they stand, take three steps backward, then turn to their right and file out of the Circle, one of them leading (this should be arranged before the ceremony).

An elder steps forward to ask a blessing or benediction. Example: "*Voices of the wilderness, be with us.*"

Another gives a short message about the importance and meaning of fire.

Then, there is the passing of the Elements.

First a chalice of Water is passed from person to person deosil around the Circle. The chalice should be as rough or simple as possible—a large seashell or wooden bowl is ideal. As it is passed to each person, the person doing the passing says, "*The gift of Water.*"

Second, a stone is passed, with the saying, "*The gift of Earth.*"

Third, a feather or stick of incense is passed, with, "*The gift of Air.*"

Last but not least, a candle is lit from the central fire and passed from person to person with, "*The gift of Fire.*" As each person holds the candle, they may pause to offer a prayer or blessing. When the candle has completed its circle, it is given to the fire.

After this, another intones (there is music to this, or it can be spoken):

Thou has made me known to friends
    whom I knew not,
Thou hast given me seats in homes
    not my own.
Thou hast brought the distant near,
And made a brother of the stranger.
I am uneasy at heart
When I have to leave my accustomed shelter
I forget that there abide the old in the new
And that where also life abidest,
In birth and death, on this world,
And on others,
Wherever thou leadest me, it is all the same.
The one commandment of this endless life,
Whoever linkest my heart with bonds of
    joy to the unfamiliar.

When one knows peace,
Then alien there is none.
Then no door is shut.
Oh answer my prayer, that I may never
    lose the bliss
Of the touch of the one,
Of the face of the many.
                (—Traditional Gregorian chant)

At this time, those in the Circle are asked to embrace those sitting next to them. At this point, the ritual can go in many different directions. For example:

• A Magick Circle can be cast, deities invoked, and magickal Workings performed.
• The event can turn into a Bardic Circle, with an ongoing ring of stories, songs, etc.
• The Fire Circle could be used for a time of recognition, passage, etc. Participants can be asked (in advance) to bring written scrolls or small items to be given to the fire.

In the end, someone should step forward to give thanks to spirits of Earth, Water, Fire, and Air, and the event formally closed. At this point, people may elect to remain seated around the fire for a casual gathering. A snack or hot beverage would be very appropriate.

Finishing:

When the evening ends, care must be taken that the fire is completely out; it must not be left unattended!

The next morning, have participants return to the Fire Circle to gather some of the ashes in a film canister, zip-loc baggie, etc. They can then use these ashes to sprinkle over their next council fire. In this way, they may carry the love and memories of a lifetime's worth of fire with them.

Spirit Naming Ceremony on Full Moon
By Ancient Singing Moon

This ritual is best done at night by fire or candlelight

All people have been asked to come dressed as one of their power animals, including the Initiate and the Shaman. As people arrive, there is one person who stands at the threshold smudging people. Once over the threshold, the participants sit down and another greeter silently washes everyone's faces and hands, and anoints foreheads, palms of hands, and, if possible, the bottoms of feet with an oil blend. The oil blend will change depending on the initiate.

The participants enter and gather around the initiate in a "village." They can softly chat, say prayers, and sing songs while all the others are entering. Gifts for the initiate may be placed in a separate area. Once everyone has assembled, the ceremony begins.

The Shaman invokes the spirits, guardians, Directions, and any special spirits who wish to be present for the initiate. The Shaman also casts the Circle, the container in which the ceremony will be held. The initiate is led by two villagers to stand at the center of the room. The Shaman will say something from the spirits if moved, such as a blessing, prayer, or direction. Then the participants are asked to find a stone and place it in a Circle around the initiate. Prayers may be said as the stones are placed. People may choose to touch the initiate with prayers and good energy, but only if the initiate is okay with this.

When the stones are placed, the participants take up drums, rattles, sticks, or any other instrument. The Shaman listens for a spirit song for the village to sing. Once that is heard and conveyed, the village begins to sing and use their instruments. They continue to sing and dance, celebrating the new spirit name. The Shaman circles the initiate while rattling, listening for songs, words, or anything else the spirits wish to convey through her. The Shaman listens for the spirit name and whatever qualities may wish to come through. (The spirit name is usually known by the initiate and communicated to the Shaman prior to the ceremony.) These things are conveyed to the initiate through song, dance, or prayer words. This continues until it feels complete.

Then the Shaman signals the village to be quiet, and touches the initiate in some way. Then, the intiate is to speak her name, saying *"I am _____, the one who _____. What I want from life is _____. The gift I bring to the world is _____."* She can say an oath or a prayer, sing a song, or convey anything that the spirit of her new name wishes to communicate to the village. Depending on what moves through her, she can become her power animal, or something else. When she is complete, she will say *"Ho"* or some other word that signals the Shaman. Then the Shaman hoots, hollers, and rattles, and the village joins in the dance and song.

The villagers then take the stones away and place them aside. When the rocks are completely gone, the initiate walks on her own back into her village, where the singing and dancing continue. Power animals may be explored, and moon rites may be acknowledged. As the Circle comes to a close, the initiate closes the Circle by releasing the spirits and guardians, offering a closing prayer or song, and declaring the ceremony complete.

Stones are returned to their place upon the land and given thanks.

Apology & Forgiveness Ritual
By Morning Glory Zell

Materials needed:
  Altar, statues of Aphrodite and Kwan Yin, water chalice, wine chalice, hourglass.
  Small fire for offerings.
  Everyone arrives at the Circle wearing a small comfortable mask.
Priestess:
  We are here to perform a ritual of accountability and forgiveness, both for our own sakes and as a spinning of the energy of reconciliation and cooperation for our family and our community.
Circle casting.
Each calls a Quarter.
Invocations:
  She changes everything she touches and everything she touches changes.
  He dances everything he touches and everything he touches dances.
Priestess says:
  Write something you want to change in the world and what you plan to do about it on a piece of paper and offer to the fire.
Each person in turn with hourglass for timing:
  There is something in my behavior that I want to change. It has hurt people that I love. One person it has hurt is....

1. Confession.
2. Reason.
3. Acknowledgement of harm done.
4. Apology.
5. Person A (wrongdoer) says: "I want to know what you experienced and offer restitution."
6. Person B (wronged party) speaks from their heart of the harm done them and then suggests restitution.
7. Person A mirrors back, with compassion and insight, what has been said.
8. Person A offers the restitution asked for, or negotiates, and then asks for forgiveness.
9. Person B offers wine, saying: *"I offer you this sweet wine of my forgiveness."*
10. They hug.
  This is repeated as often as necessary between various people. In between each all get up and dance around and sing: *"She changes...He changes..."*
  Then a Circle of gratitude is done, ending with the God, Goddess, and Quarters.
  At the end all sing: *"She changes...He changes..."* one more time with more hugs and dancing.
  Open Circle with: "All from Air into Air..."

Rebirthing Ritual
By Moose Dixon

This ritual involves individual meditation while in a large body of water (say, a small swimming pool or larger). It is intensely individual, with priest and priestess serving primarily as grounders.

There is a candle and a non-glass candle container for each participant. One priest and one priestess are needed to be "gatekeepers." One of these will hold the attendee's robe or towel and the other will hold the attendee's candle during the water immersion. Because some people may take some time, this ritual is better suited for smaller groups of people.

Participants are to chant during the walk to the ritual site and during the entire rebirthing portion of the ritual.

> The river is flowing, flowing and growing,
> The river is flowing, down to the sea.
> Mother carry me, Your child I'll always be.
> Mother carry me, down to the sea.

Full immersion into the water is voluntary, though each person will be expected to interact with the water. Full immersion is definitely a possibility, and some may find swimming underwater into their new life desirable. Concentrate on the rebirthing process and emerge at your own pace.

Leaders cast the Circle by lighting candles, and from participant to participant all candles are eventually lit. The Quarters are called, followed by Goddess and God.

Participants will be asked to consider what needs to be given a new birth in their lives, and what thing(s) or situation(s) they might need to be reborn **out of** and/or **into.** Participants should concentrate on this as they chant, enter the water, and emerge from the water.

As each participant approaches the gatekeepers, the priest (if participant is female) or priestess (if participant is male) quietly addresses him/her, saying something like this: "Are you ready to shed those things or situations that are blocking you or holding back your development, and are you ready to be reborn into those things or situations which will help you to grow?" (In the event the participant has an alternative sexual orientation, and if he or she prefers, the same sex priest/priestess may address him/her.)

Participant must answer confidently in the affirmative. If there is hesitation, the participant should be asked if they are sure. This gives the participant a chance to decide to let go of these obstructions, or to pass if need be.

Once the participant appears resolute in this renewal, the priest/priestess gently cups his/her hands around the participant's candle, saying, "This candle is your life as it is now. Blow it out." This is said firmly to impress upon the participant that this ritual is not a gentle meditation that can be put to the back of the mind and forgotten, but rather a real catalyst for change. Some participants' responses to this command may be intense; therefore priests and priestesses should be available for support during and after this ritual.

After the participant blows out their candle, they hand their robe to one of the gatekeepers. He/she takes whatever time is needed to enter (total immersion is voluntary) and emerge from the water. After the participant emerges, puts on their robe, and retrieves their candle, they are instructed to relight their candle from the priest (if attendee is female) or priestess (if attendee is male). Here again, be mindful of sexual orientation. The priest or priestess may make a statement of support or direction to the participant as Spirit moves them.

After all participants have entered and emerged from the water, the gatekeepers should complete their own immersion. The priest and priestess are the last to complete the process, being addressed by their counterpart for the questions, answers, and direction.

When this portion of the ritual is complete, the second song will be sung to lock in the energy that will magickally seal the new beginnings:

> The ocean is the beginning of the Earth;
> The ocean is the beginning of the Earth.
> All life comes from the Sea;
> All life comes from the Sea.

The priest and priestess will bring down the song with a hand signal and then release Deity. The Quarters will be released and the song will be changed to:

> The Circle is open but unbroken.
> May the peace of the Goddess be ever in your heart.
> Merry meet, and merry part, and merry meet again!

The Great Rite
By Oberon

As a ritual of sex magick, the Great Rite is the *hieros gamos*—"sacred marriage"—of the God and Goddess. Sex is a source of power, creative as well as procreative. This power is rooted in polarity, a charged attraction of opposites. But that is only one of many ways that sexual energy flows. People of similar qualities or of the same sex may also generate pleasure and power together. The giving and receiving of sexual pleasure is an endlessly varied art.

We are born out of this act of pleasure. This miracle has been a source of awe and a method of magick from the dawn of time. We all have in us somewhere the naïve and child-like belief that if sex can create us, it can create anything. Out of such simple beliefs some of the most powerful and effective magick in human experience is woven.

Our bodies are the particular piece of the Great Mother especially entrusted to us. In the experience of that sacred trust, and especially in the Great Rite, sex becomes an act of worship, awakening and engaging the God and Goddess in our partners. *"For behold, all acts of Love and Pleasure are My rituals"* (Doreen Valiente, "The Charge of the Goddess"). Thus, in the Church of All Worlds and the HOME Tradition, we sanction all loving and responsible sexual relationships between informed and mutually consenting adults, whatever their gender, number, or practice. We also advocate safe sex practices.

The following ceremony is written for a man and a woman. For same-sex couples, you will have to make your own creative adaptations.

Preparation for a Great Rite should be well thought out, including setting aside sufficient time. Make sure you have plenty of privacy, and turn off the ringers on all the phones. Arrange the place for love-making: If it is your bed, then put on fresh satin sheets, set candles all around, and select the perfect incense (rose, musk, jasmine) and your most erotic music (Ravel's "Bolero" is a traditional favorite, and Katlyn's "Beneath the Veil" by Zingaia was created just for the Great Rite). Or you might light a fire in the fireplace, and lay down cushions and a large sheepskin in front of it. Red bulbs in the lamp sockets create an exquisitely romantic and erotic lighting.

A special meal, in which you feed each other, is a perfect prelude to a romantic evening. Oysters are the traditional erotic delicacy, perhaps accompanied by a shared chalice of red wine, damiana liqueur, and/or other aphrodisiac intoxicants.

When everything is ready, begin the rite with ritual bathing of each other in a warm bubble bath with rose petals and rosewater, lit by candles and with romantic music. When you're done, towel each other dry, then adjourn to the bed and cast the Circle around it, with outstretched hand, wand, or athame:

> *I cast this Circle to purify and sanctify this space,*
> *To guard us and protect us,*
> *And to safely contain the energies we will raise herein.*
> *Aphrodite, Oshun, Hathor, Freya, Shakti, Venus…*
> *Eros, Angus, Krishna, Shiva, Kama, Pan…*
> *Bless us with your Courage, your Wisdom, and your Compassion*
> *Let our hearts and minds rejoice, relax, and be open,*
> *So that we in turn may do honor unto you,*
> *With each of our loving touches.*   (—Dave Sylvia)

Light the candles and start the music. Soul gazing, dance of veils, sacred anointing and massage—all kinds of juicy rituals could be added. Sit in a *yab-yum* position (he cross-legged, her in his lap with legs around his waist), gaze lovingly into each other's eyes, and invoke the God and Goddess in each other:

> *Awaken, my Beloved,*
> *Within this sacred vessel of thy Priest/ess.*

Fill this mortal flesh with thy Holy Spirit
That we, in our union, may be
One with You.

Caress each other gently, moving your fingertips lightly over the skin, starting with the insides of the arms and moving outwards all over
each other's naked flesh. Speak the following
to each other, in turns, and then in unison.

He: *Join me my lover*
To celebrate this night
In freedom and joy
Life's greatest rite.

She: *I'll join you my lover*
An altar we'll fashion
For this act of creation
And greatest of passion.

He: *So please you, now bare*
This temple of treasure
Great Goddess, your body
The source of love's pleasure.

She: *Thou art God, my lover*
And made with perfection
So Skyclad, be with me
For life's altar's erection.

BOTH:
Assist me, unveil me
For since time began
As Goddess and God
Have faced woman and man.

Caress me, embrace me
About me entwine
We give ourselves up
To this most holy shrine

Unfold the mystery
Bring forth ancient bliss
Awaken the fire
And anoint with a kiss.

Our passions will blend
In the spiraling dance
As our bodies merge
And unite grail and lance.

As the force from our magic
Spirals higher and higher
On the great cone of power
Soars our will and desire.

(—Avilynn Pwyll, Beltane 1990)

Finally, join together in sexual passion, holding in each of your minds the image and
thought of the God and Goddess you are
manifesting with each other in this sacred
union, as you build slowly to a glorious mutual orgasm. At this point you may also consider the use of synchronized breath, sharing
breath, and circular breathing to raise and
align energy. If there is a greater intention for
which you wish to direct the energy you are
raising, hold it in your minds at the moment
of climax.

193 The Heart of the Living Goddess

I am the first breath in crystalline space,
Like the starry heavens,
My body arches in ecstasy around the
    secret center of the Sun.
Through the circling of the spheres you
    shall know me.
For I set the star of truth upon thy brow...

I am a paradise of deep wilderness,
The soul of Nature and life of the Divine
Fragrant and fertile is my body,
Touch me in the petals of every sweet
    blossom.
Through abundance you shall know me.
I am thy oasis, pouring forth the waters of
    life

I am in the heart that rejoices
And in the body dancing forth the essence
    of immortality.
Mine are the sighs of passion and also the
    cries of birth.
Feel my presence in the pulse of thy center.
Through desire you shall know me,
For I ignite the Sacred Fire...

Through love shall you come to know me,
    beloved.
Know me in the heart of every woman,
For I am the Living Goddess,
I share the secret of life with the seed of thy
    soul.

—Katlyn Breen, 1998

Book III: Wheel of the Year

Table of Contents

The Festival Document

There shall be Four Festivals in all the World,
That will be the High Festivals of all the Faiths.
They shall be the Equinoxes and the Solstices,
And they will fall according to the Hemisphere in which they occur;
So that Spring and Autumn, Summer and Winter,
Are always in their proper place,
And do not depend upon the months and days of calendars.
Gifts may be exchanged at all of these Festivals,
And the particular symbols of each Faith may be attached,
So that these Festivals may fall in common to all.

In the Spring the Equinox shall be celebrated at Dawn,
When the sunlight falls on the Earth and quickens it to Life.
The Sunfire shall be lit, and appropriate gifts are
Candles and Seeds, Lamps and Plants.
In the Summer the Solstice should be celebrated at Noon,
When the World is in full glory and growth.
The Wine shall be bottled and drunk, and appropriate gifts are
Things to Drink, Fruits, Cups and Flowers.
In the Autumn the Equinox should be celebrated at Sunset,
When the sky begins to dim and the harvest is brought in.
Smokes are offered up, and appropriate gifts are
Scents and Seasonings, Incense and Animals.
In the Winter the Solstice should be celebrated at Midnight,
When seeds, wombs and houses are sealed like the grave.
Bread shall be baked and appropriate gifts are
Things to Eat, Cakes, Plates and Containers.

What are the Sabbats?

By She' D'Montford

Sabbats are the markers of Earth's seasonal cycle.

The word *Sabbat* comes from the same root word as the Hebrew *Sabbath,* meaning a period of rest. However, this word is originally Babylonian, designating the quarter days of the lunar cycle. That is the full, new, first, and last quarters, which occur about every seven days. It slipped into the Hebrew language to denote their day of rest and prayer which occurred every seventh day. During the Inquisition, Sabbat became the term arbitrarily assigned to the Pagan "Holy Days." In like manner, communities of Witches were described in the literature of the time as *synagogues,* lumping the Jewish people as heretics along with practitioners of the Craft; and the distinctions became blurred.. Nevertheless, this name for these eight yearly festivals has stuck.

In order to understand these festivals you must remember that they are not man-made. They are not part of a calendar anniversary of dates of historical import, nor are they randomly chosen social institutions, such as Labor Day or Father's Day. In fact, these eight Sabbats existed long before humanity, as they have always been a basic part of how this planet works. These holidays simply mark the turning points in the cycles of nature. Our planet spins on an axis that is tilted to its orbit around the sun. Once a year this creates a 24-hour period with a night that is the longest night of the year, and a day that is the shortest. This is the Winter *Solstice* ("sun-standing"). In the opposite hemisphere, we have its opposite (the longest day of the year, and the shortest night)—or, the Summer Solstice. Six months later, or halfway around the cycle of the year, we have the opposite situation. Halfway in between this, we have a balancing point, and two more days that are equally important. Each spring and autumn there comes a day when the hours between sunrise and sunset and sunset and sunrise are exactly equal. They are called the *Equinoxes,* meaning "equal night."

The year is thus split into two halves (or four quarters) for summer/autumn and winter/spring. The two halves are ruled by a Light God when the days are getting longer and a Dark God when the nights are getting longer. The year is then divided again at the cross quarters. The two Equinoxes and two Solstices are the minor Sabbats, and the cross-quarter days are the major Sabbats. These bisect the quarters, falling at the exact midpoint of each. With these in place, a diagram of the cycle of the year begins to look like an eight-spoked wheel. This image is a sacred symbol in several religions.

Thus the cycle of the Sabbats is commonly referred to as "The Wheel of the Year." It is our small wheel in the greater cycle of things. All things are cyclical, and this life is cyclical in order to fit in with the arrangement of the universe. Books often list arbitrary dates for the major Sabbats, but there exist astronomical methods for putting the cross-quarter days more precisely in-between the minor Sabbats (or you can just check with your local observatory).

These Sabbats are solar festivals, and so their mythology illustrates the life cycle of the God principle in nature, which we associate with the sun. The lunar cycles illustrate the life cycle of the Goddess principle in nature.

Cycle of the Eight Sabbats

(adapted from Larry Cornett and others; icons by Katlyn Breene)

SABBAT	OSTARA	BELTAINE	LITHA	LUGHNASADH	MABON	SAMHAIN	YULE	OIMELC
ICON								
MEANING	"Eastern Star" for Eostre, Saxon goddess of dawn & fertility	"Bel's Fire" for Belenos, Celtic god of the Sun	Litha is a Saxon grain goddess	"Games of Lugh" for Lugh, Irish Sun god	Mabon is a Celtic god of the harvest, liberation & harmony	"Summer's End" Celtic feast of the dead	"Wheel" Norse iul	"Ewe's milk" also Imbolc or Imbolg "in the belly" (pregnancy)
DATE	March 21	May 1	June 21	August 1	September 21	November 1	December 21	February 1
TIME OF YEAR	Spring Equinox	15° Taurus	Summer Solstice	15° Leo	Autumn Equinox	15° Scorpio	Winter Solstice	15° Aquarius
SOLAR FORCE	Balance of Light and Dark	Strongly increasing light, balanced heat	Peak light; darkness to come	Declining light; peak heat	Balance of Light and Dark	Strongly failing light; balanced heat	Death/birth of Sun; peak darkness; promise of light	Baby Sun, increasing light, peak cold
VEGETATIVE FORCE	Sprouting, budding	Flowering	Growth	First harvest; prep. for rest of harvest	Primary harvest	Last harvest; falling leaves; transition	Hibernation, dormancy	Life spark, germination begins
HUMAN LIFECYCLE	Child	Sexual maturity; courtship	Parent	Children up and about; attain maturity	Middle age; children weaned	Crone, elder; universal knowledge	Gestation; time in Summerland	Birth
NATURE DEITIES	Fauna (red maid), Faunus (red man), Flora (green maid), Florus (green man)	Faunus (red man), Flora (green maid), Florus (green man)	Gaia (Mother Earth), Sol (Father Sun)	Sol (Father Sun), Faunus (red man), Florus (green man)	Florus (green man), dies	Florus (green man) Fauna (red maid) Faunus (red man)	Sol (Sun god) born	Gaia (Mother Earth) Fauna (red maid) Flora (green maid)
GODDESS FORCE	Maiden returns from Underworld awakes to meet young lover	Fertility, Maiden comes of age, sexuality, marriage	Full adult, Mother aspect	Leadership, Goddess becomes reaper	Goddess enters Underworld to reign through Winter	Goddess as Crone	Goddess gives birth to Sun god	Inspiration, creativity, midwife (Brigit)
GOD FORCE	Return of Green Man	Return of Summer gods, fertility, sexuality, marriage	Sun King embraces Goddess; reborn as God of waning year	Teaching, Green Man in full adulthood	Underworld gods return	God as Gatekeeper; Lord of Underworld	Sun god reborn	Skill (Wayland)
SYMBOLS	Seeds, narcissus, crocus	Maypole, penis, May bush, Mayflower	Sun, Fairies	Last sheaf, corn dolly, bread loaf	Sickle, scythe	Pumpkin, pomegranate, apple, skull	Yule log, evergreen tree, holly, ivy, mistletoe	Candles, forge, lamb, Brigid's bed
RITUAL CYCLE	Birthing/ planting	Life/sex	Abundance	Competitive, masculine	Dying/ harvest	Death/ ancestors	Renewal	Creative/ female
SELECTED RITUAL THEMES	Welcome Nature Spirits, charge seeds, decorate/ charge eggs, celebrate Spring, symbolic breaking of bonds	Maypole dance, Nature Spirit work, regeneration of Earth, love & care, hand-fasting, crown May Queen & King, feed each other	Nurture crops, appreciate Nature, celebrate Nature's sacrifice & renewal, make changes & adjustments	Bless first fruits & tools, invoke skill, knowledge & healing, initiations, brewing, competitive games, sacred cooking fires	Going away party for Green Man, celebrate harvest, Earth healing, charge seed for next year's crop	Spiritworld contact, festival of life & death, celebrate harvest completed, dumb supper, divination, past-life regression	Giftgiving, Saturnalia, magical oaths, kindle Yule log, give birth to new projects, decorate tree with symbols & talismans	Initiation, naming, begin a new endeavor, feast of flame & waxing light

Witch Sabbaths in Gerald Gardner's Time

By Grey Council member Frederic Lamond, 2002

I was initiated into "Witchcraft," as we called it then, in the presence of Gerald Gardner on February Eve, 1957, by Dayonis (who now lives in Salt Lake City). We were taught to make a distinction between the four major *Sabbaths* on the one hand, and the equinoxes and solstices on the other.

In Gerald's day, the four major Sabbaths were called by their traditional English names: Hallowe'en, Candlemas, Beltaine, and Lammas. Gerald was trying to teach us traditional English country lore, not Celtic traditions, since Southern England had been Saxon for 1,300 years. *"In pre-Burning Times* (a favorite Geraldism) *the four Sabbaths were great big parties celebrating the end of one of the major phases of the agricultural cycle in which the whole village participated. It was only the full moon Esbats that were private to the initiated witches, because that was when spells were cast."* At the time I was somewhat cynical about Gerald's pretence that there was an unbroken line of initiations reaching back to the Stone Age, but now I realize that he was using—consciously or unconsciously—a mirror technique, in which he described a mythical past as a way of telling us what we should do in the future. So for *"pre-Burning Times,"* read *"this is what you should do when you feel safe enough to come out of the broom closet."* In line with this, he encouraged us to invite uninitiated but sympathetic friends to bonfire parties at the time of the major Sabbaths, especially Halloween and Beltaine.

We did not ignore the Solstices and Equinoxes, but celebrated these within the coven with magickal rituals to turn the Wheel of the Year and to help nature to make the transition from one season to the next. Yule, the Winter Solstice, was especially important. We had to turn the wheel so that the sun would return in the coming year: *"Unless someone somewhere in the world turns the wheel on December 21 the sun will not return!"* This may sound like astronomical nonsense but has a poetic truth to it. Unless we celebrate the passing of the seasons we may lose all awareness of them. We are already perilously close to this in North America, where 24- hour shopping and public transport has blotted out the distinctions between night and day, and air conditioning in offices insulates from the changes of temperature occurring outside.

When I asked him why we didn't celebrate the Equinoxes and Solstices with parties, he replied: *"You can if you want to, but it would not be appropriate to the English climate in which you live. The most important Pagan festival has always been the spring fertility festival, which was celebrated when it had become warm enough to make love out of doors in the fields to ensure their fertility* (on the principle of sympathetic magick). *In the Mediterranean this is shortly after the Spring Equinox: hence the dates of the Jewish Passover* (which replaced the spring fertility orgy after Moses) *and the Christian Easter. In England and countries of similar latitude it did not normally become warm enough until the beginning of May* (according to the Julian calendar, which translates into mid-May in the Gregorian calendar), *as described in this popular ditty*:

"'Hurray, hurray for the first of May, outdoor loving starts today!'

"In Scandinavia it doesn't get warm enough until midsummer, which is why Swedes, Norwegians, and Danes still celebrate midsummer with all night dancing around bonfires, with many couples disappearing into the bushes.

"Many children would be conceived around the spring festival bonfires who would be born nine months later, especially by the May Queen, and this would determine the date of the festival celebrating the return of the light: shortly after the Winter Solstices for people who celebrated the spring at the Spring Equinox, but not until February Eve or Candlemas in countries where spring is celebrated at the beginning of May."

Our coven liked the feasts we had at the major Sabbaths, whereas we had only moooncakes and wine at the full moon Esbats. So sometime in 1959 or 1960 we decided to have feasts at the Equinoxes and Solstices as well as the major Sabbaths. Talk of the Celtic eight-spoke Wheel of the Year came much later as an *ex post facto* justification, which didn't originate with us, but probably with the Druids. I am not even sure that the obsession with Celtic authenticity—including using Irish instead of English names for the major festivals—didn't originate in the U.S. sometime in the 1960s. I myself have always found this obsession with the Celts rather odd, not because I have only one-quarter Scots (and therefore Celtic) ancestry, but because the Celts were—and the Irish still are—great fighters, and therefore patriarchs. As an English poet, whose name I forget, put it in his description of the different people of the British Isles: *"The Irishman doesn't know what he wants, but is prepared to fight for it!"* What we early Witches were trying to hark back to was pre-Celtic and generally pre-Indo-European Neolithic Earth Mother worship.

Getting back to the major Sabbaths: what Gerald taught us about them implies that we should let the climate of the place in which we live dictate the dates of the major festivals, especially of the spring festival, rather than abide by what others have written about supposed old Celtic traditions.

194. Turning of the Wheel

Deep in the black of night,
Wrapped safely in the arms of the Mother
I dream,
And wish upon the coming of the child,
So radiant and bright,
That he warms the chill of Spring.
As the veil lifts, and dawn breaks,
I begin to wake, feeling my body stir.
Great passion arises, and I dance
With merriment and delight,
For this is when the Great Rite will occur.
I reach my outstretched arms
Toward the warmth of the Father.
Growing in his brilliance,
I will sacrifice myself now
Within the love of him and the Mother.
As the light begins to fade,
I begin my journey home,
Back to where I once began,
Wrapped safely in the arms of the Mother,
Deep in the black of night
I dream again.

—*Samina Oshun*

195. The Turning of the Wheel

The Wheel turns as crows take flight
Across the wintry Samhain night.
In glowing flames the Yule log burns—
Our Sun's reborn as the Wheel turns.

Imbolc chases night away
As candles change the dark to day.
The Wheel turns—Ostara's flowers
Are blessed by April's springtime showers.

On Beltaine Eve the fires burn;
Again we see the Wheel turn.
Litha brings the longest day,
When we can dance our cares away.

The Wheel turns to Lammastide,
The first fruits of our fields so wide.
And when the harvest Lord is gone,
The Wheel turns us to Mabon.

What we have sown we now shall reap
As Mother Earth returns to sleep.
The Wheel turns as crows take flight
Again across the Samhain night.

The years go by, the seasons pass.
Our lives leave shadows on the grass,
As every day we learn to feel
The constant Turning of the Wheel.

—*BellaDonna Oya, August 2002*

1. Ostara: Vernal Equinox

Introduction: Ostara
By Oberon Zell-Ravenheart & She' D'Montford

In the HOME Tradition, we have for many years been evolving a complex cycle of celebrations which have assimilated many elements of custom and folklore from our ancient Pagan heritage. We have drawn mainly from the customs of Western Europe and the British Isles, but as Greek mythology has always been a strong component of our collective Western lore, we also incorporate the Eleusinian ritual cycle into our seasonal observances. The main characters in our seasonal drama are Mother Earth (Gaia), Father Sun (Sol), and their children: the leafy Green Man (Florus) and Maid (Flora/Kore), and the hornéd Red Man (Faunus/Pan) and Maid (Fauna), keeping in mind that green=chlorophyll and red=hemoglobin.

As the Wheel of the Year forms a circle, any starting point is arbitrary, and several of the Sabbats have been regarded as New Year's Day in various traditions. For the purpose of this writing, we will begin as in casting a Circle, with the East and the festival of Spring Equinox:

Ostara (oh-STAR-ah), also called *Spring's Height,* is the Sabbat of the Vernal (Spring) Equinox, occurring around March 21, when the Earth has recovered from winter and is in full bloom. Dating back to Assyrian times, it is named for *Eostre* ("Eastern Star," or the planet Venus), Teutonic goddess of dawn and fertility, who is cognate with Ishtar, Astarte, Ashera, Aphrodite, Inanna, and Venus. The female *estrus cycle* of fertility and sexuality takes its name from her. Eggs, bunnies, and ducklings are, of course, all symbols of fertility, and are universally associated with this festival. This is the new year on the Zodiacal calendar, and the name of each 2,000-year astrological age is based on the sign in which the Vernal Equinox falls in its continuing precession. Ostara is a festival celebrating fertility and birth, when Mother Earth bears two sets of holy twins: the Green Man and Maiden, and the Red Man and Maiden, representing the plants and animals. This was considered the best time for a woman to give birth to ensure the child's survival through a harsh winter. Many ancient legends recount a goddess returning from an underworld at this time of year, spontaneously pregnant without the need of her mate. In the Eleusinian Cycle, Persephone returns from her six months in the Underworld, reborn as Koré the Flower Maiden. The Incas celebrated this festival to their goddess with a harelip. Hot cross buns *(paska)* are a traditional treat, representing the balanced sun. The gift of an egg dyed red at this time ensured that your wealth would continue to grow. And of course, this festival of birth and resurrection is known as Easter on the Christian calendar—with no change from the ancient name.

At Annwfn & Raven Haven
At Annwfn and Raven Haven, the children dye Ostara eggs, and each egg has the name of a goddess written on it. These "oracular eggs" are then chosen blindly from a basket, and each person must learn the lessons of their chosen goddess in the coming year. We also go out into the beautiful Annwfn Garden and everyone plants the first flowers, herbs, and vegetables.

At Your House
Ostara is a time of new beginnings and planting spells for future harvest. Celebrate the first day of spring by breaking the dead bonds of winter. During the week before, you should take stock of any outstanding bad feelings or arguments you may have with your family and friends. Write these down on a piece of paper, and seek to settle these with apologies, recompense, or whatever you need to do to restore the balance. At Ostara, having balanced your *karma,* you should burn the paper to wipe clean your karmic slate.

Ostara is the time we celebrate the awakening of the Earth. You can dye your own Ostara eggs and have someone hide them to be found. (You never grow too old to decorate eggs; *I* still do, and we all enjoy seeing how artistic we can make them!) This is also a particularly appropriate time to begin your magickal garden by setting the first plants into the ground. Welcome the nature spirits to your garden, and charge the seeds you'll soon be planting. Set up a garden altar with colored eggs, bunnies, and other baby animals; use a light green altar cloth and candles. You can decorate your altar in fresh spring flowers, adding a heavenly fragrance. Pastel colors are nice, as are yellow and gold, to honor the Goddess of Fertility. A bird's nest that you might have found, or even a hand-made nest, are perfect to put your dyed eggs into. And for a yummy treat, bake some hot cross buns!

Spring: Birth, New Growth, and Expansion
By Mama Donna Henes

The coming of spring has always been symbolized by the egg, representing as it does the birth of a new life. The Yoruba of West Africa use pulverized eggshell (cascarilla) to inscribe blessings of good life; you can use this to mark holy intentions on the ground, on your altar, or on your person. Magick eggs are used in China to dispel any unwanted energy in the environment, thus clearing the way for renewal.

Like eggs, seeds represent new life in springtime. In India, radkrusha seeds are worn to invite luck and spiritual growth. In Mexico, ojo de buey seeds are carried for luck and made into baby amulets to protect the little ones from harm of any sort. Throughout the African Diaspora, peonía seeds are used in ritual, placed on altars, and carried and worn to enhance the incipient power of anything they touch.

In China and Native America, it is said that the turtle gave birth to the Earth. Therefore, turtles represent Mother Earth, Gaia the Supreme Creatrix. Place a bone turtle, a rosewood turtle, or a turtle magnet on your altar to invite in the creative, generative spirit of Mother Nature. Use a turtle whistle to serenade her with prayers of supplication and appreciation.

March is also the time of the Sap Moon. Use some of these delectable tree saps to add succulent fragrance to your life: frankincense, myrrh, copal, camphor, and amber.

Spring Equinox - March 21
Also called Ostara and Eostre
Theme: Emergence[1]
By Ruth Barrett

> *Laughing Maiden is a-borning,*
> *Laughing Maiden is a-rising,*
> *Laughing Maiden is a-flying,*
> *Spring is come, Spring is come.*[2]

The arrival of the Spring Equinox marks the balancing or equal length of day and night, and the onset of warmer weather. The exact date fluctuates each calendar year with the solar cycle, usually falling somewhere between March 20 and 23. The equinoxes are times of equilibrium, of balance, of suspended activity, and when the veil between the seen and unseen is thin. Times of change such as these are also frequently times of psychological and psychic turbulence.[3] Although in spring we are poised at equilibrium, our energy and psyches are in a state of anticipation, ready to move forward into the season of rapid growth. In the Northern Hemisphere this time marked the beginning of the "sowing tide" – the time of preparing the earth for planting.

The holiday of the Spring Equinox is sometimes known as Ostara, named after the Scandinavian Goddess of Spring, or by her Anglo-Saxon name, Eostre or Ostre (from the root word *estrus,* when animals come into the fertile time of their reproductive cycle).[4] The German equivalent is *Ostern,* denoting an eastern orientation and the dawn. The Christian holiday of Easter took its name from this word, and assimilated Eostre's theme of resurrection from death into its own central narrative. Thus, Easter is typically celebrated in a ceremony at sunrise[5] on the Sunday after the first full moon after the Vernal Equinox. Decorated eggs, often dyed red, the color of life, are found all over Europe and symbolize the rebirth of nature. The chocolate rabbit is the Goddess's sacred hare in disguise.[6] It is also customary to wear a new set of clothes in celebration of the birthday of the Earth.

Spring is a time of earthly regeneration, the time of birth and rebirth. The seasonal energy is one of emergence, expansion, and the drive to implement the visions begun in winter's dreaming. The air is charged with a newness, fresh and exciting, bidding life to shake off the inner world of winter and to step fully outside into a renewed world.

In the Goddess's mythic cycle, the Maiden Goddess of spring is reborn from the Earth, emerging out of winter's confines into the bursting flowers and budding greenery of new life. As De Anna Alba writes in *The Cauldron of Change: "The world is again recreated in all its teeming diversity, and we stand in awe of Her miraculous will and the power that is woman. And a promise made to a dying world in the fall is fulfilled in the Spring. For know ye the Mystery that without life there is no death and without death no renewal, and the Great Goddess rules it all."*

Seasonal Questions and Ideas

- Ask yourself the following seasonal questions:
  Who am I becoming?
  What am I awakening within myself?
  What wisdom am I bringing with me from the dark of winter?
- Cover or confine yourself, then emerge into colors and open spaces.
- Celebrate and energize your becoming.
- Buy or make some new colorful clothes.
- Celebrate and honor the Maiden Goddess within and without.
- Do a spring cleaning of your home, altar, and mind.
- Gather with friends and play fun physical games. Dance a Circle dance and sing to honor the cycle of rebirth and return.
- Paint and decorate eggs, perhaps with symbols of your wishes for the coming season. Learn the ancient art of *pysanky* egg decorating.
- Shape sweet cookie dough into eggs, snakes, and rabbits.
- Begin your spring garden. Dig your hands into the earth and loosen the clods in preparation for planting. Plant the eggs you decorated in the soil to "grow" your intentions.
- Fill your home with seasonal flowers or branches.
- Honor the connection between mothers and daughters. Use the season to heal or honor the bond with your own mother or daughter.
- "Hatch" yourself. Create a form of pressure or resistance to simulate breaking through a seed's shell casing under the weight of the Earth. Enact becoming an active participant in your own becoming.
- Notice the flowers that begin to come out. Meditate on the courage and strength in such vulnerability.
- Spend time with a young girl or a group of girls. Find ways to support, protect, or empower them.

Ostara Ritual
By Crow Dragontree

On this Equinox, traditionally we look toward the lengthening of the day and the ongoing emergence of the Solar God's power. As he grows more virile, the Goddess blooms into full maidenhood. This is illustrated beautifully in the Sonoran desert, as plants are often coming into bloom during this time of the year. The sense that the sun's power is growing becomes quite obvious in the desert when temperatures begin to rise slightly and the air becomes just a bit drier. Just as on Imbolc, we realize that the solar energy will become a scorching blaze within a few short weeks, and our pleasurable outdoor activities will soon be somewhat limited.

It seems appropriate to take advantage of this time of youthful and developing solar vigor to energize our own goals and development. As the fruits of our seeds sown on Imbolc begin to germinate, it is no surprise to see many symbols of growth and new life, such as baby chicks and eggs, abounding this time of year. Indeed, it is a common ritual tradition to decorate an egg and hide it, to be found later during an "egg hunt." It would not be a stretch to note the symbolic nature of this act as the charging of the egg with intention ("decorating" the egg), placing it within the womb of the Mother Goddess to germinate ("hiding" the egg), and then bringing the goal to fruition ("finding" the egg).

In the ritual I am about to describe, we will be using the egg as the symbol of energy to accomplish one's goals, and will "absorb" that energy through the ingestion of the egg. You will need a hard-boiled egg that has been decorated with a symbol of your intent. This symbol can take just about any form, from a specific color, picture, rune, words, or any combination thereof.

Of course, the traditional foods of this celebration include eggs. Others might like foods sweetened with honey, and dairy products are still appropriate at this time. In keeping with the growing of the sun's power, one might try to create a dish that balances spicy and sweet flavors.

Explanation of Ostara

The High Priest or Priestess takes their position before the altar while the coveners focus on the concepts of balance and life. At the point that balance is perceived, call out:

The light and dark are balanced now,
Sun rules as long as Moon
And the night grows shorter with every hour
As the first buds start to bloom

The Maiden blossoms everywhere,
Her face shines in leaf and stem.
Her Earth-toned skin and grassy hair
Radiates from within.

The growing Sun shines warmly down,
We salute his yearly reign.
All around is growing power
And resonating strength.
Blessed Be!

Egg-Eating Exercise

Facing the celebrants, the High Priest or Priestess guides them through an empowering exercise designed to help them achieve a given goal or intent:

Take up the egg you have decorated as a symbol of your desires for this coming season of growth.
This egg is the Mother's symbol of life.
Growth begins within this shell.
Consider for a moment that which you used to decorate this egg...be it color, designs, or a combination thereof...and recall what these things represent to you personally.
The vitality of your goal for this season is embodied by this egg.
Feel the energy of this egg.
After a few seconds sensing the power of your goals within the shell of this egg, carefully peel the egg, placing the shell fragments in the bowl of Earth.
Hold the bare egg for a few seconds keeping the visualization of this egg as an embodiment of the power to grow and achieve your goals.

*It is now time to internalize your goals and
the strength to reach them by consuming
this egg.*

*As you eat the egg, know that you are absorbing
your goal. Making it a part of you and
taking in the vitality it takes to achieve it.*

You have the energy!
You have the ability!
So mote it be!

After the coveners have finished eating the egg,
you may now move on to the feast. It's possible, however, that not many will want to eat!

Here are some helpful discussion questions
to bring to the feast:

• How did you decorate your egg?
• What did that decoration mean to you sym-
bolically?
• Was the intent for your egg the same as
your seed exercise on Imbolc?
• If not, what has changed since then?
• What are some of the traditional Ostara
activities you plan to do?

After the celebration is over, the coveners may wish to save their eggshells and use them
to help fertilize their Imbolc seeds. Other activities often include spring cleaning, the perfect act
to both physically and symbolically clear out the clutter of the year as we make room for new life
and growth. Tomorrow, the sun begins to rule longer than the moon. Celebrating the first long
day of the year by greeting the sunrise is a delightful way to attune to these changes. Of
course, planting is still an appropriate activity, and some even bury charged and decorated
eggs to "grow" into fruition. Do not dig these up, however, as they tend to get rather smelly.

Eostre Rite
(Source unknown)

Materials needed: Eostre incense, cauldron or bowl of water, fire wand
(short fire-stick), firewood and kindling, plants, seeds, etc.
Circle setup: Prepare and lay fuel for the fire in North, place altar in South
or Center, and place plants, seeds, etc. around bowl or cauldron of water.

Introduction (by Priestess):
*This is the time of spring's return—
the joyful time when life bursts forth from
the Earth and the chains of winter are broken. It is a time of balance, when all within
us must be brought into a new harmony.
Developing in new directions, we see
things in a new light.*

*The God stretches and rises, eager in
his youth and bursting with the promise of
summer. Blood surges, feelings stir deep
within with the desire to grow and manifest. The Maiden, blossoming now into
womanhood, brings cleansing and renewal
with the first spring rains that, conjoined
with the growing warmth of the sun, create and nourish new life upon the Earth.*

*This is a time of love – of laughter,
dance, and play in the sunshine. Put your
trust in your vision and dance into the light!*

Cast Circle, call Quarters.
Invoking the Spring Maiden:

Priestess stands before the altar, facing
North. The Priest faces her and invokes:
*Maiden of the Earth, Daughter of
Spring
Fair Lady of the Flowers,
Come into our Circle.
Bring to us the Breath of New Life,
Fill us with music and laughter,
Let blossoms rise from beneath Thy feet,
And the sweet sounds of water by Thy voice.
I call upon Thee to descend upon this
The body of Thy servant and Priestess.*

Priest gives her the 5-fold kiss, then moves
to the North quarter and faces the centre.

Invoking and Arming of the God:
Priestess goes to stand in front of the Priest,
and invokes:
*Thee we invoke, O Lord of Light;
Be Thou a Bright Flame before us,
A smooth path beneath us,
Kindle thou within our hearts
A flame of Love and Warmth.*

Priestess takes up the fire wand, lights it with a taper from the altar candle (or Goddess candle), and hands it to the Priest, saying:

O Sun! Be thou armed to conquer the Dark!

Priest lights the fire with the wand while the others arrange themselves so that the women are in a circle in the center, and the men around the outside of them.

When the Priest has lit the fire, he leads the men in a fast, energetic dance around the outer circle, carrying the wand, while the women dance slowly and joyously around the inner circle, occasionally splashing water onto plants from the cauldron. Build energy until the Priestess calls out.

Charging of Wine & Cakes.

Discussion, sharing, music, relaxing.

Thanks and dismissal of Deities and Elements; opening Circle.

Wiccan Rite for the Spring Equinox

The place of meeting should be decorated with boughs of alder or dogwood, if possible. If there will be singing, music, and rhyme before the rite, it should concern life, death, and the summerland. If there is dancing, the Priestess and Priest shall see that the dancers shall follow them, whirling and swirling about the dancing area.

The candles on the altar shall be replaced either by clusters of 13 candles each, or by a large torch in each place. Broomsticks, stick-horses, or phallus-headed sticks shall be leaned against the altar; one shall be provided for each within the Circle. The Great Circle shall be cast in the usual manner, except that a 15-foot Circle shall be drawn.

To begin the rite, the Priestess stands to the north of the altar with the mirror behind her. She directs all within the Circle to stand at the outer part of the circle, men and women alternating. She spreads out her arms and says:

Witches all, we gather now as we rise above the flood of winter to celebrate the rite of death and life. To journey in symbol nearer to the sun and out towards the darkness, again and again, as we ourselves travel from the summerland to this world—many times—with many happenings ere we reach perfection, and finally travel beyond.

She signals for the music to start. The music should start in a slow and dignified manner, increasing in spirit and tempo. The Priestess rejoins the line just behind the Priest, who leads the coven in a line, starting a spiral inwards at a slow ceremonial pace, yet with all in step or rhythm if possible. All should chant:

Yan, Tan, Tethera, Pethera.

Continuing the chant and led by the Priest, they shall spiral inwards and outwards. Each may make his own variations in the dance, and also may follow suit with others in the Circle, as they turn, shuffle, and stamp in a growing and diminishing rhythm. As the music grows faster, the Priest may decide to seize a broomstick, and the others will follow suit as he rides, waves, and raps the stick. When the music is the fastest, they may leap and shout. The Priest shall lead in these usually, as all follow him spiraling in and out. Any who would rest must crouch by the altar. The music shall last for a long while. If there are musicians, the music shall end suddenly at a sign from the Priest. If the music is recorded it will, of course, end of its own accord.

All shall drop to positions of rest. The Priestess shall stand before the altar facing north with her arms outstretched and call:

Beltiate, solitçn cardiçn didomi. Cathçrios phylaxomençn.

All shall make the sign of the pentacle. If any of the magical catalyst* is available, she shall throw a small handful of it into the brazier.

Next should follow the rite of cakes and wine.

Finally, the Great Circle shall be opened.

Magical Catalyst: Mix less than an ounce of saltpeter with an equal amount of chamomile and powdered incense. Mix well, and place in a bowl at the base of the altar.

196. Green Season Quarter Calls

Air that blows idea-songs,
Breath of Gaia's sing-along,
The world exalts with voices ringing
Air! take our spirits winging!

Fire at growtime's blazing heart,
Quickening every living part,
We who dance to fan the flame,
Ask, Fire! let partner be your name!

Water shining in rain and river,
Thou nourisher and comfort giver.
We ask of you, Oh mother of flowers,
Gentle floods of life-stream power.

Earth, Thou art both bird and nest,
With spring-song filled and new life blessed.
We who call you are living eggs.
Earth! hatch and hold us we happily beg.
—*Olwen Fferyllt*

197. Springtime Call to the Goddess

The Crone has sighed and passed us by.
The Maiden blushes near,
In Grain and Fruit that bursts with life,
And the turning of the year.

We hear you on the whispering winds,
We see you in the flower,
This maiden of light, she now descends
To bless us with her power.

Lady of blossoms, of field and hearth,
We celebrate your youth,
Be with us as your fertile Earth
Brings forth a life renewed.
Blessed Be!
—*Crow Dragontree*

198. Ostara Goddess Invocation

Come to us, Holy Maiden,
Cloaked in the green and yellow of daffodils.
With your smile thaw the frozen springs,
Let the waters gush out,
The birth waters of the world.
Bless the buds on the apple trees, and the seeds
We hide in the dark, moist womb of our Mother.
Dance the lengthening days of Spring,
And sing the Summer into being.
—*Carolyn Clark*

199. How does one come to know the Fey?

When the journey of the day is done,
Dim twilight, soft approaching comes—
While circled round the fires some say—
"How does one come to know the Fey?"
And I dreamed of spirits, shimmering free,
Like moonlight beams that dance on streams,
In sweet Harmony's shared serenity.
There I first looked within to seek
The hope of peace that beckoned me.
So fair was she that called my name,
She shone and smiled, devoid of shame—
Beauty walks as in a candle-flame.
And once I knew this mystery,
Outside myself I then could see—
That all is Spirit, and I confess
That Life's in love with its own caress.
When the tranquil light of Spirit shines
Divisions of the realms subside—
Like the bubbling foam of surf on sand
Both here and gone, within your hands...
I ride the fragrant nightbloom drifting,
Like a whisper on the breeze.
And hear the music of a hidden world—
Of drums and pipes with source unseen......
And join the song of wonderment,
Free in Faery merriment!
I feel them as they touch my Spirit,
To find my color and my shade,
And dance with them rejoicing—
Oh, the nature of the friends I made!
They are servants of our Lady-Life
As we who turn the Wheel.
So when you come to know the Fey,
Trust deeply what you feel.
—*Bob Gratrix, Ostara, 1999*

200. Goddess/God Invocations

Hail Diana, Queen of Witches!
Huntress with Your golden arrows,
You were first of all Creation;
Walk with us between the worlds.

* * *

Hail Silvanus, God of mountains,
Lord of wild and sacred forests!
You who preserves the oak and laurel,
Walk with us between the worlds.
—*Sanura & Diane DesRochers*

2. Beltaine: May Day

Introduction: Beltaine
By Oberon Zell-Ravenheart & She' D'Montford

Beltaine (BEL-tayne) (Gaelic) or *May Day*, traditionally the first of May, but astrologically falling several days later, at 15° Taurus, is the great celebration of unashamed human sexuality and joy: *"Hooray, hooray, for the first of May! Outdoor loving starts today!"* The sacred marriage of the Red Man (Robin, Fauna) and Green Maid (Marion, Flora, Blodeuwedd, Maia) is celebrated in the Maypole rite. (May marriages among mortals are considered ill-fated, however, as they are linked to the doom of the May King.) Named for the Celtic fire god Bel, Beltane, the start of summer, is the most important Sabbat after Samhain. Its primary focus is not a fertility celebration; rather, it is a celebration of joy and life. The Light God takes over rulership from the Dark God. The lighting of fires celebrates his restoration. These fires have healing properties, and sky-clad Craft practitioners jump through the flames. Leaping the balefire (made of nine sacred woods) is said to secure protection from evil, bring good luck, and increase one's fertility; and making love in the garden will cause it to flourish.

On May Day, floral wreaths are worn and May baskets left on doorsteps for loved ones. Morris Dancers perform, the Green Man dances with the Red Man, and men may dress as women. It is traditional to wear green, the color of the Faeries. Other Beltane customs include: dancing around Maypoles, "beating the bounds" around your property and repairing fences and boundary markers, young girls bathing their faces in the dew of May Day morning for beauty and to retain youth, and milkmaids' processions with chimney sweeps and other costumed characters, as well as archery tournaments, sword dances, feasting, music, and drinking. Then of course there are the "greenwood marriages" of couples who will spend the entire night making love in the forest until they greet the new May sunrise. They will return with garlands of flowers to decorate their homes. Also called *Flora Day, Hare Day, Caedamh Dea Dia,* and *Summer's Beginning,* Beltane was Christianized as *Roodmas.*

The night before (May Eve) is called *Walpurgisnacht* (ostensibly named for St. Walpurga, an English woman missionary to Germany who died there in 780 CE; but *Walburg* is an old Teutonic name for the Earth Mother). This evening celebrates the begetting of spring by Wodan and Freya, and the bonfire must be lit using spark from flint and steel. Walpurgisnacht is traditionally regarded as a night of madness, when the veil between the worlds is particularly thin; it is the opposite hinge of the year from Samhain, and the beginning of the summer half of the year. Brocken Mountain in Germany is famed as the site of great Witches' orgies on this night. In classical times May Eve was the festival of Hades, Lord of the Underworld.

At Annwfn
At Annwfn we hold an all-night ritual and bardic on Walpurgisnacht, generally with a theme involving a journey into the mythic realm, or Faerie. We hold bawdy May games to select the Queen and King of the May, who are crowned as Hornéd Man (Robin) and Flower Maid (Marion), and who represent the men and women of our community during their reign (only until Samhain for the King, but a full year for the Queen). Children's May games are also held to select a May Princess and Prince, and the new "royal court" will convene at festivals throughout the summer season. During the year, they visit the homes of the people, bringing blessings into each.

The maypole dance is, of course, the centerpiece of Beltaine. The women prepare the Maypole crown, the Circle, the gate, and the hole, decorating them with ribbons and flowers, while the men go off to bring in the huge 20-foot Maypole. The pole is carried in procession on the shoulders of the men, led by the King. It is brought through the gate with great merriment and bawdy innuendos, then crowned, placed in the hole, raised, and anchored with rocks jammed into the hole around it. The maypole rite is a sacred marriage of the new Queen and King, and he is bound to the pole while she dances seductively around him. Everyone grabs an end of the many long ribbons hanging from the crown, and dances the weaving dance to wrap the pole and the King while pipers and drummers play a lively beat.

At Your House

Beltaine is a time of courtship, and if there is someone you especially like (including your mother), this is a perfect occasion to give them a May basket full of fresh-picked flowers. Decorate your altar with spring flowers and colorful ribbons; use a dark green altar cloth and candles. This is a time for flowers, lots of them, picked by you or bought; any varieties will do. Beltane is a great fire festival, so a group of candles on your altar bunched together in warm colors such as red, orange or pink would be a nice substitute for a small fire. You might also want to include images of the sex organs. (This doesn't have to be graphic—it can be a phallic rock and a creviced stone, or flowers, or a yin-yang symbol.) Make and wear floral wreaths. This is the festival of regeneration of the Earth. Express love and care to those close to you; feed one another in a special ritual meal. You might even crown a May Queen and King.

If you have room in your back yard, you can put up a maypole—preferably at least 10 feet tall! Ribbons should be about 1½ times as long as the pole, and fastened to the top before the pole goes up. There must be an even number, and it's best to have them in just two colors: red and green (or red and white). There has to be one dancer for each ribbon, so if you only have four people, use only four ribbons. People alternate ribbon colors, facing opposite ways: red turns to the left, moving *deosil* (clockwise), and green to the right, moving *widdershins* (counter-clockwise).

You dance the circle by alternately moving outside and then inside of the people coming towards you, weaving the ribbons over and then under theirs in turn. Finally, when the woven ribbons get too low on the pole to keep dancing, all the dancers run deosil to wrap the remainder around and tie them off as a spell for prosperity and growth in the coming year. Afterwards, when you take down the pole, you will find that the woven tube of ribbons can be slipped off the pole like a stocking, and saved as a special charm for lovers. It makes a great wedding gift!

May Eve - April 30/May 1
Also known as Beltane, Bealtaine, Walpurgisnacht
Theme: Flowering[1]
By Ruth Barrett

In Ireland, as in most parts of Northern Europe, May Eve signaled the first day of summer and hailed the "growing tide," when things begin to ripen, come to fruition, and fulfill the promises of spring. The principal customs and ceremonies of May were those that welcomed the summer. May Eve was marked by the lighting of bonfires and various rites to ensure fertility among the herds and to bring a good harvest.[2] The old name for this feast at the beginning of May

Beltane, which means "bright fire."[3] Although the holiday has various spellings, it consists of two components: *Bel* and *Tan*. "*Bel* is known to be an ancient Sun God name… *Tan* is Celtic for Fire, so here there is a double principle of God, or (good)…."[4] In old Ireland, the cattle were taken off to the summer pastures where they would remain until Samhain. All of the spring work, including tilling of the soil to produce the crops, was to be finished by May Day. The most common custom was that of venturing out after dusk on May Eve to pick fresh flowers that would be brought home before dawn on the following day. The hawthorn, or May bush, would be set out in front of the home in the same spirit in which we set out our flags on a national holiday. Sometimes the May bush would be decorated with eggshells, ribbons, colored paper, and flowers.[5] Beltane was a time of revelry and bawdiness to stimulate the sexual energy of life-making. The maypole, outlawed in Ireland in 1792, is probably one of the most overtly sexual ritual customs associated with this season.

   May Eve's dark counterpart across the wheel of the year is Hallowmas, and traditionally both holidays were the "hinge" holidays of the year, in which inhabitants of the worlds of ancestral spirits, otherworld beings, and humans might cross paths. The Faerie faith was strong in many Celtic lands, and protective measures were taken on the possiblility that mortals and immortals might encounter each other from sunset on May Eve to sunrise on May Day. Faerie abductions were feared, and it was thought that infants especially were in danger of being switched for "changelings," the children of the Faerie folk. Offerings of food or drink were left for the Faeries so that they might be kind to their mortal neighbors.

Rites of Spring: Celebrating May Day
By Virginia Johnson, Beltaine 2001

   In the spring of the year when the earth warms and the lush greening of the land begins again, joyous folk still gather to welcome the growing season as they have for hundreds of years in Europe and throughout the world.

   The ancient Romans celebrated on May 1 with a feast for the goddess Flora, called *Floralia*. Chains of flower blossoms were wound around her temples' columns. Women and girls wearing white robes scattered petals through the streets, and children made dolls of the goddess and decorated them with flowers.

   Druid priests celebrated the Celtic festival of Beltane throughout the British Isles and other Celtic lands on this day. The people built bonfires on May Eve and drove their cattle between them to protect them from disease, and the fires' embers were scattered across the fields to ensure a good harvest. Those present shared a special Beltane cake; the unlucky soul who received the burned bit was called the *cailleach-bealteine*, or Beltane churl, and was pelted with egg shells. When the Romans subjugated much of Britain from the first to the fifth centuries, they added their revels for the feast of Flora to the Beltane festivities.

   A French custom from old times is to rise at dawn and go into the woods to search for the first lilies-of-the-valley, which are considered to be lucky. The flowers are then pressed and sent to distant friends as charms.

   In certain cantons of Switzerland, May Day Eve, or *Maitag Vorabend,* brings the planting of the *Maitannli,* or May pine tree. Bachelors find these in the forest and plant them in front of their sweethearts' houses to show their affection. Young boys ring bells across the land to ward off evil, and prayers are offered to ensure good harvests.

   The English people enjoyed the May revels in medieval and Tudor times. Nobles and peasants would go to the fields and forests to gather flowers and tree boughs. The Maypole was especially prized and was carried in a procession by a team of oxen strewn with flowers. Dancers holding long colorful ribbons fastened to the top of the pole would weave in and out, braiding the ribbon about the pole. Games and pageants featured a young woman as the

May Queen, and other players as Robin Hood, Maid Marian, and Jack-in-the-Green. Morris Dancers bedecked with bells in traditional dress also performed on May Day.

May Day was not openly celebrated during the Puritans' ascendancy in the 17th century. After the Stuart kings returned in 1661, a cedar Maypole of 134 feet was erected with much celebration in London, and remained there for over 50 years.

Maypoles eventually found their way to the New World, though the power of the Puritans in the northern colonies put a chill on such festivities. In a later century, Nathaniel Hawthorne was inspired to write his short story, "The May Pole of Merry-Mount," which is based on a historical clash between easy-going Anglican colonist Thomas Morton and Puritan leader John Endecott at Plymouth colony on May 1, 1627.

Many superstitions related to May Day carried over from Britain to America. Here are a few drawn from *The Folklore of American Holidays*:

- If a handkerchief has been left outside overnight before the first day of May, the next morning the initials of your future mate will be written on the handkerchief.
- If you walk around a wheat field on the first day of May, you will meet your mate.
- On May 1 look for birds' nests. The number of eggs you find will be the number of years you will be single.
- You must go fishing on May Day. The fish will bite an almost-bare hook.
- Move your bees on the first of May.
- The first day of May is the time to go barefoot.

Another often-cited custom is for ladies to wash their faces in dew gathered from May Day morning to make themselves more beautiful.

As times changed so did how the 1st of May is celebrated. In some countries May Day has taken on a political aspect, especially in areas with strong socialist influences. These countries use the day as an opportunity to showcase their industrial and political power. And yet the rise of modern Paganism in the United States and abroad has brought a resurgence of traditional ritual reminiscent of the ancient Celts and Romans.

The May Royalty
By Oberon

There are many different aspects to what we call the "gods" and "goddesses." Some, such as Mother Nature and Father Time, are truly cosmic. Others, such as Mother Earth and Father Sun, are more finite, with material bodies to house their ethereal souls. Some, such as Pan, Eros, Yemaya, and the Green Man, are actually forces and powers of Nature. Still others, such as most of the familiar pantheons of Egypt, Greece, Ireland, Scandinavia, etc., are closely linked to the human community and embody aspects of human nature more than those of Nature Herself. There are deities that are totemic, such as coyote, eagle, and bear; these are the collective souls of particular species. Then there are the humble nymphs, sprites, naiads, dryads, fauns, Fairies, and other spirits of place.

Each of these deities, at whatever level, may have *avatars*—living human representatives who carry their energy and who manifest their spirits *incarnate* ("in flesh"), for however long they can hold it. In the Afro-Caribbean traditions, possession by the *Loa* or *Orishas* is carefully confined to the brief period of the all-night ritual. When we "call down the moon" and evoke the presence of the God or Goddess to attend our rites in the person of our priest or priestess, we always release them at the end when the Circle is opened. Being a vessel for divine energy is extremely hard on mortal flesh—notoriously so for males. Jim Morrison was a vessel for Dionysos, God of Intoxication; and Gwydion Pendderwen carried the energy of the Green Man. Neither of them knew how to let go at the right time and they were both consumed to death by the divine fire.

In the HOME Tradition, our Queen and King of the May are essentially avatars of the community, bringing together the epitome of the male and female energies and personalities of our tribe in a *hieros gamos*—sacred marriage—which is enacted on several levels in the maypole ritual. Our Queen represents the land itself as well as specifically being an avatar and stand-in for all of the women in the tribe. Thus her reign continues throughout the year, progressing in stages through the full cycle of the immanent Goddess—Maiden, Mother, and Crone. The King represents the people, bonded to the land in love and service, and is also an avatar and stand-in for all of the men in the tribe. He is the Year-King, and his reign ends at Samhain with the death of the God.

Thus it is essential that the energies of *both* genders must be represented in our avatars. The two of them (with their Princes and Princesses) hold court at the festivals of Litha, Lugnasadh, and Mabon, whereat they may hear grievances and accept vows, dispense honors and awards to those they deem deserving, as well as grant favors, dub knights, designate bards and champions, issue letters of marque, and so forth.

During the period of the King's reign, it is the privilege of the people to shower him with honors and hospitality. Every house he visits is blessed by his presence, as is every lass he loves, every field he sows, and every meal he shares. All of this goes as well for the Queen, and doubly so for the half of the year she traditionally reigns alone, when she is due support, consolation, love, and sympathy. We treat them as we ourselves would wish to be treated, for "as fare these vessels, so fare we all."

In the past few years, reluctant to lose our beloved King, and in deference to the love of his Lady, we have introduced a new ritual of transformation, of death and rebirth, whereby at Samhain we may choose to resurrect our dying May King as the Winter King (or "Rain King" in California). In such a case, he may then resume the throne with her for the remainder of the year, perhaps even taking the role of Father Winter, or Santa Claus, at Yule, when the Winter King and Wint'ry Queen may hold court together.

It is important to recognize that these offices carry no temporal authority. Our sacred royalty are not *above* us: they are *of* us. In a very real sense, they *are* us, just as the Earth is of us and we are of the Earth—that is the meaning of *immanent divinity*. Their royalty carries no right to issue orders, commands, or decrees which must be obeyed!

There is mutual honor and duty inherent in these royal offices, just as there is mutual honor and duty in the way the community relates to them. By honoring our kings and queens, we confer blessings upon ourselves and our homes. By blessing our homes and fields, they confer honor and good karma on themselves and the vessels who carry them. Various chosen couples who have carried the energies of King and Queen have added creatively to these evolving roles, and have received positive responses from the tribe. This is encouraged.

May all who sit our sacred thrones bring ever greater honor to the gods and our tribe!

201. The May Queen is Waiting

I'll prepare the furrowed earth for your sweet
    body.
The stars are rising in the moonlit sky.
The May Queen is waiting.
Her voice reaches as you sleep, can you awaken
To live the wonders of your dreams?
The May Queen is waiting.
Restless in the night, the full moon light,
Carving magic patterns in the land,
She waits for you to return again.
Do not keep Her waiting.
You startle, wake, and stare, heart is beating.

The new earth quickens as you rise.
The May Queen is waiting.
Feel the pulsing ground call you to journey,
To know the depths of your desire.
The May Queen is waiting.
Moving through the night, the bright moon's
    flight.
In green and silver on the plain,
She waits for you to return again.
Do not keep Her waiting.
Her temper stings if you refuse to taste Her
    honey.
Surrender as enchantment brings
The first light of dawning.

Move with Her in sacred dance, through
    fear to feeling,
Bringing ecstasy to those who dare.
Living earth is breathing.
Loving through the night in the bright
    moonlight,

As seedlings open with the rain,
She'll long for you to return again.
Do not keep Her waiting.
Do not keep Her waiting.
Do not keep Her waiting.

—Ruth Barrett

Beltaine Rite of Sacred Marriage
By Katlyn Breen, Desert Moon Circles

(Priest and Priestess enter from opposite sides of the Maypole, and circle slowly.)

P: *I arrive in this place filled with desire and satisfaction!*
I am he who has sought you since before the dawn of creation!

Ps: *I am she who awaits you eternally, veiled within the thin rainbow mist of dreams.*
By my motions have I coaxed the beginning to meet the end,
The inner world to mimic what lies beyond.
By my flowing waters have I guided your journeys back again to me!

P: *I have chanted your sacred names upon the silent winds,*
I have invoked you through devotion and deep desire,
Through the incense of my passion and The joyous steps of my whirling dancing Have I made the magic of your blessed names!
You are she whom I have wished for, it is for you that I return.

Ps: *Behold! The life of the world has brought forth*
A fragrant starlit temple of flowering green,
And constructed an altar of living harmony to bless our union!
May this circle of love in which we lie Be the symbolic ring of our eternal promise to one another.
Let life sing loud its joyous song like a serenade to us!
Love has purified our separate paths into the center and made sacred our touch!
Rise up unto me, reveal to me the hot red fire of the Universe that you bear!
Utter my sacred names unto me, close

and low—
Make this steaming moment, this now in time
The long encompassing all shared between us—burn all else away!
I have invoked you to the Temple that lies beyond all veils.

P: *You are the sacred Earth! You are the divine Lover! You are the Beloved!*
You are Truth, and the ecstasy of creation!
I awaken in this moment and rise, strong and sure, like the Sun.
I become a sacred fire of joy, and in this blushing moment
I share the seed and mystery of creation with you alone!
I give my light to you! Bless me.

Ps: *I am both a promise and a plea,*
With much to give- and yet my needs are many!
My desire pushes outwards even as it turns itself ever inward—
Within me lies both enigma and revelation—
A force and counter force that seeks balance
Of the delicate mysterious flower of creation!
I am the sacred chalice of sweet Life, overflowing in my joy!
I am the dark and fertile field of creation, and in this moment
I unveil the mystery of creation with you alone!
I give my cup to you! Bless me.

(Blade and cup unite in sacred marriage, in symbol or in flesh.)

(They hold the Maypole as they circle it:)
Now as cup and blade unite,
Awake the Great and Sacred Rite!

Weave the dance of perfect love,
By the horn and by the dove—
Mystery of mystery!
As our will, so mote it be!

Weave the end of separation of spirit
Weave the dance of creation—
Weave laughter and joy,
Weave beauty and harmony
Weave love for each other and for our
Earth!

We celebrate the ecstasy of union.
MOON AND SUN JOIN AS ONE!
Ps 2: *Let the maypole dance begin!*
(Maypole dance and chant.)

Ps 2: *Feel the ecstatic energy of creation,*
Bathe in this sacred fire, bask in the
glow of Beltaine!
Blessed be the union of their love!
All repeat: *Blessed be the union of their*
love!

202. Hal-an-to [Traditional]

Ch: Hal-an-to, jolly rum-ba-lo,
We were up, long before the day-o!
To welcome in the Summer,
To welcome in the May-o.
For Summer is a-comin' in,
And Winter's gone away-o!

Take no scorn to wear the horn;
It was the crest when you were born!
Your father's father wore it
And your father wore it too!

Robin Hood and Little John
Have both gone to the fair-o.
And we will to the merry green wood
To hunt the buck and hare-o!

Now blessed be our Circles,
And all our power and light-o.
And send us peace to all the world,
Send love by day and night-o!

203. Beltane Call to the God

Lord we invoke thee,
Lord, Secret of the Sun!
Thou who art the flame that burns in the
heart of every man,
And who contains the power of the fertile forest,
By rod & blade, hoof & horn, seed & stem
do we invoke thee!
Lord be present among us, Blessed Be!
—*Katlyn Breene*

204. Morris Song

Rabbits in Australia, rabbits in Australia,
We do it all day, we do it all night
Because it is a fertility rite!
—*sung by English ritual Morris dancers*

205. Beltane Call to the Goddess

Lady we invoke thee,
Evening star, soul of infinite space!
Let thy image be perfect Love.
Show us thy heart of radiant fire.
Dance the moon to fly with sun,
Dance the wind, hear harmony of heaven,
Dance the soul and we are one.
Dance the heart and the veil is lifted!
By moon and tide, earth and bud,
Flower and fruit, do we invoke thee!
Beloved be present among us, Blessed Be!
—*Katlyn Breene*

206. Bringing in the May[6]

If you survive the night of madness,
If you survive its crazy spin,
Then you shall dance around the pole,
Take what's tattered, make it whole,
And the pattern of the world you weave
before you will unfold.

Chorus (x4): Bringing in the May…

And now the quarters we must cross,
Between the equal end extreme,
We know the Morris dance is done,
So that all can feel the Sun,
As it penetrates our flesh and blood
and Spirit made as one.

A living circle cast in Love,
With friends and strangers as one voice,
A bond that's stronger, far, than steel,
We project an ancient will,
Sending power all around the world:
Protect, Renew and Heal!
—*Rick Hamouris, 1986*

Wiccan Rite for Beltane Eve

The place of meeting should be decorated with willow-boughs. A besom, or Witch's broom of willow switches, should be part of the decorations. If there will be singing music and rhyme before the rite it should concern magick, things new and fresh, and summer. Any dancing should be bright, energetic, and cheerful. Fencing and swordplay by the men are traditional, after which the winner is crowned "King of Summer" by his Lady.

A Maypole should be set up and used for mildly erotic games by the ladies and men. A "Beltane cake" containing milk, eggs, and honey should be baked; the eggshells may be saved for practical jokes, which are also traditional at this time. The atmosphere of this festival should be light, energetic, and cheerful.

Of all the festivals, this one should be outdoors if possible. If so, a magickal need-fire (actually two fires near the altar) should be struck with flint and steel.

A willow besom should be laid before the altar. A horned helmet or symbolic horned headdress should be set upon the altar. If the rite is held indoors, set up two cauldrons north of the altar, far enough apart to dance between; scented oil or spirits should be added.

The Great Circle shall be cast in the usual manner, except that a 15-foot circle shall be drawn.

To begin the rite, the Priestess stands to the north of the altar with the mirror behind her. She spreads out her arms and says:

Witches all, we meet on this, the night of Walpurgis—holy, joyous, and magick—to celebrate the return of summer, of life, of things new and fresh. I call before me he who personifies the God.

The Priest has the helmet placed on his head by a maiden within the Circle, and the sword placed in his hands. If they are available, he should wear gauntlets and sword-belt. He says:

My Lady, as the power of the God is in this season supplanted by the warmth of the Goddess, so also must I give honor to thee.

The Priestess gives the seasonal challenge:

Thou hast had thy time of dominion. Canst thou yet stand before the Lady whom I represent?

The Priest replies:

It is ordained—I cannot. For cold must yield to warmth, and death once more to life. I yield to thee my power. (He salutes.)

He bows and presents the sword to her. She sits on the south edge of the altar, and he ceremoniously places the helmet on her head, while she holds the sword upright as a scepter. He says:

To thee, with love, do I yield my reign.

She motions for him to light the two fires, and proclaims:

Thou of the joyous Craft, I do decree that thou dance! That we and those we love be free in the coming seasons of the storms of humankind and the raging of the elements. That joy of life and joy of magick be ours. As I dance, so shalt thou follow.

The Priestess puts the sword and helmet down on the altar and signals for the music to start. She and the Priest lead the circular dancing, which may be formal or free-style, as they determine. The dancing weaves around and between the fires. In this rite there is no fixed ending to the dance; it may be as determined by the Priestess and Priest.

Next should follow the rite of cakes and wine.

More dancing may follow next if so desired.

Finally, the Great Circle shall be opened.

3. Litha: Summer Solstice

Introduction: Litha
By Oberon Zell-Ravenheart & She' D'Montford

Litha (LITH-ah), also called *Midsummer* or *Summer Solstice,* occurs around June 21. Litha is the name of a Saxon Grain Goddess corresponding to Greek Demeter or Roman Ceres, and her festival is one of joy, abundance, and play. Called *Alban Hefin* by the Celts, Midsummer was Christianized as St. John's Day. Druids believed that snakes come together on the Solstice night to create the *glain,* or "Druid's egg"—said to confer great magickal powers to its possessor. Many of the ancient stone monoliths are aligned to the Summer Solstice.

Several Native American tribes mark Summer Solstice with seasonal rites and rituals, such as the *Sundance,* performed by the Sioux tribe. The Natchez honor the sun, from whom they believe they are descended, with the festival of first fruits. No one is allowed to touch the first ears of corn until after the ceremony. The Hopi also celebrate the Solstice, with masked dancers in colorful costumes representing the *kachinas,* spirits of rain and fertility.

Midsummer's Eve represented the apex of the God's life. Variously called the Oak King, Jack-in-the-Green, or Pan—with the lower torso, cloven hooves, and horns of a satyr—he was the archetypal Wild Man of the wood, and the King of the fairies. Following their King on a romp through the countryside made this night second only to Halloween in its importance to the Wee Folk, who especially enjoyed playing tricks on a fine summer's night. If you wished to see Fairy folk , this was (and is) the best night to do it. You only had to rub fern seed onto your eyelids at the stroke of midnight. Carrying a bit of rue in your pocket or wearing your jacket inside out can protect you from spiteful Fairies. If you can't do that, and you must travel on Midsummer's Eve, you must stay on the old straight ley lines until you get to your destination—otherwise you may be lead astray by the Fairy folk and get lost forever.

On this longest day of the year, picnicking, swimming, and water play are customary, as are bonfires and fireworks lit after sundown to provide light to the revellers and to ward off mischievous Fairy folk. Cakes are shared, in which one piece contains a bean or other marker; the one who gets it is considered "dedicated" and required to jump the flames three times. Throughout Europe lovers clasp hands or toss flowers to each other across the bonfire, or leap through it together before disappearing into the woods and fields ("searching for the Midsummer grass") to make love under the stars. This celebration is specifically in honor of the great Earth Mother who nourishes us with her bounty from her ever-flowing cauldron, but we may also honor the Sun Father at this time. Litha is a festival for families, marriage partners, and children. The rituals commonly celebrate the marriages of the gods, so this is the best time for marriages, and also a time for future visions and Fairy favors.

At Annwfn & Raven Haven
Annwfn is part of a much larger 5,600-acre homesteading community known as Greenfield Ranch. From the community's founding in 1972, Summer Solstice has always been the biggest party of the year, with swimming, pot-luck feasting, live bands, and entertainment. We have lots of water games in the big ranch pond: watermelon races, water ballet, rope swinging, and jumping into the water from high in the overhanging trees. A great Circle is held to spread a magickal umbrella of invisibility and protection over the entire land. Fireworks light up the night, with drumming and dancing around the great bonfire.

For eleven years (1985-1996), Morning Glory and I lived beside the Rushing River, and we used to celebrate Litha with a big skinny-dipping beach party and pot-luck barbeque. Some of our favorite things to do were inner-tubing down the river and wallowing in a "primal ooze pit." This was made by positioning an inflatable kids' swimming pool over a shallow pit dug in the sand, with a thin slick "ooze" made with water and powdered white porcelain slip we bought at a ceramics supply store. We'd let the ooze dry on our skin, and then wash it off in the river. Fireworks would light up the night, with drumming and dancing around the great bonfire.

At Your House

Litha is a classic time for magick of all kinds. Celebrate nature's sacrifice and renewal, and make changes in your own life. Make a protective solar talisman to put up on your door. Nurture your crops, and harvest magickal herbs from your garden. Decorate your altars with summer flowers and sun images; use a white altar cloth and candles, and fill your chalice with water. Some sort of fire on your altar is important, so use candles or votives. Include fresh fruits as a reminder of the Earth's bounty. A symbol or picture of Earth on your altar is a gentle reminder to honor her. Add flowers of gold, orange, and yellow; roses are traditional.

Litha is also a special time for honoring and blessing animals, so bring your pets and familiars into your Circle and give them special treats and attention.

Since Litha is just before American Independence Day on July 4, you can often buy fireworks at this time (unless they are illegal in your state, and/or you live in a very dry area with high fire danger in the summer). My favorites are fountains, which can be safely set off at a beach, around a campfire, or on the driveway. These have the colored sparkles and special effects of the high-exploding skyrockets, without the dangers of shooting them into the air. Each firework can be set off as a spell, naming the purpose before you light it. Be sure to keep a water hose handy just in case any sparks get away!

Summer Solstice - June 21st
Also called Midsummer's Eve/Day, Litha
Theme: Union[1]
By Ruth Barrett

Summer Solstice marks the peak of the solar cycle at midsummer. In the midst of the longest day of the year, we simultaneously begin our return to the dark half of the year. The exact date of the Summer Solstice fluctuates each calendar year between June 20 and 23. At Winter Solstice the underlying energy is *passive* and concerns visioning, but the seasonal energy at Summer Solstice is *active*: It's about doing and expanding, living the dream envisioned in the dreamtime of winter. At the peak point of summer bloom, prayers for blessings on the crops are asked of the Goddess. The Earth is fertile, and the womb of the Earth Mother is now ripe with life as she begins to pour forth her creations in the form of growing fields, trees, flowers, and animals.

Two fire traditions were practiced widely on Summer Solstice, sometimes called "Bonfire Night." One old Irish custom dictated that a community fire was to be lit exactly at sunset, and had to be watched and tended until long after midnight. The communal fire was built and lit by the inhabitants of a whole town, or several towns, and celebrated with music, dancing, fire jumping, singing, and other ceremonies. The family fire was a smaller fire lit by members of each household for the benefit of their particular household or farm. The family fire was a quiet affair in which protective ceremonies were the main concern. In some villages, the inhabitants took embers or ashes from the family fire, or from the community fire, and threw a portion into each field, or on the four corners of each field, in order to protect them from damaging weather such as drought or hail storms. The cattle of the farm were herded together and driven through the smoke of an outdoor bonfire. In Ireland, this was also a traditional time for medicinal herb gathering.[2]

207. Summer, Summer

Corn-doll of Beltane, Maiden of Summer
Borne up each hill and down every glen
Radiant lasses in their white dresses
We have brought only the Summer in

Ch: Summer, Summer, milk freshly flowing
   We have brought only the Summer in
   Golden Summer, opening daisies
   We have brought only the Summer in

We brought it with us from branching forest
We have brought only the Summer in
Golden Summer of Sun's descending
We have brought only the Summer in

In the sky warbling song of the blackbird
Joy without end and flowers on the trees
The cuckoo and blackbird are singing for
   pleasure
We have brought naught but the Summer in!
   —*Traditional lyrics adapted by Artemisia*
   Gaelic transliteration by Jim Duran

208. Midsummer Fires

In the Vale of Glamorgan, there I saw
A cart wheel all covered in straw
Set alight, then rolled downhill
Augur for harvest, good or ill
If out before it reaches the end
Poor harvests now bad weather send
If lighted all its fall, and still longer
Abundant crops will grow for farmer.

At Buckfastleigh is lit upon on sunset
Midsummer wheel that luck may get
If guided by sticks, it meets the stream
Fortune will shine within its beam
A flaming chariot is shown in part
Bringing delight and joy to heart
As sun now wheeling through the sky
Brings living warmth to you and I.

In Shropshire, upon St John's Eve
Three fires do they carefully weave
A bonfire of clean bones, no wood
Of wood, no bones, the wakefire should
Keep on burning through the night
Watched by all, for second sight
And lastly, made of wood and bones
St John's fire is lit upon old stones.

At Penzance, tar barrels set on fire
With music played on harp or lyre
Folk walk this way, sing loud and raucous
Holding forth torches of blazing canvas
Then link hands, and dance in circle
"Threading the needle," rhythmical
Over the dying embers, fading light
As the evening falls to night.

In Ireland, when fire dulls to reddish glow
Men leap over the flames in show
When lower still, young girls can leap
Thrice back and forth a man to keep
Married women walk upon the embers
Secure good will for family members
Then all take back within one hand
To their own house, a sacred brand.

Midsummer Eve, and fires are lit
The solar nexus reaches summit
Spoked wheel pauses, then rolls on
We chant at equinox in antiphon
Lay out the candles for spectacle
In pattern of five, a pentacle
Of customs old, and customs now
Upon the Ancient Burial How.
                    —*Tony*

209. Hail to Juno

Hail to Juno, our Protectoress!
Liberator of the people;
Patroness of babes and mothers,
Walk with us between the worlds.
   —*Sanura & Diane DesRochers*

Healing Gaia's Children
Summer Solstice 2000 at the Hog Farm
by Liza Gabriel & Oberon Zell-Ravenheart

Before ritual: Totem pole raising, teach chants and distribute song sheets.
Bardic: MC'd by Darryl, Artemisia, and others.
Food Blessing: *"Give Thanks to the Mother Gaia."*

Healing Gaia's Children Ritual

Introduction—Darryl Cherney
Priest/Priestess rap—Oberon and Liza
Grounding—Richard Ely
Circle Casting—Liza

Round like a belly, the womb of rebirth
Round like the planet, our Mother the Earth
Round like the cycles that ebb and that flow
Round us a circle from which we shall grow
Here is a circle, to work and to learn
Here is a place where we help the world turn
As magic is made upon this sacred ground
With our hearts and our will
Shall this circle be bound!
                        (—Anodea Judith)

Elements: Adey stands in the center of the circle. She invokes each Element, calling out its totem animal, a dancer, who comes in from outside the circle. She then dances with each totem and invites others grouped in that Element to dance too. Then the four Elements join hands in the center and dance together for the fifth Element. Adey coordinates. Drum and whistle accompany this.

Sun God Invocation: given by Oberon, with refrain spoken by all participants:

Oh Father Sun, source of all Earthly life,
We developed eyes to witness your radiant light,
When we crawled out of the ancient seas
Onto dry land, in search of You.
Your golden light heals us, now and always,

Ref: *YOUR GOLDEN LIGHT HEALS US, NOW AND ALWAYS!*

All living things greet You at Your rising,
And call after You as You disappear;
Birds fly to the treetops to sing
Their evening songs in Your last rays.
Your golden light heals us, now and always,

Ref: *YOUR GOLDEN LIGHT HEALS US, NOW AND ALWAYS!*

Sunflowers, Morning Glorys, all green leaves
Turn toward You as the Source.
The whole Planet yearns to be One with You
Through Her creatures.
Your golden light heals us, now and always,

Ref: *YOUR GOLDEN LIGHT HEALS US, NOW AND ALWAYS!*

We love You with Your own love,
As we rejoice together on Your longest day.
Let a new Golden Age be born for all Your
children;
May You bless our Mother Earth forever!
Your golden light heals us, now and always,

Ref: *YOUR GOLDEN LIGHT HEALS US, NOW AND ALWAYS!*
(adapted from Akhnaten's "Hymn to Aten"
—Oberon & Liza Ravenheart, 2000)

All chant: *There is a really fun God,*
            And he is the Sun God!
            Ra Ra, Ra Ra RA!

Gaia Invocation: given by Liza, with refrain spoken by all participants:

Mother Gaia, we feel You within our own bodies
Your seas quicken and swell,
Our blood pulses with Your streaming life.
Embraced by our Father the Sun,
You stir our heart's warm flow.
You are life and breath, Mother;
Help us heal one another!

Refrain: *YOU ARE LIFE AND BREATH, MOTHER;*
         HELP US HEAL ONE ANOTHER!

Mother Gaia, we see You in every person here.
Wind dances in Your sacred groves;
Our spirits move together like the trees.
Your mountains witness eternity;
They call to our ancient souls.
You are life and breath, Mother;
Help us heal one another!

Refrain: *YOU ARE LIFE AND BREATH, MOTHER;*
         HELP US HEAL ONE ANOTHER!

Mother Gaia, we know You in Earth,
Water, Fire and Air;
In every thread of the Web of Life;
In times of chaos and despair;
In our courage, our beauty, our loving—

You are there!
You are life and breath, Mother;
Help us heal one another!
Refrain: *YOU ARE LIFE AND BREATH, MOTHER;*
HELP US HEAL ONE ANOTHER!
      (—Liza Gabriel Ravenheart, 1999)
Oberon and Liza embrace & kiss.
Song: (sung by Artemisia)
   Father Sun and Mother Earth
   Through your love we find rebirth! (2X)

Statement of Intention: Bob and Darryl

Working 1: Gratitude for the Earth
Chant the gratitude chant (recited by Liza or Artemisia, chanted three times between each, and shared with rhythm or drum):
   An attitude of gratitude
   Is the guidance of the Gaia dance.

Every time someone shares, Oberon pours from the magick pitcher into a glass chalice. For brief, one-minute shares, four or five people share their gratitude for the Earth. Bob and Darryl choose people. Then everyone shouts out at once things that they're grateful for. We show the chalice; the cup runneth over.

Thanksgiving chant (Artemisia or Adey):
   Give thanks to the Mother Gaia,
   Give thanks to the Father Sun,
   Give thanks to the flowers in the garden where
   The Mother and the Father are One!
(repeat 3x, 3rd time sing "Have fun!" at end)

Working 2: Acknowledgement & Inspiration
Five people or more chosen by Bob and Darryl share acknowledgements of things that Gaia's children did to help Gaia. We invite each person to approach three people nearby whom they don't know, and say: *"Thank you for your service to Gaia."*

Chant: "She's Been Waiting" (Artemisia)
Ch: *She's been waiting, waiting,*
   She's been waiting so long!
   She's been waiting for Her children
   To remember, to return! (2x)

   Blessed be and blessed are
   The lovers of the Lady.
   Blessed be and blessed are
   The Maiden, Mother, Crone.
   Blessed be and blessed are
   The ones who dance together.

   Blessed be and blessed are
   The ones who dance alone!
   Blessed be and blessed are
   The ones who sit in vision;
   Blessed be and blessed are
   The ones who shout and scream;
   Blessed be and blessed are
   The movers and the shakers;
   Blessed be and blessed are
   The dreamers and the Dream!
      (—Paula Walowitz)

Working 3: Healing
Liza or someone else gives a brief guided meditation on healing.
Chant: "Ring the Bells," by Leonard Cohen:
   Ring the bells that still can ring,
   Forget your perfect offering.
   There is a crack, a crack in everything.
   That's how the light gets in;
   That's how the light gets in!

Everyone shares with one other person the laying on of hands, along with the ceremonial words: *"I wash your struggle with waters of compassion. I bless you with the healing power of this Circle. Be reborn!"*

Birth canal: two people at entrance: Adie & Sunshine. Liza & OZ at exit.

Chant: "The Earth shall be well" (Artemisia)
   We shall be well,
   We shall be well,
   All manner of things shall be well!
   The Earth shall be well,
   The Earth shall be well,
   All manner of things shall be well!

Chant: "Birthing Chant" (Adey)
   I am the bones of the Earth
   I am the passion of birth
   I am the flow of the sea
   I am Goddess birthing free

Working 4: What do you desire to create
   for Gaia?
Everyone splits into five groups and shares about one minute each:
   Air: Darryl
   Fire: Oberon
   Water: Liza
   Earth: Sunshine
   Spirit: Adey

Spiral Dance
Instruction and focus by Artemisia and drumming. Artemisia leads spiral dance, starting with everyone facing out and brief meditation on nature and Gaia.
Chant: "We are alive as the Earth is Alive"

> *We are alive as the Earth is Alive*
> *We have the power to create our freedom*
> *We have the courage; we are the healers*
> *Like the sun we shall rise!*

                    (—Starhawk; lyrics adapted)
Spiral dance ends with everyone facing inward.

Dismissals & Opening

Wiccan Rite for Midsummer's Day

The place of meeting should be decorated with boughs and leaves of oak with acorns. If there will be music, singing, and rhyme before the rite, it should concern the idea of sacrifice that others may live, traditions that never die, magick, "life continuing in spite of all," and the high spirits of one close to the Elements.

If there is dancing, the Priestess and Priest should lead it so that the dancers whirl and wheel about the dance floor. The dances of this ritual may be performed out of the Circle in preparation for the rite; they should, in fact, be learned by all.

Games should be played utilizing a wheel, preferably one of wood and iron, with candles or incense mounted upon it. Men and ladies, for example, might play a mildly erotic game of "spin the wheel." During the rite, this wheel should be leaned against the south side of the altar. A container of the magickal catalyst should be placed upon the altar. If a labrys (double-headed axe) can be fashioned or obtained, it should be hung upright in a dominant location both before and during the rite.

Because of the large amount of lively dancing in this rite, short and light ceremonial garb in the ancient Greek or Cretan style, or some other very minimal but appropriate clothing, may be fashioned and worn.

According to legends and traditions of the Craft, actual shape-changing of dancers some-times occurred during this rite, especially among Witches who were well-practiced in magick and experiencing the ecstasy of the Goddess in their magickal dancing. Only fragments of the rite survived the terrible time of the burnings, but this reconstruction of it is mostly complete and may again in the future be made whole through the study and practice of the modern Wicca.

The Great Circle shall be cast in the usual manner, except that a 15-foot circle shall be used. To begin the rite, the priestess stands to the north of the mirror with the altar behind her, and says:

> *Witches all, in ages far past it was the custom on this day for the King who had ruled to be sacrificed in a magical ceremony, that famine, storm, and war should not afflict the people, and that the crops would grow tall and free from blight or drought. Darkness would be removed from men's souls by the courage, pride, and magick of the one who, very willingly, walked steadily to his doom. The material rite was deeply emotional and rendingly impressive; yet the magickal portion, unseen and unseeable by human eyes, was awesomely stronger and more far-reaching. Such magick as this was cruelly pow-erful—but it worked magnificently!*

The Priestess sits, while the Priest stands in her place and with his arms out in invocation and proclaims:

> *On this night we gather here to perform again in symbol and magickal dance the rite of the Oak King's sacrifice, as it was done in ages past. In this day, our Lady no longer*

requires sacrifice of any among us, for the life she bestows is sweet, and in this season the moon must wax.

The Priest turns to the mirror, holding forth his athame in salute, calling:

Oh laughing, naked Queen, beautiful and yet terrible, thou who, like all women, canst make and then destroy thy man, and yet are beyond all blame—for thou art the Goddess—be with us here. As the holy labrys doth have two edges, so also, Lady, do we know that two faces dost thou have—one as serene, lovely, and clear as thy silver moon; the other dark and awesome, for thou art as all women.

The Priest salutes with his athame. If one is present who can play a reed-pipe or recorder, he shall at this point play a very brief minor-key tone. As the Priestess sits on the south edge of the Altar; her arms out like the limbs of the moon, the Priest comes to kneel before her, saying:

Thou who art above all adored, know that thy worshippers do give thee obeisance; the wise, the strong, the powerful, and the very princes of the world do give honor to thee.
(Sign of the pentacle)

The Priest gives her the sword, which she holds before her like a scepter. He kneels once more and continues:

The Goddess is kind when it pleases her. Thou who art the day art also the night, and at times thou dost require blood, and darkness, and strife among men for thy purpose.
(Sign of the pentacle)

The Priest stands back with the men at the edge of the Circle. The Priestess stands, puts down the sword, and motions for the music to begin. The men stand quickly while the women follow the Priestess five or more times sunwise about the Circle in a slow, graceful, and stately dance. Those led by her suddenly turn widdershins and dance and whirl and shout wildly back five times or more. Each woman returns to her man and stands arms akimbo, while the Priestess throws a handful of the magical catalyst into the incense brazier. When the sparks have ceased, she seats herself upon the altar once again, saying:

The life of a year is 13 moons, with every season round. The life of the King shall pass likewise from birth unto the ground.

The Priestess signals for the music to begin again. The women laughingly watch the men dance sunwise around the Circle, following the Priest. In the dance, the Priest chants each line (he may be prompted by the Priestess) and the men repeat, shuffling and stepping in time with the music, imitating in every manner—physical, mental, and astral—all creatures mentioned in the King's chant. They make one circle for each "change," the mood being light and cheerful.

I am a stag—of seven tines—for strength.
I am a flood—across a plain—for extent.
I am a wind—on a deep lake—for depth.
I am a ray—of the sun—for purity.
I am a hawk—above the cliff—for cunning.
I am a bloom—among the flowers—for excellence.
I am a wizard—who but I brings forth the hilltop's magic fire?
I am a spear—that roars for blood—in vengeance.
I am a salmon—in a pool—for swiftness.
I am a hill—where poets walk—for wisdom.
I am a boar—strong and red—for power and valor.
I am a breaker—threatening doom—for terror.
I am a sea-tide—that drags to death—for might.

All do sit as the Priest invokes:

Who but I knows the secret of the unhewn dolmen?

He throws a small handful of the magickal catalyst* into the incense brazier and sits. If it is desired, all may drink wine and rest at this time.

The Priestess stands with arms outstretched and calls:

When the Queen calls, there is none who would not willingly come. For Her libation must be made with love and with pain. And in the magickal chase there is no transformation which can stay her brassarids.

The Priestess signals for the music to begin again. Women join in a circle at the center around the altar, facing outwards. The men join in a circle near the outer edge, facing inwards. The men and women, led by the Priest and Priestess, will chant and imitate in very manner—physical, mental, and astral—the creatures of the chant as they dance sunwards. As the women dance, the men will stop and watch them, and vice-versa.

All: *Cunning and art he did not lack, but aye her whistle would fetch him back.*
Men: *Oh, I shall go into a hare, with sorrow and sighing and mickle care,*
          And I shall go in the Horned God's name, aye, til I be fetchéd hame.
Women: *Hare, take heed or a bitch greyhound will harry thee all these fells around,*
          For here come I in our Lady's name, all but for to fetch thee hame.
All: *Cunning and art he did not lack, but aye her whistle would fetch him back.*
Men: *Oh, I shall go into a trout, with sorrow and sighing and mickle doubt,*
          And show thee many a crooked game, ere that I be fetchéd hame.
Women: *Trout, take heed or an otter lank will harry thee close from bank to bank,*
          For here come I in our Lady's name, all but for to fetch thee hame.
All: *Cunning and art he did not lack, but aye her whistle would fetch him back.*
Men: *Oh, I shall go into a bee, with mickle horror and dread of thee,*
          And flit to the hive in the Horned God's name, ere that I be fetchéd hame.
Women: *Bee, take heed or a swallow hen will harry thee close both butt and ben,*
          For here come I in our Lady's name, all but for to fetch thee hame.
All: *Cunning and art he did not lack, but aye her whistle would fetch him back.*
Men: *Oh, I shall go into a mouse, and haste me unto the miller's house,*
          There in his corn to have good game, ere that I be fetchéd hame.
Women: *Mouse, take heed of a white tib-cat that never was baulked of mouse or rat,*
          For I'll crack thy bones in our Lady's name, thus shalt thou be fetchéd hame.
All: *Cunning and art he did not lack, but aye her whistle would fetch him back.*

At the conclusion all drop to a position of rest while the Priest says:

As one generation doth pass and the next appear thereafter, so have thy people always continued. Thou hast returned to us, oh Lady. Return, we do ask, to the world outside to bring back again the ancient ecstasy of joy and terror and beauty most sublime.

He salutes with his athame as the Priestess calls:

Achaifa, Ossa, Ourania, Hesachia, Tachema.

She throws a small handful of the magical catalyst* into the incense brazier and salutes with her athame. The rite is ended.

Finally, the Great Circle shall be opened.

*Magical Catalyst: Mix less than an ounce of saltpeter with an equal amount of chamomile and powdered incense. Mix well, and place in a bowl at the base of the altar.

210. Midsummer

Female: The Moon is full and rising
        Making the meadow bright
        And we maidens leap the circle 'round
        Clad in the moon's soft light
        A whisper in the meadow as
        We wend through oak and corn
        In fire the Oak King dies tonight
        The Holly King is born

Male: The priests have entered the Giant's
        Dance
        Of standing stone and spire
        And in the dancing night we've seen
        Fair Arianrhod's tower
        While in the fields the maidens feel
        Their skin against the corn
        In fire the Oak King dies tonight
        The Holly King is born

Female: The men shall dance the Old Sun in
    With bells and ribbons green
    While we will drive the cattle herds
    The raging fires between
    And to the barefoot meadow
    Where sheep and lamb are shorn
    In fire the Oak King dies tonight
    The Holly King is born

Male: The Morris Men are in the glen
    Their bells and ribbons gleam
    To quicken the dead with rowan
        and thread
    And thicken the harvest seed
    With sword the fool is shattered
    His clothes are tattered and torn
    In fire the Oak King dies tonight
    The Holly King is born

Male: I have built a bower love
    Where you and I may lie

Female: There to share the Harvest Dream
    Beneath the twilight sky

Male: And there we'll seal our wedding

Female: And love all lifetimes long

Both: In fire the Oak King dies tonight
    The Holly King is born!
                    —*Kenny Klein*

211. Summer Solstice Blessing

Now as the wheel, ever turning, brings us
    to its height,
And the sun begins to die in the sky,
Then must we turn inward to inner peace
    and harmony.
May this inner peace be reflected in our
    outward work,
For peace throughout this troubled world
    that we live on.
May the coming harvest be one that feeds
    all the hungry,
May all the weary have somewhere safe to
    rest their heads,
And though the warmth of the sun will
    diminish,
Let the warmth of our love be constant and
    more than that, grow.
                    —*Barbara & Peter;*
        the Coven of the Dagda's Cauldron

212. Summer Solstice Invocation

We invoke thee, Great Goddess,
You who create, animate,
And bind all elemental forces
Into Your awesome Web of relationship.
We gather at Summer Solstice
To honor and celebrate Your fire essence in
    all its forms.
We call You to our circle, into us, from
    within us,
To bless us with the passion and ability
To transform ourselves through Your gift of
    Spirit.
To heal ourselves. To heal one another.
To heal our home, our Earth.
We call You by the flame that purifies,
And by the fire of our will that burns eternally.
Blessed be the Goddess of Life who kindles
    the flame!
                    —*Ruth Barrett*

213. Sonnet for Gaia

Gaia spirit; luminous light
Spiraling out of darkest night
Casting out what doesn't hold
Bringing in the common mold

Patterns form, we see once more
Life is but an open door
Mirror held for us to see
Projections of eternity

Earth, the heart and mind and soul
The Elements that make us whole
Fate, we cast with our own hand
Seen in water, air and land

So in the Cosmos soon will be
Intertwining destiny
Dancing, weaving in and out
Spiraling magic 'round about

What we work we'll surely know
As what we reap we surely sow.
                —*Marylyn Motherbear, April 1992*

214. Mother I Feel You

Mother I feel you under my feet;
Mother I hear your heart beat!
Heya heya heya heya heya heya ho!
                —*Windsong Dianne Martin*

4. Lugnasadh: First Harvest

Introduction: Lughnasadh
By Oberon Zell-Ravenheart & She' D'Montford

Lughnasadh (meaning "Games of Lugh") traditionally falls on August 1, but astrologically falls several days later (at 15° Leo). The holiday is named for Lugh, an Irish Solar God of ritual combat. It was traditional to hold faires at this time. Marking the beginning of "Earth's sorrowing autumn," as Emer said to her husband Cuchulain, this blessing of the first fruits is also called *Bron Trogain*, or "Harvest's Beginning." As the *Feast of Bread*, it is commemorated by baking the first loaves of bread from the first grains to be harvested; the bread represents the body of the fallen God. Lughnasadh was and is the time of the first harvest, when the first fruits harvested were given as a token of thanks to the gods. Building on that ancient tradition, the Christian Church assimilated this festival as *Lammas*, or "Loaf-mass"—the day on which loaves of bread were baked from the first grain harvest and left on the altars as offerings. It is a time of sacrifice and thanksgiving for the sacrifices that allow us to continue.

Once a month-long festival held in Ireland at Teltown on the River Boyne (named for the Cow Goddess Boann, or "She of the White Track," i.e. the Milky Way), Lughnasadh (LOO-na-sah) is traditionally celebrated with competitive games among men and boys. The winners are declared champions and heroes, and held responsible for the defense of the village. The festival is dedicated to male energy, and priests representing the Green Man and Red Man preside over opposing teams. Male virility and sexuality are honored, including that between men.

The Irish Tailtean Games were originally the funeral games of the Irish Sun God Lugh, hosted to commemorate the death of his foster mother, Taillte. One feature of the festival was the once-famous "Tailltean (or Teltown) marriage"—a marriage that would last for only a year and a day, or until next Lammas. At the next Lammas, the couple could decide to discontinue the arrangement by standing back to back and walking away from one another, thus bringing the Tailltean marriage to a formal close.

Other competitive masculine games of strength and skill have traditionally been held at this time as well, including the Olympics, the Panatheniac Games, the Highlands Games, and, of course, modern football season. Lammastide was also the traditional time of year for craft festivals. A ceremonial highlight of such festivals was the Catherine Wheel. A wagon wheel was taken to the top of a hill, covered with tar, set on fire, and ceremoniously rolled down the hill. This symbolizing the end of summer, the flaming disk represented the sun as it disappeared into the valley behind the hills.

At Annwfn
We hold games of Lugh at Lughnasadh, and give special fun awards to the winners in various categories. The traditional five games (*Pentathlon*) are: running (50- or 100-yard speed race); long jumping (from a running start, over a sand pit); wrestling (gripping only above the waist, with the winner getting the other's shoulder to touch the ground); boulder heaving (a bowling ball is about the right size and weight; the winner achieving the greatest distance); and caber tossing (a long pole like a flagpole is thrown a goodly distance at a hay bale target; the winner is the one who comes closest).

At Your House
As summer passes, we remember its warmth and bounty in the food we eat. Every meal is an attunement with Nature, and we are reminded that everything changes. Lughnasadh is

the first of the three harvests and thanksgivings. Bake a loaf of special ritual bread (cornbread is good), including some berries you have picked yourself. Share it with your friends and family with thanks and blessings. Go camping if you can, or at least spend the day outdoors at the park, taking a picnic lunch and playing active physical games, such as tag, touch football, volleyball, badminton, and Frisbee. It's especially fun and traditional to play hide & seek in the evening as it gets dark. Sometimes this game leads to other nocturnal "activities."

Lughnasadh is a good time to make and bless magickal tools. Decorate your altar with summer flowers and food from the fields (especially grains, like corn and grass seeds); use a yellow altar cloth and candles. To celebrate and ensure a bountiful harvest, a loaf of bread hand made by the entire family is a nice centerpiece on the altar, surrounded by harvest figures, such as corn dollies.

Lughnasadh - August 1
Also called Lammas (Loaf Mass), Feast of First Fruits, Habondia, Threshold of Plenty
Theme: Ripening[1]
By Ruth Barrett

Sunlight is noticeably beginning to decline as the Wheel of the Year turns towards toward its darker half. The beginning of August marks celebration of the first harvest. The fertile Earth Mother is abundant with life, as evidenced by the golden fields of grain and the ripening fruits of autumn. Like the cornucopia, she pours forth her blessings of abundance. The traditional Celtic name of this holiday, *Lughnasadh,* stems from a word meaning "the commemoration of Lugh." The Celtic fire and light god, Lugh, appears in Irish legend as a leader of the Tuatha De Danann ("the peoples of the Goddess Dana").[2] Like so many of the pre-Christian gods, he undergoes death and rebirth seasonally within the eternal cycle of the Goddess. This holiday is also well known as Lammas, from the Saxon word, *hlaft-mass,* meaning "feast of the bread."[3]

In Ireland, farmers hoped to have the first crops ready for gathering at this date, which traditionally began the harvest. It was against custom to cut any corn or dig any potatoes before this day.[4] A ritual meal was prepared and eaten from the fruits and grains gathered on the first day of the harvest. This feast was usually eaten at a festive gathering that involved an excursion to some traditional site, usually a hill or mountaintop, or beside a lake or river. Garlands made from stalks of corn, which we call wheat in America, were worn in honor of the Goddess of Corn. It was a social and flirtatious time for young people, accompanied by music, dancing, and fire leaping. It was also a traditional time for weddings. In earlier times, trial marriages that lasted a year and a day began at this time. Other couples, who had decided to deepen their commitment, would join hands for life.[5]

Seasonal Questions and Ideas
- Ask yourself these seasonal questions:
  How do I share my abundance with others?
  How do I manifest my power?
  What can be, or needs to be, sacrificed for my harvest?
  How do I support myself and others in attaining or manifesting our life goals?
- Sacrifice to the Goddess as reaper those possessions, behaviors, or attitudes that will hinder the completion of your own personal harvest. Weed out, pinch back, or thin out anything not

essential that might impede its fruition. Look at the priorities in your life and review them to see if they are consistent with what you say you want or need. Initiate any necessary changes.

- Celebrate the abundance of the Earth by making and sharing a feast of fresh seasonal fruits, grains, and vegetables.
- Bake bread and taste the gift of life. Shape it into a Goddess figure, and share the bounty of her body at a seasonal ritual or feast.
- Give thanks for the gifts around you and for good fortune in your life.
- Find ways to taste what you have accomplished in the growing season.
- Honor your leadership skills or the ways in which you have supported others with wisdom.
- Take a festive picnic meal to the mountains, ocean, or a river.
- Send intentional energy through dance and song to ensure a harvest or the completion of projects, etc., which you have been nurturing along.
- Commit or re-commit yourself to animal and/or environmental activism to protect the Earth and her creatures from further pollution or extermination. Attend to recycling. Teach and encourage others to do the same.
- Find ways to give back to the Goddess for her gifts.
- Share with or provide food to those who have less than you.

John Barleycorn Ritual
By Oberon & Morning Glory Zell-Ravenheart, 1976

This ritual is a Mystery play to be enacted in pantomime while the traditional song, "John Barleycorn," is played or sung. These should be a bit of a musical interlude between each verse to allow the actions to catch up with the lyrics. Depending on how many people are available, many of the parts can be played by the same actors, with changes of props.

Characters   Notes on Costumes & Props

Three Women These are the Fates or Norns. They should wear flowing, grey, hooded robes. The 1st should carry a spindle of yarn; the 2nd a cloth measuring tape; and the 3rd a large pair of shears. Or alternatively, one large crystal ball among them.

John Barleycorn Straw-colored undergarb, with a green full-length cape overall that can be dropped at the right moment and a brown blanket to cover him at the beginning. A beardless man is preferred, with a long fake blond beard that can be hooked over his ears (this is not a requirement, as the beardless scene is only one verse). For the final verses he will also need a brown drinking cup, such as a wooden mug with a handle. This must be filled with whiskey.

Two Reapers *(May be played by the same actors as Fates, without robes)* Simple scythes for each (plastic Hallowe'en prop scythes will do nicely). 9' cord or rope.

Two Forkers *(May be played by the same actors as Reapers)* Two pitchforks (not lethally sharp!).

Loader Kid's wagon. Best if it could be one made to look like wood, with slatted sides. But anything will do.

Two Beaters *(May be played by the same actors as Reapers)* Two sticks.

Miller *(May be played by the same actor as Loader)*

Action: John Barleycorn is lying on his back on the ground in the center of the Circle covered by a brown blanket. Three women enter as the song begins, and circle slowly around him. On final line they shake hands over his body:

There were three women came out of the West
Our fortunes for to scry,

And these three made a solemn vow:
"John Barleycorn must die."

Action: Three women continue to circle, making respectively gestures of plowing, sowing, and tossing clods of dirt over John's body. Then they retreat, leaving him lying there.

They've plowed, they've sown, they've
    harrowed him in,
Threw clods upon his head,
'Til these three all were satisfied
John Barleycorn was dead.

Action: At the 3rd line, John tosses back the blanket and sits up:

They let him lie for a very long time,
'Til the rains from heaven did fall,
Then little Sir John raised up his head
And so amazed them all.

Action: John stands up. On the second line he drops his green cloak. On the third line he dons the fake beard:

They let him stand 'til Midsummer's Day
When he looked both pale and wan;
Then little Sir John grew a long, long beard
And so became a man.

Action: Reapers enter to cut John down at the knee. He falls to the ground. Then they roll him over and tie his arms to his waist, winding rope around twice, but not fully tightening knot:

They hired men with their scythes so sharp
To cut him off at the knee;
They rolled him and tied him around the
    waist,
Serving him most barbarously.

Action: Forkers use pitchforks to get John into wagon, where Loader sits him up:

They hired men with their sharp pitch-
    forks
To pierce him to the heart,
But the loader, he did serve him worse
    than that,
For he's bound him to the cart.

Action: All three wheel John around the Circle in the wagon, retuning to the center, then shaking hands over him as in 1st scene.

They wheeled him 'round and around the
    field
'Til they came unto a barn,
And there they took a solemn oath
On poor John Barleycorn.

Action: Take John out of wagon. Beaters mime beating him with sticks. Miller mimes grinding him between stones. In this process, John loses rope. Then all retreat, leaving John crouched in center:

They hired men with their crab-tree sticks
To split him skin from bone,
But the miller did serve him worse than
    that,
For he's ground him between two stones.

Action: John rises, takes drinking-cup of whiskey and passes it into the Circle. Everyone drinks and passes the cup around:

Now there's little Sir John in the nut-
    brown bowl,
And he's brandy in the glass,
And little Sir John in the nut-brown bowl
Proved the strongest man at last.

For the huntsman cannot hunt the fox
Nor so loudly blow his horn
And the tinker, he can't mend kettles or pots
Without a little Barleycorn.

Wiccan Rite for Lammas Eve

The place of meeting should be decorated with branches of holly and, if possible, a sheaf or two of grain. If there will be singing, music, and rhyme before the rite, themes should center on love cut short by death, love and sacrifice, and the "eternal triangle." If there is dancing, the Priestess and Priest shall see that it is slow and intimate. Fencing and races are traditional, with a lady consenting to be the prize to be carried off by the winner—for a kiss. She may want to put on a tongue-in-cheek show of grieving for the fallen or losing one.

The following may be recited by the Priestess and Priest, or it may be read aloud by various ones of the coven. In ancient times, a version of this rite, or one of the legends mentioned below, were mimed ceremoniously by the initiates.

The Great Circle shall be cast in the usual manner. To begin the rite, the Priestess stands before the mirror, her arms outstretched like the limbs of the moon, and invokes:

Oh Goddess—friend and sister to women, wife and lover to men, Thou who art all women, be Thou among us as we know again this ancient wisdom, sacred to Thee. (All make the sign of the pentacle.)

She lowers her arms and rejoins the Priest, who reads:

Throughout this world, and others, and the many strange and beautiful worlds of the water-sprites, the wood-sprites, the creatures of the Earth and of fire, in our many lives, in the lives of all others, in the great power of knowledge and magick, of countless centuries of time—all things are cyclic.

Kingdoms rise and fall, and others rise from them. Land comes from the sea, and after aeons, the mountains sink beneath great waves to rise yet again aeons later. The story remains the same, holding within it the greatest of truth and the greatest of magick.

At this point there will be a pause to add more incense. The incense brazier will be left open if any of the magickal catalyst is available on the altar.

Priest: *The legends of this festival are clear: Isis, Osiris, Set; Idana, Heimdall, Loki; Blodeuwedd, Llew Llaw, Gronw; Guinevere, Arthur, Lancelot; and others. It is now with the year's seasons as it is with all things.*

Priestess: *Now does the Goddess turn away Her face from the lotus-born King of the golden cup. Bright, handsome, and laughing though He be, She smiles instead on His dark and somber brother.*

Priest: *As season follows season, as snow follows summer, the change is made. For darkness must inevitably follow light.*

Priestess: *As Lady Ishtar did seal the doom of high Gilgamesh, so also does She of the flowers require the life of the smiling King. Where falls His blood, red flowers grow, as his immortal soul journeys beyond.*

Priest: *In time, in the midst of winter, He will return, incarnate once again, to know the deep love of the Lady, and to decree fate upon His brother. As day follows night this must come to pass, for all things must rise and fall, and only the Goddess remains the same.* (All make the sign of the pentacle.)

If any of the magical catalyst* is available, it is cast into the brazier. The rite of cakes and wine follows.

Finally, the Great Circle shall be opened.

*Magical Catalyst: Mix less than an ounce of saltpeter with an equal amount of chamomile and powdered incense. Mix well, and place in a bowl at the base of the altar.

---

215. Lammas

A field of grain stands, stalks tall and heavy
Beneath tall stones carved long beyond memory
Through life and deaths of aged crones
Have stood the ancient standing stones.
Now the grain grown in their shadow
Is offered in fire
To she who is both dream and desire
Mab, the forest's daughter.

Now come among the grain tall grown
Now sing the Forest's daughter home
Now dance among the standing stones
To ringing peals of laughter.

Beneath the tall stalks, wet, bedewed
Stand quietly, and look anew
Upon the stones, heavy with years
Beneath cold stars, the granite tiers
Weathered, beaten, towering high
The giant's dance beneath the sky
Their words like carven thunder;

"Come under my great tower!
I am stone, the Earth's first flower
Long I roamed in ice and fire
Shaped by the two-fold Hunter!"

In stone's shelter cool darkness grows
Through the stalks, the breeze of sunset moans

blown centuries long between the stones
In still silence, hear the tomes
The granite-carven words that tell
The story of the Horned One

I am Lugh, the twin staff wielder;
I am Lugh, the Green Man's killer!
I am son of the Forest Mother
Grown in the barley
Dark Brigit's lover
I am the master, the craftsman, the father
At Danaan's door I cried
'I am he that brings grey dawn
On harp and pipe'

I furrow, and sow
And I harvest the ripe
I reap of the mountain to fire the forge
Of iron and spirit I fashion the scythe.

I am Cernunnos, the torc giver
Wind brother, husband of the river
Bran I am, and Robin in the Hood,
Master of the craggy woods.
all with staff and sword I stand
I am Llew of the steady hand
Seek not to harm me on sea or strand
On horse, in house, or on green heathered land
Of Gwydion's magic was I sired,
Husband am I to the Maid of Flowers.

I am Osprey, I am Wren, as Crow I jest
I am suckled and nurtured in Gaia's green breast
I am born anew in the spirit of Death
And the harvest skies I crest.

So rings the tale in ancient stone
Of the two-fold Hunter, the horned one
Silently the words are borne
In the dark still breeze of twilight.

And the maidens, browned, scythes in
    hand
Naked in twilight's red softness stand
Hold to the North sky the grainy stalks
And sing the offering of care, and thought
Of seasons, of years, of death and birth,
Of flowing waters and snow dewed Earth;

"Mother, three colored, 'neath the ancient
    spires
Accept the first grain offered to the fires."
                   —*Kenny Klein*

216. Lammas Hymn

Harvest Lady, Horned Lord
Thanks we give upon this day
For the wheat and golden corn
Bountiful has come our way.

Corn and grain in ripening fields
Soon we'll bring our harvest home
Then with friends and kin we'll feast
For nothing is just ours alone.

Winter cold will soon be here
Snow and dark and fearful night
But we'll rest safe within your care
And wait for the returning light.

Mother Goddess of the Earth
Now descending into rest
To sleep until the Sun's rebirth
The dying god's eternal quest.

Harvest Lady, Harvest Lord
Thanks we give upon this day
For what has been and what shall be
Our hearts are filled with love today.
               —*BellaDonna Oya, 2002*

Lughnasadh Bread
By Lezlie Kinyon

Lammas or Lughnasadh (Lugh's Wake) is an old holiday from Celtic countries celebrating the harvest and the making of bread, ales, and whiskey. In some places, the first harvest of the grain was seen as "John Barleycorn," and as the wake for Lugh the Sun in others. In Scotland, a cattle fair was also traditionally held at Lammastide. Today, this fair is often held in conjunction with music and arts festivals.

     In early summer I grow a little barley and wheat in the back yard or in a pot. It's easy to grow, and tasty too. It looks pretty with cornflowers and tall sunflowers in a "mailbox garden" or an herb garden. If you don't have room to grow it, you can usually find whole barleycorn in the bulk section of any natural foods market.

Step one: Bless and harvest your grains. Take a handful of the stalks (you don't need more for this recipe), and set aside the remainder for other projects or put in a vase for the table and altar. Take the stalks by the handful and smack them none-too-gently against a winnowing basket placed on the ground; this will dislodge the grains from the hulls. Discard the stalks or recycle them for craft projects. Winnowing them is a group event. Use a basket to toss the grains in the air—the wind really does blow the hulls and chaff away. (You will need to pick some of the hulls out.) Soak the grains overnight so they will be soft enough to work with.

Step two: Start your yeast using the "sponge method" (yeast, teaspoon sugar, dash of salt, and 1/4 cup water, covered with one cup flour and set aside for 15 minutes or until cracks form in the flour). Make a hole in the flour in order to pour in the wet ingredients (next step).

Step three: Warm a cup of water, 1/2 cup honey, a tablespoon and a little more of olive oil (you can use butter or a mix of the two), and salt to taste. Don't heat until it boils, just until it's warm. Add to your sponge. You can add an egg as well. Add your softened grains to the liquid and mix with your electric mixer until smooth.

Knead in 4-6 cups of various flours: two parts unbleached "bread" flour and one part barley flour, and whole wheat flour. With a little practice, you will find the "mix" you like best for firmness and texture. Knead until you've sung all the verses of "John Barleycorn" that you can remember, and make up three or four more if you can. The dough should be firm and elastic, resembling a rustic Italian bread.

You can add things like chopped olives or rosemary for interest. Let rise for at least two hours (a second rise doesn't hurt, either) in a warm place, covered with a damp linen towel. Reserving a small amount, shape dough into three long baguette shaped "snakes." Braid into a ring—or any shape you like. Place on a baking sheet sprinkled with corn meal. You don't need to oil the sheet. Decorate with the reserved dough shaped into a sheaf of grains. Brush all over with warm salted water to brown it and after proving, place your bread into a moderate oven. This recipe works really well if you have access to a wood fire oven, or as a camp bread using the "Dutch oven" method. This will make a good, crunchy, crusty, "country style" bread. When it is a warm, golden-brown color, your bread is done. Eat it with butter and honey while hot.

217. Goddess/God Invocations

Hail to Gaia, Mother Earth!
Gracious Goddess, loving and strict,
Breathing Life into ALL Your children,
Walk with us between the worlds.
* * *

Hail Ceres, High Fruitful Mother!
Giver of unending bounty,
Resplendent in the colors of all the seasons,
Walk with us between the worlds.
* * *

Lugh of the Long Hand!
Hail, Lord of Light, Master of All Arts!
Teacher, Guide and Inspiration,
Walk with us between the worlds.
—Sanura & Diane DesRochers

5. Mabon - Autumn Equinox

Introduction: Mabon
By Oberon Zell-Ravenheart & She' D'Montford

Mabon, or *Autumn Equinox,* is named for the Welsh God of the Harvest, *Mabon ap Modron* ("divine son of the divine mother"). As told in the *Mabinogion,* Mabon was stolen from his mother three nights after his birth, and dwelt in *Annwfn* (the Underworld) until he was rescued by Culhwch. Because of his time in the Underworld, Mabon stayed a young man forever, and was equated with the Roman Apollo. He is the Green Man whose blood is an intoxicating beverage: Dionysos (wine), Osiris (beer), and John Barleycorn (whiskey). The bay tree is sacred to Mabon, as its magickal action is preservation, a time-honored harvest-tide occupation. Also known as *Harvest Home, Kirn Feast, Mell Day, Ingathering,* and *Harvest's Height,* this festival commemorates the ritual sacrifice of the God and his descent into the Underworld, and the brewers' art that produces the sacrament of this season. In California Wine Country, where we live, it is the festival of the Grape Harvest. Whiskey, the spirit of the barley, is also readily consumed during this festival.

In Latvia this harvest festival is called *Vela Laiks,* the "time of the dead." Just as at Ostara, the day and night are of equal length. This is the day of the year when the God of Light is defeated by his twin and alter ego, the God of Darkness. The Autumnal Equinox is the only day of the whole year when light is vulnerable and it is possible to defeat him. Harvest Home is the traditional name for this feast of thanksgiving in England, but the Plymouth Pilgrims had a late harvest, so America's Thanksgiving is celebrated much later.

The most universal tradition throughout Europe is the making of a "corn dolly" from the last sheaf of grain to be harvested. Because it was believed that the spirit of the grain resided in this doll, it was dressed in good clothes, addressed by name, and then woven into a wicker-like man form. This effigy was then cut and carried from the field, and usually burned amidst much rejoicing. Sometimes the vegetation spirit was represented by a large wickerwork figure to be burned as a mock sacrifice, as with the modern "Burning Man" festival held each year at this time in the Nevada desert. Aidan Kelly assigned this festival the name of Mabon around 1970. Historically, however, the name does not appear to have previously been attributed to any festival.

At Annwfn
The full moon closest to the Autumn Equinox is the time of the **Eleusinian Mysteries**, and since 1990 folks in our HOME Tradition have been enacting an annual re-creation of this ancient Greek festival, in which Persephone, the Flower Maid, is abducted by Hades, Lord of the Underworld, to reign as his Queen for the next six months until she returns at the Vernal Equinox. Those who are chosen to take the roles of Hades and Persephone for this rite become our Underworld royalty for the winter half of the year, holding court at Samhain and offering counsel in matters dealing with personal Underworld issues.

At Your House
Most of us enjoy this time of year for the beauty of the fall colors and the energy felt in the cool air, which seems to put an added perk in our steps. It can be great fun hunting for just the right harvest symbols. Mabon is a good time to cut new wands and staves of willow. Make a little "corn dolly" for your garden altar from an ear of corn by twisting and binding the shucks into a body, legs, and arms (you can make the head by breaking off part of the cob and leaving a short piece attached to the rest).

Your altar is a great place for fruits such as squash and apples set in an old wooden bowl. You will also want to add pomegranate, in association with Persephone. Decorate your altar with orange, brown, and yellow altar cloths and candles. Arrange colorful autumn leaves and small gourds, nuts, dried corn, seeds, acorns, pine cones, etc. Also you might want to add a bowl of water, since autumn is associated with water, emotion, and relationship. Keep in mind that this same bowl of water can be used for scrying at Samhain.

Throw a "going away party" for the Green Man, and charge seeds for next year's crop. Prepare a meal for your loved ones—or at least make some special food to share. Give thanks for all that you have harvested in this time. Remember that "an attitude of gratitude is the guidance of the Gaia-dance!" Write down on a piece of paper the things you have planted in your life this year, which you are now harvesting. Read your list aloud, saying, "For all these things, I give thanks." And then burn the paper.

Autumn Equinox - September 21
Harvest Home, Mabon, Festival of Thanksgiving
Theme: Descent[1]
By Ruth Barrett

Once again, light and dark are balanced in equal length of day and night. The exact date of the Autumnal Equinox fluctuates each calendar year between September 20 and 23. Whereas Spring Equinox symbolically manifests the equinox's equilibrium as that of an athlete poised for action, the Autumn Equinox's theme is that of rest after labor.[2] It is a time of re-balancing after intensive work. In earlier times, the Autumnal Equinox marked the middle of the harvest season and began the intensive preparation for winter. This season was known as the harvesting or reaping tide, a time of inward turning as well as celebration. It was a time of great cooperation within the community, of celebration and hard work to ensure that as much as possible of every foodstuff was carefully gathered in and preserved against the barren months of winter.[3]

In Ireland, there is Michaelmas (around September 29), which traditionally was the time of the goose harvest and a time to begin the picking of apples for making cider.[4] The Harvest Home was a feast given by the farmer for the workers, both paid and voluntary. The last sheaf of wheat was prominently displayed, generally hung in the house, and replacing the previous year's last sheaf. This last sheaf itself was called the *cailleach*, or "hag," and the way it was cut was thought to affect the destiny of its cutter.[5] The last bit of corn in the farmer's fields was the visible symbol of the end of harvest, and all over Ireland, the cutting of it was attended with some ceremony. Harvest knots—small ornamental twists or knots of plaited straw—were made and worn as a sign that the harvest was complete.

In ritual we enact the descent of the goddess Persephone into the Earth. She who has gone through her journey as the Kore, the maiden goddess daughter of Demeter, now becomes Queen of the Underworld. We cover ourselves with a black cloth as we welcome the darkness and the wisdom contained within.

Seasonal Questions and Ideas

- Ask yourself these seasonal questions:
    What is my personal harvest?
    What have I brought into manifestation this year?
    What can I do to honor the generosity of the Earth that sustains me?
    How might I thank my loved ones and acquaintances who have supported my
        creativity this year?
    How can I best acknowledge and celebrate myself for hard work completed this year?

In Search of the Lady
A Mabon Mystery Play
By Oberon & Morning Glory Zell & Diane Darling
(First performed at Isis Oasis, Oct. 1, 1988)

Characters	Props & Costumes
The Wise Woman	Flowing robes
Whale of the West	Whale mask, grey cloak, large beautiful seashell
Lion of the South	Gold lion mask, golden cloak, votive candle in red jar
Eagle of the East	Eagle mask, shawl made to imitate wings, large feather
Bison of the North	Horned bison headdress, brown cloak, large quartz crystal
Lady of Life	Green robes, crown, round mirror in ornate bowl or cauldron
Pan	Shaggy leggings, horned headgear, hoofed shoes, panpipes, filled wineskin
Green Man	Leafy mask, green robes covered with autumn leaves, leafy wreath, sheaf of wheat
Seeker Speakers	(members of audience given cue cards with all lines needed)
Guardian of East	Black covering, winged medicine skull, wand
Guardian of South	Black covering, firedragon medicine skull, sword
Guardian of West	Black covering, seadragon medicine skull, chalice of water
Guardian of North	Black covering, unicorn medicine skull, panticle paten
Gatekeeper	Black covering, red cape, demonic gorgon mask, sparklers, black crepe streamers
Queen of Death	Black robes, crown, omega mirror*, silver dagger, black satin ribbons sewn with mirrors, glass cauldron with dry ice lit from underneath by red light

*Omega mirror is made by sandwiching a sheet of 50:50 mylar (50% reflective vs. transparent) between two thin pieces of glass in a small photo frame.

Production Notes:
This mystery play is designed to be performed in the round, around a campfire. Ideally, it should begin just at sunset. There should be enough people in the "audience" to form a continuous Circle around the fire, leaving at least six feet of open space between the people and the fire. The entire play is performed within this open arena of space. Into the West side of the circle a large throne is set, with space on either side of it. Behind it is a backstage area, screened off from view, with a table on which props are kept. In front of the throne stands a small altar table, upon which is an ornate bowl willed with water with a round mirror set in the bottom. A red and a yellow spotlight are situated opposite or above the throne, to be beamed upon it when appropriate. The various archetypal characters enter the arena from their respective directions, and fade back into the Circle when their part is finished. The parts of **Pan** and the **Gatekeeper** are designed for comic relief, and should be cast and played that way. Performers should be familiar with all chants, for they will be expected to lead the rest of the group. Audience members should be encouraged to bring drums, rattles, flutes, etc. to back up the chanting. Each chant should be repeated for about three rounds before being broken by the next performer coming in. All onstage movements in the first section (through the **Lady of Life**) are deosil (sunwise). All movements in the second part are widdershins (anti-sunwise). When everyone is settled in, the play begins as if it was just a campfire sing-along. If desired, various songs may be sung prior to the one which actually opens the play ("Wind in the Pipes," by Meg Davis—see page 267, #237).

I. The Wise Woman (or Wizard)
Greetings, pilgrims, and welcome! You have come to this place in search of a Mystery.

You are children lost in the woods. All your lives you've been told all about your Father, your Father in heaven. You've been raised on his stories, of creation and destruction, of sin and redemption, of his anger and his mercy and his jealousy. But have you ever wondered about your Mother? Who is she? Where is she? 'Tis said it's a wise child that knows its own Mother. And you, poor, pitiful children, you don't even know who your mother is!

Look around you and see the mess the world is in. All the world is divided: man from woman, body from spirit, light from darkness, humanity from Nature. We feel like aliens on our own home planet, fearful and distrustful even of our own brothers and sisters. Why is this? We have lost our connection with our Mother; we are missing the half that gives us balance. Your challenge tonight is to seek out that missing part and recover your wholeness.

You are going on a journey through the world of myth and archetype—the twilight zone of the dream-time. Yours is a magickal journey, and on it you will meet denizens of the spirit realm. You will be challenged, and you must respond with the right answers when asked. You will receive power objects, and these you must pass around the Circle; on no account are you to keep more than one at a time. When the time comes to present them, whoever has them shall step forth into the center of the Circle and do so. You will learn chants to keep your spirit up, and you should play and sing along.

I can say no more; nor can I aid you on your journey, for the challenge must be for you alone. In this way you will learn and grow wise. I can only tell you now to follow the path of the heart and seek your Mother, remembering always that, in the end, the answer is LOVE.

Chant: May you walk in beauty in a sacred way;
May you walk in beauty each and every day! (3x)
(—Anodea Judith)

II. Pan

(Pipe music is heard. Pan appears in their midst, leaping into the Circle and prancing around the perimeter playing his pipes. He has a full wineskin slung over his shoulder.)

Ha! Did I frighten you, strangers? Are you panic-stricken? *(Audience response)*

Well, you know, it's seldom these days that mortals come into my forest. And when they do, they are all too often frightened of me. Perhaps it's because of my horns…it's true, I am a horny devil! *(lascivious leer, tongue waggling)* But you know who I really am, I hope—I am Pan, the lusty god of all wild things! And just who might *you* be, out in the wild woods tonight? *(Audience response)*

Seekers, eh? Well, there's one born every minute! Hey, why don't you come along with me? I'll show you my favorite swimming hole, where all the dryads go skinny-dipping! And just what did you say you are seeking? *(Audience response)*

So. It's not the dryads you're looking for. Well now, I might take you to my Lady. What do you offer me? Got any virgins among you? *(Leers at someone)* No? Well, anybody wanna get fresh? *(Audience response)*

Oh, all right. Maybe later. But I warn you about this path you're on: it ain't easy! You will encounter opposition and misunderstanding—maybe even downright persecution! You will be challenged by Elemental spirits who will threaten your very soul and sanity! But you may have a chance if you remember this clue: the answer is life! So here—have some of my mystic mead; you'll need it! *(Passes wineskin into Circle)*

(Pan then prances around the circle and plays his pipes, leading the audience in "Horned One" chant:)

Horned One, Lover, Son, Leaper in the corn—
Deep in the Mother, die and be reborn!
(—Buffalo John)

(As the following Elementals make their appearance, Pan stays in back-

ground, moving always deosil so as to be opposite them in the Circle. He then comes prancing forward and plays his pipes for the following chants.)

III. The Eagle of the East

(Suddenly an Eagle leaps into the center of the Circle, soaring around perimeter with arms outstretched as wings:)

Halt, strangers! None pass here save by leave of me! I am the great Eagle of the East, and I could rend your flesh with my talons and tear your heart out with my razor sharp beak! But I will give you one chance—you may pass unharmed if you can answer my riddle:

What is the fruit of birth? *(Audience response: "Life!")*

So. That is correct. You are wiser than you look. Who are you and why come you this way? *(Audience response)*

Ah, well, that is a noble quest indeed. Let me grant you a boon—a feather of the Air to lift your spirits. *(Passes feather into Circle)* Take this token of your natural heritage and go forth upon your quest. Blessed Be!

Chant: We come from the sky-yi, flying in the sky-yi—
Go back to the sky-yi, turn the world around!
We come from the sky-yi—
Go back to the sky-yi, turn the world around!

IV. The Lion of the South

(Suddenly a Lion leaps into the Circle and prowls the perimeter, growling menacingly:)

Halt, strangers! None pass here save by leave of me! I am the mighty Lion of the South, and I could shred your body with my claws and crunch your head between my terrible jaws! But I will give you one chance—you may pass unharmed if you can answer my riddle:

What is the flower of sacrifice? *(Audience response: "Life!")*

So. That is correct. You are wiser than you look. Who are you and why come you this way?" *(Audience response)*

Ah, well, that is a noble quest indeed. Let me grant you a boon—a candle of Fire to illuminate your spirits. *(Passes candle into Circle)* Take this token of your natural heritage and go forth upon your quest. Blessed Be!

Chant: We come from the fire, sitting round the fire—
Walk upon the fire, turn the world around!
We come from the fire—
Walk upon the fire, turn the world around!

V. The Whale of the West

(Suddenly a Whale slips into the Circle, moving low along the ground at first, then rearing up majestically to full height:)

Halt, strangers! None pass here save by leave of me! I am the awesome Whale of the West, and I could smash your boats to splinters with my tail and swallow you whole down my prodigious gullet! But I will give you one chance—you may pass unharmed if you can answer my riddle:

What is as old as the sea? *(Audience response: "Life!")*

So. That is correct. You are wiser than you look. Who are you and why come you this way? *(Audience response)*

Ah, well, that is a noble quest indeed. Let me grant you a boon—a shell from the sea to refresh your spirits. *(Passes seashell into Circle)* Take this token of your natural heritage and go forth upon your quest. Blessed be!

Chant: We come from the water, swimming in the water—

Go back to the water, turn the world around!
We come from the water—
Go back to the water, turn the world around!

VI. The Bison of the North

(Suddenly a raging Bison charges into the Circle and stamps around the perimeter, menacing with all his horns:)

Halt, strangers! None pass here save by leave of me! I am the powerful Bison of the North, and I could gore your belly with my horns and pulverize your bones beneath my pounding hooves! But I will give you one chance—you may pass unharmed if you can answer my riddle:

Wht is the heart of the mystery? *(Audience response: "Life!")*

So. That is correct. You are wiser than you look. Who are you and why come you this way? *(Audience response)*

Ah, well, that is a noble quest indeed. Let me grant you a boon—a crystal of the Earth to support your spirits. *(Passes crystal into Circle)* Take this token of your natural heritage and go forth upon your quest. Blessed Be!

Chant: We come from the mountains, living in the mountains—
Go back to the mountains, turn the world around!
We come from the mountains—
Go back to the mountains, turn the world around!

VII. The Lady of Life and the Green Man

*(During the last chant, Pan is dancing at side of Circle opposite throne, drawing audience's attention to him. The **Lady of Life** and the **Green Man** surreptitiously slip from behind the throne to take their places: She sits on throne, while he kneels beside her. At end of chant, a yellow spotlight illuminates the throne and tableau: they are clasping hands and mooning over each other. A certain sadness is felt. She sees audience and they rise together, still holding hands.)*

Pan: Hail, Lady. These seekers have come from a far away place on a noble quest.

Lady: Welcome, beloved ones. How lovely you are and how brave! Greetings, Lord Pan! Are you behaving yourself with these gentle folk?

Pan: Alas, my Lady, that I am.

Lady: *(Gazes longingly and with regret at the Green Man, steps away from him and says:)* So, my children, and what is the object of your quest? *(Audience response)*

Perhaps I am she whom you seek—Let me tell you who I am, that you may decide for yourselves *(recites "Hertha" by Algernon Swinburne)*.

G.M.: *(To the audience)* If you claim the Queen of Life as your true Mother, then bring forth the Elemental tokens of your natural heritage and offer them to her in fealty. *(The four people holding the feather, candle, seashell, and crystal bring them forth.)*

Speak, and tell the meaning of each. *(Pan cues the audience and urges the right people to come up if necessary. Lady takes each one and lays it on the small table with the bowl, as each person says a few words relating the significance of the object.)*

Lady: A feather of the air, a candle in the darkness, a shell from the sea, and a crystal from the Earth. These are indeed the gifts of Nature to her children. Truly, you must be mine. I recognize you, my children; can you tell me my name? *(Audience responds by calling out names of the Goddess.)*

Well done, my children! Truly, it's a wise child that knows its Mother! And yet I have other faces you must come to know also, if you would truly know me. Take hands together, and let Lord Pan lead you in a spiral dance inward to view the mystery in my scrying-bowl. Come, children, and behold my reflection! *(Pan leads audience in spiral dance, taking the hand of one closest to left side of throne and leading everyone, hands linked, deosil around Lady and Green Man in a wide circle, then in to view reflections in bowl, then back out widdershins to original places in the Circle.)*

So you see that I am in you and you are in me. But of course even this truth is only half of the answer that you seek. You would get quite another perspective from my sister. If you would truly penetrate to the depths of the mystery, you must seek her face as well. *(Turns back to the Green Man; they hold each other tenderly.)*

Pan: *(To the audience)* Ah! The leprous White Lady, Queen of the Underworld, her dark and cold magnificence! She who will hang your corpse like a side of beef in her great hall, where worms and beetles may consume it. She who casts your mortal soul into her great boiling cauldron and stirs and sings over it until you forget who you were. The fey and beautiful Queen of Death! I advise you not to seek her dread company until, at the last, you must.

Seeker: Oh, but we must know the entire answer to our mystery—Lord Pan, we implore you to take us to her dark castle.

Pan: Not on a bet! I've fulfilled my part of our bargain, now you're on your own!

Seeker: What may we offer you to take us there?

Pan: Seekers, there ain't enough virgins in the entire animal kingdom to make it worth my while to take you on that journey. The way is dark, dangerous, cold, and dry. The Elementals there are ferocious and have no mercy. And, were you to make it past them, you would then face the Keeper of the Gates of Hell, whose appetite for flesh is boundless, whose face is all your nightmares, whose heart is devoid of warmth and who has no known sense of humor! No thanks. That ain't my idea of how to spend a fine autumn evening. You're on your own and I'm out of here. *(Splits)*

Seeker: What will we do now? We can't find our way alone and we can't find peace until we complete our quest.

(Lady looks sadly and lovingly at the Green Man. He steps forward and addresses the seekers:)
G.M.: I am the Green Man, who is born in the spring. Ancient folk called me Tammuz; nowadays some call me John Barleycorn. I love the Lady the whole summer long and then I am cut down with the grain in the fall. Now the harvest nears completion. There is singing in every threshing room, the hay ricks stand for the drying, the corn and turnips fill their bins, and my father the sun rides ever lower in the sky. I myself depart this day for the realm of the Dark Lady, there to abide with her pale grace while the green world sleeps beneath the winter storms. Since you be true seekers, I will guide and conduct you to the Underworld, where that Lady waits to welcome me back to her side. But I cannot vouch for your safety, for she is ancient, wise, and ruthless, and in her domain none may say her nay. Yet I'll give you a clue that may aid you: within her realm, the answer is always 'Death.' Do you still wish to come with me?

Seeker: Yes, with fear and trembling, but with steady hearts we thank you and will follow at your command.

G.M.: *(To Lady)* Then I must bid you farewell, my Lady and my love, until the spring, when I will, as always, return to you. *(They embrace lovingly and tearfully.)* My parting gift to you, my Lady: grain which will nourish our folk through the winter, and the seed from which I will spring. Farewell! *(He brings a sheaf of wheat from under the small table and hands it to her. She cradles it and weeps as they part. As he passes the table, he blows out the candle.)*

Come with me now, children, as we seek the Queen of Darkness. *(The spotlight is turned off. Under cover of the sudden darkness, she slips offstage.)*

Chant: We are one with our Mother, we are one with the Earth
We are one with each other by our lives, by our birth!

(As the following Guardians make their appearance, the Green Man stays in background, moving always widdershins so as to be opposite them in the Circle. He then comes forward and leads audience in the following chants.)

VIII. The Guardian of the North

(A shadowy figure appears, draped shapelessly in black, and holding a Unicorn medicine skull in front of its face)

Halt, strangers! None pass here save by leave of me! I am the Guardian of the Northern Gate, and I could shatter your works with earthquakes and bury you beneath avalanches! But I will give you one chance—you may pass unharmed if you can answer my riddle:

What is the fruit of birth? *(Audience response: "Death!")*

So, death you say? That is correct. But you are fools to enter here. Who are you and why come you this way? *(Audience response.)* Well, you may pass, but you'll be sorry. Yet, I will grant you a boon—a pentacle of the Earth that you might retain your materiality. It is a symbol of your inner magickal heritage. *(Passes pentacle paten into Circle.)*

Go now upon your quest; so mote it be!

Chant: Down, down, down, down,
Decomposing, recomposing…

IX. The Guardian of the West

(A shadowy figure appears, draped shapelessly in black, and holding a seadragon medicine skull in front of its face.)

Halt, strangers! None pass here save by leave of me! I am the Guardian of the Western Gate, and I could drown you in the watery deeps and the waves would wash over your bones! But I will give you one chance—you may pass unharmed if you can answer my riddle:

What is as old as the sea? *(Audience response: "Death!")*

So, death you say? That is correct. But you are fools to enter here. Who are you and why come you this way? *(Audience response.)* Well, you may pass, but you'll be sorry. Yet, I will grant you a boon—a chalice of Water that you might retain your emotions. It is a symbol of your inner magickal heritage. *(Passes chalice into Circle.)*

Go now upon your quest; so mote it be!

Chant: Down, down, down, down,
Decomposing, recomposing…

X. The Guardian of the South

(A shadowy figure appears, draped shapelessly in black, and holding a seadragon medicine skull in front of its face.)

Halt, strangers! None pass here save by leave of me! I am the Guardian of the Southern Gate, and I could blast you with lightning and consume you with unquenchable flames! But I will give you one chance—you may pass unharmed if you can answer my riddle:

What is the flower of sacrifice? *(Audience response: "Death!")*

So. That is correct. But you are fools to enter here. Who are you and why come you this way? *(Audience response.)*

Well, you may pass, but you'll be sorry. Let me grant you a boon—a sword of Fire that you might retain your power. It is a symbol of your inner magickal heritage. *(Passes sword into circle.)*

Go now upon your quest; so mote it be!

Chant: Down, down, down, down,
Decomposing, recomposing…

XI. The Guardian of the East

(A shadowy figure appears, draped shapelessly in black, and holding a winged medicine skull in front of its face)

Halt, strangers! None pass here save by leave of me! I am the Guardian of the Eastern Gate, and my hurricane could blow you away and scatter your souls like smoke upon the winds! But I will give you one chance—you may pass unharmed if you can answer my riddle:

What is the heart of the mystery? *(Audience response: "Death!")*

So, death you say? That is correct. But you are fools to enter here. Who are you and why come you this way? *(Audience response)* Well, you may pass, but you'll be sorry. Yet, I will grant you a boon—a wand of the Air that you might retain your inspiration. It is a symbol of your inner magickal heritage. *(Passes wand into Circle.)*

Go now upon your quest; so mote it be!

Chant: Down, down, down, down,
Decomposing, recomposing…

XII. The Keeper of the Gates of Hell

(Suddenly a demonic figure leaps into the Circle from behind the throne, brandishing lit sparklers. It may be dressed in black, red, or even more flamboyant colors, and wears a hideous oriental-style demon or gorgon mask:)

Gatekeeper: Halt!

G.M.: Let us pass, O Gatekeeper!

Gatekeeper: Greetings, sir! You may indeed pass through the gate once again, where my Lady eagerly awaits your touch. But these—why, they're not even dead! None may enter here without the sacrifice.

Seeker: O, please, great Gatekeeper, let us pass, for we seek audience with your Queen. We have passed through many trials in our travels from a far-off place.

Gatekeeper: Funny, we had another group from there just last week. They're still down in the pit. Nope. Sorry, I have my orders. Now, begone, for soon enough shall you each return to this gate, stripped of all save memory!

G.M.: *(To the audience)* Perhaps if you offered him a bribe… Who dares bribe the Keeper of the Gates of Hell?

(Green Man encourages members of the audience to make offers to Gatekeeper, even including the Elemental objects. Gatekeeper nonetheless remains firm, rejecting all. Finally, with Green Man's encouragement, someone offers a kiss, kisses the hideous Gatekeeper really good, and he sweeps off his mask, revealing that he is really Pan, who gleefully rejoices that he got what he really wanted in spite of the Seekers' refusal.)

Pan: Ha! That's what I wanted! But I never thought I'd have to go to hell for it! Foolish seekers you may be, to have come so far on such a quest. I fear that you know not what you do! Still I have abetted your folly by imbibing the fruit of the vine—provided by my brother here *(nudging the Green Man)*—with the real Gatekeeper, who now lies unconscious in the darkness like one who has felt the cold hand of Death. In short, I drank him under the table, and I myself am feeling a bit fluffy! But let us not proceed ungirded! Look what I have, uh, borrowed from the Guardian: Shadows! We will pass through the labyrinthine halls of the Underworld unnoticed, guided by his Lordship here, who knows them well indeed! *(Passes out black crepe streamers, which each seeker drapes around neck.)* Lead on, my brother!

XII. The Queen of Death

(Green Man leads on, with Pan bringing up the rear, looking around nervously all the

while. They circle widdershins to opposite the throne, attracting all eyes while the Queen of Death slips onto the throne from behind. Suddenly she is illuminated by the red spotlight. Her skin is white, her eyes are black and her lips are blood red. She is gazing into the omega mirror.)

Queen: How strange! My Lord the King comes to sojourn the winter with me, as he does each year. But lo! He is followed close on by trembling mortals—and they are yet alive! How can this be? Where is my Gatekeeper? ...Oh, here also is Lord Pan, stinking of wine and barley malt. Curiouser and curiouser. Ah, well—all who come here pay the price, be it before they pass my gate or after! Still, how extraordinary!

(Green Man and Pan come before the throne. Green Man and Queen have eyes only for each other, and meet in a passionate embrace. She smiles and seems softened, kisses him again, then leaves his embrace. Her face is mocking.)

Queen: Well, what have we here? Living mortals intruding into the kingdom of the dead? Ignorant fools! You know not what you have wrought for yourselves.

Pan: O great Queen, these harmless idiots have traveled from a faraway place, through travail and hardship, faced fierce Elementals, etc., etc., you get the picture. They were sent here by your sister, the Lady of Light, and now they beg your indulgence to ask a burning question. *(Pulls forward seeker spokesperson and nudges spokesperson broadly.)*

Seeker: Oh, mighty Queen who devours all, we are humble seekers and we wish to know the truth, no matter how dreadful it may seem. Is it true that you are our Mother also?

Queen: My sister sent you. Aye, I might have known. Your innocence and sincerity are refreshing, like the waters of my deep, deep wells. But you must also be the bearers of keen wits and powerful desires if you are truly my children. Let me tell you who I am that you may decide for yourselves. *(Recites "Charge of the Star Goddess," by Doreen Valiente.)*

Queen: *(continuing)* So, if you are truly my children, bring forth the symbols of your inner magickal heritage.
(Seekers bring the wand, pentacle, chalice, and sword forward, urged by Pan if necessary, and lay them at the feet of the Queen with any appropriate words they choose to speak.)

Queen: Well done, I see that you are truly *my* children as well. And to prove it, you may gaze into my magick mirror and see the face of our souls combined. Be not afraid, for you are in me and of me, and when you have merged with me then you need never fear the face of Death, for you will see through her veil and know her secret. Thus, when you see our faces become as one, then speak to me my name. *(Queen of Darkness passes around the Circle carrying the omega mirror to each person and allowing time to adjust it to each person's viewing. She prompts the seekers if necessary, asking "What is my name?" During this process the Circle sings "Children of the Night," by Phillip Wayne:)*
We are the Children of the Goddess,
We are the Children of Delight,
We are the Children of Her pleasure,
We are the Children of the Night!

Pan: A thousand thanks, my Lady, for your kindness towards these mortals. We now ask your leave to depart this place, leaving you to the pleasures of the marriage bed.

Queen: Don't be ridiculous, Pan, as if you can help it. None depart this place as they entered it. No mortal departs at all, save by way of my crystal cauldron, gateway to the Infinite. *(Indicates large punch bowl with many glowing red light sticks and dry ice boiling within)*
(Addressing the seekers:) You may now abandon your bodies, let them fall where they may, and be cast by my hand into the well of souls, there to be cleansed of all memory of self, ultimately to be reborn into new mortal bodies. *(Shocked silence)* Well? Do you need help?

(Queen draws an athame.)

Lady: Greetings, sister!

Queen: *(turning, astonished, to the Lady, not lowering the blade)* My sister! You! Here in my chamber! Will wonders never cease! You, who are the Lady of Life, how is it possible for you to enter this realm of death?

Lady: I come with these, my children. For wherever two or more are gathered in my name, there am I also.

Queen: O night of joy! Our husband returns to me hale and well, and you, my beloved sister, appear as if by magic in my chambers. Let us raise our cups to this rare and exquisite moment! Let us... oh, fie! I must finish with my mortal children. I won't be a moment...

Lady: Wait, sister! Grant me a boon!

Queen: A boon!?! From the Lady of Death to the Lady of Life? Whatever you wish, my sister! If it be in my power, it is yours.

Lady: Spare these mortals, for they are my children as well and much beloved of me. It was they who brought me into your presence, fulfilling the true purpose of this quest to restore the great balance of light and darkness.

Queen: Alas, you ask that which is not mine to give. For by those very laws of balance, none may enter the realm of the dead and exit again unchanged, unsacrificed. They must die if ever they are to live again; for the answer to the great riddle may be life in your realm, but we are in my domain, dear sister, and the answer here is always death.

G.M.: *(Cutting in)* It has always been so, my loves, yet there be a third answer encompassing this duality, and if we can satisfy the riddle test once more, then I too beg that these poor souls be ransomed. For I am Lord of Love, and by my presence and claim on them, and in the name of LOVE, may they die only the small death tonight, sworn as they are to return inevitably to your land, my Dark Queen, in their proper time.

Queen: As you well know, I am most fond of surprises. I accept this challenge. *(Turning to seekers)* Answer me now:
What is the fruit of birth? *(Audience response: "Love!")*

G.M.: What is the flower of sacrifice? *(Audience response: "Love!")*

Pan: What is older than the sea? *(Audience response: "Love!")*

Lady: What is the heart of the mystery? *(Audience response: "Love!")*

Queen: *(Amused in spite of herself)* Very clever and very true. How did you come to learn this?

Lady: *(With a laugh)* 'Tis the Green Man who teaches us that love alone is greater than either life or death. Now, let us gaze into the omega mirror, my sister, I and thou together, and with the power of our love let us once again restore the balance of light and dark. *(They raise the mirror between them and gaze into the images there, pivoting so that both images are seen by seekers as they slowly turn. Both Queens begin an "om" chant.)*

Together: *(when the "om" becomes quiet)* So mote it be.

Lady: My children, you may return to your lives, but you must die the small death by leaving a sacrifice here in my sister's cauldron. Therefore, knot into your shadows those things which you willingly leave here in darkness, and do not carry back with you into the world of light. Cast away old habits and outworn beliefs and any other things that would destroy your own balance.

Queen: These I accept as sufficient sacrifice—for now. Do not hesitate! Bind your sacrifice into your shadow and cast it into the cauldron! *(All do this and go forward at random to let their crepe paper fall into the cauldron.)* It is done, and bravely! Therefore, I grant you passage from this place. Mark well the way, my children, for you will walk this path again! And that you pass safely the hungry ghosts and demons who feed on mortal flesh, I give you this gift: new shadows and true faces! *(Black satin ribbons with tiny mirrors sewn on)* Go, now, for the moment of your respite from here may pass sooner than you wish! But will you stay and feast, my sister? We have much to talk about!

Lady: Alas, my work is unfinished until winter lays its cloak upon the land. So I will accompany my children to our home in the great world above. *(They embrace.)* Come, Pan, give me your arm. Perhaps we can find a bite to eat and some time for a game…of chess.

(Pan grins and winks at the seekers. The Lady smiles and winks at the Queen and Green Man. All exit and join in the Circle.)
(Enter the Wise Woman/Wizard)

Wise Woman/Wizard: Well met now! You have completed your quest to meet the Lady and you got more than you bargained for, perhaps. Still, they do say: All's well that ends well. As you leave the Circle and return to the world, remember these lessons you have learned this night and use them wisely as you seek the balance in your lives and for the Earth. The Circle is opened with these words:

> All from air, into air
> Let the misty curtains part.
> All is ended, all is done,
> What has been must now be gone
> What is done by ancient Art
> Must merry meet and merry part—
> And merry meet again!

Wiccan Rite for Fall Equinox

The place of meeting should be decorated by wreaths and wrappings of grape or blackberry vines, as well as mushrooms and possibly a barley sheaf and some quince, if they are available. If there will be singing, music, and rhyme before the rite, it should concern drinking, celebrations, and good times. If there is dancing, the Priestess and Priest should see that it is fast, bright, and cheerful. Pork, mushrooms, roast apples, and wine aplenty are traditional.

The Great Circle shall be cast in the usual manner. To begin the rite, the Priestess stands before the mirror, facing it with her athame held out in salute. She invokes:

Lady of the Willows, Mother of the Sacred Child, grant to the witches of thy Craft an understanding of thy mysteries.

She drops her arms after the salute. The Priest comes beside her and also looks into the mirror, saluting with his athame and saying:

Thou son of the Goddess, half-divine and yet half-human, whose shape did ever change into any manner of beast, whose body is as barley and wine and whose soul is as the bright sun, grant unto these witches thy strength, thy passion, thy joy, and the visions and prophecy which are thine.

They turn about and the Priest begins preparation for the dance as the Priestess proclaims with cheer:

Oh sweet upon the mountain the dancing and the singing, the madding, rushing flight. Oh sweet to sink to Earth outworn to be one with the Godling, to know all of his powers, to know all of his ecstasy. It is for this we dance; to know the freedom and the magick of the horned son of the Lady.

The dance shall be accompanied entirely by drums, starting with a strong rhythm and becoming yet faster. In addition to the drums, the Priest or one chosen by him should read and chant the following, over and over again, in time to the dancing:

Oh witches come, oh come! Sing ye, Horned One. Sing to the timbrel, the deep-voiced timbrel. Joyfully praise Him, He who brings joy. Holy, all holy music is calling. To the hills, to the hills fly oh witches, swift of foot, on, oh joyful, be fleet!

The music shall last for a long while. If there be drummers, the rhythm will end suddenly at a sign from the Priest. If it is recorded, the finish will, of course, come of its own accord.

All shall drop to positions of rest. The Priestess shall stand before the altar facing north, her arms outstretched, and call:

Mete us out joy, strength and magick, oh knightliest one!

If any of the magical catalyst* is available, she should throw a small handful of it into the incense brazier.

Next should follow the rite of cakes and wine.

Finally, the Great Circle shall be opened.

*Magical Catalyst: Mix less than an ounce of saltpeter with an equal amount of chamomile and powdered incense. Mix well, and place in a bowl at the base of the altar.

218. Second Harvest

The sun makes His descent
From the heavens and all that is above,
To caress the face of the One he loves;
To lay upon Her hills and mounds—
Earth! in all her green and growing splendor!
He enters Her valleys and caves,
Awakening Her inner fire.

Now all that is to be, held safe, within Her Body,
Alive within the space of Her Breath,
Fed by the running of Her Streams and
    Hidden Wells,
Within the horizon full of stars,
The moon lifts a reflective face
Speaking the name of the Beloved.

Listen well for that name.
What you will
Is what you gain.
    —*Marylyn Motherbear Scott, 9/17/2002*

219. The Strength of the Magick

In this time of the Falling Leaves,
The Magician unweaves her warp and her weft.
Meticulous and nimble, her fingers untie the
    knots in her web.
She honors it all, alone, she silently grieves.

Carefully pruning the tree of her birth,
She ponders new life that will grow.
She cuts and she trims, she gathers her wood,
To place in the stove of her soul.

Rolling and turning the threads of her weave...
Her fingers touch life, they touch death.
Sifting and turning, this web that's been made,
She separates wheat from the chaff.

Serenely she chooses what's to be saved.
She lets fall the dirt of her dead.
Out in her garden, she digs a deep hole.
She buries the flesh of her pain.

Into her pestle fall hardened old ways,
Thru grinding, she softens her soul.
Kneading and turning, she bakes us a bread
Made from the bones of her past.

She stands in her kitchen, alone in the night,
Smelling the spices of life.
She takes out her blade, she carves out a slice.
The rest she leaves for me and you.
    —*Mz Imani, 1996*

220. Mabon God/Goddess Invocations

Hail Dionysus, God of vineyards!
Lord of laughter, wit and wine,
Lord of the Dance who lifts our burdens,
Walk with us between the worlds.
                * * *
Cosmic Womb of all Creation,
Queen of Harvest, Queen of Heaven,
Ever changing yet remaining,
Walk with us between the worlds.
    —*Sanura & Diane DesRochers*

6. Samhain: Hallowe'en

Introduction: Samhain
By Oberon Zell-Ravenheart & She' D'Montford

Samhain (meaning "summer's end") is the Celtic Feast of the Dead, when the veil between the worlds is thinnest, and departed spirits may return to commune with the living. Bonfires are lit and blazing straw from the fire is carried through the villages and over the fields. Traditionally celebrated on October 31, Samhain (SOW-in) falls several days later astrologically, at 15° Scorpio. It is the "hinge" of the year opposite from Beltane, and is the Celtic New Year, marking the beginning of the winter half of the year. Also called *Third Harvest* or *Winter's Beginning,* this festival has been thinly Christianized as *All Souls' Day,* with the night before being called *All-Hallows, Hallowmas,* or *Hallowe'en.*

This is the most magickal night of the year, as it is a time to commune with otherworldly beings. The Goddess mourns her marriage to the Dark Lord for the duration of winter. She visits the Earth with her fairy minions from the Underworld, and the veil between the worlds stands open for them for the night. The Dark Lord takes up the rulership of winter, leading the underworld minions of the fairy realms on a wild hunt upon the Earth. Exactly opposite Beltane on the Wheel of the Year, Samhain is Beltane's dark twin. Samhain is also the Celtic New Year and the Feast of the Dead. Yet, as death is necessary for rebirth, the New Year has always been celebrated with chaotic, noisy, and joyous festivities bringing on a symbolic end of the world and a birth of a new. The trick-or-treating of Hallowe'en is an echo of this and of the Wild Hunt.

This has long been a favorite holiday for Pagans of all ages, and an occasion for masquerade, pumpkin-carving, and trick-or-treating. In Mexico it is called *Dia de los Muertos,* the "Day of the Dead." Shrines to the beloved dead are put up everywhere, along with sugar skulls and dioramas featuring tiny posed skeletons. In many lands, candles are lit in every room and food and drink put out for the souls. It is a time to honour our ancestors, remember our beloved dead, and hail our descendants, as we set a place for them at the evening meal. The most important element of Samhain Eve is the rite of the Dumb Supper, a meal of "underworld" foods (mushrooms, nuts, black olives, pork, beans, chocolate, etc.) shared in total silence, wherein the spirits of the beloved dead are invited to join the feast and be remembered in honor and love.

At Annwfn & Raven Haven
At Annwfn, the King and Queen of the Underworld hold court, presiding over the dumb supper and the laying down of the May King's crown (an alternative to his ritual sacrifice). One of our ritual dramas has the Red Maid seeking her lost love, the Green Man, who descended into the Underworld at Mabon, and now reigns there as King. *Scrying* may be done at this time, with a crystal ball or concave black magick mirror. The Samhain Circle is considered to be held in the Underworld, and the energies move *widdershins.*

At Raven Haven, we go all out in this season to completely redecorate our entire Victorian house with spider webs, plastic skeletons, masks, black draperies, purple string lights, and black lights. In the garden, the cornstalks are bundled together, and we carve some really strange pumpkins. In our back yard we have created a special "family graveyard" to honor our beloved dead. I've made a number of Styrofoam tombstones with names, dates, and epitaphs for people we've cared about who have died. Then in mid-October we throw an annual "Addams Family Reunion" party, inviting all our friends to dress up in their best Goth gear and Victorian ensembles.

At Your House

There are so many things you can do for Samhain! Spook up your home with Halloween decorations, carve weird pumpkins, hang "ghosts" (balloons covered with cheesecloth) from trees, and throw a costume party for your friends. One very special thing you could do at this time is to make up your altar to honor your beloved ancestors. Get small photos of departed grandparents or anyone you love and admire who is no longer living. Frame them nicely, each with a little label, and arrange them on your altar, along with other mementos. Use a black altar cloth and candles, black feathers, a small sand timer, a pomegranate, a carved pumpkin, apples and nuts, and other items that symbolize death. If you've collected any small animal skulls or bones, you might display them here. You also may want to place candy on your altar as offering to all of the children who have passed on. It's fun to make and decorate traditional Mexican "Day of the Dead" sugar skulls, and these can also be part of your ancestor altar. Samhain is an especially good time to do divinations and necromancy, connecting with the spirit world; you might want to put a bowl of water on your altar for scrying.

Hallowmas – October 31st
Also known as Samhain, All Soul's Night, All Hallows Eve, Hallows, and Halloween
Theme: Deepening[1]

By Ruth Barrett

Night is noticeably lengthening as the dark half of the year marks the first day of winter. With the last of the harvest gathered and stored away, the livestock were brought in from the summer pastures close to home. Those animals not likely to survive the winter were slaughtered and their meat preserved for winter stores. In earlier times, this was a time of sacrifice, divination for the new year, and communion with the dead. To the ancestors, this season was a time of endings and rest, and the night of October 31st was a moment in time that belonged to neither past nor present, to neither this world nor the Otherworld.

In Ireland, the customs of November Eve varied greatly from village to village. The beloved dead were remembered and honored by candles that were formally lit, one for each departed relative. If the deceased had died in the family home, a candle was lit in the room where the person died. It was a night when communication with the dead was possible and one could ask favors from the ancestors. It was also the time to escort the souls of those who had passed through the veil between life and death.

Halloween was also called "the night of mischief or con," when bands of young people would go door to door begging for bread or money. The holiday was taken very seriously: Because the people knocking at the door might be real Faeries or ghosts in disguise, it was of utmost importance to give them something. Pranks were played on persons generally held to be mean or unpleasant. Divination customs included the lighting of bonfires and scrying into the hot coals or ashes to foretell the future for personal reasons, such as marriage or the success of the next season's crops. Especially important was the foretelling of weather for the coming year, often done by observing the winds at midnight, which would indicate the prevailing wind during the coming season and warn of storms.

The practice of "trick or treat," in which children disguised as ghosts and goblins walk from door to door asking for donations of candy, is still celebrated in the majority of neighborhoods in the United States. Seances, scary stories, and spooky games to foretell the future are still played at today's Halloween parties by young and old alike. The image of the Old Crone riding her broom across the moon is displayed in store windows and in homes. Although most people are unaware that these images and customs survive from ancient Pagan religions, most Americans have yet to let go of the holiday that acknowledges the place of death in life.

Mexico's Dia de los Muertos is celebrated in many parts of the United States and "is the result of a fusion between a medieval Spanish-European tradition honoring souls of the dead and pre-Columbian indigenous rites of the dead."[2] In the mid-tenth century, Pope Gregory IV established All Souls' Day and the Feast of All Saints on November 1st and 2nd respectively. Dia de los Muertos is a time set aside in many families to honor their ancestors by bringing offerings of yellow marigolds, photographs, copal incense, fanciful toys, food, and alcoholic libations to special altars and to the gravesides of relatives for family reunions. The atmosphere of this festival is light-hearted and loving.

Quest through the Shadows
A Samhain Mystery Play
By Oberon & Morning Glory Zell, and Candice & Alan Campbell, 1975

Props: The most important prop is the Scarecrow Throne, set in the West edge of the Circle. This is a straight-backed chair with arms. Four 6-foot-tall poles are taped securely to the legs, arms, and back of the chair, and brought inwards at the top to support a 6-inch square platform. Then a thin black drape is arranged over this frame, to close or open all the way down the front. Cornstalks are placed over the drape around three sides, and tied at the top below the platform, leaving the front open. Finally, a lit Jack-O-Lantern carved like a skull sits atop the platform, supported on the sides by the tops of the cornstalks (this could be a plastic Hallowe'en prop). Before anyone enters the ritual area, the Green Man takes a seat inside this Scarecrow, and closes the black drape around him so that nothing of him shows. He should be able to see through the material enough to follow the action. He remains utterly still until his surprise appearance at the climax of the rite.

Thirteen numbered cue cards are prepared before the ritual, with lines of the Riddle. These will be handed out by the Crone to 13 people around the Circle, in order, along with 13 lightsticks, of which one is red and 12 are green. The red one goes to the first person, who gets cue card #1.

All people in the Circle will need to be seated for this rite, either in chairs or cushions on the floor. No one may sit behind the Scarecrow Throne. A low black-draped altar is set in the center of the Circle, with a platter of nutcakes and a chalice of apple-pomegranate juice. Animal bones, skull, etc. are on the altar, along with a deer antler, dead leaves, an apple, and half a pomegranate.

(The Circle is cast by whatever method is preferred; all motions are conducted widdershins. Enter the Witch-Crone with a Black Book, cue cards, and 13 lit lightsticks in a basket.)

Crone: Come hither all beings mortal and immortal, living and dead. We welcome you to this celebration! We are gathered this evening in a Circle outside of time and space. Here at Summer's ending, the magick door between the worlds opens and we find ourselves in the hall of the Lord of Shadows. *(lights switch to red)* I have cards for some of you. When you are questioned, you must give the answer on your card. *(Crone goes around the Circle widdershins, handing out cards and lightsticks, starting with the red lightstick and card #1. When all the cards are handed out, she reads from the Black*

Book, remaining always on the opposite side of the Circle from Fauna.)
Hear then the tale of the Goddess Fauna—
Who is the sovereign of all creatures:
Our Lady of the Beasts…
(At the beginning of this invocation, Fauna enters dressed as a huntress in animal skins and makeup. She carries half a pomegranate, cut open to expose seeds. Circling widdershins, she begins a mime of the actions described by the Crone while very soft drum, bells, and finger cymbals add accent:)
She, who is at once the vixen and the hen.
Hawk-eyed, deer-footed, cat-whiskered Lady;

She floats on silent owl-feathered wings,
Celebrating with the voice of larks,
Howling with the dirge of wolves,
Her voice sings the lonely music of the
  whale song.
She awoke from restless and empty dreams,
turning to Her Lover for His nourishing
warmth. Lying in the hollow nest His body
had formed She found the red ripe heart of
a pomegranate, each seed a drop of His
precious blood. She began Her search, over
hill and under hill. She searches for Him
with the migrating herds of deer and bison.
She seeks Him under drifts of fallen leaves,
where squirrels cache their winter stores.
Outside the Circle of firelight Her restless
eyes sweep the barren landscape.

*(Crone closes Book and retreats offstage as
spotlight hits Fauna.)*

Fauna: Where is He—
My fair and tender Lover?
I hunger for His touch
And for the smell and taste of Him.
Long and fruitless has my search been.
I have asked the stones, but they are silent.
I have asked the wind, but it only sighs.
I have asked the fire,
But it snapped at me impatiently!
I have asked the rain,
But it only mirrors my weeping.
Am I not the Mistress of all magick?
I shall make a spell!

(She spins, slowly, then faster)
By the Starlight dream I spun, By the
Moon and by the Sun,
All things concealed shall be revealed,
As I do will so be it done!

*(She flings out Her arms...Fauna walks out
to the first person sitting in the Circle, who
holds the red lightstick. She points at the
person and demands:)*

Fauna: Have you seen my true Love?

1ˢᵗ Person: *(reading from card by glow stick)*
I haven't seen Him since the beginning of
August. He was just fine then—strong and
tall as corn, golden as the sun, Ripe and
lusty and spilling seed upon the ground.

*(Fauna hands the person some pomegran-
ate seeds, then goes widdershins to next person in Circle with green glow light.)*

Fauna: Have *you* seen my Lover?

2ⁿᵈ P: I saw Him towards the end of September. He wore all the colors of a rich harvest.

*(Fauna will hand each speaker some pome-
granate seeds as she goes on, one by one
around the Circle, asking and being answered
by the people with green lights. As she asks
each person: "Have you seen Him?" she varies her voice and phrasing. Sometimes laughing, sometimes bullying, sometimes teasing,
sometimes changing the wording altogether:
'Come on, how about you? Are you hiding
Him under your seat?' etc.)*

3ʳᵈ P: I saw Him in early October. He
looked tired and spent. What have you
been doing to Him?

4ᵗʰ P: I saw Him back when we had that
cold snap. He was cold and pale and
hardly said a word.

5ᵗʰ P: I saw Him in the field after harvest; he
wore a bandage and walked with a limp.

6ᵗʰ P: I saw Him beneath an Oak tree,
fallen in a blaze of blood.

7ᵗʰ P: I saw Him shivering in the long
autumn rain.

8ᵗʰ P: I saw Him in the city, where he
hardly stood a chance.

9ᵗʰ P: I saw Him completely silent under a
waning moon.

10ᵗʰ P: I saw Him the morning of the first
frost. His face was wrinkled and His
hair was white.

11ᵗʰ P: I thought I saw Him moving
through the fog like a will-o-the-wisp,
but I couldn't catch up with Him.

12ᵗʰ P: I didn't see Him. There's nothing left
of Him but bones rattling in the wind.

13ᵗʰ P: He's gone to the Kingdom of Death.
Lady, look for Him in the Underworld.

Fauna: *(At this point Fauna begins a spi-
raling dance, singing and chanting:)*
I circle around, I circle around,
The boundaries of the Earth.
Wearing my long wing feathers as I fly,
Wearing my long wing feathers as I fly.

*(The audience joins in and the drummer be-
gins to pick up the beat. The audience joins*

in the familiar chant, which goes on until Fauna reaches the center of Her spiral and drops in front of the Scarecrow. Drum roll and chant ends. She begins to investigate the Scarecrow, poking him here and there. Suddenly a sepulchral voice emerges from the effigy, startling her and everyone.)

GM: Welcome to the Kingdom of Death, Lady. Blessed be thy feet that brought thee on this path. Why have you come to the land of Shadows?

Fauna: I come in search of my True Love…have you seen Him?

GM: He exists—but why seek the dead? I am King here, and would take you for my Queen. Abide with me and let me place my cold hand upon your heart.

Fauna: I do not love *you*! Where is the one I truly love?

GM: He is here, at my hand and by my will.

Fauna: *You!* Why do you cause all things I love and take delight in to fade and die?

GM: Lady, it is the way of Nature. As your cat devours your mouse, so age causes all things to wither. But when mortals die at the end of their time, I give them rest and peace. And as for your Lover, He too must be numbered with those that go down into the Earth.

Fauna: Give Him back to me, or I'll cut you down and grind you up and scatter you to the winds!

GM: Fierce you may be, but all things surrender to Death.

Fauna: Not so, for I am my Mother's daughter and my necklace is the Circle of Rebirth. Love alone does not surrender to Death. Whatever you take from me I will reclaim; whenever you kill one I will give birth to a thousand more. For that too is the way of Nature! Now I ask you for the last time… Where is my Lover?

GM: Your question will be answered if you can answer my riddle:
A yellow eye in a blue face
Sees a yellow eye in a green face.
That eye is like to this eye
But in a low place, not a high place.

Fauna: A yellow eye in a blue face
Sees a yellow eye in a green face.
That eye is like to this eye
But in a low place, not a high place?
The answer to your riddle is a simple daisy in the Sun. It is the token of My True Love, who is know by many names: Tammuz, Adonis, Osiris, and Dionysos. Beloved of all and most of all by Me.

GM: *(He throws back the black shroud to reveal a man with face and beard painted bright gold and wearing a green velvet robe and an autumn wreath. He hands her a bunch of daisies, saying:)*
Welcome, Beloved! Your quest is ended; your quick wits have answered both my riddle and the challenge. The power of your love has set me free. For indeed, I am the Green Man. In Springtime, I am Jack-in-the-Green, John Barleycorn at Harvest, and Jack O'Lantern at Summer's end. I am the spirit of all green plants, and it is my fate to be cut down in the Fall. So I go and rule in the Underworld this season. Come live with me and be my love. We will hibernate here beneath the Earth, and we will sleep together and keep each other warm through the cold dark months, when I shall reign as Jack Frost.

Fauna: Yet as Spring follows Winter in my Circle of Rebirth, now that we are united by the power of Love, no mortal need ever again fear death. *(Fauna and the Green Man kiss amid cheers, hoots, etc. from audience. They turn and bow to the audience hand in hand, then go to the altar to serve the Sacraments. The Green Man raises a platter of cakes:)*

GM: This is my body, the grain of the field; ripened by the Sun. I give you stored sunlight to eat.

Fauna: *(Blesses the cakes with antler.)*
All my creatures bless your gifts.

GM: *(Feeds Fauna, then picks up chalice)*
This is my blood, pressed from the fruit of vineyard and orchard. I give you liquid sunshine for your drink.

Fauna: *(Dips the antler into the chalice in blessing.)*

All my creatures bless your gifts.

GM: *(Holds the chalice to her lips.)*
Let all the Earth rejoice in the abundant harvest!

Fauna: So mote it be! *(Audience responds: "So mote it be!")*

And as a token of my power, I will give beads from my necklace of rebirth. Let those who will, wear them in Love, remember-

ing that they need never fear death. *(Faerie helpers pass around the Circle with chalice or cups of apple-pomegranate juice, platter of nutcakes, and a bowl containing a loose string of beads.)*

All: Hoof and horn, hoof and horn,
All that die that be reborn.
Vine and grain, vine and grain,
All that fall shall rise again!

The Rite of the Dumb Supper
by Morning Glory Zell

This is a ritual of amatory necromancy for the purpose of calling forth the Beloved Dead. It may be performed as a Sabbat ritual at Samhain, or as a solitary personal rite, or a funeral commemoration. It should be done at midnight. When invoking the beloved dead, only invite those shades who are appropriate to attend. Do not name your great aunt Flossie who was a minister's wife and looked down her nose at you, even if she did die this year. Be wary of famous dead political figures who tried to conquer the world. And for Goddess' sake do not mention the names of any mass killers or axe murderers, even if they were your personal friends! These kinds of shades would be uncomfortable at a Pagan Sabbat, or else unwelcome if not downright dangerous! Give this part of the ritual careful thought. Hopefully, you should know whom you plan to invoke in advance.

Keep in mind that the focus of the Dumb Supper is remembrance of the Dead, human or otherwise. It is not the time to invoke Astral Guides, personal Totems (unless extinct), Faerie or Elemental Guardians, etc. This ritual, The Dumb Supper, is to begin the process of opening the Door Between the Worlds, and by starting with those nearest and dearest we call our dead to return to us by ties of love and affection. And with those ties, stronger than death, we begin building the bridges that connect us to All Time and Space.

After appropriate purification and banishing spells, the ritual chamber should be hung and decorated with black ribbons, flowers, black candles, skulls, and pictures of the Blessed Dead to be invoked. The altar should have the customary tools, plus a bell, and also a dark mirror, crystal, or other device for scrying and to act as a materialization focus. A door or window to the West should be left open as a Gateway for the Spirits' return. A supply of charcoal and Amatory Necromancy incense should be near the thurible. A trestle board should be set below the altar containing the Feast. The foods should be of the following nature: mushrooms, root crops, potatoes, carrots, cooked pumpkin in some form, pork or ham, poppy seed pastries, chocolate and other black-colored foods, and a ripe pomegranate. All dishes should consist of bite-sized finger foods and only in token amounts.

When all are gathered, the candles and incense are kindled and the Circle is cast in silence, backwards and widdershins. Quarters are invoked from the North. God and Goddess are invoked in their aspects of Guardians of the Dead: Hades, Shiva, Arawn, Osirus, Legba; Kali, Morrigan, Cerridwen, Hecate, Persephone, etc. Replenish the incense at this point.

The Priestess takes up the bell to recite the Grand Necromantic Citation:

By the mysteries of the deep *(strike)*
By the flames of Banal *(strike)*
By the power of the West *(strike)*
By the silence of the Night *(strike)*
And by the holy rites of Hecate

We call thee by ties of Love
Oh Spirits of the Blessed Dead!
Come and break thy eternal fast this Night.
So mote it be!

The Priestess first invokes three specific names of the Beloved Dead, rings the bell and passes it to the person on her left, who then invokes some more names, striking the bell to finish, and passing it on widdershins around the Circle until it returns to the Priestess. When the bell returns to the Priestess, she begins the great Necromantic Charge:

Allay Fortission Fortissio Allynson Roa!
Allay Fortission Fortissio Allynson Roa!
Allay Fortission Fortissio Allynson Roa!
(strike)

She repeats the words the first three times alone, striking the bell to signal the end of the first sequence. For the second sequence everyone joins together, repeating the words three times aloud, after which the bell is struck. The third sequence is repeated together in **silence**. *The silence extends into a meditation where we have a chance to mentally greet those spirits we have summoned and commune with them. The meditation ends with the bell.*

The Cup of the Dead is then sent around widdershins, with a silent libation and toast to the Spirits. When the Cup has made its round, the servers begin passing around the wine and other substantial dishes, and the Dumb Supper commences. All things are passed and consumed in silence and widdershins, for only thus do we walk in the paths of the dead. An empty plate is set in the West along with the Cup of the Dead; and as others are served, so is the Plate for the Dead, but with **tiny** *portions (the Dead don't eat a lot, even when they do have much of an appetite).*

The food is passed around only once: begun with wine, ended with wine, and finally with the Cup of the Dead. The incense is replenished and the Priestess repeats the license to depart:

Go, go, departed Shades,
Or linger if you will.
By the Lady of Darkness,
And the Lord of Silence,
We license thee to depart
Into thy proper place.
And be there Love between us evermore.
So mote it be!
(Bell is struck three times)

An astral doorway is made and people can now speak or come and go, but casual conversation should take place outside the Sanctuary itself.

The Dumb Supper, whether celebrated formally as a group or less formally as a solitary rite, has ancient shamanic origins, and most parts of the world have some analog of it. The most familiar for us perhaps is the Celtic Feast of the Hollow Hills with Arawn the Samhain King. We should enjoy this Silent Communion without reservations, for contact with those we love and respect who are gone is a precious and fleeting experience that enriches us. I have taken this form of the Dumb Supper from Paul Huson's Mastering Witchcraft, *and have altered what is intended as a solitary ceremony to contact a dead loved one into a more Pagan-oriented ritual to be used by a group for Samhain Sabbat. Blessed Be.*

Amatory Necromancy Incense

1 part Verbena *(finely reduced)*
1 part Wormwood *(finely reduced)*
1 part powdered Sandalwood
1 part Dittany of Crete *(finely reduced)*
1 part Gum Benzoin
Moisten with a few drops of: Rose oil, red wine, honey, your own blood.
You may also add the optional: Poppy seeds, Mullein, Pomegranate juice, Cedar oil.

---

221. Gypsy Song for Calling the Dead
By Marylyn Motherbear Scott, 9/21/91
(This is a song and a ritual; the music may be obtained from author at: POB 85, Calpella, CA 95418)

It is the time of year
It is the time to cast away your fear

And enter deep within the Earth
Where spirits play the bones for birth
Laughing, we dance together
Holding hands with death
Weeping, we greet our loved ones
Who from the Earthly plane have left
Weaving the circle from garlands of love
Binding all life from below and above

(softly) Sing out their names now
    Give their memories breath
(softer) Sing out their names now
    Give their memories breath
(even softer) Sing out their names now
    Give their memories breath
(If there is music, let it continue. If not, hum the Gypsy tune while the names of the Beloved Ones that have crossed over are sung or spoken out. When the calling is complete, begin to sing:)
    Their names have been sung

And they must be moving on
The ship must leave the misty shore
Before the light of dawn
Fare thee well, your lessons I will take
Fare thee well and blessings on this place
(Hum some more to permit departure time, then clap your hands and speak!)
    Spirits be gone.
    Pilgrims, to thy path.
(You may end with quiet or a diminishing drum beat if drum is present throughout; or muffled hand-claps.)

Food for the Dead
By D.J. Clark, 11/3/2000

The food for the dead is taken from Homer's *Odyssey* (Book IX):

...I poured a libation to all the dead, first with a mixture of honey and milk, then with sweet wine, and a third time with water; over this I sprinkled white barley.... When I had finished entreating the host of the dead with prayers and supplications, I seized the victims and cut their throats, and their dark blood flowed into the pit.

...Then the soul of Theban Tiresias came up, '...But step back from the pit, and hold aside your sharp sword so that I may drink the blood and speak the truth to you.'

At our table, plates for the dead will be set with a bowl of Odysseus's Libation.

    1 part milk and honey   1 part sweet wine
    1 part water   1 part blood
    and sprinkled with white barley.

Wiccan Rite for All-Hallow's Eve

The place of meeting should be decorated with wreaths and vine of ivy. If there be singing, music, and rhyme before the Rite, it should concern death, ghosts, and magic, yet ever return to being comforted and cheerful. The Priestess and Priest shall lead the dancing so that the dancers spiral slowly inwards and outwards about the dance floor in a cheerful manner. Traditional Hallowe'en games and practices apply. A cauldron shall be featured in the decoration.

A henge of stones should be set about the ritual Circle. Brooms, willow-besoms, or riding-sticks should lie next to the altar; one shall be provided for each within the Circle. A horned helmet or symbolic horned headdress should be set upon the altar.

The Great Circle shall be cast in the usual manner, except that a 15-foot circle shall be drawn. The cauldron shall be placed near the altar.

To begin the Rite, the Priestess stands to the north of the altar facing the mirror, and invokes:

Oh Goddess of things living and growing, our time of warmth and fair winds is ended for now. As the day has passed, so must the night also come, and for seven full moons must the dark Horned One have dominion. (Sign of the pentacle.)

She turns about and calls:

I call Thee forth, Oh Thou who personifies the God.

The Priest stands at the south; he should be wearing gauntlets and sword-belt, if they are available. He answers:

I hear and come, my Lady. For as now must Fall and Winter's darkness return, so must I again resume my power.

The Priestess motions for him to be seated on the southern edge of the altar. She then ceremoniously places the helmet on his head, saying:

On this, the holy eve of Samhain, do I cede dominion to thee, Oh Horned One of the dark realm.

She walks sunwards to the front of the Priest and briefly drops to one knee, presenting the sword to him and saying:

And for Thy season, do I cede Thee power, oh Thou of the Underworld.

The Priest holds the sword upright as a scepter. He says:

I do thank Thee, gracious Lady, and in my duties I shall ever owe loyalty to Thee.

The Priestess retires, and the Priest stands, saying:

Oh thou of the ancient craft, this night in ages past was the year's ending. On Samhain's Eve were the Sylphs, Undines, Salamanders and Gnomes, and Sprites of the wood free everywhere—as they are now. On All Hallow's Eve did the mighty dead return from their graves, remembering warmth and comfort and joy of friends—as they do now.

The Priest removes his helmet and sheaths or puts down the sword. He says:

For all do love joy and cheer. So therefore, Witches all, give honor and love to those who before us have passed into the Summerland. Let us dance and make merry for our comrades who have gone beyond—and for our other friends from their strange and beautiful realms. As I dance, so shalt thou follow.

The Priest signals for the music to start; it should be fast and bright. He and the Priestess should lead the coven in a line, spiraling inwards and outwards. Each may make his own variations on the dance and also may follow suit with others as they turn, shuffle, stamp, in a growing and diminishing rhythm. After awhile, the Priest may seize a broomstick, and the others will follow suit to ride and shout and leap as the dance grows faster. In this Rite there is no fixed ending to the dance; it may be as determined by the Priestess and Priest.

Next should follow the Rite of Cakes and Wine.

The rest of the night shall be spent by all in divination with the mirror, with cards, with crystal, or by other means.

Finally, the Great Circle shall be opened.

Morning Glory's Apple Spider

A Witchy Samhain treat, or just keep a pot going on the stove all through the fall to warm up cold tummies and make your whole house smell homey and magickal.

To one gallon of organic apple juice, add:

1/4 cup whole allspice
1/4 cup whole cloves
1/4 cup whole cardamom
1/4 cup whole nutmeg broken into pieces
1/2 cup fresh sliced ginger

Prepare your spices beforehand:

Ginger root is measured in standard medium-sized widths by about finger's length. Slice ginger root into 1/8-inch round slices and cut into halves.

You can cut your nutmeg with a paring knife (use an old one). If nut is too tough to cut, then use a nutcracker.

Add these two spices together into a deep bowl, along with the cloves, cardamom, and allspice.

Pour apple juice into a stainless steel cookpot and set on a medium temperature stovetop burner. Allow juice to just come to barely a simmer, then stir in all spices and turn burner down to low (never boil!). Simmer covered for about 15 minutes then uncover for another 15 minutes.

Serve by dipping out of cookpot with a heatproof ladle and pouring into a mug through a small tea strainer.

For that extra special fun touch, decorate the mug handles with black plastic spider ring party favors.

Presto, Apple Spider!

222. Samhain Prayer

Lord of Shadows, Lady of Life
Open wide, I pray thee,
The Gates through which all must pass.
Let our dear ones who have gone before
Return this night to make merry with us.
And when our time comes, as it must,
O Thou the Comforter, the Consoler,
The Giver of Peace and Rest
We will enter Thy realms gladly and unafraid,
For we know that when rested
And refreshed among our dear ones
We will be reborn again by Thy grace.
Let it be in the same place
And the same time as our beloved ones,
And may we meet, and know, and remember,
And love them again.
—*Janet & Stewart Farrar*

223. Samhain Kyriele

October month of Samhain,
Omen of the holy unseen
The Hunt will come to claim us all,
    Our Dead we call!

Death must provide the food for Life,
Fat cattle fall beneath the knife,
To nourish us through winter's pall,
    Our Dead we call!

In Summerland the Wise do wait,
To meet again their kin in fate,
Rejoicing in our King's fair hall,
    Our dead we call!

On Samhain night the gates yawn wide,
Giving glimpse of the Summerside,
Tonight we our grieving devall,
    Our Dead we call!

Come feast with us, our loved Dead,
Savor our wine and share our bread,
You have but gone where we go all,
    Our Dead we call!
—*Maryanne K. Snyder*

224. Samhain Goddess/God Invocations

Hail Hecate, Triple Goddess!
Guardian of moonlit crossroads,
Weaver of nocturnal visions,
Walk with us between the worlds.

* * *

You are Herne, Leader of the Wild Hunt.
Keeper at the Gate of Time,
Awakener of our deepest Heart,
Walk with us between the worlds.
—*Sanura & Diane DesRochers*

225. Samhain Round

And as the light around us fades
In golden shadows through the glades,
Like distant echoes down the hall,
We answer Samhain's ancient call.

From everlasting times 'til now,
To storied lands, we all must bow;
Where magic rings within our souls
And as we shatter, we are whole.

This is the night to join the Dance,
Partake in all-renewing trance;
Where worlds within and out are One,
Our sacred journey now begun.

To greet the ones we loved before,
Our kith and kin from days of yore,
Forgiven foe and long-lost friend—
We dwell among you yet again.

For now the worldly veils are thin,
Where hope and healing can begin.
Our deeds are done; the hour is late.

By fin and feather, leaf and bark,
As sun now banks to sheltered spark;
This year of trial and joy is past
Within the Circle we have cast.

And as the light around us fades
In golden shadows through the glade,
Like distant echoes down the hall,
We answer Samhain's ancient call...
—*Marc Hirsch, October, 1997*

226. Farewell to Spirits

Spirits here now, are loved ones gone by.
And you may stay here with us 'til the last
    candle dies.
When the last tiny flame has guttered and
    gone,
You must leave and continue your journey
    beyond.
—*Melanie F. Stoehrer*

7. Yule (Winter Solstice)

Introduction: Yule
By Oberon Zell-Ravenheart & She' D'Montford

Yule (meaning "wheel" in Norse) is the Festival of *Winter Solstice* and the longest night of the year, occurring around December 21-23. One of the most universally celebrated festivals, Yule is the most important in the northern countries, as it commemorates the birth of the infant Sun God from the womb of Night. Yule is also known as the Festival of Lights, for all the candles burned on this night. In ancient Rome it was called *Natalis Solis Invicti*—"Birthday of the Unconquered Sun"—and it took place during the longer festival of the *Saturnalia,* the greatest festival of the year, and from which we get our New Year's image of old Father Time (Saturn) with his scythe. Yule is opposite from Litha, and while the emphasis now is on the newborn Sun God, Mother Earth is still honored as the *Madonna* (mother with child on her lap).

In Ireland, the sun does not even crest the horizon on Winter Solstice. It is a day without sunlight—truly the Longest Night! The Yule Log is burnt in our darkest hour, representing the god Lug laying down his life in the battle to maintain warmth and life for us. On this day, the wise god Lug does battle with the darkness on its home territory and dies on the 23rd, the "No Name Day," the day without sun. Then late on the 24th the sun/son rises and is reborn again. Celebrated on the 25th, Christ's birth (or "Christ Mass") is the Christianized narrative and celebration of this event, which finds its culmination in the crucifixion and regeneration of Eastertide.

Yule was the first Pagan festival to be Christianized, in 354 CE, when the birthday of Jesus (probably in late September) was officially moved to the date of the Winter Solstice and called *Christmas.* The many customs associated with Yuletide (candles, decorated trees, the Yule log, wreaths, pine bough decorations, gift-giving, *wassail* and caroling, costumed mummers' plays, mistletoe, "decking the halls with boughs of holly," etc.) are all Pagan, and provide a rich store of material for our contemporary celebrations. This is Yuletide. 'Tis the season to be jolly. The sun is reborn—it is generous to all, and we are its children. Evergreens, holly, ivy, and mistletoe all symbolize immortality and resurrection—and the eternal life of nature—as they are still living and green in the dead of winter. These Pagan customs were forbidden to Christians, but in 1644, they had become so widespread in England that they were outlawed by an act of Parliament. There is no record of Christians decorating their homes with evergreens, holly, ivy, and the "Christmas" tree before 1605.

At Raven Haven
We set up a big Yule tree and hang it with special decorations we've been collecting and making for decades. Often I have climbed up into an oak tree and cut down a big mistletoe ball, decorating it with foil ribbons and hanging it from the rafters.

A ritual drama may enact the story of the first Yule, when the sun went away and the children had to go and bring it back. Some of the characters in our Yule ritual may include the Wint'ry Queen, the Queen of Night, Father Winter, Father Time, Lucia (a maiden with a crown of candles), and always, of course, the young Sun God. We bring in the Yule log amid singing and toasting. We have a big pot-luck feast; drink hot mulled cider and *Atholl Brose* (traditional Scotts wassail); exchange gifts; and share songs and stories around the fire, holding vigil until the dawn. We maintain that *somebody* has to stay up all night to make sure the sun comes up in the morning!

At Your House
Since Yule is the original version of Christmas, practically anything you might do for

Christmas is appropriate for Yule as well. Make a wreath for your front door, and decorate your house with string lights. "Deck the halls with boughs of holly," fragrant pine, ivy, and mistletoe. The Druids revered the white berries of the mistletoe as the semen of the God, and this can also be placed on your altar, or hung in doorways for the traditional kissing beneath it. (Probably our ancestors did more than kiss under this symbol of fertility!) *NOTE: Mistletoe berries are highly poisonous, so be sure to keep them away from children and animals!*

Set up a Yule tree, and decorate it with special symbols, amulets, and hand-made talismans (blown-out eggshells are great to paint and decorate). Citrus fruits (lemons and oranges) to represent the sun are also traditional to hang on your tree. Put up a sun symbol as a reminder of the sun's return. If you have a fireplace, you can decorate and burn a special Yule Log. As you light it, make pledges for new projects you wish to give birth to.

Fix up your altar with a Santa Claus figure, reindeer, and little decorations in the shapes of animals, trees, presents, snowflakes, icicles, etc. Use a red and green altar cloth, or put a sheet of cotton down for an altar cloth that looks like snow. Acorns, nuts, apples, cinnamon sticks, and pomegranates are also appropriate for decorating your Yule altar. Burn lots of green and red candles, since this is a celebration of light. And most important, make special gifts for your loved ones. These can be artwork, crafts, projects, or collages (pictures made by cutting images out of magazines and gluing then onto a background of cardboard or wood).

Give Yule presents to the birds and Faeries by hanging ornaments of fruits, nuts, seeds, and berries on the branches of outdoor trees. Strings of popcorn and cranberries are fun to make, and the wild creatures will love them! You can make them for your own inside tree first, and then take them outside later.

Winter Solstice - December 21st
Also called Midwinter or Yule ("Wheel")
Theme: Conception/Communion[1]
By Ruth Barrett

Winter Solstice comes at the dead of winter and marks the longest night. Being a solar holiday, the exact date fluctuates each calendar year between December 20 and 23. The ancestors saw this season as a time of faith and the rebirth of spirit. In ancient celebrations of midwinter, fires were lit with ceremony on hilltops and in homes. People huddled around the blazing Yule log and lit ritual fires outside to encourage the sun to return. In many old Pagan traditions that were later adopted by the Christian calendar, it was at this time of the year that the Star Child, sacred son of the Mother, was born. He represented hope during the hard months of winter.[2] By projecting and energizing hope for the sun's eventual return and the Earth's renewal, the people made a "spiritual cradle," or psychic space, for the newly conceived light to eventually fill. In Norway, people still wish each other *Gott Jul*, literally meaning "Good Wheel," a winter holiday blessing for a "good turn" around the Wheel of the Year once again.

In the darkest part of the year when the days are shortest, Nature asks us to slow down and enjoy a cup of warm tea, to be with loved ones, to listen rather than to speak. Under the ground, the Earth silently sleeps. Seeds rest in suspended animation and the animals hibernate. In contrast, we humans rush frantically to the malls, stressing ourselves with activity when we really yearn to rest, dream, and gather strength in our bodies for the coming season of renewal. For many people living in the United States, taking time to rest and dream is seen as a sign of laziness. However, nature teaches us that resting, drawing inward for a time is present in all living things. Rest is necessary for growth that comes later in its season.

The sun *will* return: Our modern knowledge of astronomy tells us that this is a fact we can depend on. Unlike our ancestors—to whom the cycles of light and dark and heat and rain meant life or death, and food or starvation—we need only go to the supermarket and buy everything we need. Urban dwellers usually forget about the farmers who provide our food, and overlook our continued dependency on the cycles of nature. As modern people we know we don't actually have to make magick in the darkness to encourage the sunlight to return, but with that knowledge we have lost the awe and wonder of the darkness. Because of the pervasive use of electricity, especially in urban areas, we often have to *create* the experience of darkness in order to illuminate the light. With such ingrained cultural and religious emphasis on the light—always the light—we forget to value the dark. Half of the year moves toward darkness and then rests in it—indeed, "Death belongs to life, half of day is night,"[3]

Midwinter invites us to dream in the dark, to become still and listen to the wise self within, the Old Wise Hag, present in every woman. Winter is her season, and she lives on the edge of Spirit, able to access both this world and the next. It is the Old One who is already in your future looking back into this moment at the choices you made, the values you chose to follow, the paths you took. Dreaming is her power, and she patiently waits in the dark with wisdom and guidance. It is often this wise self that we try to avoid in our constant rushing toward the light, and which we choose not to see with our inner eyes.

The dark season challenges us to surrender to our dreaming, to trust that the strength of the Earth will support our weight as we sleep. It is out of the darkness that flowers eventually emerge, babies are born, and inspiration for poetry and ideas are nurtured toward the page and through our voices. In the deep dark places in ourselves, we find the inner truth about ourselves. In this winter season of so many people prematurely rushing toward the light, remember to slow down and do winter's inner work. Celebrate the dark, where the inner life is honored and nurtured. Sometime during this season, take some time for yourself to go inward to find out what your dreams are.

Seasonal Questions and Ideas

- Ask yourself these seasonal questions:
  - What am I visioning, hoping for?
  - What dreams do I carry inside?
  - How do I keep my faith alive?
  - What can I do to encourage the rebirth of spirit in my life, my family, and my world?
- Light a candle in the dark to honor a dream or long-term vision you have for the coming year. Remember that the flame is symbolic of your inner spirit light, representing hope and faith. Pass the flame to others.
- Make or give candles as gifts of spirit, faith, and hope.
- Stay up all night in the darkness and wait for the sunrise.

Grandmother, Give Me Shelter
A Yuletide Mystery Play
By Morning Glory & Oberon Zell, 1975

Props

Enough birthday **candles** for everyone, with holed pieces of card to place them through to catch the melting wax.

Usual **altar implements,** including several large **chalices** filled with apple juice and/ or wassail, and a plate of fancy **Yule cookies**.

Yule Log, appropriately decorated with ribbons, sprigs of holly, and ivy, and set with three lit candles: red, white, and green.

"The King" —a beautiful little box containing a lifesized feathered effigy of a wren wrapped in red and gold ribbons, with a gold foil crown on its head, and reposing in a little mossy nest.

Costumes

Winter King: grey cloak over red robe or Santa suit; Santa hat; scythe and hourglass; holly wreath for head.

Wint'ry Queen: voluminous white cloak over black robe; headdress of stars and icicles.

Corn King: an ear of dried Indian corn with shucks attached.

Madrone: a madrone branch with berries.

Bear: a bear mask.

Coyote: a coyote mask.

Woman: a fringed scarf.

Jesus: a white robe and crown of thorns.

Lucia: a huge red candle and ivy wreath; bright Yule garments.

Ritual begins with procession of the Yule log, carried by several children, and led by a small boy carrying "The King." Rather than having the candles set in and lit, a very small child ("The Robin") may ride the log in. Traditional song is sung:

> Joy, health love and peace
> Be all here in this place
> By your leave we will sing,
> Concerning our King!
> Our King is well dressed in silks of the best
> In ribbons so rare, no king could compare!
> We have traveled many miles
> Over hedges and stiles
> In search of our King, and to you we bring
> Joy, health love and peace
> Be all here in this place (etc.)

The Yule log is set on the hearth in front of the fireplace, and the King is placed on the altar. All the people find their places around the room and settle down. The Circle is cast and the Elements are invoked in the usual manner. Gwydion's song. "The Wint'ry Queen," is played. Then the one who is to be the **Winter King** *comes forward, wearing a grey cloak with the hood down, and a wreath of mistletoe and ivy, and evokes the* **Wint'ry Queen.** *She, in turn, evokes the* **Winter King** *in him, whereupon he raises his hood and lowers it to his eyes. They bow formally to each other, then retreat to their respective places, he by the Yule tree, and she by the doorway into the hall, where her cloak will serve as a portal for the comings and goings of various actors.*

Priestess: *Comes forward to explain the significance of what is to come by telling a little story about the time of year, and what it means in the natural world, and that as the year turns, so do the ages...*

Recording: "Shelter From the Storm" by Bob Dylan (from *Blood on the Tracks*) *After song ends, a series of Supplicants approach the* **Wint'ry Queen:**

Corn King: Grandmother, give me shelter! I am tired and I want to rest. I have spent my pollen and begotten a bountiful harvest.

Wint'ry Queen: Well done, my good and faithful son! As the Corn King, you have given your all and many have been fed by your sacrifice. Enter my doorway. You have earned the peace of repose. *(Corn King enters into the* **Wint'ry Queen***'s cloak.)*

Madrone: Grandmother, give me shelter! My limbs are weary and my bark has fallen away. I am lonely, and naked to the cold winter wind.

Wint'ry Queen: No, my daughter Madrone, your task is not done. For though your bark has fallen away, your berries are just now ripening. You must provide winter food for the birds and squirrels. *(Madrone leaves.)*

Bear: Grandmother, give me shelter! The land is barren and cold, and my bare feet are freezing on the icy ground. I have grown fat on the summer salmon and blackberries, but now the stream is frozen over and the berry patch is only sharp brambles.

Wint'ry Queen: Poor Bear, come in from the cold, and sleep in warmth and comfort, dreaming of ripe summer berries and salmon leaping in the running streams. *(Bear enters into the* **Wint'ry Queen***'s cloak.)*

Coyote: Gramma, gimme shelter! All my prey are hiding in their nests, safe from the cold where I can't reach them. I sing to the moon and she only brings me rabbits! If I eat one more rabbit, my nose will start twitching!

Crone: Coyote, Trickster, Teller of Tales, you told the rabbits in the dark of the moon that they must hasten her return by making more rabbits. Now there are so many rabbits there isn't enough food for all.

You must stay out and eat those that die of starvation and so be punished for your greed. *(Coyote leaves.)*

Jesus: Grandmother, give me shelter! I am here, for I can do no more. My 2,000-year experiment has failed. Were it only myself I could abide my failure. But it is the people—the women, the men, the children who suffered on my account. I wanted to change the world for the better, to aid the advancement of man and create a world united in peace. Verily, I say, my dreams have turned to gall and ashes, and all the natural world has been twisted and poisoned in my name. Grant me rest and forgetfulness.

Wint'ry Queen: My son, your burden must still be borne. The men who followed you, and who built on what you started, were not the same quality as yourself. They could not have followed your example and built the dream you had, for they never understood it, or you. I pity you, but the law is immutable. You have had your age of glory and now you must stay and help clean up the mess that was made in your name. You have a final cup of bitterness to drink. *(She offers him a drink from the chalice.)* Go. But first...let me take your crown of thorns. *(He bows to her, and she removes the crown of thorns. He leaves.)*

Woman: Mother, give me shelter! I am weary unto death of the cruelty of humanity. I have given my love and nurturing to all the world and I have been repaid with betrayal and lies. I was raped by my brothers and sold into slavery by my father. I was seduced by a lover and then denounced as a whore by my sisters. I have given birth to many children who have taken all that I had and not even repaid me with gratitude, and finally the whole family left me alone to clean up the terrible mess they made of my life. All my life I have lived for others, only to find that my best efforts were all in vain. I no longer know what to believe, so I have come to seek peace in your shadow.

Wint'ry Queen: Beloved daughter, my door is always open to you. You sold your freedom for security when this age began, and found it was only lies and illusions. Come in and rest and be renewed. Your time is coming soon. Your task is first to learn the wisdom of the Sybil. Lulled by my poppies, sleep to dream the healing and teaching dreams. For when the time is fulfilled, you will take my place as the ancient Crone. *(Woman enters into the Wint'ry Queen's cloak.)*

Winter King *(comes forward, circling in a spin, sweeping the room with his scythe:)* I am the winnower, I am the reaper, I am the shadow behind your back. I take the living in their prime, and I await at the end of time. After me comes but the darkness; after me comes but the cold. Through the long and lonely nights you feel the fear of growing old. *(He then fades out of the circle to stand in the shadows by the Yule tree like the specter at the feast.)*

Priestess: And darkness now enfolds the sleeping world on this longest, darkest night. *(She extinguishes all lights, including altar candles and candles on Yule Log. Then she begins Ayisha's chant for all to join in:)*
> Deepest darkest longest night
> Gather round the fire bright
> Singing power unto the sun
> Rise again when morning comes!

Wint'ry Queen: Granddaughter, awaken! *(She slowly unfolds cloak to reveal young girl—**Lucia**—within. She is dressed in bright Yuletide garments and wears a wreath of ivy leaves. She holds a very large red Yule candle, which the **Wint'ry Queen** lights as she opens her cloak.)* Your beauty rest has ended and the time of the Koré has come. The world is weary of strife and longing for love. Now at this darkest time when the need is greatest, innocence must re-enter the world and be the bearer of light and truth. Someday, my child, you will return to this door and wearily seek entrance. I will be sleeping the sleep of metamorphosis and your mother will sit in my place, welcoming you with the promise of renewal. But today is your quickening and all the world rejoices. Evoe Kore! Evoe Lucia!

Lucia comes forward with the lit candle, and lights the candles on the Yule log. Lucia then brings her candle to the Priestess, who lights her small candle from the larger one. Then Priestess passes the light to another, who continues, until everyone in the room is holding up a lighted candle. Then the tenders of the log ceremoniously place it onto the fire and light it. Everyone sings "Light is Returning," by Charlie Murphy.

Winter King then comes forward again, circling in a spin, faster and faster, finally throwing off his cloak to reveal Santa suit underneath. Then with a merry "Ho ho ho," the Winter King and Queen turn to the distribution of the presents under the tree.

Wiccan Rite for Yule

The place of meeting should be adorned with the traditional decorations of this season, with the addition of birch bark and branches. Songs, music, and rhymes may be seasonal but should all be slanted toward Witchcraft. If there will be dancing before the rite, it should be bright and gay. The traditional foods are to be eaten, with the addition of pork in some form. A piece of oak log with 13 red candles in it should be in a central location before the rite, and placed north of the altar for the ceremony, A Yule tree, fully decorated, should be placed at the north outside of the Circle.The Great Circle shall be cast in the usual manner.

To begin the rite, the Priestess stands to the north of the altar with the tree behind her. All in the Circle may light the candles of those near them and the Priestess shall light the candles on the log. She spreads her arms outwards as the limbs of the moon and invokes:

The ghost of the old year is with us yet. Let us call him forth with rite and dance; let him feast with us as we bid him farewell.

For in this season the sacred child is born of the Goddess, He of the sun, who shall reign in joy with bounteous seasons of life, ever rich, for all. With song and dance shall we worship both—the Mother ever gracious, and the Child of Promise most glorious. Blessed Be the Goddess most noble, the same through the ages of time, everlasting through eternity. Io Evohe! Blessed Be!

All salute. The Priestess calls for fast music and all follow her and the Priest about the Circle in a fast and cheerful dance which becomes ever faster. All shall chant:

Io Evohe! Blessed Be! Io Evohe! Blessed Be!

If the coven members are carrying candles, the last one shoes candle goes out as the dance proceeds shall be called "Nick," and must light candles, pour wine, and replenish the incense for the rest of the night. At the end of the dance, the Priestess or Priest will call for all within the Circle to drop to a sitting position. The Priestess shall stand before the altar facing north and say:

All blessings to the Lady, and to her sacred Child. Blessed BE! (Sign of the pentacle.)

All: *"Blessed BE!"* (Sign of the Pentacle.)

Priestess throws a small handful of the magical catalyst* into the incense brazier.

Next should follow the rite of cakes and wine.

Before opening the Great Circle, the Priest shall give the salutation of the year. He shall say to those of the coven:

Oh friends of our coven, I do bid you to charge your cups and join in the salute to the year.

When all are holding form their cups in salute, the Priest shall call:

Thirteen moons are waxed and waned,
Dancing in the starry vault.
Ancient year is running low—
Day of days draws to a halt.
Greet the Hag and bid her go—
Farewell to the ancient Crone,
For tonight the old guard changeth;
Bid the Maid to take the throne.

Rejoice, rejoice, it is reborn,
the olden curse is washed away—
Shining bright the thirteen moons
Shall rise to greet the newborn day.
A joyous new year! Blessed Be!
All: *"Blessed Be!"*
All shall drink deeply.
Finally, the Great Circle shall be opened.

A Celebration of Light
(An Interfaith Solstice/Yule Celebration)
Developed by the CUUPS group of First Unitarian Society of Denver,
the Insight Buddhist Meditation Group of Denver, and Rev. Joan Van Becelaere.

Candles for the New Year/Yule Log Ritual

(For the Yule Log, you need a nice looking log, about 18 inches long and about 4 inches or more in diameter. Drill three holes in it—votive candle or tea light holder size if possible, or smaller for taper candles. You can decorate the log, but beware that nothing is too near the candles. (Experience proves that it is more than a bit disconcerting if the decorations catch on fire during the ritual.) Place multiple tea lights in holders or multiple votive candles around the log. Or you can use a large bowl filled with sand and plant small tapers into the sand as they are lit.)

This is the time of the solstice, the longest, darkest night of the year. Being without light is one of the most unsettling of experiences for those of us who have become accustomed to living with the gift of electricity. To be in the dark is to be disoriented, without a sense of direction. *(Turn off the lights.)*

At the Solstice, the darkness triumphs, and yet gives way and changes into light. The breath of nature is suspended: all wait while the darkness is transformed into the reborn light. We watch for the coming of dawn, the bringer of hope, and the promise of the summer.

Even though we live in a time of modern conveniences, a time of electricity and central heating, we still yearn for the light and warmth of the sun. The Wheel of the Year turns to bring us the light. The word "yule" means "wheel." As the wheel turns, we call upon the sun, reborn from the womb of night.

To welcome and strengthen the reborn light at the new year, it is custom to burn the Yule Log on Solstice night. This evening, instead of burning the log, we will light its three candles:

The first candle is to honor the year that is past. It leaves us with all of its memories—good and bad, happy and sorrowful. We light this candle to symbolize, to honor, to celebrate the ways, great and small, that each of us has triumphed over forces that would have us abandon our beliefs, give up our faith, or lose our identity.

The middle candle is the light of the present, the moment of change and rebirth of the life force. It honors the now, this moment of transformation.

The last candle is for the new year, for life reborn and growth of peace and love. We light it to honor hope and the anticipated future. At the solstice and the coming of the new year, the past, present, and future are all layered upon each other and intertwined.

If you have a joy or concern for the year that is past, for the present, or the year to come, please come forward, share it with us, and light a candle to honor your joy or concern.

227. Deepest, Darkest, Longest Night

Deepest darkest longest night
Gather round the fire bright
Singing power unto the sun
Rise again when morning comes!

Deepest darkest longest night
Gather round the fire bright
Deep inside we face our fears
Feel our pain and cry our tears!
—*Ayisha Homolka*

228. The Turning Song

The Sky has gone dark, the winter is deep;
Our season of cold is reaching its peak.
The stars have gone out, the greyness is here;
The bottom has come, the turning is near.
The wheel has stopped, it turns not at all;
Oh spirit begin a new cycle for all!
The wheel will turn, the season will too;
The sun will restore his blessing to you.
—*Tom Bruce, 2002*

229. 'Twas the Night of the Solstice

'Twas the night of the Solstice, the party was done
Soon we would gather to call back the Sun;
The season of Winter was half the way through,
We called for the Mother to birth Him anew.

The children were quiet or now fast asleep,
The elders drew nigh then, the Solstice to keep;
All were prepared and the Circle was raised,
In peace and in silence as deep as a cave.

The Priestess then lifted the sword upon high,
The Priest made the ancient call to the sky;
So ancient, that cry that asks for rebirth,
As Mother and Sun Child are called to the Earth.

Then what to our wondering eyes did appear?
The Lord and the Lady our folk all revere!
"What is your need that you call us this night?"
"Bring us," we chorused, "the Child of Light!"

"Lady, Who art the seasons of birth,
Come to us, bless us, dear Mother Earth."
"We hear you" She answered, "and so it shall be,
As Solstice is here, I return Him to thee.

"But remember your promise and cherish
    your land,
For He gives both the seed and the death
    by His hand."
The silence was total, the Priestess bowed low.
The Priest gave salute, asking, "What do we owe?"

"You owe Us your laughter," He said, "and
    your love.
And in all of your magics, respect for her grove:
Rape not Her body, nor pillage Her soil,
Labor with love and give free of your toil.

"And follow the seasons of Moon and of Sun,
Do so with love and We always will come
To comfort and guide you, to bring you rebirth;
So give of your love to your land, Mother Earth!"

So saying, They faded; we wondering looked on,
The Solstice rite done with the morning birdsong.
The message They gave was of love, not of pain,
That the land that we cherish be fruitful again.

The Circle was ended, the peace yet abides,
Through cycles of seasons and love we'll not hide;
Her children who met Them that night in the grove,
Still cherish the land and Their message of love.
                            —Suncat of Hearthfire
                    (with apologies to Henry Livingston)

230. Light is Returning

Light is returning,
Even though this is the darkest hour
No one can hold back the dawn!
Let's keep it burning—
Let's keep the light of hope alive!
Make safe our journey through the storm.
One planet is turning—
Circle on Her path around the sun
Earth Mother is calling Her children home!
                            —Charlie Murphy

231. Silent Night

Silent night, Solstice Night
All is calm, all is bright
Nature slumbers in forest and glen
Till in Springtime She wakens again
Sleeping spirits grow strong!
Sleeping spirits grow strong!

Silent night, Solstice night
Silver moon shining bright
Snowfall blankets the slumbering Earth
Yule fires welcome the Sun's rebirth
Hark, the Light is reborn!
Hark, the Light is reborn!

Silent night, Solstice night
Quiet rest till the Light
Turning ever the rolling Wheel
Brings the Winter to comfort and heal
Rest your spirit in peace!
Rest your spirit in peace!
                            —Ellen Reed

232. Blessings of Yule!

Slow and slow turns the Wheel of the Year.
To the season of silence, cold, bleak and drear.
Hope's to be born, from the dark, wintry night
The feast is prepared, and the Yule-Log alight.

Round is the wreath, as the year turns round;
Green is the Holly—Life midst Death found;
The berries red as the Sunrise of Birth
Of Hope to the world, and Joy to the Earth.

Bright blessings of Yule! May they
    shine on your life!
May you feast, and rejoice, and set aside strife!
Hope and gladness be with you, gloom and
    misery fly
Away, at the Birth of the Lord of the Sky!
                            —Ken Humphreys

233. Yule Blessing

This is the long night.
This is the dark night.
This is the cold night.
This is the night of last hope.
This is the night of the little spark.
This is the night of turning from darkness.
This is the night of turning toward light.
This is the night of wonder.
The long night is here:
Come to us, you spirits;
Together let us fill the long night with light,
Calling all beings to warm themselves at our
    fires.

—Ceisiwr Serith

234. Gods Rest Ye Merry Pagan Folk

Gods rest ye merry Pagan folk,
Let nothing you dismay.
Remember that the Sun returns
Upon this Solstice day.
The growing dark is ending now
And Spring is on its way.
    O, tidings of comfort and joy,
    Comfort and joy!
    O, tidings of comfort and joy.

The Winter's worst still lies ahead
Fierce tempest, snow and rain!
Beneath the blanket on the ground
The spark of life remains.
The Sun's warm rays caress the seeds
To raise Life's songs again.
    O, tidings (etc.)

Within the blessed apple lies
The promise of the Queen
For from this pentacle shall rise
The orchards fresh and green
The Earth shall blossom once again
The air be sweet and clean!
    O, tidings (etc.)

The Goddess rest ye merry, too,
And keep you safe from harm.
Remember that we live within
The circle of Her arms,
And may Her love give years to come
A very special charm.
    O, tidings (etc.)

—Elexa of Sothistar

235. Ye Children All of Mother Earth

(tune: It came Upon a Midnight Clear)

Ye children all of Mother Earth
Join hands and circle around
To celebrate the Solstice night
When our lost Lord is found
Rejoice, the year has begun again
The Sun blesses skies up above
So share the season together now
In everlasting love!

—Ellen Reed

236. Wheat that Springeth Green

Once the world was young
And all our songs were new.
Once our songs were sung
And all the words were true.
Look deep within;
The song is still in you
Love will come again,
Like wheat that springeth green!

When the world was dark
And all the skies were cold,
Then our hearts did hearken
To the wisdom old.
In frozen soil and snow
Does the sleeping seed unfold
Love will come again,
Like wheat that springeth green!

Now the world is turning,
Turning from the dark.
And our heart-fires burning,
Burning with a spark.
Though the flame has died low,
The light has left a mark.
Love will come again,
Like wheat that springeth green!

—Farida Fox

Atholl Brose (Scots Wassail)

Morning Glory's famous recipe:
    1 gallon water   4 cups oats
Soak 24 hours. Strain oats (we use nylon stockings or pantyhose). Save oatwater! (Eat oatmeal for breakfast over next week!) Add to oatwater:
    1 qt. whipping cream   1 fifth of scotch
    1 pound honey   salt to taste

8. Oimelc (Brigantia, Candlemas)

Introduction: Oimelc
By Oberon Zell-Ravenheart & She' D'Montford

Oimelc, Imbolc, and **Imbolg** are variants of the name for the cross-Quarter Sabbat that is traditionally celebrated on February 2, but falls several days later astrologically, at 15° Aquarius. *Oimelc* (EE-melk) means "ewe's milk," and *Imbolc* or *Imbolg* means "in the belly," referring to this as a festival of pregnancy, birth, and lactation ("got milk?"). It is the celebration of the bursting of the locks of frost, and the breaking of waters as the sacred sets of twins lower in the womb of the Earth Mother. This is a festival of waxing light and fertility, once marked with huge blazes, torches, candles, and fire in every form.

The Romans called this Irish holy day *Brigantia,* as it was dedicated to Brigit (also called Brigid or Bride), goddess of fire, the forge, inspiration, creativity, poetry, herbal healing, and especially midwifery. At her shrine in the ancient Irish capitol of Kildare, a group of 19 priestesses (no men allowed) kept a perpetual flame burning in her honor. The Roman Church could not very easily call the great goddess of Ireland a demon, so they canonized her instead. Henceforth, she would be "Saint" Brigit, patron saint of smithcraft, poetry, and healing.

Since she symbolized the fire of birth, the glow of good health, the fire of the forge, and burning poetic inspiration, Brigit came to personify the new warmth and life of spring. The Roman Church adopted this symbolism as *Candlemas* or *Candelaria,* the day to bless all the church candles, which are then used to bless the throats of parishioners, keeping them from colds and sore throats. Maidens dressed in white were adorned with crowns of the blessed candles. Bonfires were lit on the beacon tors, and chandlers celebrated their special holiday. Other customs of Brigantia include making a little Brigit's bed and a Brigit doll to sleep in it.

This festival marks the beginning of both the lambing and plowing season. Opposite the men's festival of Lughnasadh, Oimelc is celebrated with Women's Mysteries of birth and menstruation, and rites of passage into womanhood. It is a time of Dianic and Wiccan initiation, celebration of sisterhood, and woman-to-woman loving. Called *Lady Day* in some Craft traditions, Oimelc has been popularized in America as *Groundhog Day.*

At Annwfn & Raven Haven
Brigit fires up the forge and leads us to each forge talismans in token of our pledges to complete some creative project during the year. The goddesses reign, and two priestesses may take the parts of the Red and Green Maids. At the Brigit bardic in front of our cozy hearth fire, we share poetry, songs, and stories attributed to her inspiration. In honor of Brigit's healing arts, we give each other massages and foot rubs.

At Your House
The fires of Brigit represent our own illumination and inspiration as much as light and warmth. The primary magickal tool of this Sabbat is the candle. Invite your friends and family to a bardic Circle in honor of Brigit. Ask them each to bring poetry, songs, short stories, and even jokes to tell—best, of course, if they have written these themselves! If you have a fireplace in your house, you should light the fire and some red candles, and turn out all other lights. Fill a drinking horn or chalice with apple juice, and pass it around the Circle deosil. As each person drinks in turn, they must share something they've written, or at least tell a joke.

With the promise of spring and rebirth in the air, fix up your altar to Brigit. Include a statue of the Goddess, with a red and white altar cloth and candles. Red, pink, white, and gold candles are also appropriate. Use a small set of lights to brighten your altar and acknowledge the fire festival. Fill your chalice or a bowl with milk and include a small bowl of seeds and sprouts as a symbol of fertility and rebirth. A *besom* (witches' broom) and cauldron would be suitable to display. A very traditional Brigit doll can be made with nothing more than a simple old-fashioned clothespin, wrapped in red cloth for a gown. A traditional Brigit bed is just a small box lid with a little pillow, mattress, and blanket made from scraps of cloth. You can make little "feet" for the bed with push-pins. If there is snow outside, fill your chalice with it, set it on your altar, and let it melt to hasten the end of winter and the beginning of spring. Sweep out your temple with the besom ("sweeping out the old").

Brigid - February 1st
Also known as Imbolc, Oimelc, Festival of the Waxing Light, Bride/Brigid's Day, Groundhog Day (in the U.S.), Badger's Day (in the U.K.), and Candlemas Theme: Stirrings/Quickening[1]
By Ruth Barrett

The Earth begins to waken from winter's sleep as the pale sunlight grows stronger with each passing day. The first signs of renewal appear as the crocuses bloom and early lambs are born in the snow. The hope and faith sustained through the winter cold and darkness has turned to a certainty. Seeds that have been resting in the earth crack their casings and send out a root, initiating the discovery of individuation.

In ancient Ireland, this Cross-Quarter day marked the first day of spring and the first stirrings in the womb of Earth Mother, as farmers started their preparations for spring sowing. Like all of the Cross-Quarter day fire festivals, divination was done at this time to predict the prevailing wind and weather conditions in the season to come. To see a badger or hedgehog (or groundhog in the U.S.) emerging from its burrow to forage was a sign of good weather. If the critter stayed out, it was a sign that mild weather was coming. If it saw its shadow and returned to its burrow, the winter would be longer.[2] In the U.S., we still carry on this tradition on February 1st, when people gather in Pennsylvania to see "Punxsatawney Phil," the famous groundhog, emerge from his burrow.

The time between Yule and the Spring Equinox was called the "cleansing tide." It was a time of thinking and planning, of assessing what had been achieved and what unfinished work could readily be cast away. It was a time when all things were washed clean or swept away.[3] In ancient Rome, February was cleansing time, "the month of ritual purification."[4] During the season, a new tide of life started to flow through the whole world of nature, and people had to get rid of the past and look to the future. Thus, spring cleaning was originally a nature ritual.[5]

An Irish folk tradition that continues to this day, St. Brigid's Day is still celebrated on the first of February. In addition to being a goddess of poetry, inspiration, divination, smithcraft, and healing, Brigid is also a patroness of cattle and dairy work, and is closely bound up with food production.[6] Traditionally, a young girl dressed in white and wearing a crown of rushes was escorted from house to house by a group of other young girls. She would give a blessing for an egg, a penny, bread, sugar, or cakes.[7] During this time, seed saved from the previous year's crops were mingled with the new. Water from wells dedicated to Brigid or Bride was sprinkled on the house and its occupants, farm buildings, livestock, and fields, to invoke the blessings of the goddess, so powerful and beloved she was transformed in later years into a saint by the Catholic Church.[8] Many old customs associated with the Celtic goddess Brigid continue to this day, such as picking rushes and weaving them into sun wheels, also called Brigid's crosses.

Ritual of Brigit's Forge

This is a fusion of two similar rituals created in 1993 and 1998 by Diane Darling, Tom Lux, Linda Johnston, Anne Bogner, Ace Greenfield, Oberon, Morning Glory, and Liza Gabriel.

Props:
charcoal brazier & charcoal
altar stuff: bread, mead
small cauldron of water
copper rings for all
anvil, iron mallet
cord for charms
tongs, bellows
wire hooks

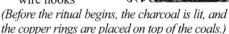

(Before the ritual begins, the charcoal is lit, and the copper rings are placed on top of the coals.)

Introduction to the Ritual:
P: *(Rap about self-empowerment—being your own captain, steering your own ship; Explain that we will be invoking Brigid, honored teacher, to ask her to teach us a skill we need; think about what to ask for; be brief, as Brigid does not suffer fools or wordy students lightly.)*

Circle Casting
Ps: Round like a belly... *(—Anodea Judith)*

Grounding of the Elements
P: *(holds incense)*
This is the first breath you took.
This is the dance of will in your hands.
This is the dance of the worlds in your mind.
This is the song that gives you life.
This is the wind that will scatter your days.
This is the Truth.
(holds flame) This is the fire that forged you.
This is the flame of life in your veins.
This is the flame of love in your loins.
This is the fire of the hearth and the heart.
This is the flame that will consume you
     and make you new.
This is the truth.
Ps: *(holds water)*
This is the womb that carried you.
This is the healing well.
This is the fall of rain on parched earth.
This is the sea of all making.
This is the wine-dark tide
That will carry you into the dream.
This is the truth.
(holds salt) This is the earth that bore you.
This is the bread that feeds you.

This is the law you live by.
This is the hand that holds
All the days of your life.
This is the tomb that will cover your bones.
This is the truth.

Evocations of Brigit & Wayland Smith
(Ps turns towards where Brigit stands in the Circle.)
Ps: Brigid, Brigantia, Bride, Brigandu,
     Bright Arrow,
Beloved Goddess of all Smiths of the
     Sacred Metals
Springsource of the great poetry of the
     Celts,
Whose cauldron holds the light and heat
     of inspiration,
Healer, physician, Lady of Kildare.
Brigid, excellent Goddess, sudden flame
Emerge from your sanctuary behind the
     impassable hedge
Do us the honor of taking the form of
     your priestess
To be with us, on this, your night.
                    (—Morning Glory)
(Brigit *enters Circle.)*
Ps: Hail Brigit of the triple face!
Your songs do rise on the lilt of grace
Your blossoms beautiful ever bloom
On the wings of poetry's sweet
          perfume!   *(—Sharon Knight)*
Brigid *greets the people with an appropriate welcoming rap.*

Brigit: Hail Wayland, ye coal black Smith!
(Wayland *enters Circle with hammer and bellows, stands before forge, and builds up the heat with the bellows)*
Forge our best intentions to a worthy gift
As the circle of our lives turns round again
Strengthen our bonds where bound we
     would be
And where we would not, let us be free!
               (—Morning Glory)
All: Hello, hello, hello again ye coal black
     Smith! (3x)
Wayland *greets the people with an appropriate welcoming rap.*

Working:

Brigit sits on chair with cauldron of water between her legs, for quenching the hot metal.
Wayland: *gives rap about the power and magic of the forge:*

> When metal is forged in very hot fire, it becomes malleable and plastic. With a considered and well-directed strike of a hammer, a purposeful shape can be realized. The smith transforms this hot shape into a tool to perform useful work. Just so do the gods fire and shape their worshippers into instruments well-suited to their sacred purpose.

Ps: Let us pay homage to Brigit, our teacher. Tonight let us ask her to teach us a skill, the particular skill we each need to transform our lives in the forge of the new time that spring and the flow of human events bring. (*turns to* **Brigit**) Great Brigit, let me learn_____. Teach me, please, I vow to be your willing student.

Drums rise to soft background while supplicants come forward one at a time. Brigit retrieves one ring from coals, places on anvil, hands seeker mallet. Seeker strikes copper once. Wayland places copper on hook, hands to Brigit, who quenches it in the bucket of water and hands it to seeker, dismissing him/her. After last one, drums rise to crescendo, then halt.

Cakes and Mead

P: From the seed of the Father (*raises athame above plate and wine goblet*)
Ps: To the body of the Mother (*holds goblet and plate with cakes*)
Together: From this union worlds are nourished.
(*Ps offers cakes and P offers mead to Brigid.*

She takes them and offers them back to P&Ps, who then take them to Circle.)
May you never hunger.
May you never thirst.

Bardic

This part of the ritual is hosted by **Brigit** *herself. She fills a large chalice with mead, takes a sip, and instructs everyone on how to conduct the bardic:*

> When the chalice comes to you, you are invited to make a bardic offering to Brigit. You may sing a song, read, or recite poetry, lead a chant, tell a *short* story or joke, or display a piece of artwork you have created in the past year, with a little explanation. Keep the chalice until you are finished, take another sip, and then pass it on. If you do not wish to make a bardic offering at this time, you may take a sip and just pass the chalice on to the next person.

Brigit passes the chalice to Ps, and they begin the bardic by singing the "Well Song":

> We will never, never lose our way
> To the Well, of Her memory
> And the power, of the living flame,
> It will rise, it will rise again!
> Like the grasses, through the dark, through the storm,
> Towards the sunlight, we shall rise again!
> We are searching, for the Waters of Life;
> We are moving, we shall live again!
> *(—Starhawk)*

(Like any MC, Brigit may intervene at any time to sing a song or chant of her own, or call for something in particular from someone as she thinks it appropriate. Bardic continues as long as Brigit feels like it, and may be ended by her when she wishes, in consultation with Ps.)

Dismissals and Opening of Circle

A Bardic Circle for Brigit
By Oberon

For the Festival of Brigit (Brigantia), the most traditional rite is a *Bardic Circle*—a sharing of songs, stories, poetry, or even jokes. Well ahead of time, in the invitations to the event, the host should let everyone know that a Bardic Circle will be held and that they should bring appropriate stuff to share. These may be original compositions or not. If an offering is to be musical, invite guests to bring instruments.

When the bardic is to begin, everyone gathers into a circle, seated comfortably. The most important element is a large chalice or drinking horn filled with an appropriate thirst-quencher: water, wine, or apple juice is acceptable, but mead is by far the most traditional! Be sure to keep enough more on hand to refill the cup when it gets low!

Bardic Circles are often begun, now as in olden times, with an invocation and dedication to Brigit (Irish saint and goddess, patron of all creative endeavors) or the Muses (Greek patrons of the arts and sciences). Begin by explaining the idea of a Bardic Circle:

In ancient times, the bards dedicated themselves to memorizing the lore of the people in stories, poetry, and song. Thousands of years before there was TV or movies, the best entertainment in the village was a bardic performance. Through these, children and adults learned the history of their ancestors, the myths of the gods, the adventures of heroes, and the lessons of the legends.

But you don't have to be a professional bard to participate in a Bardic Circle! Anyone can tell a story or a good joke, or read a favorite poem—even if you can't sing or perform in other ways. A Bardic Circle is a sharing experience, like a potluck, in which everybody gets to contribute something.

Now, it's well known that barding is thirsty work! So we will pass the horn (or chalice) around the Circle. When it comes to you, take a drink, and enter the center to offer your contribution. When you are done, take another drink, and pass it on to the next person. If you aren't ready when the horn/chalice comes to you, just say "pass" and hand it on to the next in line.

As host, you take a drink and begin with the first offering, and then pass the horn/chalice to the person on your left. In the HOME Tradition, we commonly like to begin our Bardic Circles with "Wind in the Pipes," by Meg Davis (page 267, #237).

Imbolc

By Crow Dragontree

This day typically marks the recovery of the Goddess after giving birth to the God. The daylight hours are getting longer and the sun's power is just about to peak. In the Sonoran Desert, we begin to feel the sun/son's growing power as it begins to get warmer and drier and the first stirrings of the seed sprouts become evident. We know that soon it will become too hot to fully enjoy such solar brilliance as is common in the desert, but for now we celebrate the growing warmth while it is still temperate.

This is a fantastic time to plant seeds, both literally and figuratively. Planting connects us to the Great Mother as well as the Growing Son. Both God and Goddess are deeply involved in the continual fertility of the Earth. While we plant our seeds into the ground, we may also "sow" our intentions for the coming year and take advantage of the burgeoning symbolism of the first signs of manifest power.

Toward this end, have ready a seed or handful of seeds with which you will charge your intent in the present ritual. If doing this spell indoors, bring a bowl of Earth to the altar. This ritual is written as if it is performed indoors in such a manner. Feel free, however, to adapt it in any way that is appropriate for your setting. In either case, be sure to ritually cleanse the seed and bowl of Earth (if used) in the manner with which you are most comfortable.

The foods used during this ritual have traditionally been dairy products. This is likely because of the Western European association with animal lactation during this time. While such an association still holds true to this day, even in the Sonoran Desert, you may also wish to celebrate the Sun God's rise to power with the bold, spicy foods that are common to our area.

Explanation of Imbolc

The High Priest or Priestess stands before the altar while the celebrants perform some gesture that connects them to the Earth (e.g., holding the seed between your palms, touching the bowl of Earth, etc). Feel your energy merging with the Earth. While doing so, intone:

The fertile Earth stirs once more
And Spring leaps into view
Brings back the life we knew before
The world begins anew

The Young God's strength grows in us all
And all around, we see
That the Springtime Goddess starts to warm
And Winter's a memory

Just as the lands are fertile now,
Let us be fruitful, too
Creative and bold, we chart our course
And to our selves stay true
Blessed Be!

Seed Planting Exercise

The High Priest or Priestess faces the celebrants. Instructing each of them to take up their seeds and think about their intention for the seed, he or she provides direction to guide their exercise and experience:

It is now time to plant the seeds of this spring's hopes and dreams. Holding the seed you have chosen and hold it between your palms, consider what this seed means to you symbolically.

This seed is the seed of your own inspiration.

This seed is your own creativity.

It is the symbol of the starting point of your goals for this season.

Think upon the specific goal you wish to accomplish this spring.

Imagine yourself having achieved that goal.

Consider how your life may change and evolve in the upcoming spring while you are achieving this goal.

Realize that every seed faces challenges in its growth, and that you will meet these challenges with capability.

Now envision your seed germinating, growing, and becoming to its full potential ...just as your goals shall.

With that visualization firmly set in your mind, slowly press the seed into the bowl of Earth.

It is fertile, warm, and welcoming.

Hold your hands over the bowl for a few seconds, continuing the visualization, until you are ready to release it.

When all of the celebrants have released their energy into their respective bowls of Earth, you may wish to begin the feast.

Finishing Touches

During the feast, these discussion questions regarding your experience of the celebration may be helpful:

- What kinds of things do you hope to foster this spring (i.e., what was your "seed?")?
- Of course, we have to strive to meet our goals. What kinds of steps do you intend to take to make sure they come to fruition? That is, how do you intend to "make your seed grow"?
- What are some of the traditional Imbolc activities you plan to do?

After the Feast is finished, you will wish to plant the seed with the bowl of Earth outdoors. Other traditional activities that may connect you to the change of the year may be to turn on all of the lights in the house at sunset, symbolizing the growing longevity of the sun. In a similar spirit, some celebrants prefer to set a red candle in every window. Perhaps even a fire could be lit on these still cool nights, either outdoors or safely in a fireplace, for purposes of purification symbolic of the new life that just now begins to sprout around you.

Wiccan Rite for Candlemas Eve

The place of meeting should be decorated with berries and boughs of rowan, or mountain ash, if that is possible. If there will be singing, music, or rhyme before the rite, it should concern the return and quickening of new life. If there is dancing, the Priestess and Priest shall see that it is slow and sensuous. The decorations for the meal before the ceremony should feature red-colored paper.

A small ship model of archaic design should be placed on the altar for this ceremony, symbolizing the return of the Goddess after many cold months, after many cold years, and after many cold centuries. The ship should be placed between the God and Goddess figures.

The Great Circle shall be cast in the usual manner.

To begin the rite, the Priest stands before the mirror to the north of the altar, holding the ship up before him. He looks within the mirror for the space of five heartbeats, then calls:

Three ladies came out of the East, with rhyme and herbs and iron wrought fair.
Return again, oh thou White Swan, pride of the golden hair.

The Priestess, from where she sits in the eastern part of the Circle, responds in a low voice:

The times are ill, and thou of my Craft shall someday make them right.
Sad the town yonder, sad those that are in it;
I am the White Swan who shall again someday be Queen of them all.

The Priest, still facing the mirror, says:

I will voyage in the Lady's name in likeness of deer, in likeness of horse, in likeness of serpent, in likeness of king, to bring back the High One once again. More powerful will it be with me than with all the others, Oh thou gracious Goddess, so may it be in Thy name." (All make the sign of the pentacle.)

The rite of Drawing Down the Moon shall follow. Then the rest of the night shall be spent by all in divination with the mirror, with cards, with crystal, or other means. Blackberry wine shall be drunk.

Finally, the Great Circle shall be opened.

Customs of Candlemas
By Mike Nichols

One of the nicest folk customs still practiced in many countries—especially by Witches in the British Isles and parts of the United States—is to place a lighted candle in each and every window of the house (or at least the windows that face the street) beginning at sundown on Candlemas Eve (February 1), and allow them to continue burning until sunrise.

Make sure that such candles are well seated to prevent tipping, and guarded from nearby curtains, etc. What a cheery sight it is on this cold, bleak, and dreary night to see house after house with candle-lit windows! And, of course, if you are your coven's chandler, or if you just happen to like making candles, Candlemas Day is the day for doing it. On this day some covens hold candle-making parties, and try to make and bless all the candles they'll be using for the whole year.

Other customs of the holiday include: weaving "Brigit's crosses" from straw or wheat to hang around the house for protection, performing rites of spiritual cleansing and purification, making "Brigit's beds" to ensure fertility of mind and spirit (and body, if desired), and making crowns of light (i.e. of candles) for the High Priestess to wear for the Candlemas Circle (similar to those worn on St. Lucia's Day in Scandinavian countries).

All in all, this Pagan festival of lights, sacred to the young Maiden Goddess, is one of the most beautiful and poetic of the year.

An Imbolc Dedication Candle
By Lady MoonDance

As a holiday dedicated to the Celtic goddess Brigid, this is the season to ask for inspiration, creativity, wisdom, and healing. Known as a triple goddess as well as a patroness of poetry, healing, and smithcraft, she is also the "Lady of the Sacred Flame" who guards the spark of life. So beloved was she and so widespread was her worship that the Catholic Church adopted her as St. Brigid and declared February 1 her feast day. Even today her sacred flame continues to burn at her well in Kildare, and priestesses around the world dedicate themselves to her service. On February 2 (Christianized as "Candlemas"), the year's supply of

Creating Circles & Ceremonies

candles were blessed, and some were burned to honor Christ as the light, the truth, and the way—once again symbolizing the flame of Spirit showing the way out of the passing darkness. Traditionally a time for dedications and initiations, this is the season to decide on and formalize your commitment to focus on a specific aspect of your path for the waxing year. Decorating and blessing a candle to help you on your path is a natural way to mark this holy day. This activity can be done alone, or as part of a larger solitary or group ritual.

In the days and weeks from Yule (Winter Solstice) to Imbolc, consider what you wish to pursue during the upcoming year: working on your relationships, reclaiming your power, expressing your creativity, starting a new career, etc. Try to choose a specific area of your own spiritual, emotional, or psychological journey, rather than that of the world or of those around you. In honor of Imbolc, this should be a dedication to yourself and to your own personal path. You may wish to perform some divination or to spend time journaling, meditating, and reflecting on recent events before finding your focus.

Now select a candle for this purpose. You will need either:

- A pillar candle in an appropriate holder, and a toothpick, pencil, or small knife, or
- A glass-enclosed "novena" (7-day or 9-day) candle, craft paper and drawing supplies, catalogues and/or magazines, scissors, and nontoxic, clear-drying craft glue.

You may want to choose a color based on the following list:

Red - Love, passion, emotions, courage, sex, strength, power, blood, fire, energy
Pink - Honor, love, romance, femininity, friendship
Orange - Attraction, encouragement, stimulation, fire, courage
Yellow - Attraction, charm, confidence, happiness, joy
Green - Fertility, prosperity, abundance, growth, luck, healing
Blue - Success, material/earthly destiny, patience, tranquility, healing, clarity, wisdom
Turquoise - Healing, balance
Purple - Spirituality and spiritual destiny, power, peace, royalty
White - Purity & oneness—contains and reflects all colors—positive, active Yang energy
Black - The Void—negates all colors and energy—receptive, passive Yin energy
Gold - The "masculine" aspects of the Divine, the Sun, prosperity & abundance
Silver - The Goddess or Lady, the Moon, prosperity and abundance

Above all, select the color that draws you to it whenever you meditate on your desired goals. If you cannot find one that seems to fit, try selecting white or a basic color. Then, while meditating on your purpose, imagine the colors and images you would associate with this purpose swirling around inside your candle until they resolve into a design. By personalizing your candle in this way, you are also further imbuing it with your purpose.

For the Pillar Candle:

Use the implement of your choice to carve words, runes, pictures, and other symbols representing your dedication onto your candle. One of my own favorite techniques is to form a crossword-puzzle style pattern, interlocking the names of qualities I am seeking to develop within the next year. Similar to a bind rune, this ties the individual ideas together, making for a stronger whole.

For the Glass-Enclosed Candle:

Designed to burn for a week or more, these types of candles can sometimes be found in the ethnic food section of major supermarkets, but the best selection is often found at local Hispanic or international food stores. A printed plastic wrap on the candle can easily be removed by cutting it off, whereas other coverings are often much more difficult to remove. It is also a good idea to consider the meaning depicted when making your selection, as its energy has already been infused into the candle. I generally look for plain candles for this reason, although sometimes a (Goddess) Mary or luck candle can be just the right touch.

Look through magazines and catalogues, cutting out phrases and images that reflect your focus and the qualities associated with it. If you have problems finding the right ideas, you might want to consider the types of magazines you are reading! In the meantime, feel free to draw on blank paper or to piece together words and letters from magazines as needed. Using the craft glue, create a collage on your candle, bringing together the images that represent your purpose.

When You Have Decorated Your Candle:

Hold it out away from you and admire your creation, rolling it around in your hands. Then close your eyes and meditate, envisioning yourself walking on the path to which you are dedicating yourself. Let scene after scene flow from you, through your hands, and into the candle.

Burn your candle as you make your dedication to your path and purpose. Each night before bed, take a few minutes to look at your candle and then burn it for at least fifteen minutes while you envision the things that you are working toward. (Glass-enclosed candles can be left burning in a safe place for several hours, all night long, or continuously, as desired.) Continue to burn it nightly, pouring off wax as needed, until it is gone. Bury any leftover remnants. If you decorated a glass-enclosed candle, you may wish to keep the container near your altar or workspace as a reminder of your dedication. It can later be used to hold dried flowers, incense, and other items, as appropriate.

Imbolc Soda Bread
By Nagia

3 cups unbleached wheat flour
1 Tbs. baking powder
2 Tbs. caraway seeds (optional)
1 cup dried black currants
   or dried blueberries

2/3 cup sugar
1 tsp. salt
1 1/2 cups buttermilk
6 Tbs. butter
2 eggs

Preheat oven to 350°F (about 180°C), and grease a 10" cast iron frying pan with butter. Set aside. Mix dry ingredients in large bowl, then blend liquid ingredients in a separate bowl. Add wet to dry, and mix thoroughly. Add currants and seeds if desired. Pour into pan, shape into loaf, and cut a deep "X" into the top. Bake for 40–50 minutes. Allow to cool for a few minutes, then serve.

237. Wind in the Pipes

Welcome to a moonfilled night
Of strange and wondrous tales,
Of ancient kings and mystic rings
And ships with painted sails.
Of how I came to be here
And where I wish to go,
And all my deepest secrets
Which you will come to know.

Settle back and dream awhile
And come along with me;
We will walk the ancient forests
And sail the deepest seas.
O let your heart go rambling,
There's much we have to see,
From what we are this moment
To what we hope to be!

—Meg Davis

238. Bright Poet Queen

Spirit of Earth, Spirit of Air,
Water and Flame come to us as we share.
Bright Poet Queen, we seek your advice—
Brigid return from the kingdom of ice.
The Imbolc flame burn higher and higher—
Brigid our Mother, the Goddess of Fire.
We drink the milk and light every light—
Brigid please come to our home on this night!

—Cerderaff

239. Brigit Invocation

Hail Brigit, healing Goddess!
Patroness of crafts and poets,
Be our Light and Inspiration;
Walk with us between the worlds.

—Sanura & Diane DesRochers

Appendix A: The Church of All Worlds Tradition

By Liza Gabriel, Morning Glory & Oberon Zell-Ravenheart

I. Basic Principles

The Church of All Worlds Tradition is an eclectic tradition of Neo-Paganism. Its practices are intended as a means towards the best outcome for all. The CAW tradition is ever-evolving with basic, inclusive practices as follows:

Reverence for the Earth

Practitioners of the CAW Tradition revere, honor, and protect the Earth. Most believe that our planet is a conscious living being. Most revere Her as a manifestation of the Great Mother Goddess worshipped by human beings from the dawn of time.

Thou Art God/dess

Practitioners of the Church of All Worlds Tradition honor the God and/or Goddess as immanent in every human being, voiced in the common greeting, "Thou Art God," or "Thou Art Goddess." The deepest experience of the Divinity in other people and things comes through the process of *grokking*. Literally, *grokking* means "drinking." In practice it means expanding one's identity to include the whole being of another person or thing.

Sharing Water

In harmony with the process of *grokking,* the water that is essential to all life is the primary Sacrament of the Church of All Worlds Tradition. Water is Blessed and passed in a chalice, or otherwise shared. Often the last drops are offered to the Divine. Usually when a chalice is passed, the person passing blesses the person receiving the chalice by saying, "Never Thirst," "Thou Art God," "Drink Deep," "Don't spit in the cup," or other appropriate words. This ritual, more than any other, is the common practice of the CAW Tradition.

Water Kinship

The intention of the Water Sharing ritual is to affirm bonds of kinship. Depending on the intimacy of the circle, four levels of this bond are common:
1. Affirming our connection to each other and to all life;
2. Affirming belonging to a tribe or tradition;
3. Affirming friendship;
4. A lifelong Commitment of deep communion, friendship, love, and compassion, which may or may not have an erotic component.

Nests

Nests are the basic grouping of the CAW Tradition and are usually composed of at least three people who have a consistent commitment to the Tradition. At least one member, the Nest Coordinator, should have at least one year experience and the blessing of other long-term practitioners of the Tradition. A Nest may begin with no experience and work towards the ideals of Nesthood. Some Nests are families. Others are social networks, or ritual working groups. They are usually small and intimate. Sometimes several Nests may form a Branch.

Freedom of Expression in Intimacy & Family

The Church of All Worlds Tradition is associated with open attitudes towards intimacy and sexuality. How this is practiced differs widely from person to person and Nest to Nest. Practitioners of the CAW Tradition affirm and support the broadest diversity of intimate and familial expression consistent with a sustainable and ethical life. For example, CAW practitioners support same-sex bonding through marriage, handfasting, or other means. While quite a number of practitioners of the CAW Tradition are monogamous, all support the full range of choice in relationship, including intimate relationships and familial bonds that contain more than two adults; in other words, polyamory.

A Tradition that Looks Equally to Future and Past

Four of the five practices above derive directly from *Stranger in a Strange Land*, the 1961 science fiction novel by Robert Heinlein in which the name "Church of All Worlds" first appeared. Some members of the CAW Tradition glow with pride over this fact, while others are embarrassed and do not wish to be identified with the book. There is no question that many aspects of the book are increasingly outdated.

What will never be outdated, however, is the Church of All World's embrace of the mythology of the future and of science and technology as sources of wisdom as valid as the sacred traditions of old. The CAW Tradition honors the ancient past and looks, with equal reverence, to the future.

Fun

Humor, enjoyment, play, fantasy, and all forms of pleasure are central to the ways that practitioners of the Church of All Worlds Tradition come together.

II. Practices of other Neo-Pagan Traditions shared in common by the Church of All Worlds Tradition

1. Polytheism. Most but not all practitioners of the Church of All Worlds Tradition believe that Divinity takes many forms and worship whatever form is meaningful to the individual. The Myths and Mysteries of many Deities provide deep sources of initiation and wisdom for practitioners of the CAW Tradition.

2. The Wheel of the Year. Like almost all Neo-Pagan traditions, the CAW Tradition celebrates the cycles of the seasons, especially the Quarters and Cross-Quarters: Ostara, Beltaine, Litha, Lughnasadh, Mabon, Samhain, Yule, and Oimelc.

3. Magick. Practitioners of the Church of All Worlds Tradition sometimes use traditional and untraditional means to influence the course of events through the focus of personal will. They acknowledge, honor, and use unseen forces beyond rational human understanding.

4. Wiccan Rede. Church of All Worlds practitioners support the *Wiccan Rede* as an ethical foundation: *"'An it harm none, do as you will."* However, in the CAW Tradition, it is understood that *all magick, whether it serves personal ends or not, is intended to move toward the best outcome for all.* The CAW Tradition looks beyond the perennial spiritual value of nonharming, and actively contributes to the evolution of the whole. What form this takes varies widely.

5. Casting a Circle. Practitioners of the CAW Tradition frequently cast a circle by ritually drawing it with a blade, wand, or other power object. The circle then serves as a place of protection, holiness, and power in which religious and magical acts are accomplished. The ideal of every action and relationship inside the circle is *perfect love and perfect trust.*

6. The Five Elements. Practitioners of the CAW Tradition often use the traditional elements, Air, Fire, Water, Earth and Spirit and the corresponding directions East, South, West, North and Center as important parts of religious practice.

7. Evoking the God and Goddess. Practitioners of the CAW Tradition often choose individuals in their Circles to serve as focal points and expressions of the Divine Male and Female. Divinity is also invited into the ritual Circle on its own without being invited into a particular individual.

8. Bardship. The Church of All Worlds Tradition is a rich source of song, chant, ritual, art, lore, scholarship, vision, and so on. The practitioners of the CAW Tradition who have made major contributions to the creative life of the Neo-Pagan Movement and the broader culture

are too numerous to name. Innovation and creativity are valued and nourished.

9. The Influences of Other Traditions. The CAW Tradition enjoys and embraces influences from all the world's religions and traditions in ways that complement its basic principles and practices.

Foundations of the Arte
By Ian Corrigan

The Four Pillars of the Witch's Gate

Will—The Magician must have strength of mind, to always seek to overcome.

Imagination—The Wizard must be able to bring to mind any image or feeling that is needed.

Faith—The Witch must be confident of her power, ready to set aside doubt when needed.

Secrecy—Magick must never be revealed to those who have no part in it.

The Four Powers of the Magus

To Know—Knowledge is power, and we must seek knowledge of the myths and stories, of the ways of herbs and stones and natural things, of spells and charms, of healing and blessing, and of how to turn aside ill.

To Dare—No magick is made without the courage to act. The Magician must be prepared to risk failure, to look into the unknown, to discover strange things about themselves and about the world.

To Will—Every Wizard needs the strength to seek goals with determination, to focus on one thing at a time. The Magician must train the mind to serve the will, and not follow the blind habits of life.

To Be Silent—Magick is a secret Arte, not because it is forbidden, but because it works with the hidden paths of the world. No deed of magick—no spell, no charm—should be revealed to anyone who is not working it.

Nine Magickal Virtues

Wisdom—to seek knowledge, and know its meaning.

Vision—to see truth in the world and in the Otherworld.

Strength—of body, mind, and spirit.

Courage—to face fear and overcome.

Honor—to serve the good, and keep one's word.

Diligence—to work hard and get a good reward.

Hospitality—to be kind to strangers, and share what you have.

Pleasure—to enjoy your life and the world around you.

Appendix B: Pantheons of Various Cultures & Religions

By Oberon & Morning Glory Zell-Ravenheart

Afro-Caribbean Pantheon

Afro-Caribbean religions are a mixture of Roman Catholic ritual elements from the period of French colonization, and African theological and magickal elements brought to Brazil, New Orleans, Haiti, and Cuba by African slaves formerly belonging to the *Yoruba, Fon, Kongo, Benin,* and other tribes. These blendings created many regional variations, including *Voudun, Santeria, Candomble, Catimbo, Umbanda, Palo Mayombe, Batuque,* and *Xango.* The common name for these faiths is *Ifa.* The *Loa* or *Orisha/Orixa* are a group of African Nature divinities who are concerned with the lives of humans. Fon/Vodouisants believe all Loas originate from the Goddess-God co-Creators, **Mawu-Lisa.** The Loa are invoked by *vévé* (magickal sigils) drawn on the ground, and by singing and dancing, during which they may *possess* certain of their worshippers.

Here are the Orixa, with their feast days:

Ayida Weddo— Rainbow goddess and wife of *Damballa.*

Damballa— Serpent god who is the father and leader of all the Loa.

Elegua (Legba, Exu)— Orixa of crossroads, doorways, and gates, he is the messenger of the gods. He loves all things in excess: wine, spicy foods, singing, dancing, sex, and big cigars. June 29, Sept. 29.

Erinle— Healer of the sick and injured. Oct.24.

Ghede— Loa of the dead. Nov. 1-2.

Mama Watu— Mermaid goddess of the sea.

Obatala/Babalu Aye— The creator god, of whom all the Orixa are but aspects. Bringer of peace and calm, and protector of the crippled and deformed, he wears all white and drinks no alcohol. June 21, Sept.24, Dec. 17.

Ogun— Metalsmith and warrior, he is the patron of civilization and technology. Jan. 17, April 23.

Orunmila— Orisha of wise counsel and protection. Oct. 4.

Osanyin— Orisha of deciduous vegetation. March 19.

Oxosi— Lord of the forest, the Horned Hunter and Green Man. May 15.

Oxun (Urzulie)— Beautiful river queen of fresh waters, she is the goddess of love, sexual passion, fertility, sensuality, and luxury. March 25, Sept. 8.

Oya— Goddess of storms, tornadoes, lightning, and cemeteries. She epitomizes female power and righteous anger. Feb. 2, Nov. 25

Pomba Gira— The sacred whore, and feminine face of *Elegua.*

Xango— Orixa of lightning, dance, passion, and virility. He is the epitome of all things masculine, and the dispenser of vengeance on behalf of the wronged. Sept. 30, Dec. 4.

Yemaya (Yemoja, Iemanja)— Loving sea-mother and goddess of the moon, and guardian of women, childbirth, fertility, and Witchcraft. She rules the subconscious and creative endeavors, and is worshipped by millions in Brazil. Dec. 31.

Celtic-Gaelic Pantheon

The gods of the Welsh and Irish Celts were called the *Tuatha de Danaan* ("children of Dana"). **Dana** or **Danu** was Mother Earth and the Lady of Fresh Waters, and her husband was **Bilé,** a god of the Underworld. The Tuatha were a group of people who migrated into Ireland from their original homeland in the area of the Danube River. They were the fifth in a series of waves recorded in the Irish *Book of Invasions.*

The Tuatha de Danaan are:

Angus— God of youth and love. He plays sweet music on his golden harp, and his kisses become little birds which hover around lovers.

Boann— Cow goddess, wife of Daghda. She bore him *Brigit, Angus, Mider, Ogma,* and *Bodb the Red.*

Bodb the Red— He succeeded his father, Daghda, as king of the gods.

Brigit— Goddess of fire, forge, hearth, poetry, inspiration, healing, sacred wells, gold, wealth, and midwifery.

Camulus— War god who delights in battle and slaughter.

Daghda ("good god")— Father god of the Earth, who succeeded Nuada as king. His harp changes the seasons, and his cauldron is always full. Known for his prodigious appetites, his wife is *Boann.*

Dian Cecht ("swift in power")— God of medicine. He has a spring of health in which wounded gods are healed.

Goibnu— Metalsmith of the gods. He forges their weapons and brews a magick potion which renders them invisible.

Lugh— Grandson of Dian Cecht, and god of the sun. He is the master of all arts and crafts.

Lyr— God of the sea.

Manannan/Manawyddan— The son of Lyr, he is the great Wizard of the Tuatha, and patron of merchants and sailors.

Mider—A god of the underworld whose wife, Etain, was carried off by Angus.

Morrigan, Macha, and **Nemain**— Triple Goddesses of war and destruction.

Nuada— Son of Dana and chief of the Tuatha. He lost a hand in battle, and *Goibnu* made him one of silver.

Ogma—God of eloquence and literature, he invented the Ogham alphabet used in sacred writings.

Some other Celtic & Gaelic Deities:

Aine— Goddess of sex and fertility.

Ana/Anu— "Mother Earth."

Arawn— God of the Underworld (*Annwfn*).

Arionrhod— Moon goddess: "Arionrhod of the Silver Wheel."

Belenos— Sun god.

Bilé— God of the Underworld, husband of Danu.

Blodeuwedd—Flower goddess created by Gwydion.

Cernunnos— Stag-antlered god of animals, the Underworld, and wealth.

Dana/Danu— Great mother goddess of the Tuatha. The Danube and Don Rivers are named for her.

Epona— Horse goddess.

Flidais— Huntress and protector of deer.

Grainne— Sun goddess.

Mabon— Harvest god, son of Modron.

Modron— Great mother goddess of the land.

Rhiannon— Bird goddess and lady of the Faeries. The wife of King Pwyll, kidnapped by *Arawn*.

Robur— Green Man; god of vegetation.

Taranis— God of storms, thunder, and lightning.

Tethra—God of death.

Wayland— Smith god.

Chinese Pantheon

Chinese mythology is believed to have originated in the 12ᵗʰ century BCE (around the time of the Trojan War). The myths and legends were passed down orally for over 1,000 years, before being written down in early books such as *Shan Hai Jing* ("Tales from the Mountains and Seas"). Other myths continued to be passed down through oral traditions such as theatre and song, before being recorded in the form of novels such as *Fengshen Yanyi* ("The Creation of the Gods").

Chang'e— Goddess of the moon. Unlike other lunar deities who personify the moon, Chang'e just lives there.

Dragon Kings— The four divine rulers of the four cardinal seas. They can shapeshift into human form and manipulate clouds and rain. When angered, they can cause floods.

Eight Immortals— These are represented as a group; rarely individually. Each Immortal's power

can be transferred to a tool of power (the "Covert Eight Immortals"), that can give life or destroy evil. The Eight Immortals are:

- **Cao Guojiu** ("Royal Uncle Cao")— Patron of actors, he is shown with castanets or a jade tablet of admission to court.

- **Han Xiang Zi** ("Philosopher Han Xiang")— Patron of musicians, he is often shown with a flute.

- **He Xiangu** ("Immortal Woman He")— She is shown with a lotus blossom or flower basket.

- **Lan Caihe**—Patron of florists, he is an effeminate and eccentric youth who carries a flower basket.

- **Li Tieguai** ("Iron-crutch Li")— Emblem of the sick, he carries a crutch and a gourd.

- **Lü Dongbin** (755-805 C.E.)— Patron of barbers, he is a scholar with a magic sword.

- **Zhang Guo Lao** ("Comprehension-of-Profundity")— Emblem of old men, he rides a mule and carries a tube-drum.

- **Zhongli Quan**— Official leader of the Immortals and a military figure, he carries a fan.

Erlang Shen/Yang Jian— War god with a third true-seeing eye in the middle of his forehead. He carries a three-pronged, two-edged polearm and is followed by his Celestial Hound.

Fu Hsi— First of the mythical Three Sovereigns of ancient China. He invented writing, fishing, and trapping.

Kuan Yin— Bodhisattva of compassion, known in the West as the *Goddess of Mercy*. Her name is short for *Kuan Shih Yin* ("Observing the Sounds of the World").

Hotei/Bu-Dai ("Calico Bag Arhat")— Known in the West as the obese *Laughing Buddha*. Based on an eccentric Chinese Chan monk, in China he is called the *Loving* or *Friendly One*.

Huang Di or **Yellow Emperor**— One of the Five Emperors, he is said to have reigned from 2698-2599 BCE, and is believed to be the ancestor of all Han Chinese.

Jade Emperor— Ruler of Heaven and among the most important Taoist gods, known informally as *Grandpa Heaven.*

Three Pure Ones— Three Taoist deities:

- The **Jade Pure,** "Heavenly Worthy of the Primordial Beginning."

- The **Upper Pure,** "Heavenly Worthy of the Numinous Treasure."

- The **Great Pure,** "Heavenly Worthy of the Way and its Virtue."

Matsu ("Mother-Ancestor")—Popular Taoist goddess of the sea, who protects sailors and fishermen.

Meng Po ("Lady of Forgetfulness")— She serves in *Feng Du*, the Chinese realm of the dead, where her "Five Flavored Tea of Forgetfulness" ensures that souls who are ready to be reincarnated do not remember their previous lives or their time in hell.

Nezha— The terrible Trickster, depicted as a flying youth with a wheel of fire under each foot, a golden hoop around his shoulders, and a spear in his hands.

PanGu— The first living being and the creator of all.

Shang Di or **Shang Ti** ("Lord Above" or "Lord On High")— The Supreme Deity.

Shennong ("the Divine Farmer"), the **Yan Emperor**— He taught the ancients the practices of agriculture. He is credited with identifying hundreds of medicinal and poisonous herbs, and discovering tea (in 2739 BCE).

Zao Jun ("Stove Master")— The kitchen god, the most important of the domestic gods (gods of courtyards, wells, doorways, etc.). Just before each New Year, he returns to Heaven to report the activities of every household over the past year to the Jade Emperor, who rewards or punishes each accordingly.

Sun Wukong, the **Monkey King**— Magician, priest, ruler, sage, and warrior in the shape of a monkey. He is the mischievous protagonist of *Journey to the West,* based on popular tales dating back to the Tan Dynasty.

Xi Wangmu ("Queen Mother of the West") — Ruler of the Western Paradise and goddess of everlasting happiness, fertility, and immortality.

Yan Luo— God of Death and the ruler of the Underworld *(Feng-Du).*

The Endless

In his award-winning Vertigo comic book series, *The Sandman* (1989-1996), Neil Gaiman conceived seven archetypal entities called "The Endless." Older and more universal than the gods of any pantheons, these "anthropomorphic personifications" are a family of immortals who embody the things all mortals must face. Some very effective rituals have been created around these. The family members, in descending order of age, are:

Death— The eldest sister, and the kindest of the Endless. She is the last person any of us will ever see. She shows up to guide your soul to wherever you're going next. Sort of a "compassionate reaper."

Destiny— The eldest brother. He walks alone in his garden, leaving no footprints and casting no shadow. Chained to his wrist is the great Book in which is written all that was, all that is, and all that will be.

Dream— *Morpheus,* the Sandman, the Master of Dreams. He rules The Dreaming and can make your sleeping hours a peaceful fantasy or a living hell. But at least you can talk to him in person.

Desire— To know him/her is to love him/her— passionately, painfully, and exclusively. Never a possession, always the possessor, Desire is everything you ever wanted. Everything.

Despair— Pathetic, bloated twin sister of *Desire.* The windows of her bleak domain are mirrors in our world. Everyone looks into her wet grey eyes at least once in their life. The trick is to tear your eyes away.

Destruction— He got fed up, abandoned his post and went into hiding. Now he just wants to be left alone. Things are still destroyed, but it's no longer his fault or responsibility. Mortals are now perfectly capable of creating all the destruction they want.

Delirium— The youngest of them all, she was once *Delight.* Her appearance varies from moment to moment, and she cannot concentrate for long on any one thing.

Egyptian Pantheon

Isolated along the fertile Nile river, bounded by the sea at the north, the cataracts (falls) in the south, and burning deserts to the east and west, Egyptian culture was continuous for about 3,000 years before the Roman conquest.

Ra, the Sun-god united with his own shadow to beget **Shu** (dry air) and **Tefnut** (rainclouds). These two then united, bringing forth **Nut** (the heavens) and **Geb** (the Earth). They were held apart by Shu during the day, while Ra journeyed across the sky, but at night, Nut descended to rest upon the body of Geb. They became the parents of **Isis** and **Osiris, Set,** and **Nepthys**, thus completing the *Ennead* ("the nine")—the basic pantheon recognized in every temple of Egypt.

The nine members of the Ennead are:

Geb— God of the Earth.

Isis/Aset— Great goddess of the moon, she is the universal Goddess, both in Egypt and throughout the Roman Empire. Her symbol is a throne. Festival Aug. 27.

Ra/Khepri— God of the sun, patron deity of Egypt, god of laws and the kingship. His symbol is the scarab beetle rolling a ball of dung. Festival Aug. 30.

Nepthys— Protectress of children and comforter in the afterlife. Wife of *Set* and mother of *Anubis.* Festival Aug. 28.

Nut/Nuit— Goddess of night and the starry heavens.

Osiris— Lord of life, death, and rebirth. Ruler of *Amenti* (the Underworld), and husband of *Isis.* Their son is *Horus.* The Egyptian *Dionysos,* he is bread, beer, and wine. Deceased Pharoahs were identified with him. Festival Aug. 24.

Set/Seth— God of chaos, storms, darkness, violence, the uncreated universe, and the burning red desert. He is the antithesis of *Ma'at* and nemesis of *Osiris* and *Horus.* Festival Aug. 26.

Shu— God of hot dry winds and the atmosphere, and the breath of life, who holds apart the heavens (*Nut*) and the Earth (*Geb*). At other times, he is a god of the Fire Element.

Tefnut— Goddess of cool moist afternoon breezes, gentle rains, and the Water Element.

Other important Egyptian Deities include:

Ammon/Amen— God of generative powers, "The Invisible One." Chief god of upper (southern) Egypt, he represents the secret power that creates and sustains the universe ("The Force"). His wife is *Maut*. Festival Sept.13.

Anubis— Jackal-headed god of embalming and the Underworld, son of *Nepthys* and *Set*. Adopted by *Osiris* after Set's defeat by *Horus*, he become *Osiris'* messenger into the world of the living, spirit guide for the dead, and our guardian during sleep and astral travel.

Bast— Cat-goddess of the kindly warming rays of the sun. Festival Jan. 24.

Bes— Dwarf-like ithyphallic fertility god, he was a popular spirit of joy often depicted in amulets.

Hapi (Greek *Apis* and *Serapis*)— God of rivers. Represented as a sacred black bull, he is regarded as an *avatar* (incarnation) of Osiris. As the Greek *Serapis*, he is the god of healing. Festival July 9.

Hathor— Cow-goddess of love, beauty, and music, she is the Egyptian *Aphrodite*. Her symbol is the *sistrum*. Festival July 24.

Heket— Frog goddess and midwife. Some say she is the precursor of Greek *Hekaté*.

Horus/Harakte— Hawk-headed lord of light, son of *Isis* and *Osiris*. The reigning Pharoah was worshipped as the living incarnation of Horus and personal savior of all Egyptians. Festival Aug. 25.

Khem— Lord of the harvest and patron of agriculture, he is the Egyptian Green Man. Represented as a mummy, his name is also that of Egypt itself. He eventually became subsumed into *Osiris*.

Khnum— Lord of the sources of the Nile, he has a ram's head. He was the potter who fashioned all living things out of Nile mud.

Ma'at— Goddess of truth and justice, law, morality, and the pre-existing order of the universe. Her symbol is an ostrich feather.

Maut/Mut— Vulture goddess, mother of the gods and mistress of the sky. Wife of *Ammon*. Festival Jan. 1.

Mesergert— Lady of the mountains.

Neith— Goddess of outer space, and mother of *Ra;* chthonic sun goddess, goddess of the loom, the warrior mother. Also the Earth-mother of the Nile Valley. Her husband is *Khem*.

Nekhbet— Goddess of protection.

Nun— Goddess who is the primeval ocean.

Ptah— Master of artisans, who made the moon, sun, and Earth. God of engineers, doctors, and politics, he was invoked in Memphis as the father of all beginnings. Festival Feb. 25.

Sekhmet— Ferocious lioness-goddess of the burning sun; goddess of power and protectress of women.

Selket— Scorpion goddess and guardian of tombs and mummies.

Taurt/Tauret— Hippopotamus goddess, protectress of pregnant women, and patroness of midwives.

Tehuti (Greek *Thoth*)— Represented as an ibis or a hamadryad baboon, *Thoth* is the god of writing, wisdom, magick, arts, and sciences; the patron god of all Wizards—the Egyptian *Hermes*. Festival Sept. 17-18.

Wadjet— Cobra Goddess who protects the Sun and the royal family. She is represented by the *uraeus* symbol.

Etruscan Pantheon

The original Etruscan pantheon of pre-Roman Italy mirrors the duality of nature, with deities for practically everything! Here are some of the numerous gods and goddesses of ancient Etruria. Many of these became minor gods in Rome, and are still worshipped in *Stregheria*, or Italian Witchcraft.

Anteros— God of passion.

Aplu— Water god.

Astrea— Goddess of justice.

Belchians— God of fire.

Cautha— Sun god; he is depicted rising from the sea.

Charun— God of the Underworld; he leads the dead to enjoy a happy afterlife.

Comus— God of revelry, feasting, and drinking.

Corvus— ("crow") Messenger of the gods.

Copia— Goddess of wealth and plenty.

Diana— The triad goddess: Maiden, Mother, & Crone; the goddess of all Witches.

Dianus—Nature god of fertility, horned god of the woods, consort of Diana.

Egeria— Goddess of fountains, she possesses the gift of prophecy.

Fana— Goddess of the Earth, forests, wildlife, and fertility.

Faunus— Nature god of the forest, wildlife, and fertility.

Februus— God of purification, initiation, and fevers. February is named for him.

Felicitas— Goddess of good luck.

Fortuna— Goddess of fortune, fate, blessing, luck, and fertility.

Fufluns—God of wine, vegetation, vitality, and gaiety.

Horta— Goddess of agriculture.

Jana— Goddess of the moon.

Janus/Giano— God of the sun and of all beginnings, portals, doorways and thresholds; associated with journeys.

Laran— God of war; depicted as a youth wearing a cape and armed with a lance and helmet.

Losna— Moon goddess.

Lupercus— God of agriculture, the wolf god. Roman festival (*Lupercalia*) February 15.

Menrva— Goddess of wisdom and the arts.

Munthukh— Goddess of health.

Nethuns— God of fresh water; identified with wells and springs and depicted as a naked and bearded figure.

Nortia— Goddess of healing and fate.

Nox— Goddess of the night.

Pertunda— Goddess of sexual love and pleasure.

Picus— Woodland god; agricultural deity associated with the fertilization of the soil with manure.

Sentinus— God who gives sensibility.

Summamus— Storm god; he is responsible for lightening and thunderbolts.

Tagni— Most ancient name for the god of Witchcraft.

Tana— Star goddess.

Tanus— Star god, consort to *Tana*.

Terminus— God of boundaries and fields, protector of personal property. Related to Greek *Hermes*.

Thalna— Goddess of childbirth; depicted as a youthful woman.

Tinia/Tin— Supreme sky god, married to *Uni*.

Tuchulcha— Goddess of death; she is part human, part bird, and part animal, with snakes in her hair and around her arms.

Turan— Goddess of love, health, and fertility; usually portrayed as a young woman with wings on her back.

Turms— Messenger god.

Umbria— Goddess of the shadows and of things which are hidden or secret.

Uni— Goddess of marriage and magick.

Vanthi— Goddess of death; she is depicted with wings, a cap on her head, and a key to open tombs in her hand.

Vesta— Goddess of the hearth and fire.

Virbius— God of outcasts and outlaws, guardian of sanctuaries.

Vertumnus— The Etruscan Green Man of vegetative growth and springtime.

Greco-Roman Pantheon

Achaean Greeks first settled into various areas of Greece around 2000 BCE The Romans adopted the Greek gods pretty much intact, though giving them different names. The Greek versions of their origins and stories are found in Hesiod's *Theogony* ("birth of the gods"), and in Homer's *Iliad* and *Odyssey*. The primary collection of the Roman versions is Ovid's *Metamorphoses* ("transformations").

Gaea, Mother Earth, was the eldest of all Greek deities—born out of **Chaos**, which also brought forth **Erebos** (the Underworld) and **Nix** (Night). After this, several generations proceeded. The first were called the *Titans*. These were followed by the Olympian Gods, who gained ascendancy after their victory in the *Titanomachia* ("Battle of the Titans").

These are the twelve Olympians—and their Roman equivalents:

Aphrodité (Roman *Venus*)— Goddess of love, beauty, and sex. Husband: *Hephaestos*. Symbols: mirror and dove. Planet: Venus.

Apollo—God of the Sun, music, and prophecy. Twin brother of *Artemis*. Symbol: lyre. Planet: the sun.

Ares (Roman *Mars*)— God of war. Symbol: Spear and shield. Planet: Mars. Roman festival (*Equiria*) February 27, March 14.

Artemis (Roman *Diana*)— Goddess of the moon and the hunt. Twin sister of *Apollo*. Symbols: bow drawn like crescent moon, deer, hounds. Planet: the moon.

Athena (Roman *Minerva*)— Goddess of war and wisdom. Symbols: shield, spear, *aegus* (breastplate with head of Medusa).

Demeter (Roman *Ceres*)— Queen of the Earth, goddess of grain and all cultivated plants. Symbol: cornucopia.

Hades (Roman *Pluto*)— Ruler of the Underworld; the dead, all things buried, and the wealth of mines. Wife: *Persephoné*. Symbol: two-pronged scepter. Planet: Pluto

Hera (Roman *Juno*)— Queen of the gods, wife of Zeus. In charge of marriage, women, families. Symbol: peacock tail-feather.

Hermes (Roman *Mercury*)— Messenger of the gods. In charge of communication, magick, arcane knowledge, hidden things, thievery. He is the patron god of all Wizards. Symbol: caduceus. Planet: Mercury.

Hestia (Roman *Vesta*)— Goddess of hearth and home. She is always invoked first in any Greek ritual.

Poseidon (Roman *Neptune*)— Ruler of the seas; waves, tides, sea-monsters; also horses and earthquakes. Wife: *Amphitrite*. Symbol: three-pronged trident. Planet: Neptune.

Zeus (Roman *Jupiter*)— King of all the gods; ruler of the sky, clouds, thunder, lightning, judgment, authority. Wife: *Hera*. Symbols: thunderbolt and eagle. Planet: Jupiter.

Other important Greco-Roman deities include:

Aesculapius— God of physicians and healers. Once mortal, he was granted immortality for the number of lives he saved. Symbol: staff entwined by single serpent.

Amphitrité— Goddess of the sea, wife of *Poseidon.*

Dionysos (Roman *Bacchus*)— God of the grapevine, wine, intoxication, and inspiration. Son of *Persephoné* and *Hades.*

Eros (Roman *Cupid*)— God of love, and the primal force of attraction in the universe. Originally born of Chaos, he later incarnated as the son of *Aphrodite.* Symbol: cock.

Hekaté/Hecaté— Goddess of crossroads and transitions: birth, weddings, aging, death. Daughter of the star goddess, Astra, she is the goddess of Witchcraft and the Dark Moon.

Hephaestos (Roman *Vulcan*)— Smith god, son of *Zeus.* He is the great artisan, forging all the weapons and tools of the gods. Symbols: hammer and tongs.

Kronos (Roman *Saturn*)—Titan father of Olympians; god of time and harvest—the original grim reaper. Symbols: scythe and hourglass. Roman festival (*Saturnalia*) December 17-23.

Pan— One of the most ancient gods, representing the wildness of all nature. He is half-man and half-goat. Symbol: the *syrinx,* or panpipes.

Persephoné (Roman *Proserpina*)— Daughter of *Demeter,* wife of *Hades,* and queen of the Underworld. Symbol: the poppy.

ʜindu Pantheon

The Hindu pantheon is as vast and ancient as the people of India. Based on sacred writings called the *Vedas* (composed between 1500-600 BCE), it encompasses many diverse sects, philosophies, and practices. Many Hindus venerate a complex array of deities, and consider them as manifestations of the one supreme cosmic spirit called **Brahman,** who is the Ultimate Reality, the Absolute or Universal Soul, without beginning or end, who is hidden in all and who is the cause, source, material, and effect of all creation.

The numerous celestial entities in Hinduism are called *Devas*—usually translated into English as "gods," but more accurately as demigods, deities, celestial spirits, or angels. These all emanate from the Triune Godhead comprised of **Brahma** the Creator, **Vishnu** the Preserver, and **Shiva** the Destroyer. Many Devas are seen as *avatars,* or incarnations, of these three.

Here are some of the most important Devas:

Aditi— "The Void," gateway and birth-mother to all limitless possibilities. Lady of space and infinity.

Agni— God of fire and the hearth, protector of *Sita,* the wife of Rama. He blesses all weddings.

Brahma— Creator god; primary of the triune godhead, whose priestly caste are called *Brahmins.*

Ganesha— Elephant-headed son of Shiva and Parvati. He is the laughing god who breaks down all obstacles and brings good fortune.

Hanuman— Monkey god who is both messenger and trickster. As told in the *Ramayana,* he helped *Rama* rescue *Sita* from the demon *Ravenna.*

Indra— Vedic god of lightning and thunder.

Kali— The great mother goddess of time, personified as the Destroyer. The death-bringing aspect of the triplicity of destructive goddesses (along with *Durga* and *Parvati*). She is the protector of abused women, and her festival in the fall is called *Mahankali Jatara Bonalu.*

Kama— God of love and desire, his book is the *Kama Sutra.*

Krishna— Youthful, dancing, laughing god of joy and wonder. Later he became a great warrior, as described in the *Bagavadgita.*

Laksmi— The *Shakti* or wife of *Vishnu,* and first created of "The 17 Beautiful Things." Rising on a lotus flower from a sea of cosmic milk, she is the goddess of love, marriage, joy, wealth, and general good fortune. The swan and the elephant are sacred to her.

Maya— The great mother goddess, she represents life and reality as the great illusion.

Prithivi— "Mother Nature." She is the living spirit of all that is wild and beautiful.

Rama— An avatar of Vishnu, his story is told in the *Rama Yana.*

Ratri— Goddess of the night, she is the wife of *Kama,* god of love.

Rudra— The red god of storms and war.

Saraswati— Goddess of music and craftwork, she played the sitar and sang the "om" which began the vibration that led to all creation. The peacock is her bird.

Shakti— The female half of all Divinity and all gods; sometimes thought of as the Divine Wife.

Shiva— "The Destroyer," who clears the way for new growth. Third of the Great Triune Gods.

Sita— Wife of *Rama,* kidnapped by the demon *Ravenna.*

Soma— God of bliss and desire fulfilled.

Tara—Goddess of the stars, and of healing and mercy.

Ushas— Goddess of the dawn and springtime.

Vishnu— "The Preserver." He is the second in the great trinity; he keeps the wheel of karma turning.

Yama— God of death who takes mortals into his realm in the Underworld until they are reincarnated.

Japanese Pantheon

Although influenced by the ancient Chinese, much of Japanese mythology and religion is uniquely their own. It embraces Shinto and Buddhist traditions as well as agriculture-based folk beliefs. The Shinto pantheon alone includes more than 8,000 *kami* ("gods" or "spirits"). The 8th century CE *Kojiki*

("Record of Ancient Things") is the oldest recognized book of myths, legends, and history of Japan. The *Shintoshu* explains the origins of Japanese deities from a Buddhist perspective, while the *Hotsuma Tsutae* by Waniko Yasutoshi (1887) portrays a substantially different version, contending that Amaterasu, the Shinto sun deity, is male rather than female. Japanese mythology also affirms the divine origin of the Imperial Family. The word for the Emperor of Japan, *tennô*, means "Heavenly Emperor."

Amaterasu— Sun goddess. She was born from the left eye of *Izanagi*, and went on to become the queen of heaven *(Takamagahara)*. She was considered to be ancestor to the Imperial household and the emperor.

Amatsu Mikaboshi ("August Star of Heaven")— God of evil and of the stars, specifically the pole star.

Ama-no-Uzume— Fertility goddess of dawn and revelry. She charmed *Amaterasu* out of hiding.

Chimata-No-Kami— Phallic god of crossroads, highways, and footpaths. Phallic symbols were often placed at crossroads.

Inari— God of fertility, rice, and foxes. Inari's pure white foxes, or *kitsune*, are his messengers.

Izanagi ("He who invites")— Creator god. He and his wife *Izanami* bore many islands, deities, and forefathers of Japan.

Izanami ("She who invites")— Goddess of both creation and death, as well as the former wife of *Izanagi*.

Kagu-tsuchi— God of fire. Born from *Izanagi* and *Izanami*, who died from the burns in giving birth to him. His father cut him into eight pieces and the eight body parts became eight mountains, and from Kagu-tsuchi's blood came eight gods.

Konohana— Cherry-blossom princess and symbol of delicate earthly life. She is the daughter of the mountain god Ohoyamatsumi.

O-Kuni-Nushi— God of sorcery and medicine. Originally a mortal governor, he became ruler of the unseen world of spirits and magick.

Seven Gods of Fortune— Gods of good fortune. Each has a traditional attribute:

1. **Ebisu**— God of fishers or merchants, often depicted carrying a cod or sea bass.
2. **Daikokuten**— God of wealth, commerce, and trade. Ebisu and Daikoku are often paired and represented as carvings or masks on the walls of small retail shops.
3. **Bishamonten**— God of warriors.
4. **Benzaiten**— Goddess of knowledge, art, and beauty.
5. **Fukurokuju**— God of happiness, wealth, and longevity.
6. **Hotei**— Fat and happy god of abundance and good health.

7. **Juroujin**— God of longevity.

Susanoo— God of sea, storms, and thunder; also snakes and farming. He is brother of *Amaterasu* (sun) and *Tsuku-Yomi* (moon).

Tsuku-Yomi— God of the moon, brother of *Amaterasu*, the Sun Goddess.

Uke-Mochi— Goddess of foods, who produces food from her own body.

Judeo-Christian Pantheon

Although Judaism and Christianity both acknowledge only one Supreme Creator God, called **Jahveh** or **Jehovah** (meaning "I Am That I Am"), their traditions also include large numbers of lesser *angels, demons,* and *saints,* which are analogous to the pantheons of other peoples. Moreover, Christianity envisions the Godhead as *triune,* or threefold: a *Trinity* consisting of Father (**Jehovah**), Son (**Jesus Christ**), and Holy Ghost (**Shekinah**). In Christianity, of course, the most important deity is Jesus Christ, the son of God, born of the Virgin Mary, and *messiah* (savior) of mankind. His crucifixion and resurrection is the foundation of Christianity.

Angels ("messengers") comprise the "Hosts of Heaven." There are thousands of them, organized in ten ranked "choirs." Each choir is ruled by an archangel. The ten archangels in order of rank are:

Metatron— "Angel of the Presence." King of all the angels, and the youngest, he was once the Hebrew patriarch Enoch. He is the link between God and humanity, and his female counterpart is *Shekinah.*

Ratziel— "Delight of God." Prince of knowledge of hidden things, who is called the Angel of Mysteries.

Tzaphqiel— "Contemplation of God." Prince of spiritual strife against evil.

Tzadkiel— "Justice of God." Prince of mercy and beneficence who guards the Gates of the East Wind.

Kamael— "Severity of God." Prince of strength and courage who bears the flaming sword.

Raphael— "Physician of God." Prince of healing, with *Michael* as his lieutenant.

Haniel—"Grace of God." Prince of love and harmony, his female counterpart is *Hagiel.*

Michael—"Protector of God." Prince of art and knowledge, with *Raphael* as his lieutenant.

Gabriel—"Strength of God." Most beloved of all the angels, he appeared to Mary in the Annunciation and dictated the Quran to Mohammed.

Sandalphon—"Co-brother." He is the twin of *Metatron,* and was once the Hebrew prophet Elias.

Other important angels include:

Azrael— Black-winged angel of death, whose scythe cuts free the souls of the dying.

Hagiel— Beautiful green-eyed angel of love and beauty, appearing exactly as the Greek Goddess *Aphrodite.*

Shekinah— "Mercy of God." She comes forth on the Sabbath and blesses the union of husband and wife. She is considered the mystical Bride of God.

Sophia— Spirit of wisdom; she is not an angel, but rather is considered to be an emanation of the Godhead.

Uriel— Angel of salvation, with dominion over thunder and terror. Uriel was sent to Noah to give warning of the coming flood.

Demons are fallen angels who were cast down into *hell* (the Underworld) after the great war in heaven, in which the rebellious **Lucifer** ("Light-bringer") was defeated by Jahveh. As with the angels, demons also are ranked in ten orders, each ruled by an arch-Demon. The arch-demons in order of rank are:

Satan & Moloch— "Twins of God." Rulers over *Shahul,* the "triple hell," or grave hell of supernals.

Beelzebub— Supreme chief of hell and demon of the hinderers.

Lucifuge Rofacale— Lucifer, "King of Hell," administrator of justice; demon of the concealers.

Astaroth— Demon of fertility and the smiters.

Asmodeus— Demon of arsonists and wrath.

Belphegor— Demon of hagglers, discoveries, and ingenious inventions.

Bael— Demon of the ravens of death; makes men invisible and gives wisdom.

Adramelech— "Poison of God." High chancellor of hell and president of the high council of devils.

Lilith— The first woman, created before Eve; refused to submit to Adam; mother of *succubi* and *incubi;* demon of the obscene ones.

Nahema— Demon of "The Five Accursed Nations."

Saints were once living men and women whose exemplary lives and posthumous miracles earned them spiritual immortality as patrons to be called upon by the faithful. They are primarily associated with the Roman Catholic Church, which claims sole power to sanctify. Here are only a few of the thousands of saints recorded, and their feast days:

St Augustine of Hippo— Patron of brewers. Aug. 28.

St Barbara—A martyr who became the protector of women who resist oppression.

St Brigit— The "Mary of the Gael," she is buried at Downpatrick with *St. Columba* and *St. Patrick,* with whom she is the patron of Ireland. Her name is also written as *Bridget* and *Bride.* Feb. 1.

St Christopher— Patron of travelers, invoked against storms, plagues, etc. July 25.

St Dominic— Patron of astronomers. Aug.8.

St Francis of Assisi— Patron of animals, merchants, and ecology. Oct. 4.

St Joan of Arc— Patroness of soldiers and of France. She was condemned to death as a heretic, sorceress, and adulteress, and burned at the stake on May 30, 1431, at 19 years of age. May 30.

St John the Baptist—Last of the Old Testament prophets and the precursor of the messiah. June 24.

St Jude— Patron of desperate causes. Oct. 28.

St Luke—Patron of physicians and surgeons. Oct. 18.

St Mary the Blessed Virgin— "Mother of God," mother of Jesus, wife of St. Joseph, and greatest of all Christian saints. Feast of Immaculate Conception Dec. 8. Feast of the Assumption Aug. 15.

St Mary Magdalen the Penitent— Patroness of prostitutes and repentant sinners. July 22.

St Monica— Patroness of wives and abuse victims. Aug. 27.

St Nicholas— Patron of children, prisoners, and captives. Patron saint of Russia. Dec. 6.

St Peter— "Gatekeeper of Heaven." Prince of the apostles and the first pope; June 29.

St Valentine— Patron of love, young people, happy marriages. Feb. 14.

Norse-Teutonic Pantheon

There are two races of Norse gods, the *Aesir* and the *Vanir.* The Vanir may have been the gods of a more advanced grain-raising people who moved into the territory of the worshippers of the Aesir, who mostly lived by herding cattle. After a long conflict, the two groups made truce. To ensure this peace they traded hostages and intermarried. The Vanir were given their own dwelling-place of *Vanaheim* in Asgard.

The twelve Aesir are:

Odin— God of wisdom, inventor of the runes, and chief of all the gods, he is called "All-Father." He traded one eye for a drink from the Well of Wisdom. His two ravens *Hugin* (thought) and *Munin* (memory) bring him news from all the worlds. His wife is *Frigg.*

Frigg— Wife of Odin, goddess of love and fertility, and patron of marriage and motherhood.

Vili— Brother of Odin and co-creator of humans.

Ve— Brother of Odin and co-creator of humans.

Vidar— Son of Odin, god of silence and revenge, the second strongest of the gods (after Thor).

Loki— God of fire and ally of the frost giants, he is the chaotic trickster, crafty and malicious, always plotting against the gods. His wife is *Sigyn.*

Hoder— Blind god of winter, twin brother of *Balder.* His wife is *Skadi,* the queen of northern snows and skiing.

Balder— God of beauty, light, joy, purity, innocence, and reconciliation. His wife is *Nanna.*

Bragi— God of eloquence and poetry. His wife is *Idun.*

Heimdall— Watchman of the gods and guardian of the rainbow bridge, *Bifrost.*

Forseti— God of mediation and justice, son of Balder.

Thor— God of thunder, and strongest of the gods. Lightning flashes whenever he throws his hammer *mjollnir.* His wife is *Sif.*

And here are some of the Vanir:

Njordh — God of the sea, winds, fire, and the hunt. Husband of *Skadi.* When he was killed by mistake, she demanded of the gods a new husband.

Nerthus— A Frisian Earth-goddess whom many believe to be the sister-wife of Njordh and mother of *Freyr* and *Freyja.*

Freyr— God of sun and rain, and the patron of bountiful harvests, son of Njordh. His wife is the beautiful Giantess *Gerd.*

Freya— Goddess of love, beauty, fertility, prosperity and magic. Daughter of Njordh and twin sister of Freyr, she likes love-poetry, but she also chooses slain warriors for her great hall, *Sessrumnir.*

Idun— Goddess of eternal youth and keeper of the apples of immortality. Wife of Bragi.

Skadi— Originally the wife of Njordth. When her husband was slain she demanded justice of the gods. She was blindfolded, and chose Hoder, but he loved the sea and she loved the mountains.

Sif— Golden-haired fertility goddess (some say giantess), wife of Thor.

Tyr— Original Germanic god of war and justice, the precursor of Odin.

Ullr— God of the hunt, famous for his skill in archery. Son of Sif.

Other Norse deities and beings include:

Mimir— Keeper of the Well of Wisdom.

Hel/Hella— Goddess of the Underworld, daughter of Loki and sister of *Fenris.* She is a terrible icy cold keeper of the unworthy dead.

Fenris— The huge and terrible wolf who will destroy the gods in the Battle of *Ragnarök.*

Norns— Goddesses who determine fate. The three best known are *Urd* (what has been), *Verdandi* (becoming), and *Skuld* (what shall be). One's fate, or *wyrd*, was the result of what one was given at birth as well as the choices one made.

Valkyries— Daughters of Odin who select dead heroes and bring them to *Valhalla*, home of the Gods. They fly on winged steeds, singing songs of victory; Freya sometimes leads them.

Phoenician (Canaanite & Carthaginian)

The belief system of the western Phoenicians or Punic peoples—that is, the Carthaginians and the people of the other Phoenician colonies along the coast of Africa, Iberia, and the islands of Sardinia, Corsica, Malta, and the western portion of Sicily—was very similar to that of the old city-states of Phoenicia or Canaan, as it is referred to in the Old Testament. Carthaginians worshiped a pantheon of gods and goddesses similar to those of the cultures with which they had contact. They even adopted some of the gods of their neighbors. The Phoenician pantheon includes:

Adon/Adonis— God of youth, beauty, and regeneration. He dies, is mourned, and is reborn each year.

Anat/Anath— Maiden goddess of love and war. She rescued her husband *Baal* from the Underworld and slew the god *Mot.*

Asherah/Baalat Gubl— Goddess of Byblos; the "Upright One," goddess of the fertility of flocks and fields, and represented by the Tree of Life. She was particularly hated by the Hebrew prophets, who forbade her worship in any form.

Astarte/Ashtarte— "Queen of Heaven," goddess of love and pleasure, her offerings were honey cakes. Her priestesses were *qadistu* ("sacred prostitutes"), and her temples were sanctuaries for doves and fishes.

Baal/El—"Almighty," "Lord of the Earth," "Rider of the Clouds." Ruler of the universe, god of the sun, and fire of summer; high god of sacrifice. Son of *Dagan.*

Baal-Hammon— God of fertility and renewer of all energies.

Dagan/Dagon— God of fishes and the deep ocean, patron of fishermen. Father of mighty Baal.

Eshmun/Baalat Asclepius— God of healing.

Kathirat— Goddess of marriage and pregnancy.

Kothar/Hasis— Skilled god of craftsmanship.

Melqarth/Melqart— Lord of the Underworld and the cycle of vegetation.

Mot— God of old age, death, and decomposition; keeper of the Underworld.

Shahar— God of dawn.

Shalim— God of dusk.

Shapash— Sun goddess.

Tanit/Tanith—"Queen of Heaven" or "Mother Goddess." Goddess of Carthage, good fortune, wealth, abundance, and bountiful harvest. She received infant sacrifice.

Yamm— God of the sea.

Yarikh— Moon god.

Sumerian-Babylonian Pantheon

Mesopotamia ("land between the rivers") is the fertile plain of modern Iraq through which the

Tigris and Euphrates rivers flow. From about 3500 BCE, this was the home of the Sumerians, Babylonians, Assyrians, and Chaldeans (in that order). The most complete stories we have are from the Babylonian period (612-538 BCE), but these built upon the older Sumerian mythology, as the Romans did with the Greeks.

Tiamet was the great dragon-serpent of the chaotic primordial ocean. After a great battle, she was slain by **Marduk**. He cut her body into two parts, thus creating heaven and Earth. He set the stars and planets in the heavens, and established their motions. Then, on the advice of his father, **Ea,** he created humanity. **Ninhursag** ("Earth-mother") planted the Garden of Eden, and in it the two trees of Life and Knowledge. **Enki** raided her garden prematurely and she struck him down, but later healed him.

The gods of Babylon include:

Adad (Sumerian *Hadad*)— God of thunder, lightning and rain. His wife was *Shala*.

Allatu (Sumerian *Ereshkigal*)—Ancient dark Earth goddess, queen and keeper of the Underworld. She struck down her younger sister *Ishtar/Inanna* for her hubris, then was later tricked into allowing her to be resurrected.

Anu— God of the heavens, and father of all the gods. Eldest of the gods, his was the North Star, and he ruled destiny.

Asshur— God of war.

Dummuzi— Sumerian shepherd god of flocks and fields, consort of *Inanna*. He was cast into the Underworld for six months of the year; when the Earth grew cold in winter, all the world mourned with *Inanna*.

Ea— God of the waters: sea, springs, and rivers. He was also god of air, wisdom, and life, and a potter who formed both gods and humans.

Enki— Sumerian god of wisdom who favored Inanna. He raided the Garden of *Ninhursag* when he was a very young god of irrigation. She struck him down but later healed him, whereupon he was enlightened and became the god of wisdom.

Enlil— "God of the Great Mountain" (Earth), and ruler of the Golden Age.

Geshtinana— Sister of *Dumuzzi* who volunteers to take his place in the Underworld for the other six months of the year.

Girru— God of fire in all aspects.

Gula— "Great Physician." Goddess of healing who could restore life.

Ishtar (Sumerian *Inanna*)— Queen of heaven and goddess of beauty, love, and war; she was the daughter of Anu, and the most powerful goddess of Sumer. She tricked Enki into giving her the *mei*, which represent the powers of all social or-

der. As Inanna, she descended into the Underworld to confront her sister, Ereshkigal; but as Ishtar she encountered *Nergal* as the dark lord. As Ishtar, her consort was *Tammuz*, but as Inanna, her consort was *Dummuzi*.

Lilith/Lilitu— Winged screech owl goddess who warned of impending death and carried the souls of the dead into the Underworld.

Marduk— God of the spring Sun, prudence, and wisdom; also of war and lightning. He was the son of *Ea,* and his wife was *Zarpanit*.

Nana— Goddess of waters, wife of *Ea,* and mother of *Inanna*.

Nanan— Sumerian god of the Moon. He is seen as sailing in his crescent-shaped boat. The origin of "the Man in the Moon."

Nebo— Son of *Marduk,* he was the god of learning and inventor of writing.

Nergal— God of pestilence and destruction. He married *Allatu* to become lord of the Underworld.

Ninib—God of fertility and healing. His wife was *Gula*.

Ninlil— Wife of *Enlil*. Goddess of winds, clouds, dew, rain, and all fertile moisture. A gentle goddess who rose in wrath when she was raped.

Zu— God of the storm. He stole the Tablets of Destiny from Enlil.

Sin (Sumerian *Nannan*)— God of the moon and son of Enlil. His queen was *Ningal*.

Shamash— God of the sun, champion of justice, and giver of law. He was also a healer and life-giver.

Tammuz— God of vegetation, consort of Ishtar.

Sources for information on these Pantheons

Alternative Religions: http://altreligion.about.com

Budge, Sir Wallis. *Egyptian Religion,* Bell Publishing, 1900.

"Catholic Online: Saints & Angels": www.catholic.org/saints/ (2006).

Decker, Roy, "Religion of Carthage," http://ancienthistory.about.com/cs/nemythology/a/deckercarthrel1.htm (accessed 2006).

de Plancy, Collin. *Dictionnaire Infernal* (Illus. by L. Breton), 1863. Editions 10/18 (1999).

Encyclopedia Mythica: www.pantheon.org/ (2006)

Monaghan, Patricia. *New Book of Goddesses & Heroines (3rd ed.).* Llewellyn, 2002.

The Mystic's Wheel of the Year: A Multifaith Calendar Reflecting Eco-Egalitarian Spirituality, PO Box 77167, Washington, DC 20013. www.WheeloftheYear.com

Robinson, Herbert Spencer & Knox Wilson. *Myths & Legends of All Nations.* Littlefield, Adams & Co., 1976.

Wikipedia: http://en.wikipedia.org/wiki (2006)

Appendix C: Ritual Resources

Here are just a few of our favorite CDs of Pagan ritual music and chants:

The Best of Pagan Song compiled by Anne Hill. Serpentine Records, 2004. A splendid introduction to contemporary Pagan music, mostly songs with some chanting.

Bending Tradition by Emerald Rose. 2000 (studio release). Mostly songs, some suitable for ritual use; the chant "Freya Shakti" is a delightfully fresh take on the popular "Isis Astarte."

Be Pagan Once Again! and *Avalon is Rising* by Isaac Bonewits

Carry Me Home: A Collection of Old & New Pagan Songs by Todd Alan & Friends. The group has done several albums; this one has songs and chants, some of them more spoken than sung in presentation.

Caution Horses by the Cowboy Junkies, 1990 (studio release).

Chants: Ritual Music, 1987, and *Second Chants: More Ritual Music from Reclaiming & Friends,* 1994, by Reclaiming, Serpentine Records. Starhawk and Reclaiming have given us some of modern Paganism's best poetry; these albums offer beautiful songs, chants, rounds, and invocations.

A Circle Is Cast by Libana. Spinning Records, 1986. One of many albums by this famous women's chorus, it features a variety of songs, rounds, and chants—traditional and original, in English and other languages.

Circle Round and Sing! Songs for Family Celebrations in the Goddess Traditions by Anne Hill. Serpentine Music Productions, 2000. Accompaniment for the book of the same name; this album features an exquisite selection of songs, chants, rounds, blessings, and invocations both old and new.

A Dream Whose Time is Coming by Assembly of the Sacred Wheel, 2001 (studio release).

The Enchantment, by Gaia Tribe, Earth Tones Studios, 2004.

Enchantress by Gypsy Ravish, White Light Pentacles, 2001.

Faerie Goddess by Elaine Silver, The Orchard, 1999. Has the most beautiful version of "Burning Times" we have ever heard.

Fire Dance! by MotherTongue. EarthSpirit, 1992. One of many albums by this famous performance group, it includes a variety of chants, songs, and rounds.

Gaia Circles by Gaia Consort, The Orchard, 2001. One of Oberon's all-time favorites.

I'll Have My Chants This Time a Round: Rounds and Chants for Everyday Mystics by Chris Wagner (Khrysso), Worldberry Jam, 1996. Features a selection of wonderful songs, chants, and rounds from around the world.

Pagan Saints by Flesh & Bone, Intersound Records, 1999.

Pasha & the Pagans, Familiar Productions, 2002. Jones St., San Francisco, CA 94102, 537 Songs both moving and amusing.

Pick the Apple from the Tree by Francesca De Grandis, 1997 (studio release).

Rime of the Ancient Matriarch by Holly Tannen, 1999 (studio release). Serious and humorous Pagan songs and ballads.

Rumors of the Big Wave by Charlie Murphy. Warner Brothers, 1983.

Early Years by Ruth Barrett & Cyntia Smith, Aeolus, 2000.

Songs for the Old Religion and *The Faerie Shaman,* 1982, by Gwydion Pendderwen. Serpentine Records, Pagandom's first recorded bard. Essential!

Welcome to Annwfn, 1987, and *Chorus of Life,* 1991, by our own Gaia's Voice. Inspired by decades of CAW and HOME rituals at our sacred land, Annwfn. From Serpentine Records.

The Wolf Sky by Australia's awesome Wendy Rule, Shock, 2006. Her 5th major release, it's a wild, epic, dark, and beautiful album. It opens with an elemental invocation and ends with a chant.

Wytches, 2003, and *Belatane,* 2005, by Inkubus Sukkubus.

There are many lovely and moving songs of the Goddess and the God available on tapes and CDs. Here are just a few that are particularly wonderful, and great to play for rituals:

"Jack in the Green" by Martin Graeve, from Jethro Tull's *Songs from the Wood.*

"John Barleycorn" recorded by Jethro Tull, Steeleye Span, Fairport Convention.

"Shelter from the Storm" by Bob Dylan, from *Blood on the Tracks.*

"Hymn to Her" by the Pretenders, on *Isle of View*

"Danu" by Ruth Barrett, on *Parthenogenesis,* Dancing Tree Music.

"Every Woman Born" by Ruth Barrett, on *The Early Years,* Ruth Barrett & Cyntia Smith, Dancing Tree Music.

"Ancient Mother" and "From the Goddess/O Great Spirit," by Robert Gass, *On Wings of Song,* Spring Hill Music.

"Creature of the Wood" by Heather Alexander, SeaFire Productions.

Some excellent online sources for CDs of Pagan music and chants are:

Heather Alexander (SeaFire Productions): www.heatherlands.com/seafire
Alula Records: www.alula.com/PeterWendy.htm
Appleseed Recordings: www.AppleseedRec.com
Mark Unger & Leanne Hussey (Avalon Rising): www.moremoose.com
Blackmore's Night: www.BlackmoresNight.com
Brociliande: www.flowinglass.com/broceliande/disc.html
Claddagh Records: www.CladdaghRecords.com
Clannad: www.clannad.ie/
Dancing Tree Music: www.DancingTree.org
Emerald Rose: www.emeraldrose.com/
Francesca De Grandis (3rd Road Productions): www.well.com/user/zthirdrd/music.html
Jesse Wolf Hardin (Earthen Spirituality Project): www.EarthenSpirituality.org
Earth Tones Studios: www.PaganMusic.com
MotherTongue: www.earthspirit.org/mtongue/mothertongue.html
Gaia Consort: www.GaiaConsort.com
Inkubus Sukkubus: www.InkubusSukkubus.com
Kenny Klein: www.KennyKlein.net
Ladyslipper Music: www.ladyslipper.org
Loreena McKennitt: www.wbr.com/McKennitt
Sharon Knight, Pandemonaeon:

www.TranceJamRecords.com
Reclaiming Collective: www.Reclaiming.org
Serpentine Music: www.SerpentineMusic.com
Abby Spinner: www.spinner@mcbridemagic.com
Spring Hill Music: www.SpringHillMedia.com
Holly Tannen: www.HollyTannen.com
Tempest: www.TempestMusic.com
Gypsy Ravish (White Light Pentacles): www.wlpssp.com
Wendy Rule: www.wendyrule.com/music.php
Zingaia (Sequoia Records): www.SequoiaRecords.com

There are a number of excellent books that list pantheons of deities in encyclopedic form that are very useful to consult in designing a ritual, and deciding whom to invoke. Here are some of our favorites:

Farrar, Janet & Stewart. *The Witches' Goddess,* 1987; *The Witches' God,* 1989, Phoenix Pubs.
Monaghan, Patricia. *New Book of Goddesses & Heroines (3rd ed.),* Llewellyn, 2002.
Robinson, Herbert Spencer & Knox Wilson. *Myths & Legends of All Nations,* Littlefield, Adams & Co., 1976.
Hugin the Bard. "Songs from the Mabinogion." In *A Bards Book of Pagan Songs,* Llewellyn, 2002.

Indispensable collections of ancient invocations of the Greek Gods and Goddesses are the Homeric and Orphic hymns. Various excellent translations of these are available online.

Appendix D: Credits & References

Book I: The Magick Circle

NOTE: Much of the material in Book One is reprinted from *HOME Cooking: Rites & Rituals of the Church of All Worlds,* by Oberon Zell, Holy Order of Mother Earth, Laytonville, CA, 1997.

1. Welcome to the Circle of Magick!

Crowley, Aleister, *Magick Without Tears,* Chap. 1: "What is Magick?" Falcon Press, 1982.
"History of Theatre." www.tctwebstage.com/ancient.htm. 2006

3. Quarter-Callings

Barrett, Ruth. "Invocation and the Power of Sound." *Women's Rites, Women's Mysteries: Intuitive Ritual Creation.* Llewellyn, 2007.
Ashleigh, Moira. "Invocation." *Fire Dance!* by MotherTongue (1992). The EarthSpirit Community: POB 723, Williamsburg, MA 01096.

Arthen, Andras Corban. "Air I Am." *All Beings of the Earth* and *Fire Dance!* by MotherTongue (1992). (From "The EarthSpirit Community")
Hamouris, Rick. "We Are a Circle." *Welcome to Annwfn* (http://music.msn.com/album/?album=42202408).
Mc Bride, Abbi Spinner. "Behold, There is Magic All Around Us." *Fire of Creation* (2006). (To hear an MP3, visit: www.vegasvortex.com/vortex.php?page=3)
Bonewits, P.E.I. "Winged One" (1992). www.neopagan.net/Contents.html#PartTen.

4. Invoking the Deities

Apuleius, Lucius. *The Transformations of Lucius (The Golden Ass).* Translation by Robert Graves. London: Farrar, Straus & Giroux, 2000.
Mahabharata. Translation & preface by Kamala Subramaniam. Bharatya Vidya Bhavan, 1997.
Barrett, Ruth. "Lady of Three" and "Invocation." *The Year is a Dancing Woman: Goddess Songs,*

Chants, and Invocations for the Wheel of the Year. Dancing Tree Music, 2003.

___. "Goddess Mother of the Earth." Women's Rites, Women's Mysteries (op. cit).

___. "Ocean Queen." Heart is the Only Nation. Dancing Tree Music, 1996.

Anderson, Raymond T. "The Essence of Air." Circle Network News, Vol. 20: No. 4.

Daly, Mary & Jane Caputi. Webster's First New Intergalactic Wickedary of the English Language. Beacon Press, 1987: 65.

Reilly, Patricia Lynn. "Mother's Day Prayer." A God Who Looks Like Me. BB (1995). www.openwindowcreations.com.

Jaynes, Julian. The Origin of Consciousness in the Breakdown of the Bicameral Mind. Mariner Books, 2000.

5. Working the Magick

Middleton, Julie. Songs for Earthlings: A Green Spirituality Songbook. Emerald Earth Publishing, POB 1946, Sebastopol, CA 95473, 1998. www.EmeraldEarth.net.

Campbell, Don. The Roar of Silence. Quest Books, 1989.

Spinner, Abbi. Enter the Center (2001). www.spinner@mcbridemagic.com.

6. Communion

Heinlein, Robert Anson. Stranger in a Strange Land. Avon Books, 1961.

Judith, Anodea. "Whither Water Sharing?" Church of All Worlds Membership Handbook, 3rd Ed. Autumn 1997.

Kaufman, Ted & Jean. The Complete Bread Cookbook. Coronet Communications, Inc./ Paperback Library, 1969.

Zell, Oberon & Liza Gabriel. "Sacraments in the CAW." Church of All Worlds Membership Handbook (op. cit).

7. Ending the Ritual

"Young Father Goose." From The Annotated Mother Goose. Introduction and notes by William S. Baring-Gould and Ceil Baring-Gould. World Publishing Company, 1967.

Book II: Rites & Rituals

Perrigo, Gale. "Pagan's Way" (1984). From HOME Cooking: Rites and Rituals of the Church of All Worlds (op. cit.).

Sala, Luc. "The Fire-Ritual: Heaven's URL."

1. Rituals for Recurrent Occasions

Barrett, Ruth. "Birthday." Women's Rites, Women's Mysteries (op. cit).

"Chinese New Year." http://www.educ.uvic.ca/ faculty/mroth/438/CHINA/ chinese_new_year.html (accessed 2006).

Leland, Charles Godfrey. Aradia: The Gospel of Witches. 1889. Book Tree, 2004.

NASA's Eclipse page: http:// sunearth.gsfc.nasa.gov/eclipse/eclipse.html.

"The Origins of Hogmanay." www.rampant scotland.com/know/blknow12.htm (2006).

Pesznecker, Susan "Moonwriter." "Drawing Down the Moon." Companion for the Apprentice Wizard. New Page Books, 2006: 218-220.

Wikipedia: http://en.wikipedia.org/wiki/New_Year (accessed 2006).

2. Blessings, Dedications, & Consecrations

Darling, Diane. "A Meeting of Church (of All Worlds) and State." Green Egg, Vol.26, No.101. Summer 1993.

FireFox, LaSara. "Goddess in the Mirror." Sexy Witch. St. Paul, MN.: Llewellyn, 2005.

3. Rituals of Protection & Healing

Breene, Katlyn. "Warding, Blessing or Protection Ritual." Grimoire for the Apprentice Wizard. New Page Books, 2004: 301.

Buckland, Raymond. Advanced Candle Magick. St. Paul, MN.: Llewellyn, 1996.

Cunningham, Scott. Cunningham's Encyclopedia of Magical Herbs. Llewellyn, 2005.

FireFox, LaSara. "A Witch's Banishing Ritual." Sexy Witch. Llewellyn, 2005.

Fox, Selena. "9/11 Prayer for Peace." http:// www.circlesanctuary.org/liberty. (Permission to pass on to others is granted – please include this credit line & permission to share if you do.)

4. Elemental Rituals

Fox, Farida Ka'iwalani. "Harmonious Living with the Environment." Green Egg, Vol. 23, No. 89. May, 1990.

___. "The Sweet Water of Life." Green Egg, Vol. 23, No. 90. August, 1990.

___. "Air: The Invisible Sword." Green Egg, Vol. 24, No. 92. March, 1991.

___. "What is to Give Light Must Endure Burning." Green Egg, Vol. 23, No. 91. November, 1990.

Starhawk. "The Four Sacred Things." Green Egg, Vol. 23, No. 91. November, 1991.

5. Rites of Passage

Barrett, Ruth. "Croning Rituals." In "The Power of Women's Ritual." Women's Rites, Women's Mysteries (op. cit.).

Campbell, Joseph. The Hero of 1,000 Faces. Bollingen, 1972.

Moonoak, Paul. "Rites of Passage." Church of All Worlds Membership Handbook (op. cit.).

Spence, Lewis. "Gypsies." *An Encyclopedia of Occultism*. George Routledge & Sons, Ltd., 1920.

6. Handfastings

Kingsbury, Donald. *Courtship Rite*. Pocket Books, 1983.

Zell, Morning Glory & Oberon. "Neo-Pagan Handfasting Rite...Church of All Worlds." *Green Egg*, Vol. 7, No. 63. June 21, 1974.

Waterbearer by Sally Oldfield had a song on it called "Fire & Honey" that seemed written for handfastings and May Day/Midsummer rites featuring love.

7. Meditations, Initiations & Mysteries

Pesznecker, Susan "Moonwriter." "The Vision Quest." Works Consulted:

Alexander, Jane. *Sacred Rituals at Home*. New York: Sterling/Godsfield, 1999.

"Breitenbush Hot Springs. A Center for Consciousness in the Oregon Wilderness." *Breitenbush* 2005. www.breitenbush.com.

Crystal, Ellie. "Vision Quest." *Crystallinks Metaphysical and Science Website*. www.crystalinks.com/visionquest.html (2005).

Kavasch, B. & K. Baar. *American Indian Healing Arts*. Bantam, 1999.

"Native Americans—Religion." *American Old West Culture*. www.thewildwest.org/native_american /religion/Quest.html (2005).

8. Other Rituals

Santer, Lynn & Peter Andrew Wright. *Professor Midnight*. Zeus Publications, 2005. www.zeus-publications.com/midnight.htm.

Book III: Wheel of the Year

"The Festival Document." *Green Egg,* Vol. 26, No. 101. Summer 1993.

"Cycle of the Eight Sabbats." Chart by Larry Cornett, from *Amaranth*, Vol. 1, No. 48. Jan. 1991.

1. Ostara (Spring Equinox)

Barrett, Ruth. "Spring Equinox." Excerpted from *Women's Rites, Women's Mysteries* (op. cit). Works cited:

[1]Mountainwater, Shekhinah & Mooncat. "The Chakras and the Wheel of the Year." From *Ariadne's Thread*.

[2]Chant by the author from *The Year is a Dancing Woman* (op. cit).

[3]Green, Marian. *A Calendar of Festivals*.Element Books, Inc., 1991.

[4]Kindred, Glennie. *The Earth's Cycle of Celebration* (self-published). Appletree Cottage, Dale End, Brassington. NR

Matlock, Derbyshire, England, DE4 4HA.

[5]Guiley, Rosemary. *Encyclopedia of Witches & Witchcraft*. Facts on File. 1989: 281.

[6]Green, Marian. *A Witch Alone*. The Aquarian Press, 1991: 52.

[7]Alba, De Anna. *The Cauldron of Change*. Delphi Press, Inc., 1993: 183.

Book of Shadows: Outer Court (Original copy in personal collection of authors. No author or publication information given.)

D'Montford, S. "Spell Craft." November 7, 2005 Sydney Australia

Zell, Oberon. "The CAW Wheel of the Year." *CAW Membership Handbook* (op. cit.).

2. Beltaine (May Day)

Barrett, Ruth. "May Eve." *Ibid*. Works cited:

[1]Mountainwater, Shekhinah, & Mooncat, *Ibid*.

[2]Danaher, Kevin. *The Year in Ireland*. The Mercier Press, 1972: 88.

[3]Davidson, H.R. Ellis. *Myths and Symbols in Pagan Europe*. Syracuse Univ. Press, 1988: 39.

[4]Green, Marian. *A Calendar of Festivals*. Element Books, Inc., 1991: 49.

[5]Knightly, Charles. *The Customs and Ceremonies of Britain*. Thames & Hudson Ltd., 1986: 159.

— "The May Queen is Waiting," from the CD, *The Heart is the Only Nation,* Aeolus Music.

Book of Shadows: Outer Court

D'Montford, S. *Ibid*.

Zell, Oberon. *Ibid*.

An easy-to-learn version of the traditional May song, "Jack in the Green" (not Jethro Tull), done by John Wesley Harding, Kelly Hogan, and Nora O'Connor is on *Songs of Misfortune* (Appleseed Recordings): www.appleseedrec.com/lovehalltryst/cd/.

3. Litha (Summer Solstice)

Barrett, Ruth, "Summer Solstice." *Ibid*. Works cited:

[1]Mountainwater, Shekhinah, & Mooncat. *Ibid*.

[2]Danaher, Kevin. *The Year in Ireland*. The Mercier Press, 1972: 134-149.

—, & Smith, Cyntia, "Summer, Summer," from the CD, *The Heart is the Only Nation*. Chorus translated from the Gaelic by Jim Duran.

Book of Shadows: Outer Court

D'Montford, S. *Ibid*.

Zell, Oberon. *Ibid*.

4. Lughnasadh (First Harvest)

Barrett, Ruth. "First Harvest." *Ibid*. Works cited:

[1]Mountainwater, Shekhinah, & Mooncat, *Ibid*.

[2]Farrar, Janet & Stewart. *Eight Sabbats for Witches*. Phoenix Publishing, 1981: 102-105.

[3]*Encyclopedia of Wicca and Witchcraft* (p. 227).

[4]*The Year in Ireland* (p. 166).
[5]*Cauldron of Change* (p. 209).
Book of Shadows: Outer Court
D'Montford, S. *Ibid.*
Zell, Oberon. *Ibid.*
Eva Cassidy's "Fields of Gold" (covered by Sting) is wonderful for Lughnasadh: evacassidy.org/eva/fog.htm.
Caliban did a great variation of "Bold John Barleycorn" on their debut CD, *Caliban*: www.tempestmusic.com/html/calibanalbum.html.

5. Mabon (Fall Equinox)
Barrett, Ruth. "Autumn Equinox." *Ibid.* Works cited:
[1]Mountainwater, Shekhinah & Mooncat. *Ibid.*
[2]*Eight Sabbats for Witches* (p. 116).
[3]Green, Marion. *Natural Magic.* Element Books Limited, 1989: 102.
[4]*The Year in Ireland* (p. 190).
Book of Shadows: Outer Court
D'Montford, S. *Ibid.*
Zell, Oberon. *Ibid.*

6. Samhain (Hallowe'en)
Barrett, Ruth. "Hallowmas." *Ibid.* Works cited:
[1]Mountainwater, Shekhinah & Mooncat. *Ibid.*
[2]"Dios de los Muertos" from Museum of Cultural History, Los Angeles, Cal., 1982.
[3]Hart, Nett, & Lee Lanning. *Dreaming.* Word Weavers, 1983: 130.
Book of Shadows: Outer Court
D'Montford, S. *Ibid.*
Snyder, Maryanne K., "Samhain Kyriele," *Green Egg*, Vol. 27, No. 106; Autumn 1994
Zell, Oberon. *Ibid.*
One of our favorite pieces is Loreena McKennitt's "All Soul's Night" on *The Visit.* Her "Tango to Evora" is wonderful to dance to in Circle and makes a lovely processional for handfasting & such. www.quinlanroad.com

7. Yule (Winter Solstice)

Barrett, Ruth. "Winter Solstice." *Ibid.* Works cited:
[1]Mountainwater, Shekhinah & Mooncat. *Ibid.*
[2]*A Witch Alone* (p. 49).
[3]Armstrong, Frankie. "Out of the Darkness." Song heard by the author in the mid-1970s.
Book of Shadows: Outer Court
D'Montford, S. *Ibid.*
Pagan Yule Carols www.sacred-texts.com/bos/bos509.htm
Serith, Ceisiwr. "Yule Blessing." *A Book of Pagan Prayer.*
Zell, Oberon. *Ibid.*
This Winter's Night by MotherTongue is a fabulous CD of Yuletide songs and stories. www.earthspirit.org/mtongue/mothertongue.html.
"Beautiful Darkness, Celebrating the Winter Solstice," by Lisa Eckstrom, Jessica Radcliffe, & Martin Simpson, recorded by High Bohemia Records: www.cduniverse.com/search/xx/music/pid/2229618/a/Beautiful+Darkness.htm.
This is a lovely winter song: "Winter, Fire & Snow" by Anuna, from the album *Winter Songs* (Claddagh Records): www.claddaghrecords.com

8. Oimelc (Lady Day)
Barrett, Ruth. "Brigit." *Ibid.* Works cited:
[1]Mountainwater, Shekhinah. & Mooncat. *Ibid.*
[2]*The Year in Ireland.*
[3]*Natural Magic* (p. 102).
[4]*Eight Sabbats for Witches* (p. 65).
[5]Ibid (p. 66).
[6]*The Year in Ireland* (p. 13).
[7]Ibid (p. 25).
[8]Ibid (p. 37).
Book of Shadows: Outer Court
D'Montford, S. *Ibid.*
Zell, Oberon. *Ibid.*
A song seemingly made for Imbolc: "Light That Beauteous Flame," with legendary fiddler Johnny Cunningham & singer Susan McKeown, on the wonderful CD, *Peter & Wendy* (Alula Records, 1997). www.alula.com/PeterWendy.htm.

Art Credits

Appendix E: Index

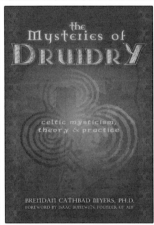
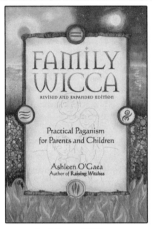
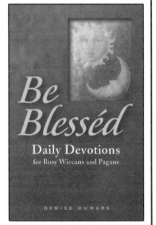
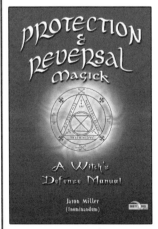

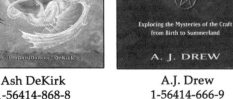

About the Authors

Oberon Zell-Ravenheart is a renowned Wizard and elder in the worldwide magickal community. In 1962, he co-founded a Pagan church with a futuristic vision, and he has been involved in the founding of several other major groups and alliances. First to apply the term "Pagan" to the newly emerging Nature Religions of the 1960s, and through 30 years of publishing *Green Egg* magazine, Oberon was instrumental in the coalescence of the Neo-Pagan movement. In 1970, he had a profound Vision of the Living Earth, which he published as an early version of "The Gaia Thesis." He has traveled throughout the world, celebrated Solar eclipses at ancient stone circles, raised Unicorns, and swam with Mermaids. His first book was *Grimoire for the Apprentice Wizard* (New Page Books, 2004). Living in NorCalifia, Oberon is Headmaster of the online Grey School of Wizardry, and lifemate to Morning Glory, his beloved wife of 32 years.

Morning Glory Zell-Ravenheart is a Witch, Priestess, Loremistress, and Goddess historian—famous for her rituals, songs, poetry, and her Goddess Collection of over 150 votive figurines. For over 30 years she has traveled, lectured, and taught college courses with her husband and soulmate, Oberon, on Neo-Paganism, the Gaia Thesis, and Goddess re-emergence. Morning Glory has been involved in creating ceremonies of every kind and scale, from simple rites of passage, to spectacular events such as the 1979 Solar eclipse at the Stonehenge replica in the Oregon Dalles. Her journeys have taken her to the Australian Blue Mountains, the depths of the Coral Sea, the jungles of New Guinea, the ruins of ancient Greece, the caves of Crete, and Taoist Goddess Temples of China. She is a published poet, songwriter, and author, with short stories included in two volumes of Marion Zimmer Bradley's *Sword and Sorceress* anthologies; and she was an acknowledged consultant for MZB's *The Mists of Avalon*. She is the founder and proprietor of Mythic Images and Headmistress of the Grey School of Wizardry.